GW00835955

# NASSER

## ALSO BY SAÏD K. ABURISH

*Saddam Hussein: The Politics of Revenge*

*Pay-off: Wheeling and Dealing in the Arab World*

*The St. George Hotel Bar (*paperbacked as *Beirut Spy)*

*Children of Bethany*

*Cry Palestine*

*The Rise, Corruption, and Coming Fall of the House of Saud*

*A Brutal Friendship: The West and the Arab Elite*

*Arafat: From Defender to Dictator*

# NASSER

## THE LAST ARAB

SAÏD K. ABURISH

DUCKWORTH

First published in the UK in 2004 by
Gerald Duckworth & Co. Ltd.
90-93 Cowcross Street, London EC1M 6BF
Tel: 020 7490 7300
Fax: 020 7490 0080
inquiries@duckworth-publishers.co.uk
www.ducknet.co.uk



A catalogue record for this book is available from the British Library

ISBN 0 7156 3300 7

Printed and bound in Great Britain by
CPD Ltd, Wales

To another Arab, my friend Abdul Bari Attwan.

To Linda with love.

# ACKNOWLEDGMENTS

No list of the people who helped me research and write *Nasser: The Last Arab* is provided. I owe a huge debt of thanks to all of them. However, the opinions expressed in the book, like its shortcomings, are mine alone.

# CONTENTS

# NASSER

# INTRODUCTION

## The Painful Truth

Gamal Abdel Nasser, universally known by his last name, was the towering Arab leader of the twentieth century. A pro-West Egyptian army colonel who assumed power in 1952 with the knowledge of the CIA, Nasser later became the embodiment of the historical confrontation between the Arabs and the West.

What separated Nasser from Arab leaders of his time is still with us today. The others depended on Western support and ignored their people. But the voices of the people seemed to reside within Nasser's person. His inability to reconcile his responsibility to his people with his natural pro-West inclinations was his undoing.

A similar conflict has faced the traditional Arab leaders since September 11, 2001, and President George W. Bush's demand of unqualified adherence to his new policy, "the war on terror." "Either you are with us or you are against us," announced the president, without considering the delicate position of America's Arab friends in the Middle East. Because their people dislike the United States, especially its pro-Israeli policy, it is impossible for Arab leaders to openly support Washington against fellow Muslims, even Muslim terrorists. Caught unexpectedly in a no-win situation, the leaders of Egypt, Saudi Arabia, Jordan, and other pro-West countries were exposed and without protection. Other than declaring war against Israel in 1948, the pro-West Arab leaders had never had to disagree with their protectors so openly.

In fact, President George W. Bush wasn't asking for anything new. Telling Arab leaders what to do has been the norm for Western governments since the First World War. Both accepted the idea of Western dominance, which allowed Arab leaders to dismiss the aspirations of their own people and become dictators. This is the background to the political, cultural, and spiritual decline that has afflicted the Arab Middle East for more than eighty years. The decline followed Britain's and France's creation of fourteen countries made up of chunks of real estate that lacked religious, ethnic, and linguistic cohesion. The new countries—Syria, Iraq, Lebanon, Jordan, Palestine, Kuwait, Saudi Arabia, Bahrain, Qatar, the United Arab Emirates, Oman, Yemen, Egypt, and the Sudan—were placed under sheikhs, emirs, and kings in accordance with colonial interests. The Arab people tried their utmost to change this situation. Decades of turmoil followed as they expressed their rejection of the new Arab rulers and their sponsors. But, judged by the lack of results, the various rebellions and coups produced, and the continuing dominance of unpopular pro-Western leaders, the Arab people have not succeeded in liberating themselves. More important, the majority of the Arabs are no longer trying to create a democratic political process in their countries, while small groups are now resorting to violence.

Today's Arab leaders—Fahd of Saudi Arabia, Mubarak of Egypt, Abdullah of Jordan, and the heads of the tiny Gulf statelets—are more dependent on the United States and its system of using them as deputy sheriffs to control the oil-rich region than their predecessors were on the British and French, who were behind the creation of this system early in the twentieth century. The British and French showed a minimal basic concern for the Arab people and things were easier in the 1930s, 1940s, and 1950s, but this is no more. When the United States assumed the role of the major power in the region, it not only extended the original system, it exercised tighter indirect control and retarded any chance of introducing democracy. Despite attempts to blame some Arab countries without examining America's role, what the September 11 terrorist attacks proved—that the "arrangement" fell short of representing a working system—is what we are facing today.

The only way to judge this or other theories that purport to explain the decline of the Arab Middle East to its present sorry state is to examine the records of the Arab leaders of the twentieth century. Whether in a modern or a traditional mold, the dictators' behavior represents a visible and consistent pattern. Moreover, it is axiomatic that dictatorships leave us with no institutions to examine; the cult of personality created by dictators excludes the development of durable political organizations. Writing a book about Arab parliaments would be tantamount to playing trick or treat; they existed only briefly and were created by leaders who did not believe in democracy. In fact, not a single one of these leaders has left behind any institution of lasting value. Even the legendary unifier of the Arabian Peninsula, Ibn Saud of Saudi Arabia, left us with nothing but a family of awesome statistical proportions. The House of Saud fails to qualify as an institution, unless perpetuating despotism is elevated to an accepted form of continuity. So the absence of institutions places the Arab leaders in the unique position of being the sole representatives of their time.

In writing a political biography of Nasser, I am continuing to examine the history of the Arab Middle East in the twentieth century through the lives of its leaders. I began with the House of Saud; *The Rise, Corruption, and Coming Fall of the House of Saud* showed that the dynasty's mere presence represents an impediment to progress, or even the potential for progress. I followed up by examining the Hashemites of Jordan (and until 1958 of Iraq as well) in *A Brutal Friendship: The West and the Arab Elite*. The Hashemites had, and have, "Made in the West" stamped on their rule. Left with only poor Jordan, they continue to depend on outside powers to survive. After that came my biography of Arafat *(Arafat: From Defender to Dictator)*, a study of the betrayal of an Arab people—the Palestinians—by a popularly chosen leader who eventually emulated the traditional ones and placed his responsibility to the powerful West ahead of that to his people. And the latest effort was a biography of Saddam Hussein *(Saddam Hussein: The Politics of Revenge)*, an examination of tribal megalomania using modern methods—and why the West supported and used Saddam and then opposed him. Western support for Saddam depended on his usefulness, as when he invaded Iran and, with substantial support from the West, interrupted Khomeini's plans to convert and control the Middle East.

Naturally, all the Arab governments of the Middle East came out against my efforts. Two resorted to physical threats, then gave up when the threats didn't work. One offered a substantial bribe, which I turned down. When these traditional methods didn't work, I was subjected to a campaign of slander in which Western news correspondents and former diplomats participated. Many establishment Arabs who live off corrupt Arab regimes accused me of being in the pay of the Israelis. The United States and British governments made their displeasure known. At one point it became difficult for me to make a living.

The case for writing a biography of Nasser is clear. Thirty-two years after his death, the man who waged war against political Islam needs to be studied. The Arabs of the street and souk, those who supported Nasser while he was alive, have now turned to Muslim fundamentalism. It was Nasser who saw the Islamic danger first and never wavered in his opposition to Islam as an instrument of governance. This and other factors tell a great deal about how and how much the Arab Middle East has changed since his death.

Reexamining Nasser with the benefit of hindsight is necessary to determine why the efforts to free the Arab masses by the most charismatic leader since the Prophet Mohamed failed while he was alive and why his Islamic enemies became his heirs.[1] He left no political heritage behind him. Nasser depended on the support of the Arab people more than any Arab leader of modern times—even in the hours of his darkest defeats. But while the masses on occasion pressured their governments to follow him, he never succeeded in molding them into effective political parties or movements, and his vision disappeared with him. Perhaps that is why the Arab people have stopped trying. Or perhaps a popular leader expressing the wishes and hopes of the Arab people and possessing all the abilities needed to make them truly independent is a combination beyond attainment.

It is a sad and disturbing comment on our times that today's most popular Arab leaders are Saddam Hussein, Yasser Arafat, and Osama bin Laden—a thug, an incompetent, and a charlatan. As a Saudi taxi driver once told me, today's Arab leaders "can go on trying—but if Nasser couldn't do it, then nobody will ever be able to do it." Even former guests of his harsh prison system agree that what he had to offer was greater than what preceded and followed him.[2] The time to find out what this elusive factor is has come. What is it that Nasser tried to achieve that so endeared him to an Arab people who, in desperation, have turned to Islam for solace? What is the factor that has changed to the point of rendering today's Arab leaders impotent and unimportant? While it is now some thirty years since his death, a reexamination of Nasser's life can tell us much and shed light on the dark questions that plague the Middle East today.

# 1

# The Dreamer from Nowhere

Gamal Abdel Nasser shared a single, odd trait with other Arab leaders of the twentieth century: like Hafiz al-Assad of Syria, Saddam Hussein of Iraq, and Yasser Arafat of Palestine, he adored his mother but had an uneasy relationship with his father. Beyond that character-forming quality, however, he had nothing in common with the others, not even in the way he manifested his dictatorial inclinations (or indeed, on occasions, his lack of them). Moreover, unlike most other Arab leaders, he unpretentiously continued to celebrate his own ordinary background as a man from and of the people.

Nasser's hometown of Beni Mur in the district of Asyut was and remains utterly lacking in distinction. It could have been mistaken for any of hundreds of medium-size villages in Lower Egypt, or the "Said," as Egyptians call that part of their country. Though Beni Mur was where his family came from and he considered it home, Gamal was not born there, but in the Bacos district of Alexandria on January 15, 1918. He was the firstborn of thirty-year-old Abdel Nasser Hussein, who had been transferred to Alexandria as a postal clerk.

The fact that his father's position merited his being transferred from one part of Egypt to another suggests a middle-class status, but it was only marginally within Egypt's small middle class. At the time, only the upper classes had family names; the rest of the population—the peasantry (which included most Egyptians) and other nonaristocrats—were named after their fathers. Gamal, without a family name, began as one of the people. Abdel Nasser was Gamal's father's given name, and he was called Abdel Nasser Hussein after his own father. Hussein Sultan, Gamal's grandfather, belonged to a small class of petty local notables and owned a few acres of land in a village where most of the inhabitants tenanted the land of rich pashas in Cairo.

In the 1930s the pashas, less than 2 percent of the population, owned more than 65 percent of the land and employed and exploited over four million peasants who tenanted for them. A tenant farmer usually lived off two acres of land and his small share of what they produced. He had hardly any rights, and when elections were held he was supposed to vote in accordance with what the pasha told him. Because banks did not deal with poor people, there was little social mobility, and very few ever overcame their peasant background. Historians have rightly described Egypt as a "hydraulic society," totally dependent on irrigation from the Nile River. But only 5 percent of the landmass of Egypt was cultivated, and this land was intensively farmed. Then as now, the country had no resources beyond agriculture, and it was poor. In addition, there were years of drought, so the few people like Hussein Sultan who owned small plots of land found other vocations to protect themselves against crop failure.

Educated at an American missionary school, the Wissa Charitable Secondary School, Abdel Nasser was tall, dark, sturdily built, and handsome, characteristics he bequeathed to his son, who improved on them by having piercing black eyes which twinkled. Abdel Nasser's awareness of status drove him to wear the fez, a relic from Ottoman Turkey which symbolized belonging to the city bourgeoisie. He drew a line between himself and the average citizens of Beni Mur, the tenant farmers, and in a way this justified assigning local notability to the Nasser family.

Abdel Nasser Hussein married above his station. Gamal's mother, Fahima, was the daughter of a relatively well-to-do coal merchant, Mohamed Hamad. Beyond that and the accepted fact that she was typical of her generation, a good housewife and mother who obeyed her husband, we know very little about her. Even her grandchildren, Nasser's children, do not have much information about their grandmother. This is understandable;

Fahima died in 1926, leaving Abdel Nasser with eight-year-old Gamal and three younger brothers. Interestingly, at the time of her death, Gamal was living with his paternal uncle Khalil in Cairo.

Legend has it that Abdel Nasser Hussein did not tell his son of his mother's death for months and that Gamal did not have the chance to attend her funeral. But why was Gamal in Cairo anyway? Either Fahima had been ill and unable to take care of him, or his parents saw a special spark in him and decided to send him to the big city and a better school. Because there is nothing to suggest that Gamal objected to his Cairo exile and he did apply himself to his schoolwork more than most, one assumes that the reasons for his Cairo presence suited him. But there is no definite answer to this and other questions—and the family sidesteps the subject.

Nevertheless, there is little doubt that Fahima contributed to her son's well-being and influenced her children's lives. She used the forty-dollar monthly income (a substantial sum then) she received from her family to educate her four children,[1] and Gamal's attachment to learning implies that he noted his mother's noble gesture and responded to her hopes. While there is no record to suggest this, it is possible that Fahima was behind sending Gamal to a school superior to the Koranic one which existed in Beni Mur. The Beni Mur School taught local students the Koran and other religious tracts and the basics of reading, writing, and arithmetic over a period of three years.

According to most of his biographers, Gamal adored his mother, and the injury of her death and not being informed about it deepened when his father remarried a mere two years later.[2] But in Arab societies, including Egypt, it is hardly unusual for widowers to remarry after short periods of widowerhood, and withholding bad news from people is quite common. Most of the time, widowers need someone to attend to their children from the previous marriage, while the carrier of bad news, such as the death of a loved one, has always been frowned upon. Yet, the whole episode left an indelible imprint on Gamal's psyche even though for the most part he continued to live with relations. Abdel Nasser had not committed any violation of what was normal and one is forced to conclude that Gamal was an unusually sensitive child who behaved differently from most Egyptian children his age.

Gamal's father moved from one village to another without moving higher in rank. Gamal Nasser, or "Victorious" (Gamal Abdel Nasser translates into "handsome servant of the victorious, Allah"), as he later in life became known, was shunted back and forth from his uncle Khalil to his maternal grandparents, and eventually lived with his father and stepmother. Nothing detailed exists regarding his relationship with either of them, and there is less about his relationship with her seven children. Whatever turbulence there was in these relationships was kept beneath the surface, showing in hurt rather than in argument or open disaffection.

The impressionable youngster lived in Beni Mur, Cairo, Alexandria, Katatba, Ismailia, and Demanhour among other places. After completing the three years of Beni Mur's Koranic school he studied at the Khoronish, El Nahda, Nahasseen, and Ras al-Tin schools, as well as others. At the Koranic school, when Gamal was between the ages of seven and nine, his first achievements were noted. The sheikh in charge of the school later encouraged his students to be "like Nasser."[3] Indeed, he was not only a good student, he became an observing Muslim at a very early age, something which must have pleased the sheikh; and throughout his life, Nasser never acquired any vices except smoking. His Islamic ways were reinforced by one of his uncle's neighbors, Hassan al-Bakry. Deeply religious and well versed in Islamic teachings, Bakry liked the young Gamal and taught him a great deal. Like everybody else, Bakry was captivated by the charm of his young neighbor.

The combination of living in so many places with different people and attending so many different schools did not dislocate Nasser, it broadened his horizons—he got to know Egypt well. This meant becoming aware of the class divisions which racked it. Gamal traveled from one place to another by train, and he must have seen how inhumanely crowded the third-class compartments were and noted the conditions of the poor fellahin, or peasants, who traveled in and even on top of them. Most fellahin traveled with all their earthly belongings gathered in one bundle which they carried on their backs, and most suffered from obvious eye and tooth diseases. At the age of twelve he lived at Uncle Khalil's when the latter lived in the Khan al-Khalili district near Al Azhar, the foremost Muslim university in the world. This added to a natural inquisitiveness, and by reading a great deal about Al

Azhar and its students, he became aware of conditions in many Islamic countries.

On another occasion he was living with his father and stepmother when they rented half a house in the Khamis al-Ads district of Cairo. The house belonged to the Jewish Shmuel family, who lived in the other half, and young Gamal befriended the young Shmuels and behaved toward the elders with the same deference and respect he accorded Muslim neighbors. In addition, he seems to have been aware of the international atmosphere of Alexandria, where one out of three people did not speak Arabic. French, English, Italian, Greek, and Armenian were spoken regularly, by foreigners as well as pretentious Egyptians. The people who spoke Arabic, the natives or fellahin as the upper crust called them, lived in the poor quarters of the city. Most of them were workers and servants for members of the city's international community.

By all accounts, Gamal was a model guest when with his relations. His uncle Khalil, an unassuming family man and an official of Al Waqf Islamic Endowment, a charitable establishment, and his prosperous maternal grandparents had nothing but praise for his obedience, helpfulness, and good manners. He dressed correctly but modestly, and his eating habits were simple. He could live on the staples of the average Egyptian: cheese, rice, meat, and cucumbers and other vegetables. These habits were to stay with him throughout his life. His only indulgence was going to the cinema on a regular basis. Gamal's self-denial was voluntary, particularly when he was with his maternal grandparents, who tried to spoil him by being generous with the pocket money they gave him.

The most telling part of his personality was his ability to maintain scholastic continuity despite the many moves from school to school. He had an insatiable hunger for knowledge. All his biographers (Lacouture, Nutting, Stephens, Mansfield, Abdel Malek, Tikriti, Woodward, Stewart, Wynn, and eighteen others) agree that he spent most of his spare time reading, especially in 1933, when Uncle Khalil happened to live near the National Library, from which young Nasser started borrowing books. Though the source of his mastery of English remains a mystery, he read in English as well as Arabic, and he read serious periodicals as well as books.

In addition to the Koran, the sayings of the Prophet Mohamed, and the lives of the Sahaba (Mohamed's earliest supporters), he read Carlyle, Napoleon, Gandhi, Dickens, Voltaire, Hugo, Lord Cromer (onetime British governor of Egypt), Liddell Hart, and many others.[4] He read mostly the biographies of great men, especially favoring the literarily competent and the pacifists among political leaders. Cruel dictators did not fascinate him the way Stalin captured the imagination of Saddam Hussein, the only other modern Middle Eastern leader who was well-read. In fact, Nasser even had literary pretensions that went beyond the usual nationalistic essays written by Egyptian teenagers of his generation. In secondary school he started a novel called "For the Sake of Freedom."[5] (Just about everything he wrote had the word *freedom* in it.) This attempt at writing a novel appears to have been influenced by Mustapha Kamel, the late-nineteenth- and early-twentieth-century pamphleteer and founder of the Egyptian National Party. The antiestablishment and anti-British Kamel and the nationalist poet Ahmed Shawki were to remain two of Nasser's idols for the rest of his life.[6]

Whether it came from Kamel, Shawki, or his pious uncle Khalil, the model student had something mysterious within him that considerably influenced his future life.[7] According to Nasser's late, able biographer Robert Stephens, the Beni Mur tribe hailed from the Hejaz, the western and more advanced part of the Arabian Peninsula. In other words, their Arab and tribal inclinations and sense of personal loyalty differed from those of the average Egyptian. Their slogan is supposed to have been "We never attack unless attacked." Furthermore, although his formative years were spent in Alexandria and Cairo, he considered himself the son of Beni Mur, and his thinking belonged to the countryside. The Saidis are proud, generous, emotional, and manly. So Nasser had that rare combination of tribal Arab and Saidi characteristics.

Nasser's daughter Huda, the guardian of his legacy at *Al Ahram*'s Center for Study of the 1952 Revolution (*Al Ahram* is Egypt's leading daily), admits that she never spoke to her father about his lineage, but she suspects that Stephens was right.[8] She and others also speak of the legendary pride and hospitality of the Beni Mur people and how open and straightforward they are. Half Egyptian myself (my mother hailed from the Saidi town of Sanhud al-Kubra), I recognize these traits as totally valid and very evident in the everyday life of the Saidis; my Al Azhar–educated maternal grandfather subscribed to them.

Also, very much like the author, Dr. Huda Abdel Nasser is intrigued by the fact that one of her uncles was called Izz al-Arab, or "glory of the Arabs." Stephens claims that only someone who believed in the Arab notion of glory would give a child such a name. Dr. Huda Abdel Nasser is not aware of anyone else in Egypt called Izz al-Arab, nor am I. In fact, even in countries which wear their Arabness more openly than Egypt, such as Palestine, Syria, and Iraq, it is difficult to find a name that implies an equal attachment to the Arabs and their history. As we will see later, Nasser believed in and spoke of the glory of the Arabs regularly.

It is obvious that very early in his life, Nasser acquired the notions of freedom, dignity, and glory. With nothing else to go on beyond what Stephens, Huda Abdel Nasser, and others believe, it also seems possible that the disaffection Nasser developed toward his father did not stop the family, most likely his uncle Khalil, from imparting to him a sense of Arabness, which merged with Saidi pride and other elements he discovered through reading later in life. However, this sense of Arabness is not as strange as some promoters of Arab disunity would suggest. A majority of Egyptians celebrate their Arab identity without hesitation. In fact, throughout the 1920s and 1930s, Egyptian schoolboys, Nasser included, marked the anniversary of the November 1917 Balfour Declaration promising the Jews a homeland in Palestine by striking. In Cairo there were organizations such as Jimaat al-Wihda (the Unity Group), the Arab Writers Union, Rabitat al-Arab (Arab Union), and many more. Even Egyptian women had a committee to support the Palestinians in the mid-1930s.

So what we have is a sensitive, introverted child who was polite and accommodating but never warm and outgoing, who read voraciously and incorporated what he read into an Arab-Saidi attitude toward pride and dignity and indeed religious tolerance. Moreover, the prevailing conditions of obscene wealth and extreme poverty which existed in Egypt at the time would not have escaped his sensitive eye. The single recorded incident which provoked his outrage at the denial of dignity to the Egyptians was to come later, in 1942; but there must have been many more incidents which burned within him but did not unsettle him. After all, in addition to being the oldest nation-state in the world, Egypt was also the oldest feudal dictatorship in the world. It had been ruled by the Greeks, Romans, Persians, Byzantines, Kurds, Arabs,

Circadians, Turks, French, British, and even King Farouk's Albanian dynasty for over three thousand years.

It was of dignity, glory, and freedom that Nasser spoke and wrote to his closest secondary-school friend, Hassan al-Nashar.[9] It was with Nashar that the brooding, well-read student and elected high school class chairman tried to act on the frustration which afflicted his generation. All Egyptian teenagers of the 1930s resented the corrupt monarchy and feudal class system which denied the average Egyptian dignity. But unlike most fun-loving and sympathetic Egyptians, Gamal was constantly, even morbidly, preoccupied. There was no playfulness in him; when he ran out of books he borrowed a book from Nashar or other people.

Of course, the colonial British were still in Egypt, where they were hated for being an alien, infidel force and for supporting the criminal establishment. To Nasser's generation, Britain was behind all the problems which afflicted Egypt. "Oppose them with all the force you can muster," Nasser wrote to Nashar in 1936.[10] The reference to "them" was all-inclusive and covered all direct and indirect oppressors of the Egyptian people: the British, and behind them their servants, the monarchy and the pasha class of feudal landlords. The all-powerful British topped the list because they were easier to identify and, unless one directly depended on them for livelihood, their presence was impossible to defend. As we will see, though the British ostensibly gave Egypt her rights in accordance with a treaty between the two countries, they still had a military presence in the country and were not shy about using it.

Gamal was ahead of his generation in several ways. He was an educated revolutionary who merged a sense of tribal honor with the teachings on equality and freedom of the Koran, Voltaire, and Gandhi. Lenin, Nkrumah, and Trotsky were other models who shaped his thinking and inherent anticolonialism. And though he succumbed to teenage indulgences or letting off steam through the usual shouting and joining demonstrations, his quiet nature also impelled him toward unsophisticated but deliberate action. He and Nashar did join demonstrations without knowing what their purpose was, but they also read all the books about freedom together, and on at least one occasion they accosted politicians entering a building to ask for their help in joining a political party bent on action.

In February 1936, Gamal was wounded during a demonstration the purpose of which, except for being anti-British, escaped him in later years. The wound, which he earned when the students tried to cross Cairo's Al Rodah Bridge to the other side of the Nile, was superficial, but it won him a mention in the press, and a baptism of fire. He was also jailed for two days.[11] Most of the people arrested with him belonged to the fascist Young Egypt, or Misr al-Fatat (later renamed Hizb Masr al-Ishtiraki, or the Egyptian Socialist Party), the Egyptian Green Shirts of the 1930s. In fact, some historians claim that Gamal joined this party in 1933.[12] Whether or not he joined the party cannot be verified and is not important except to denote a restless state of mind. There isn't even a hint that he ever acted on orders from the party, nor was its fiery leader, the uneducated rabble-rouser Ahmed Hussein, his type of man.

In 1937, aged nineteen, Nasser applied for entry to the country's leading officers' cadet school, the Obassia Military College. Egypt had no aristocratic military tradition, and the opening of the school to the middle class had produced a huge number of applicants. What followed was to strengthen the feelings that produced his essays on freedom, his letters to Nashar, his participation in demonstrations, and—unusual for an Egyptian—his attachment to chess rather than sports as a pastime. Lacking a *wasta,* an influential intermediary to promote his application against dozens of others, Nasser was turned down. Disappointed and embittered, he enrolled in law school, in all likelihood without having the means to finish the course and become a lawyer.[13] After that he tried and failed to enter the police academy, again because he had no wasta.

So a military or paramilitary career, with all it implied in terms of Egyptian and Arab manliness, was uppermost in his mind. His family had no background in this area, or for that matter any interest in politics, but he had read Clausewitz and Liddell Hart and was smitten with the idea of conquering heroes, not as lovers of war but as liberators. Essentially a practical person, he accepted the need for a wasta, and he mysteriously managed to see the secretary of state, Ibrahim Kheiry Pasha, who sponsored his second attempt at entering the Obassia Military College.[14] From then on, with little contact with family except for a rare visit, he never looked back. The well-behaved, conservative rebel finally had a home. In fact, but for the army he never belonged to a social group.

The pictures of Gamal Abdel Nasser at the military college show a young man uneasy in front of the camera. He is never smiling; instead, with or without a rifle in his hands, he is staring at the photographer with attractive black eyes while holding back on expressing himself. One gets the feeling that he wanted to say something, to transmit something, but that he did not trust the camera to convey his thoughts. Shyness and an inner compulsion to speak out are in apparent conflict. What he wants to say gains importance; it is what remains with the viewer long after the picture is put away.

At the military college, Nasser's horizons were expanded further. The cadets with him came from all walks of life: the lower aristocracy and the upper middle class, and now and then a member of the royal family. Except for Hassan al-Nashar, he appears to have had no close friends in previous schools—perhaps because he moved in and out of them quickly—but at the military college he was to meet many of the people who would later join him in conspiring against the government he so detested. Among them were some who remained friends throughout his life. One of them was Abdel Hakim Amer, his lifelong best friend; another was Anwar Sadat, the man who succeeded Nasser as president of Egypt in 1970.[15]

Nasser was a good student, but not a brilliant one except in the course which reflected his commitment to method, the one about administration.[16] For an Egyptian or an Arab to excel in administration is rare, and this attribute gives us another glimpse into why Nasser represented something unusual. His first posting was to the town of Mankabad in the district of Asyut, not far from Beni Mur. It was here sometime during 1938–39 that the first whisperings of military unhappiness with the state of the country and a willingness to overthrow the monarchy began.[17] Nasser, Abdel Hakim Amer, Abdeel Rauf Hussein, Anwar Sadat, and other members of the officers' group which eventually controlled Egypt were there, and they talked and talked about the corruption consuming their country and the need for change. In Mankabad, Nasser was the natural leader of the group, the one who spoke little and listened a great deal. According to the man who succeeded him and, driven by jealousy, tried to undo his legacy, Anwar Sadat, "his energy, his clear thinking and his balanced judgement"[18] made him a leader. They were always with him.

But while Mankabad was the beginning of contacts between kindred spirits, it did not produce an organization or a solid commitment to changing the government and the makeup of Egypt.

Discussing the corrupt conditions surrounding them always came easily to lower-ranking army officers in the Middle East, but organizing to overthrow a government was something else. While it contained many of the Mankabad bunch, by all accounts, the group which formed the nucleus for the Association of Free Officers military conspiracy headed by Nasser did not become an organized entity until much later.[19]

Furthermore, at the time there were several similar groups within the army and other branches of the military. In fact, except for Nasser's presence, what happened in Mankabad represented no more than a debating society among junior officers who were touched by the plight of their country. But they were too few and too junior to think of overthrowing a government or of establishing a group which would eventually do that. Even then, according to others beside Anwar Sadat, Nasser was the most serious among this diverse group.[20] He was a natural leader, and his personality left an indelible impression on all of his fellow officers. What is more telling in terms of how things happen in the Middle East is that from then on, except for the impulsive Sadat, nobody ever acted without his approval.

After Mankabad, Nasser was posted to the Sudan in 1941. He was accompanied by Abdel Hakim Amer, who was his junior in rank and who was to have a considerable influence on Nasser's public and private life and through that on modern Egyptian history. The conservative Nasser lost no time in turning Amer into a full-time protégé, and the easygoing, likable Amer accepted his role and proceeded to convince Nasser that being a serious soldier need not interfere with enjoying life. They played chess for long hours. Nasser called Amer "Robinson," after Daniel Defoe's hero, while Amer called Nasser "Jimmy." It was a case of opposites attracting, and, except for his wife and children, no one would be that close to Nasser in his life. No one was ever that familiar.

If 1941 and life in the Sudan affected Nasser's personal behavior, it was 1942 which was to haunt him and a whole generation of fellow Egyptians, those in the army in particular. The Second World War was in progress, and early in 1942, the panzers of Field Marshal Erwin Rommel were making progress in Libya and poised to strike at Egypt and perhaps occupy it. Egyptian prime minister Ali Maher and the young King Farouk were suspected of having pro-Axis sympathies, not because they loved Hitler and Mussolini but because most Arabs (including Sadat) thought the

Axis would give them their freedom. With the German military danger to the Middle East augmented by the presence of the two sympathizers and the Arab street cheering with every Rommel success, the British decided to act.

On February 4, 1942, the British ambassador to Egypt, Lord Lampson, marched into Al Abdin Palace and ordered King Farouk to dismiss Maher and appoint the more pro-British Mustapha Nahas prime minister. This act, a blatant violation of Egyptian sovereignty, was made worse by the military threat it contained. Lampson's demand was backed by a battalion of British troops which surrounded the palace and threatened to storm it and arrest the king.[21] Some historians claim that Lampson called the king "boy."[22] True or not, he certainly threatened him, and very openly, and that is what the average Egyptian believed.

In Egypt time stood still. The people did not love Farouk or even like him, but he was their king, and the crown represented their national honor. Lampson had humiliated them; Britain, obviously indifferent to Egyptian feelings, had committed an unforgivable crime. Sadly, Mustapha Nahas, the leader of the hitherto popular Wafd Party, the representative of anti-British Egyptian national aspirations earlier in the century, did not share the feelings of the people. The man who was more nationalistic than other politicians and who had signed the 1936 Anglo-Egyptian Treaty limiting the British presence in Egypt to the Suez Canal area returned to office backed by British bayonets. For most Egyptians, there was no longer any political party in the country that spoke for them, since the other political parties were at least as subservient as the Wafd.

Nasser was devastated. He recorded his thoughts in a letter to Nashar, and as usual, he did not mince words: "I am ashamed that our army has not reacted against this attack."[23] He adds to this in his 1954 book, *Philosophy of the Revolution*, where he states that he prayed to Allah for "a calamity to overtake the English." Clearly he wanted the Egyptian army to confront the British to stop them from forcing a prime minister on Egypt. Considering his knowledge of military affairs, he must have known that the Egyptians would be defeated, but what was at stake was Egyptian dignity, and that always meant a great deal to Nasser. Simply stated, he was ready to start an unwinnable war and die defending Egyptian honor and dignity. For the rest of his life, though a practical man, winning or losing came second to honor and dignity.

Even officers of higher rank felt the same way, though many of them had connections to the king, who controlled high-level army appointments, and they were as corrupt as he was. Brigadier Mohamed Naguib, the man who would later become Nasser's comrade and then his competitor for power, was among those who protested. Naguib offered his resignation to King Farouk because of the army's failure to defend Egypt's national honor.[24] Farouk thanked him but turned down his request. Many other officers expressed similar feelings, including practically all of those who had been stationed at Mankabad. Anwar Sadat, the most hotheaded among them, was involved in an attempt to flee Egypt and join Rommel, but he was captured and imprisoned.

The extremist nontraditional political parties in Egypt, the Muslim Brotherhood of Hassan al-Bana and Ahmed Hussein's Young Egypt, made substantial gains at the expense of the traditional parties. Mustapha Nahas and his Wafd never recovered. For them and the mainline political parties it was the beginning of the end. It was also the beginning of the end of the corrupt and obese Farouk, the king whose personal behavior resembled Nero's and who unashamedly went to sleazy nightclubs hiding behind nothing more than dark glasses. Practically all Egyptians were willing to die defending him, but he gave in too easily and manifested no courage. The feeling among Egyptians that Farouk should have led a call to arms was so widespread that it is difficult to speculate on what might have happened had Farouk reacted differently.

Later in 1942 Nasser, the model officer, was admitted to the staff college. He performed even better than he had at military college. Besides that he brooded, read, and smoked more cigarettes. The one officer with whom he was constantly in touch was Robinson, Abdel Hakim Amer. But sometime during that period he was to befriend an officer by the name of Khalid Mohieddine. From a solid upper-middle-class family, Mohieddine was a leftist, a member of the Communist Party; he would go on to play a leading role in Nasser's life and in Egyptian politics. How many of Nasser's socialist ideas came from Mohieddine is impossible to tell, but Nasser listened to him more than to most. And the well-read and worldly Mohieddine always had something to say.

Nasser's energy was boundless. His contacts with the old Mankabad group were kept alive from a distance at a time when he read several hours a day and applied himself so assiduously to his military career that he was appointed instructor at the military college. There he combined his command of military matters with his knowledge of history and enlivened the curriculum of the college by citing example after example of events in history that resembled conditions in Egypt during his teaching years. The depth of his teaching made him the envy of other instructors and the idol of the students. All cadets wanted to attend his classes.[25]

In 1944 Nasser became engaged to and married Tahiya Kazem, the daughter of a well-to-do rug merchant of Iranian origin.[26] One Nasser biographer, the French journalist Jean Lacouture, states that Abdel Hakim Amer introduced Nasser to Tahiya and her family, and considering Tahiya's high social status and Amer's extensive contacts, this is quite possible.[27] However, it appears that Nasser decided on his own to marry and did not go through his family, as was the wont of people of his class in a traditional Muslim society. Tahiya's many attributes and solid character must have appealed to him. Because of her higher social status, one is forced to assume that her family approved of her suitor because they were impressed by his character and manners, the things most other people noticed. But though Tahiya was a highly educated and attractive woman who spoke fairly fluent English and French, she was a retiring, observant Muslim committed to the idea of family and support for her spouse.

Superficially it was a relatively quiet time, the calm before the storm. The Allies were winning the war, and Egypt was in a state of suspense awaiting the final outcome. The traditional political parties were waiting for things to return to "normal," but the hearts of the Egyptian people were with those who advocated an immediate ejection of the British and radical change in the social system. In 1944, the Arab states got together to create the Arab League, which finally came into being in March 1945. It is now accepted that the idea for the League originated in the Colonial Office in London and represented an attempt by Britain to maintain its monopoly on power in the Middle East. The League was set up as a body to promote cooperation among the Arabs in lieu of the total unity or the confederation advocated by some Arab leaders. But at the time, the Arab public did not know of the British involvement, and most Arabs assumed that the League was a first step in the direction of total Arab unity, or at least unity of purpose. Nasser, the young man who had solid Arab inclinations and who never failed to remember the Balfour Declaration, was pleased.

Among other things, the creation of the League and making Cairo its headquarters put an end to an intellectual argument which had raged in Egypt for a generation. Like Nasser, most Egyptians followed their religion and culture and thought of themselves as Arabs, but there were intellectuals who promoted Egyptian nationalism and others who believed Egypt belonged to a Mediterranean culture.[28] With its acceptance of the Arab League and the appointment of the Egyptian Abdel Rahman Azzam as its first secretary-general, the Egyptian government made a decision which was popular with most of its people. The advocates of a non-Arab Egypt, always a small minority of intellectuals, fell silent.

As the war ended, the Egyptian people were clamoring for the British to leave their country, and the old, discredited political parties continued to lose ground to the Muslim Brotherhood and Young Egypt, the militant organizations which had once been considered fringe groups, similar to some Islamic groups of today. The Brotherhood, founded in 1928 and led by supreme guide Hassan al-Bana, was a right-wing organization which did not object to the ways of the king and the landlords provided they toed an Islamic line. To this day, it is a right-wing organization which does not accept the merest amount of social justice in the area of wealth sharing.

Nasser, the restless officer-politician looking for a political home, had flirted with the Brotherhood after his brief contact with the Green Shirts, but he broke with them over their secret contacts with King Farouk[29] and because they were vague regarding their attitude toward the feudal landlords. The practicing Muslim who prayed five times a day found fault with and refused to accept the political Islam that was preached by the Brotherhood. But the practical politician who began to develop in him knew better than to end all contact with members of the Brotherhood or to oppose their organization. After all, the Brotherhood was the one organization which had penetrated the Egyptian army, and many of Nasser's would-be collaborators belonged to it. What was needed was an act of conversion: the officers who belonged to the Brotherhood had to be convinced that their duty as officers capable of changing the course of Egyptian history superseded their oath of allegiance to Bana. Not only that, but he was not yet ready to confront the Islamists.

Simultaneously with his political activity, Nasser the happily married man emerged. The arrival of his daughter Huda in 1946 enchanted him. Photography was one of his few hobbies, and he took hundreds of pictures of her; later he bought a movie camera and used it regularly. Though the arrival in 1947 of his daughter Mona filled him with joy, Huda was to remain the apple of his eye for the rest of his life. He appears to have been free of the Arab favoritism toward sons. (Sons Khalid in 1951, Hamid Abdel in 1952, and Hakim Abdel in 1953 followed.) Meanwhile, mainly through Amer, Nasser stayed in touch with the old Mankabad officers group, and he had his eye on recruiting others. Most of the others were people whom Amer discovered in the various branches of the Egyptian armed forces, and Amer always presented a full file on each of them to Nasser. Unlike the home-bound Nasser, Amer was social and charming, and he appears to have known everybody in Cairo, certainly in the army.

In November 1947 the United Nations voted to partition Palestine between the Palestinian Arabs and the Jews, the first step toward the creation of the state of Israel. Riots broke out in Egypt and throughout the Arab world. Using the Arab League as a forum, the Arab governments, despite pressure to the contrary by the friends in the West, announced that they would not abide by the UN's partition resolution and threatened to go to war. Helping the Palestinians, including sending armies to fight in Palestine, was popular throughout the Arab world, and Egypt was no exception, but behind the scenes competition was developing between Arab leaders, several of whom, like scavengers, saw in the impending war an opportunity to enhance their regional position and become leader of all the Arabs. Certainly King Abdullah of Jordan did nothing to disguise his ambitions in this area, and Farouk of Egypt thought that way too.[30]

The period between the UN partition decision and the entry of the Arab armies into Palestine was a time for militias, paramilitary groups, and nongovernmental military organizations to operate in the contested country. The mufti of Palestine, Hajj Amin al-Husseini, presided over the all-Palestinian Arab Higher Committee and fielded a force of Palestinian irregulars called the Holy Strugglers. The Arab League, waiting for the British army to leave Palestine before dispatching the Arab armies, created a force of volunteers from all over the Arab world called the Liberation Army. Headed by Fawzi al-Kawakji, a Turkish-trained Syrian officer, its mostly Syrian and Iraqi troops infiltrated Palestine in small numbers. The third group that joined the fray on the Arab side was the Muslim Brotherhood. The attitude of Islamic groups toward outsiders such as the Jews has always been clearer than their attachment to some social causes such as wealth distribution, and thousands of members of the Brotherhood trekked to Palestine to fight, inspired as they were by the prospect of martyrdom.

In fact, the Palestine war was a good opportunity for the Muslim Brotherhood to shine. For years the Brotherhood had trained the Secret Apparatus, its underground military organization, in the use of weapons. The instructors were Egyptian army officers who secretly belonged to the Brotherhood. Marching into Palestine to resist infidel designs on the holy city of Jerusalem and its shrines was a chance that could not be missed. In fact, one of the Brotherhood's recruits was Egyptian-born and -educated Yasser Arafat. (Whether Arafat was a full-fledged member remains unknown.)

Despite a life of bliss with Tahiya and his devotion to his two daughters, Nasser was itching to join the fray. Because of his doubts about the Brotherhood and his lack of respect for the governments behind the Liberation Army, he decided to offer his services to the Arab Higher Committee and the mufti, who had accepted a few non-Palestinian volunteers. By then an army major, Nasser visited the mufti in his offices in Hilmayat al-Zeitoun and volunteered to fight with his Holy Strugglers.[31] Though impressed by Nasser's person and rank, the mufti felt obliged to consult the Egyptian government; he did not want to alienate Egypt by "stealing" one of the army's promising officers. According to the mufti, the Egyptian government turned down his request to have Nasser seconded to his forces. For Nasser it was a major disappointment.

But there is something in this incident which is unusual. The Egyptian government had released many of its officers, mostly to fight with the Liberation Army. Among them were two people who were to become Nasser's comrades in arms and fellow members of his government, air force officer Abdel Latif Boghdadi and army captain Kamal Eddine Hussein. So why not release Nasser? There is little doubt that his term of instruction at the military college had earned him a reputation and that he had become known within army and government circles. But there is more to it, and as we will see later, the movements of Nasser and his contacts with other officers had become known to the authorities. However, the number of antigovernment officers and groupings was considerable, and the government did not want to call attention to their existence, and that may explain why the government limited itself to keeping him out of Palestine and away from the chance to become a hero. On the other hand, the mufti practiced nepotism and appointed members of his family to command the Holy Strugglers; it could be that he did not want someone who could outshine them. In either case, the refusal had more to do with Gamal the person than it did with existing policy.

Meanwhile King Farouk swung between wanting to run for king of all the Arabs through fighting in Palestine and simply using the whole thing as a diversion from the problems besetting Egypt.[32] Following either option meant sending the Egyptian army to fight in Palestine, and that is what Farouk decided to do in May 1948, immediately following the withdrawal of the British forces in that country. The Syrians, Iraqis, and Jordanians (Trans-Jordanians then) followed suit. Sadly, there was no coordination between the Arab armies, and except for the British-trained and -led Arab Legion, no other Arab army was prepared for war. The noted Egyptian journalist and writer Mohamed Heikal states, "The Egyptian army had enough material to enter [the war], but not enough material to win."[33]

In fact, the situation was much more serious than Heikal's lament indicates. Major Gamal Abdel Nasser wrote to his friend Hassan al-Nashar of the total unpreparedness of the Egyptian army and how "our soldiers were dashed against fortifications."[34] Not only were they dashed against fortifications but they were using defective arms which had been purchased by the king's cronies, a collection of petty crooks who profited from the war by realizing huge commissions from arms deals. The worse the arms, the higher the commission they realized. Of course, they passed some of the money on to the inconstant Farouk. Nor was there any realization of how unprepared the army was, though the soldiers and the nonpolitical low- and middle-rank officers were to prove themselves gallant men. The army had no maps or tents,[35] and overall logistical support was lacking. When engaged in actual fighting, its soldiers were subjected to contradictory orders, and much of the time "palace officers," men who had attained high rank through a connection with the royal palace, issued orders which had no value except that of publicity. And to add insult to injury, the Egyptian press, mostly relying on government publicity releases, mostly originating in the palace, misled the Egyptian people and turned each defeat into a resounding victory. Nasser knew better.

The Iraqis and Syrians were equally unprepared. But despite all that, the Arab armies were putting pressure on the Israelis and pushing them back toward a narrow strip along the coast of Palestine. Units of the Egyptian army reached Hebron and Bethlehem; the Iraqi army was a mere eight miles from the Mediterranean and cutting Israel into two. The Arab Legion had surrounded Jerusalem, and some Israelis spoke of surrendering the holy city to the Arabs.[36] Suddenly, on June 14, 1948, the Arab governments—in the case of Egypt and Jordan, without soliciting the opinions of their field commanders—buckled under Western pressure accepted a UN call for a truce. The king, who had sent an unprepared, ill-equipped army to war, denied that army its small successes, which were earned by precious blood. For Nasser and other officers it was a simple case of betrayal, the beginning of the legend of being stabbed in the back by Farouk, his corrupt circle of friends, and his government.

A month later the war resumed, but the initiative had passed from the Arabs to the Israelis. Reequipped with new weapons mostly from Czechoslovakia and capitalizing on divisions among the Arabs, the Israelis took the offensive and began by attacking the Egyptian army. They pushed the Egyptians back into a pocket near today's Gaza Strip. Nasser was the deputy commander of the brigade which was surrounded at the town of Faluga. The Egyptians fought valiantly, and Nasser suffered his second minor wound on July 12, 1948. Desperate, the Egyptians appealed for help to the Arab Legion and the Iraqi forces, whose sectors were unusually quiet. They wanted them to attack the Israelis to ease the pressure on their forces. But, except for an unorganized and doomed attempt to relieve them by the irregulars of the Muslim Brotherhood, the calls to the organized Arab armies went unheeded. King Abdullah of Jordan and his cousins in Iraq were happy to see the army of their competitor for Arab leadership defeated.[37] Abdullah was in secret negotiations with the Israelis to divide Palestine between them,[38] with the knowledge of his British chief of staff, Glubb Pasha.

The second truce, in August 1948, left Nasser and his brigade surrounded by Israeli forces. But Nasser refused to surrender.

When the Israelis and Egyptians negotiated for the Egyptians to withdraw and cede to Israel the areas they still occupied, Faluga and Iraq al-Manshia, Nasser had his one chance to directly assess the enemy. He met with two Israeli officers, future chief of staff Yigal Allon and a junior officer by the name of Mordechai Cohen. Years later both men were to praise the young Egyptian officer they had met and to speak of his curiosity about their organization and the methods they used. Both spoke of Nasser's bravery and dignity.[39]

Nasser never recorded his impressions of this encounter with the enemy, but there are statements of his thoughts at the time. Desmond Stewart cites him writing to Nashar, "Our country is a second Faluga."[40] And in his *Philosophy of the Revolution*, Nasser quotes the martyred Egyptian officer Ahmad Aziz, obviously a kindred spirit: "We were fighting in Palestine but our dreams were in Egypt." On careful analysis, the dreams Nasser had in mind were more like a nightmare; he was contemplating what to do in Egypt to remedy the betrayal of the Egyptian army in Palestine. He had always believed that social conditions in Egypt were unhealthy and needed to be corrected, and he and his army comrades had discussed the prospect for change in Mankabad; but it was the defeat in Palestine which traumatized them. It provided the spark for later action against the gang of politicians running Egypt, Farouk above all.

In his despair over the Egyptian army's defeat, perhaps because of it, Nasser made one try to overcome the differences that separated him from the Muslim Brotherhood.[41] Back in Cairo in October 1948, he sent an emissary (either Anwar Sadat or Abdel Munim Abdel Raouf) to the Brotherhood's supreme guide to once again investigate the possibility of cooperation between army officers and the Brotherhood. But it soon became apparent to Nasser that the Brotherhood's agenda was not a nationalist one; Bana had no place in his organization for anyone except people who blindly obeyed him. From that time on, Nasser took steps to protect everything he did from the influence of the Brotherhood, and that was well before the Association of Free Officers was formalized and became a real entity.[42] This, however, was not known to the Brotherhood, who, strong and popular, still thought in terms of incorporating Nasser and his group into their ranks.

The effects of the defeat in Palestine were not limited to army officers. With the magazine *Rose al-Yussuf* clamoring for an investigation of the purchase of defective weapons and pointing an accusing finger at the royal palace and Farouk, the Egyptian people began looking for the reasons behind the humiliating performance of their army. Following street riots in December 1948, a member of the Muslim Brotherhood pretending to be a police officer shot and killed Egyptian prime minister Mahmoud Fahmy al-Nakrashi. A mere two months later, the Brotherhood's supreme guide, Hassan al-Bana, was assassinated, almost certainly on the orders of Nakrashi's successor, Ibrahim Abdel Hadi. It did not stop there; Abdel Hadi, who belonged to the conservative and monarchist Saadist Party, behaved like a dictator and in a period of official terror imprisoned thousands of Brotherhood members. Like today, it was the Egyptian government versus the Islamists.

It was at this time that Nasser was to experience three small incidents which prompted him to put into action whatever was whirling in his mind. In February 1949, Nasser was sent to the Greek island of Rhodes as part of the Egyptian delegation negotiating, under United Nations supervision, a formal cease-fire with the Israelis. It was another humiliating experience, made more so when during the talks the Israelis violated the truce and occupied Um Rshrah, today's Elat. However, upon returning to Cairo in March 1949, he followed the news of the Syrian army's overthrow of its country's government, the Husni Zaim coup d'état, with considerable interest. He was impressed by the Syrian people's support for the army coup and their obvious disdain for their old rulers.[43] Encouraging as that was, Nasser soon discovered what might await if he didn't speed up what he had in mind. Nasser was summoned and interrogated by Prime Minister Abdel Hadi himself, though it was done in the presence of the chief of staff of the army.[44]

The interrogation happened when Nasser had decided to turn the common inclinations which bound him to a number of army officers into a concrete organization. He put Amer to work contacting old and new comrades, and the new ones got to see Nasser only after an initial screening by the charming Robinson. Obviously someone Amer had tried to recruit squealed on them. Abdel Hadi asked Nasser about "his" group of officers and what they had in mind. Nasser denied the existence of any such group. The available secondhand reports indicate that Nasser behaved very coolly and was convincing. This is probably true, but also true is that Abdel Hadi was reluctant to extend his harsh measures to the army. As mentioned before—and this was more true after the humiliating experience in Palestine—there were many army officers' groups in existence or in the making, and there is no record of the government provoking them by arresting any of them.

Immediately after the interrogation, Nasser decided to turn the loose ties of his officers' group into a formal organization. Again using Amer as legman, he created the Association of Free Officers. All members had to swear allegiance to the aims of the organization and to the Egyptian people and they took a vow of secrecy with one hand on the Holy Koran and the other on a revolver.[45] There is disagreement as to the original number of officers and the exact date of the founding of this association, whether it was four, five, or six officers and in May or June, but this is irrelevant because the number increased right away and the reason behind excluding some officers from the original group was their posting outside Cairo. Eventually, the founding committee of the Association of Free Officers comprised fourteen men. Some (Abdel Munim Abdel Raouf and Kamal Eddine Hussein) belonged to the Brotherhood; others (briefly Sadat and Hassan Ibrahim), to Young Egypt; Mohieddine was a Communist; and the Salems, Mohieddines, and Sarwat Okasha were aristocrats.[46] Bringing this group together and depending on their loyalty despite their diverse beliefs and background is a testimony to Nasser's organizational genius.

There was no question as to where Nasser belonged in this group: he was unanimously elected chairman of the Association of Free Officers. Soon, underground leaflets with the name of the organization, the Voice of the Free Officers, began appearing throughout Egypt. They addressed themselves to two basic issues: the British presence in Egypt and corruption in government.[47] Other things may have been on the officers' minds; Palestine was to Nasser what the Dreyfus case was to the founder of Zionism, Theodor Herzl.[48] That is why the Egyptian writer and journalist Mohamed Heikal testifies that Palestine "defined Nasser."[49] But the Free Officers cleverly settled on the two things which all Egyptians understood and to which all Egyptians related. It was Nasser the politician and not Nasser the officer who was one of the editors of the leaflets, and Nasser the politician knew that there was no way of forcing the British to leave or ending corruption without changing the Egyptian government. Moreover, the politician in him knew other things could wait.

# 2

# The Encounter with Power

In modern Egypt, the absence of military tradition was important. The army was not connected to the circles of power, neither running nor influencing the leadership of the country. Though political movements, the Muslim Brotherhood in particular, recruited army officers, the prospects of using them to give the army political direction did not exist. What Nasser did was new and unique.

Unlike the only other army that belonged to a semi-independent Arab country, the Iraqi army, the Egyptian army had no political history until it was politicized by the 1948 war. Officers such as onetime chief of staff General Aziz al-Masri (and the impetuous Anwar Sadat) sought to change this picture, but they failed. The response from within the ranks was less than enthusiastic. Pampered, privileged, and unprofessional, the officer corps was happy leaving politics to the politicians. In return, the people in power did not pay the army serious attention. The appearance of the bulletins of the Association of Free Officers did not alter this picture. The king, pashas, and out-of-touch political parties of Egypt, using Masri and an unimpressive collection of also-rans as models, continued to act without looking over their shoulders.

Outsiders shared this attitude. Foreign journalists stationed in

Egypt treated the bulletins with some disdain, not seeking their source and ignoring their content. Though aware of the diminishing popularity of the traditional parties and the increase in political violence, most foreign correspondents living in Cairo accepted the punching-bag theory, the historical belief that the Egyptian people were incapable of reacting to their worsening political and economic conditions. To these outsiders, the growing Muslim Brotherhood, which by then had 1.5 million members, represented the only potential challenge to the ruling establishment. The contest as to who should run Egypt was restricted to the monarchy, pashas, and traditional feckless and corrupt political parties.

But the situation was getting worse. In January 1950, King Farouk sought to distance himself from the harsh dictatorial measures of Prime Minister Ibrahim Abdel Hadi by dismissing him and calling for new parliamentary elections. Despite the imprisonment of thousands of Brethren (members of the Muslim Brotherhood), the overt branch of the movement had flourished, and the Secret Apparatus of the society, the military branch, had continued to assassinate judges and minor government officials as well as set fire to some Jewish-owned stores. The king—and contrary to reputation, Farouk was not a stupid man—wanted a way out of the cycle of violence. By dissolving the government, he absolved himself from responsibility for the deteriorating security situation and put the blame on Abdel Hadi.

The Wafd Party, though it had boycotted the previous elections because of the king's questionable dissolution of another parliament, was the most popular among the traditional political organizations, despite its 1942 collusion with the British against the monarch. As expected, especially after the Brotherhood insisted that it was a religious organization and not a political party, refused to contest the election, and backed the enemies of Abdel Hadi, the Wafd won an overwhelming victory. The king asked its leader, Mustapha Nahas, to form a new government.

Because the Wafd had run on a platform of easing oppression, eradicating corruption, reforming the bureaucracy, and ending the British presence in the country, the election of Nahas represented a threat to the raison d'être of the Association of Free Officers. At least outwardly, except for agrarian reform, the Free Officers' demands and those of the Wafd were one and the same. But any potential for the Wafd to preempt Nasser and his Association was vitiated during the swearing-in ceremony of the new cabinet. In an expression of loyalty and supreme subservience, Nahas asked Farouk for the favor of kissing the royal hand.[1] Farouk agreed with relish, and with that the monarchy once again became the final, perhaps only, authority in Egypt. That simple, gratuitous act ceded the power invested in the Wafd by the people to the king.

In March 1950, the Wafd government and the British started renegotiating the 1936 Anglo-Egyptian Treaty, which granted the British the right to station their forces along the Suez Canal. The treaty would have expired in 1956, but the Egyptian people were clamoring for it to be abrogated—they wanted the immediate departure of the British. Except for the attention-grabbing moves of demanding the departure of the British and the release of thousands of Muslim Brotherhood detainees by way of thanking the society for its support, the Wafd failed to address the problems racking the country. Either its leadership forgot its promises or they did not know how to tackle the difficulties facing them.[2] Certainly, the idea of structural reform aimed at giving the majority of the people their economic and political rights was ignored. In focusing only on ejecting the British from Egypt, the Wafd confirmed that it was a nationalist party, but not a reformist one.

Nor was the Wafd government concerned with international problems or regional ones. Among other things, it totally ignored the Palestinian question. The May 1950 tripartite (U.S., British, and French) declaration placing an embargo on the shipment of arms to the Middle East and opposing the use of force to alter state borders went almost unnoticed. Even British recognition of Israel and acceptance of Jordanian annexation of the West Bank passed without a protest from Egypt. Egyptian forces were still in the Gaza Strip and the Sinai, and the army blocked the passage through the Suez Canal of ships heading for Israel, but these anti-Israeli policies were inherited from the old government. But for its (ultimately failed) internal reform program and the focus on the 1936 Anglo-Egyptian Treaty, one might describe the Nahas government as inept and inward-looking.

In fact, one of the problems uppermost on the Egyptian people's minds, that of corruption, became worse. Nahas's attractive young wife, Zeinab al-Wakil, managed to forge an alliance with commodity traders and was involved in an attempt to manipulate the Alexandria cotton exchange.[3] Zeinab's expression of greed was not an isolated incident: even Fuad Sarrag Eddine, the powerful deputy leader of the Wafd and minister of the interior, offered to sell the incomparable gold treasures of King Tutankhamen to repay some government debts.[4] King Farouk, never one to forget his 1942 humiliation and aware that a "clean" government was a natural threat to his ways, was happy to see the decline in the Wafd's fortunes. Preoccupied with an imaginary Communist threat to the country[5] (the USSR was too far away and the local Communists were too few and divided), Farouk secretly established contacts with the equally anti-Communist Muslim Brotherhood—a move which undermined the Wafd further.[6]

It was a sick, confusing situation, which bred an atmosphere of rumor and suspicion, and it was pushing the Free Officers to the forefront of politics well before they were ready for action, or had even considered moving against the government. The recruiting continued and the number of officers who belonged to the Association of Free Officers expanded, but there was no plan for a takeover of the government.[7] According to one of the founders of the association, Khalid Mohieddine, "The number of officers reached ninety, but nobody knew all of them and where they belonged in the hierarchy except Nasser, perhaps Amer also, but I doubt it."[8] It is clear that despite the abyss into which Egypt was sinking, the calculating conspirator who never tired of recruiting fellow officers to his cause was committed to a conservative course of action. Or perhaps—and this is not far-fetched, considering the constant changes in conditions—Nasser simply lived day to day.

Interestingly, none of his eventual co-conspirators who later in life wrote their memoirs, including Sadat, who tried to undermine the Nasser legend after he became president, criticized Nasser for being cautious. As one of them told me on a nonattribution basis, "The Egyptian people don't boil over like the rest of the Arabs, but when they do they stay angry for a long time." According to others, Nasser knew what the situation required and was aware of the Association's unreadiness to move against the government, and the people's unpreparedness to accept such a move. Above all, the Wafd government was still renegotiating the 1936 treaty and demanding that the British evacuate Egypt immediately. It would have been unpatriotic to act against a government when it was dealing with an outside enemy, and on enmity toward the British all Egyptians agreed.

So for nearly two years, Nasser did little beyond recruit officers, issue his underground bulletin, and mark time. He saw a great deal of Amer, and once again, the latter's contacts gave Nasser a new channel of communication to individuals who might help the cause. Through Amer, armored corps officer Sarwat Okasha joined the Association; and through Okasha, Ahmad Abul Fath, Okasha's brother-in-law and the editor of one of Egypt's leading dailies, *Al Misri* (*The Egyptian*), began publicizing the allegations and demands of the Free Officers. Coupled with what was being published in the crusading *Rose al-Yussuf* weekly, the revelations electrified the already tense atmosphere of the country. No one could overlook an accusation of treachery against the royal palace when it contained detailed accounts of the defective weapons bought in 1948 and how they had contributed to the death of Egyptian soldiers in Palestine. In fact, even the Wafd government thought better of stopping *Al Misri* and its editor, though it briefly imprisoned *Rose al-Yussuf* editor Ihsan Abdel Kudus.

Meanwhile, the Wafd-British negotiations dragged on and the British manifested no willingness to evacuate their bases along the Suez Canal. Finally, on October 11, 1951, Nahas abrogated the 1936 treaty. This not only canceled the legal basis for the British presence in Egypt, it also ended the condominium arrangement through which Egypt and Britain governed the Sudan together. By abrogating the treaty, Egypt claimed exclusive sovereignty over its southern neighbor. Of course, the British counterclaimed that this was a unilateral act, unacceptable and illegal. Behind the British attitude was the cold war; Britain was preoccupied with defending the Middle East against the Communist threat, something toward which the average Egyptian manifested an utter lack of concern. Ignoring all new military considerations, such as that an atomic bomb would block the canal completely, the British insisted that Suez was a viable line of defense without which they could not do.

The Wafd's move was a popular one, but it wasn't enough. The government felt obliged to do something concrete about the British presence. Immediately after the abrogation of the treaty, hundreds of young Egyptians, with the encouragement of their government, volunteered to join what the Egyptian press called Liberation Squads, paramilitary groups who traveled to the Suez Canal area to wage a guerrilla war against the British forces. Except for the Muslim Brotherhood, which fielded members of its

Secret Apparatus, in this case renamed Rovers, the volunteers came from the major cities and tended to be educated, with many college graduates and students among them. Meanwhile, fifty thousand Egyptian laborers stopped working for the British forces, adding to the British predicament. The Association of Free Officers issued pamphlets and exhorted people to join the fight against the British, and some of its members helped train the guerrilla fighters.[9] But that wasn't enough; this time the pressure on Nasser to do something was too heavy to resist.

According to Sadat, Nasser had to act but was still uncertain regarding the wisdom of doing anything overt, anything which might expose and endanger his organization. Instead, he decided to wage "a large scale assassination campaign."[10] While there is some question as to how large-scale this campaign was meant to be, Nasser admitted to participating in one assassination attempt in January 1952. Without telling his colleagues, he and others unknown tried to kill royalist general Hussein Sirri Amer by attacking his car with submachine guns as he drove through one of Cairo's streets at night. The attempt did not succeed, but an innocent woman passerby was wounded and started wailing and shrieking. Nasser recalled the wails of the woman in his *Philosophy of the Revolution* and stated that it haunted him and turned him against all similar action in the future.[11] He lived up to his word; from then on, the Free Officers followed him and rejected the practice of assassination.

The background to this attempt deserves examination. It is an example of Nasser's resorting to uncharacteristic behavior when under pressure, a tendency that dogged him for the rest of his life. Sirri Amer was very close to Farouk, a true royal palace general. In December 1951 he was nominated for the presidency of the Officers' Club. Normally this was a ceremonial office, and the elections for it went unnoticed. But this time, first the royal palace, then Nasser, decided to make an issue out of the election of a club president. To show that it controlled the army, the palace wanted a royalist; in return, Nasser and his comrades were determined to establish the independence of the army from the monarchy. Using Amer as an intermediary, Nasser and his Free Officers decided to field their own nominee without revealing their identity. They settled on General Mohamed Naguib, the fatherly, pipe-smoking, popular general with both a law and a doctoral degree, who had offered his resignation to Farouk when the British humiliated him in 1942 and who was thrice wounded in Palestine.

Naguib won overwhelmingly. Abul Fath lost no time in publicizing the victory of Naguib and his unknown backers and praising the nationalistic spirit of the army. To Farouk it was a personal defeat; to the rest of the country, mostly through whispers, it was an announcement that there was more to the unknown officers than pamphleteering. The guerrilla war against the British was gaining momentum—daily there were dozens of casualties—but the prospect of controlling the conflict looked dim. In the background the Egyptian government was broke and teetering on the edge of economic and political disaster. The Free Officers had it on good authority that to spite them, Farouk was thinking of compensating Sirri Amer for his loss of the Officers' Club election by offering him the position of chief of staff of the army. This was when Nasser tried to kill Sirri Amer. Because it was the one instance of his personally resorting to violence, it could have been a deviation and not an expression of policy, as Sadat alleged. In either case, the inner, all-consuming anger of the people was to lead to developments early in 1952 which were to change all of Egypt, including the plans of the Free Officers.

On January 25, 1952, the British once again demonstrated that their presence in Egypt was backed by brute force. The commander of the British forces along the Suez Canal, General George Erskine, supposedly tired of the Egyptian police force's support for the Liberation Squads and Rovers, issued an ultimatum to an Ismailia police post to surrender to his troops and demanded that all Ismailia be cleared of armed men. The contents of the ultimatum were conveyed to Minister of the Interior Fuad Serrag Eddine. This time, the Egyptians showed no hesitation: Serrag Eddine ordered the police to resist.[12] As expected, the better-equipped British forces used artillery and armored personnel carriers and got the upper hand. In fact, they did not stop until they had killed forty Egyptians and wounded seventy, most of them policemen.

One day later, Saturday, January 26, 1952, the Egyptian state cracked. In what is now called Black Saturday, the Egyptians of Cairo took matters into their hands. Protesting mobs in the thousands roamed the streets killing, looting, and burning foreign-owned establishments or ones frequented by foreigners and members of the Egyptian establishment. They burned the Shepherd's Hotel, the Thomas Cook and British Overseas Airline Corporation (BOAC) offices, the Rivoli and two other cinemas, the Turf Club, Gruppi's tearoom, and hundreds of smaller and less significant places.[13] From a distance it looked as if the whole of Cairo were on fire. Seventy-six people, including nine British subjects, were killed, and the overall cost was too extensive to calculate.

Why the government made no attempt to control the situation and whether a specific party or person instigated the violence remain mysteries to this day.[14] Future investigations proved inconclusive. Perhaps it was a genuine, spontaneous show of anger by a whole people. The government did declare martial law the next day, but it was too late, and King Farouk felt justified in dismissing the Wafd government and dissolving parliament. He replaced Nahas with one of his cronies, the unpopular Najib al-Hilali. In essence, the monarchy shed all pretense and ran the country directly.

Demonstrating the total lack of touch with events that always characterized the French-speaking, champagne-drinking Egyptian upper classes, Hilali sought to control the situation by giving members of the armed forces and police a raise in salary.[15] Nasser's reaction was more to the point. The Free Officers published (probably not for the first time) their six-point program for Egypt. Nasser and Khalid Mohieddine's handiwork is worth reproducing in full:

1. Regarding the British army stationed in the Suez Canal Zone, the first principle was the liquidation of colonialism and the Egyptian traitors who supported it.
2. Regarding the feudal despotism, which controls vast territories, the second principle was the liquidation of feudalism.
3. Regarding the attempt to preempt the revolution by capitalists, the third principle was to end the domination of power by wealth.
4. Regarding economic exploitation and despotism, the fourth principle was to establish social equality.
5. Regarding the plots aimed at weakening the army and using whatever remained of its power to threaten the rising popular discontent, it was decided to build a powerful army.
6. Regarding the rigged electoral methods, which falsified elections, it was decided to establish a healthy democratic atmosphere.

It was a naive program, and so general in tone and content and punctuation as to be laughable. However, this time it was taken seriously and the source was noted. Could Nasser and his followers have come through with a list of more focused, exact demands without making them sound like a threat that would have led to a premature confrontation with the government? Could they have pointed the finger at the palace and the pasha class without adding "or else" to each of their allegations? The answer is no, and in view of Nasser's reluctance to act prematurely, the diluted nature of the officers' demands was understandable—and served its purpose. What is remarkable about the vague six-point program was not its content but, once again, that the remaining members of the Association of Free Officers accepted it because they were committed to Nasser and trusted his leadership. Of course, *Rose al-Yussuf* and *Al Misri* made much of it. However naive, the six-point program promised a structural change in Egypt and catapulted the officers to the center of Egyptian politics.

Unable to cope with the unrest, there were four different cabinets in Egypt during the period between January and July 1952. They began and ended with Hilali, who presided over the first cabinet after Black Saturday and was prime minister for twenty-four hours of the last one. Public pressure kept mounting, and even Farouk's most ardent supporters found it impossible to ignore the calls for reform emanating from the street. At one point the king, probably realizing the unhappiness among army officers, offered the popular General Mohamed Naguib the post of minister of war. Naguib declined the offer. A short time later, in late May 1952, Nasser received word that the king knew the names of the members of the Association and that he intended to arrest them.[16] How the king learned the names of the officers remains unknown, but Nasser was told by Association member Major Sarwat Okasha, who had been told by his pro-officers brother-in-law, *Al Misri* editor Ahmad Abul Fath. It was a case of the antagonists recognizing each other.

Whatever intentions Nasser had were put forward to preempt a Farouk move and meet the new conditions. The methodical Zakkaria Mohieddine was entrusted with drawing up plans for an army takeover of the government,[17] the actual deployment of army units loyal to the Association. This, however, did not call for the officers to install themselves as the new government. Instead, the Free Officers wanted to recall parliament and entrust it with dealing with the country's problems.[18] Their aim, as articulated by their leadership, was to reestablish parliamentary democracy. The one thing Nasser personally decided and did not leave to Zakkaria Mohieddine was the selection of a known, acceptable-to-the-public general to lead the move against Farouk. Nasser thought—and to this day the surviving members of his group agree—that unknown or relatively unknown officers of low rank would not be acceptable to the Egyptian people and thus would be vulnerable against officers loyal to Farouk.

The lieutenant colonel was willing to cede his position of leadership to a known soldier of higher rank. In selecting his "boss," Nasser, as usual when in uncharted territory, depended on the reliable Amer, the man many thought of as the second member of the Free Officers. The first candidate for a leader of the planned coup d'état was General Fuad Sadek.[19] But Farouk had just made Sadek chief of staff of the army, and Sadek felt obliged to decline the offer. Amer then suggested Mohamed Naguib and, upon Nasser's agreement, contacted the well-known president of the Officers' Club and hero of the Palestine war. Naguib, as when he was selected for the presidency of the Officers' Club, did not hesitate to accept the offer. But, amazingly, he was not told much about the coup, and appears to have been agreeable but not curious. Certainly he knew nothing about the group's specific plans, nor was he asked to participate in the actual effort to take over the government. This substantiates the assertion made by all members of the Association, that Naguib was never anything but a figurehead.

With the acceptance of Naguib and the finalization of the Zakkaria Mohieddine plans to occupy all key bridges, the Post, Telephone, and Telegraph (PTT) building, the radio station, and army headquarters, the army units led by the Free Officers were ready to move. Hilali had been entrusted with forming a new government on July 21; Nasser and his comrades started their move on the night of the twenty-second and declared themselves successful on the twenty-third. But two days before ordering loyal army units into the streets, Nasser had completed his plans by contacting Britain, the United States,[20] the Muslim Brotherhood, and the the Democratic Movement for National Liberation, a group in the Communist Party.[21] According to Khalid Mohieddine, Free Officer Ali Sabri informed the American assistant military attaché, David Evans. The American's reaction to the news of the impending coup was "If you are not Communists then go for it." There is no record of the British and Communists' reaction, but the Muslim Brotherhood is supposed to have welcomed the news wholeheartedly.

The whole business of exposing their plans to outsiders, though necessary both to forestall any British or American attempts to help Farouk, and the need to obtain the support of the Communists and the Muslim Brotherhood, tells a great deal about the condition of Egypt, and about the Free Officers and the nature of their coup. First, the leaks to the officers, certainly the one suggesting that Farouk intended to arrest them, demonstrates how truly sick and in need of cure the king and his various governments had become. But it also shows the coup to have been a move against the excesses of the monarchy, an attempt to limit its political action, rather than a conspiracy to remove it. According to William Lakeland, then an intelligence operative attached to the American embassy in Cairo, "We didn't know of the coup but we had an inkling."[22] This means the Americans were told there would be a move against Farouk, but not the details showing the date, manner, and time. Contrary to some allegations, there was no direct American support for the coup, beyond refusing to help the monarchy, because there wasn't any need for it.

If General Sadek, the Americans, the British, the Muslim Brotherhood, and the Communists knew of an impending move by the army, then surely the news must have reached the secret police and the palace. Therefore, Nasser did carry out a coup, but it was a preemptive strike aimed at thwarting Farouk's plans to arrest him and his comrades, perhaps to stop Farouk from installing a military government loyal to the monarchy. The key factors, the timing and the nature of the takeover, were unknown. As it were, army units took to the streets during the early evening of July 22 and occupied the already mentioned strategic centers and buildings in the city without encountering any resistance while air force planes circling Cairo supported them. Khalid and Zakkaria Mohieddine, Gamal Salem, Abdel Latif Boghdadi, Ahmad Hussein, and Hussein al-Shafai commanded their units in both the army and air force. To avoid detection by opponents, Nasser and Amer donned civilian clothes and moved from one part of Cairo to another to see that all was going according to plan. Sadat, lowly and not expected to participate directly in the takeover, had been kept in the dark regarding everything and was in the cinema with his wife.

Luck was with the rebels every step of the way. On entering the Abbasiya Barracks ahead of schedule, a Free Officers army unit encountered the high command of the Egyptian armed forces, who were there to discuss rumors of a coup de'état.[23] After a brief scuffle, the generals there, all Farouk loyalists, were arrested. Army units whose officers had no connection with the Association began supporting the rebels voluntarily.[24] Anwar Sadat would later sum up the situation correctly and concisely when he wrote of "no one rising to protect the monarchy."[25] He, after watching the movie, managed to join the army unit occupying the army headquarters, but only after someone recognized him, demanded and got the password, and let him in. The wandering duo of Nasser and Amer, still in civilian clothes and driving Amer's small car, successfully used the password *nasr* ("victory") and appear to have visited every single army unit loyal to the movement, perhaps every corner of Cairo.

After determining that all was under control, Amer was sent to inform Naguib and bring him to the army headquarters while the first proclamation, written by Nasser and Khalid Mohieddine, was read on Egyptian radio by Sadat. It was written in the name of the Revolutionary Command Council (RCC), with Naguib identified as its chairman and leader and Nasser reduced to vice chairman. By then it was the morning of July 23, 1952. Though they had little inkling of what the army had in mind, the people of Egypt were joyous. Peaceful demonstrations, already in evidence in some poor neighborhoods, broke out everywhere. The crowds shouted the name of Naguib and carried his picture, probably supplied by *Rose al-Yussuf* or *Al Misri*. Later, the coup leaders would call on the people to control their enthusiasm and stop their shows of support, but very few listened to this. Crowds chanting support for the army and against the king and politicians appeared everywhere. However, this time they needed no coaxing to be peaceful.

When the fatherly Naguib, identified while he was on his way to join the officers as the leader of the coup, arrived at the army headquarters in the company of Amer, he discovered that all the work was done. He looked at the young men around him, all of whom belonged to a younger generation, and said, "*Mabrouk*": Congratulations.[26] The coup d'état was an easy military operation that cost the lives of only two soldiers, killed more because of their ineptitude rather than because they resisted. Meanwhile, except for an emphasis on restoring dignity to the people, Sadat was reading vague proclamations in the name of the Revolutionary Command Council and its chairman. This left most Egyptians confused. The inexactness, the absence of a clear-cut definition of the army's aims, and rumors that the officers had met with leaders of the Muslim Brotherhood led many to think the coup was a Muslim Brotherhood operation.[27] Moreover, there was reason to speculate on what the coup meant, because initially Hilali and other members of the cabinet remained free. Even the resented Ismael Shirrin, Farouk's brother-in-law and an honorary colonel whom the king had appointed as his last minister of war, was still free. The proclamations spoke of the people's honor and rights, but the officers did nothing.

But if Naguib had no idea what should follow, Nasser certainly did. Communicating with the king through Hilali and others, he demanded the appointment of Ali Maher, an independent politician with a relatively clean record, as prime minister. Farouk readily accepted the demand. According to Anthony Nutting and others, even then the officers did not want to govern Egypt, just to stop the slide toward anarchy.[28] Except for the natural appointment of Naguib as Maher's minister of war, an office Farouk had offered him in the past, the officers certainly manifested no inclination to elevate themselves or participate in the government. Nor did Naguib present them with his own ideas as to what should be done. He was happy posing for the cameras and pretending he was the leader of the officers' coup.

But the original group of officers expected to succeed through implementing the promises of their six-point program. While no record of their expectations exists, it seems that they expected to become the guardians of the people's interests against the monarchy and pasha class while leaving the day-to-day business of governing to others. Maher was conducting negotiations to form a civilian government, but army units were moving on Alexandria, the summer residence of the king. Maher knew nothing about this move, and Naguib was told about the new deployment of troops only after the fact. Still, most pictures of the heady days of July 22 and 23 show Naguib in the center of a group of officers, with Nasser deferentially to his side. The difference in their ages is obvious. Naguib looked relaxed and amiable, while Nasser, wearing an open-necked shirt, looked Hollywood handsome but impatient. Most of the time, Nasser was watching Naguib as if waiting for him to do or say something. It looked as if Naguib were the boss, and that was what the Egyptian people knew and accepted.

On July 24, Nasser delegated Zakkaria Mohieddine and Anwar Sadat to tell Maher of their demand for Farouk to abdicate in favor of his seven-month-old son, Prince Ahmad Fuad.[29] Initially the conservative Maher refused to deliver the abdication ultimatum. But he changed his mind on July 25, after Alexandria's Ras al-Tin Palace, the summer residence of the king, was surrounded by troops loyal to the Free Officers, and after he heard the people celebrating and became convinced that the country expected the king to abdicate. This was when Maher realized that Nasser and not Naguib was the leader of the coup. There was one last-minute quibble: Farouk wanted the announcement of the abdication to go beyond stating that he was bowing to the will of the people, which the text written by the officers stated. He wanted the statement to include something about the abdication reflecting the royal will. Nasser turned down his request. With a shaky hand—his signature is barely legible—Farouk signed the abdication document that sent him into exile later that day. Whether, as some allege, Farouk asked for American help and was refused cannot be confirmed.

The royal yacht *Al Mahrussa* left Alexandria late on July 25, after arrangements for its return after delivering the king to Italy were made. With the king were his second wife, Queen Nariman; their young son and pretender to the throne; and a few lowly servants. Although he had requested that some of them accompany him, none of his corrupt aides, the people accused of being involved in the defective arms scandal, were allowed to leave with him. But the king, acting in character, did take 204 pieces of luggage into exile.[30] Except for Gamal Salem, all the Free Officers and Naguib were there to salute Farouk and bid him a final good-bye. Again, to the Egyptian public, it looked as if Naguib were behind the end of Farouk.

Accounts differ as to what Farouk actually told the officers who saw him off. Many state that he wished them well, while others say that he alluded to the difficulty of their task. Boghdadi and Khalid Mohieddine, who were there for Farouk's departure, claim that he told them that he had thought of "doing the same thing they were doing."[31] If so, then it confirms what Nasser had learned and supports his decision to act before the king did. It was obvious that he had not known why Gamal Salem was absent. Salem, a hothead who was to cause Nasser many problems in the future, wanted Farouk summarily executed for treason, but

Nasser and the clear-thinking Khalid Mohieddine turned him down.[32] When Salem persisted, Nasser used his personal authority to deny Salem's demand, removed him from the farewell ceremonies, and then refused to debate the issue.

Because U.S. and British diplomats had asked for the king's life to be spared[33] and because some believe that was behind Nasser's decision to spare Farouk's life, this is the time to examine the degree of American involvement in the coup, if indeed it was a direct one. Miles Copeland, a onetime CIA operative in Cairo, always insisted that the Americans knew all about the coup, that Nasser consulted them and got the green light.[34] Copeland claimed that he and Nasser had been quite friendly and were on a first-name basis. Arab historian Butheina Tikriti claims that the American ambassador to Egypt, Jefferson Caffrey, referred to the officers as "my boys."[35] Another historian of Egypt, the authoritative P. J. Vatikiotis, states that senior CIA operative Kermit Roosevelt contacted the officers soon after the coup,[36] and indeed there is a picture of Roosevelt with Naguib and Nasser which supports this historian's assertion.

But former members of the Free Officers insist that the group's first contact with the Americans was the already mentioned link between Sabri and Evans. They see nothing in Roosevelt's visit and state that any representative of the United States would have been received in a friendly fashion. Judging by what happened during the two years following the coup, both sides are right. Nasser admired America, its films and its democratic ways, and for a number of years he did believe that he could do business with America because it was not an imperialist power.[37] However, it is also obvious that he did not disclose whatever plans he had for Egypt. Those who see in all of this a conspiracy are wrong: Evans was told openly, and conceivably informing the U.S. followed earlier contacts with other American elements. Perhaps the mere existence of these contacts did permit Caffrey to exaggerate American involvement and use the "my boys" expression, to associate America with an obviously popular movement. America was then new to the Middle East, but it had determined that the British regional role was over, and the United States was replacing the British throughout the region. As Evans had said, America's only interest lay in fighting Communism. It was already thinking of a Middle East alliance to keep the Soviet Union out of the region and to stop the growth of the local Communist parties. Totally preoccupied with the Communist threat, America, deliberately or through neglect, overlooked that of the Muslim Brotherhood. The U.S. government cooperated with the Free Officers by not opposing the coup, but that fell short of agreeing with the motivation behind the coup or of understanding its impact on the whole Middle East.

The sequence of events that accompanied and followed Farouk's departure demonstrates how tentatively Nasser exercised power and supports those who claim that his eventual assumption of power was improvised. The establishment of a three-man Regency Council to rule Egypt until the crown prince came of age was announced in Farouk's abdication proclamation. The council's members represented Egypt's bases of political power. Brigadier Rashad Muhana was an army officer with Muslim Brotherhood sympathies. Bahieddine Barakat Pasha was a lawyer and judge who belonged to the aristocracy. And Prince Mohamed Abdel Munim was a member of the royal family. Such inclusions, betraying a commitment to continuity, prompted the *Times* of London July 24, 1952, to describe the coup as nothing more than an internal affair. But creating the Regency Council with the idea of dissolving it later probably was among the acts Nasser planned ahead of time. The Association of Free Officers and an effective Regency Council could not live side by side. However, besides ending the monarchy and land reform, little else was planned. The Free Officers possessed an attitude, but they had no practical plan, just a six-point program.

The first major problem to face Nasser and his colleagues—in fact most of the early problems—was with one of the groups on whose support they had thought they could count. In August 1952, less than a month after the army's takeover, riots broke out at textile factories of Misr Fine Spinning and Weaving at Kafr al-Dawar near Alexandria. The Communist-led workers, emboldened by the change in government, wanted to take over the factories and run them along Soviet lines. When the police and army tried to restore order nine people were killed and more than twenty were wounded. A summary military court tried the responsible workers and sentenced two of them, Mustapha Khamis and Mohamed Bakri, to death.[38] Nasser and Khalid Mohieddine stood firmly against carrying out the sentence, but the rest of the officers, Naguib included, insisted on making an example of the two accused lest commuting the sentence encourage others. To them that would have doomed the whole movement before it was established.

Thus Nasser, always a firm believer in the precept that blood begets blood,[39] lost the first confrontation within the RCC. Of course, the conservative Ali Maher and members of the Regency Council agreed with the majority of officers. The repercussions of the workers' challenge to the authority of the RCC were great. After the executions, the Communist Party began issuing bulletins attacking the Association of Free Officers. To the Communists, the coup and the modest change in government which followed it were no more than a fascist attempt to mislead the people and preempt a real revolution. How could a government led by Maher and beholden to a Regency Council which included a member of the royal family be anything else? The party went further and pointed out the Association's Muslim Brotherhood connections. Though the Brotherhood responded initially by backing the RCC, Nasser had already lost one of the parties which had supported him.

And the Muslim Brotherhood's support was short-lived. The RCC's differences with the Brotherhood started after the October 1952 resignation of the Maher cabinet. Asked to join the new government, dominated by members of the RCC, the Brotherhood demanded four portfolios,[40] including an important one for supreme guide Hassan Ashmawi. After consulting with the original members of the RCC, including Brotherhood members Kamal Eddine Hussein and Abdel Munim Abdel Raouf, Nasser turned down the demand. He then adopted a policy of divide and conquer and included two Muslim Brotherhood members in the cabinet who were willing to serve individually but not as representatives of the Brotherhood, Ahmed Bakhouri and Ahmed Husni. They respectfully occupied the minor posts of minister of waqf and minister of justice.

While the Communists were small in number and posed no threat, the Brotherhood commanded a huge following and was determined to have a say in the direction the country was heading. The Brotherhood's chance to challenge the RCC and its policies was sparked by the adoption of the land reform law in October 1952, which forced Prime Minister Maher to show independence and resign. He refused to back Law 178, the decree which limited land ownership to two hundred acres per person, and a serious crisis developed. For Nasser, the land reform act gave the RCC identity and transformed the events of July 23, 1952, from a coup to a revolution. The Brotherhood and its sympathizer on the Regency Council, Rashad Muhana, supported Maher and came out against the "un-Islamic" land reform program.[41] On this Nasser would not compromise. He hit back. The RCC demanded and got Muhana's resignation, after his feeble attempts to use the Brotherhood failed because the Brotherhood refused to back his confrontational schemes and considered him a weak character. Later he was arrested, tried for trying to overthrow the government, and imprisoned. Ultimately he was released because he had no following and represented no danger.

When several well-known civilian personalities refused the invitation to become prime minister and form a new cabinet and Egyptian professionals (doctors and lawyers) asked for the army to return to barracks, it looked as if the new regime were doomed. But it was obvious to all that the only group capable of replacing the RCC was the Muslim Brotherhood. It was here that Nasser, an observing Muslim who believed in secularism, showed nerves of steel. To him what mattered most was to create and enfranchise 1.5 million new landowners,[42] even if it sounded un-Islamic. He refused to accommodate the Brotherhood and moved ahead audaciously. When all the civilian candidates approached refused to form a cabinet, Maher was replaced by the ever willing and very popular Naguib, a man who loved the trappings of power and the cheers of crowds. Nasser became deputy prime minister and minister of the interior. Cleverly, Nasser made no other anti-Brotherhood moves. Both sides remained in their corners, ready to fight another round. Nasser was happy to use time to chip away at the huge following of the Brotherhood, but their leadership knew that and was anxious for immediate confrontation.

The third major confrontation, following those over land reform and the issue of representation in the government, came soon enough. In January 1953, Nasser, after overcoming Naguib's opposition, sided with the majority of his fellow officers and abolished all political parties and created a one-party system, the Liberation Rally, which was meant as a national movement that would replace all parties. Though the Communists and the Brotherhood were not included in the party-dissolution decree (the Communists because including them would have added to their importance), neither accepted the principle of a one-party system, and both were determined to block the move. Nor was the Brotherhood pleased that Nasser had described it as a strictly religious organization. Riots led by the Brethren broke out, but the police and army responded firmly and put them down. There were a small number of casualties. This prompted the first crackdown by the RCC.

Simultaneous with dissolving the parties and the reaction to it, Nasser began using the more willing among the ulemas of Al Azhar, as a counterweight to the Brotherhood.[43] There was nothing new in this: Farouk and his family had used the institution of higher learning, perhaps the leading Muslim university of all time, for generations. Yet it was a clever attempt to draw a line between religion and the state, and it gained Nasser some support among the more educated Egyptians and the press. But it was a move which the Muslim Brotherhood noted with dismay.

Nasser's manipulation of power and Naguib's seeming subservience occurred against a background of debate among RCC members as to what their mission was. According to Sadat, Nasser was the lone officer who, even after the dissolution of the parties, supported the return to democracy.[44] The rest of them were for a dictatorship because only a dictatorship would implement their six-point program. Boghdadi describes Nasser as being more specific and wanting to hold elections six months after the coup, early in 1953.[45] Outvoted, Nasser still advocated a return to democracy after three years, which he thought long enough to evict the British army, eradicate despotism and its causes, and build a strong Egyptian army. For a while, the RCC exercised power with the three-year deadline in mind. Clearly, either Nasser was naive or he was pretending and hoping that his fellow officers would invest all power in his person. While no one accused him of coveting power at this stage, perhaps he was actually rejecting the principle of a dictatorship in order to create one; or perhaps he was just hedging his bets in case of a Muslim Brotherhood takeover. It was certainly difficult to govern while the Brotherhood, the most popular and best-organized movement in the land, withheld support from the government.[46]

At this point nothing was said about Palestine; it was relegated to a secondary issue, a decision with which all members of the Association agreed. Not only that, but Nasser thought that peace between the Arabs and Israel was only a matter of time,[47] and this incredible change of direction for Egypt, the exclusive commitment to internal matters, was very popular. Among other things, it allowed Nasser to lower the military budget and use the money saved to set up the apparatus entrusted with helping small farmers manage the land sold to them by the government. Israeli prime minister David Ben-Gurion held a view similar to Nasser's and thought peace was only a matter of time.[48] Of course, the Brotherhood added this to its long list of objections to Nasser, after land reform, the creation of the Liberation Rally, the rejection of its demands to be seriously represented in government, and his failure to eject the British from the Suez Canal area. As a matter of fact, Nasser and the Islamists disagreed on everything, and once again the Brethren sought to penetrate the army and police and threaten him. New Muslim Brotherhood recruits were called "assistants," above that was the rank of a "related" individual, then came active membership, and after that the member became a mujahid, or holy struggler.

Early in 1953, in a move which contradicted what they preached (but has since become the trademark of Islamic movements everywhere), the Muslim Brotherhood contacted the British and sought their help[49]—without stopping its campaign to have them ejected from Suez. Little is known about the nature of the contact, but it is assumed, probably correctly, that the Muslim Brotherhood presented Nasser as representing the Communist danger. The Brotherhood also sought and received support from a new player on the Middle Eastern stage, the conservative monarchy of Saudi Arabia[50]—another country preoccupied with an imaginary Communist threat and willing to bankroll its opponents. To endear itself to the Saudis, the Muslim Brotherhood began advocating the closure of cinemas and the wearing of the veil for women. This did nothing except add to Nasser's mistrust of Britain, his hatred of traditional Middle Eastern regimes, and his loathing for the Brotherhood. He expressed his feelings by working with the ulemas of Al Azhar to broaden the curriculum of the university and introduce some of the new sciences. But Nasser still did not feel strong enough to ban the Brotherhood. His flanks were not secure, and there was sympathy for the Brotherhood among the original members of the RCC. Also, for the first time, Naguib held a different opinion on a strategic issue, opened contacts with the Brotherhood, and opposed any crackdown against them. Nasser, in his duty as minister of the interior, settled for imprisoning more of them, without consulting Naguib.

The opposition to the land reform act was widespread, and members of the dissolved political parties added their voices to Maher, Muhana, the Brotherhood, Naguib, and others. When the dissension threatened to get out of hand, Nasser confronted

Naguib and secured his reluctant approval for another popular measure: the creation of a special court to try members of the old regime for corruption. One of the more dependable members of the RCC, the one who played a quiet role in the background, Wing Commander Abdel Latif Boghdadi, was made chairman of the court. In addition to Farouk's old entourage of arms traders and high-class pimps, people such as former prime minister Ibrahim Abdel Hadi, General Sirri Amer, Wafdist minister of the interior Fuad Sarrag Eddine, and Farouk's cousin Abbas Hilmi were put on trial. Most got heavy sentences but were later reprieved. But it was another sign that Nasser would not compromise on what he considered the cornerstone of the revolution, land reform, what he proudly called economic freedom.[51] But once again, the Egyptian people attributed the measures to Naguib, which made the general more popular and difficult to manage.

Even the CIA, though it knew who the original RCC members were, accepted Naguib's popularity and thought that he had become irreplaceable. More important, by the middle of 1953 Naguib himself was beginning to show signs of acting independently and of trying to steer the government toward adopting conservative policies. He began by moderately opposing land reform, and he did not back the dissolution of the Regency Council and the abolition of the monarchy.[52] But he suffered from two shortcomings: he had no organization within the army on which to depend, and he was not clear regarding what he wanted. Even the vague program of Nasser and his comrades was more developed than Naguib's political thought.

Nasser viewed Naguib's attachment to the monarchy with disdain and used it against him. Journalists Abul Fath and Mohamed Heikal, a new but valued acquaintance, ran stories which diminished Naguib's street support. Meanwhile Naguib and Nasser were touring the country on any pretext, giving speeches as if they were running for office in a functioning democracy. The younger officer was the better speaker and his thoughts were clearer. Though in June 1952 Nasser bribed Naguib by installing him in the office of president while settling on being vice president, the differences between the two were too fundamental to die. Afterward, Naguib's independence began to show in other areas. In the field of foreign relations, in June 1953 he used the visit of Secretary of State John Foster Dulles to promote his own image as

Egyptian head of state. Thinking that allying himself with the United States would help him against Nasser, he told Dulles that he would look with favor upon the presence in Egypt of a U.S. military mission,[53] and he failed to say anything about Palestine. The first high-ranking foreign personality to visit Egypt since the revolution, Dulles gave Naguib a gold revolver as a present from President Eisenhower.

Nasser, occupied with the negotiations with Britain to replace the 1936 treaty with an agreement to end their occupation of the Suez Canal area and determined to make his foreign policy mark there, wanted to be identified with this primary demand of the RCC and the Egyptian people. He wanted to oversee the departure of all foreign troops. He personally led the Egyptian negotiating team, which began meeting with the British in March 1953. Simultaneously he initiated another move, which revealed his commitment to internal reform and to relieving the external pressure on Egypt. He established secret contacts toward achieving peace with Israel. At first Nasser used Sarwat Okasha to contact the small, unrepresentative Arab-Israeli Peace Committee, the ad hoc group made up of intellectuals in Paris.[54] When the Israelis welcomed Okasha's move, Nasser decided to give the contact a more permanent form and put the initiative in the hands of Abdel Rahman Sadeq, an attaché at the Egyptian embassy in France.[55]

Before long Naguib and Nasser openly competed for control of Egypt. The younger man was itching to replace the idol he had created. However vague the six-point program of the officers, it did call for structural changes in Egypt's social and political system, and the land reform program did turn a nearly bloodless army coup into a social revolution. This commitment to change was confirmed by abolishing the monarchy. Naguib had nothing to offer that could match these moves. All we know is that he wanted a corruption-free government through the use of the old governmental system, the monarchy, the old political parties, and an elected parliament. The man who personified the revolution and who had the people behind him stood for nothing. But sensing his strength on the street level and the consequent weakness of Nasser and his young comrades, Naguib tried to get rid of them.

As already stated, Naguib's first move was to establish contact with and win the support of the Muslim Brotherhood.[56] The general and the Islamic group were bound together by their common hatred of Communism and their opposition to anything that smacked of socialist ideology. The Naguib-Brotherhood contacts took place throughout 1953 and during the early part of 1954, a time which witnessed many street and university clashes between members of the Brotherhood and supporters of the RCC-backed Liberation Rally. Though this meant that followers of Nasser and supporters of Naguib were battling each other daily throughout the country, Naguib went further in soliciting the backing of old political institutions. Foolishly, he met with Mustapha Nahas, the old leader of the Wafd Party who had been granted amnesty and allowed to live in peace with the implicit understanding that he would undertake no political activity. This provocative move, made in the open as a challenge to Nasser, sealed Naguib's fate.[57] Nasser was determined to get rid of him. The contest became one between a progressive colonel and a reactionary general.

In February 1954, army units loyal to Nasser kidnapped Naguib and announced that he had been relieved of all his duties.[58] In the streets of Cairo pro- and anti-Naguib demonstrations broke out. Followers of the Brotherhood and the Wafd, and others who believed he was the actual leader of the revolution, were for Naguib's reinstatement. The numbers produced by Nasser's Liberation Rally could not match those who rose in support of Naguib, and it looked as if Nasser and his supporters might have to use the army against the people. But the decisive support for Naguib, a move that halted the slide toward civil war and anarchy, came from an unexpected source, RCC member Khalid Mohieddine. The very popular major ordered units of the armored corps to free Naguib immediately, even if that meant fighting the pro-Nasser troops which had kidnapped him.

With Mohieddine breaking rank and most of the people clamoring for the release of Naguib, Nasser relented and allowed the general to reassume his duties, or to look as if he were. But it was not a total loss for Nasser. He withheld the announcement reinstating Naguib until March, then appointed himself prime minister and promoted Abdel Hakim Amer, the man who seemed to control his success, to general and gave him the command of the armed forces—two positions formerly occupied by Naguib. In fact, this time all the cabinet posts except two were filled by reliable members of the RCC. Naguib was surrounded but did nothing, even when several high-ranking officers resigned to protest the Amer appointment and promotion, which they called an attempt to politicize the army and keep it loyal to Nasser. It most definitely was, and soon Amer, with Nasser's open connivance, used Naguib's absence in the Sudan to purge the army of all those who might support Naguib. For Naguib, this was a major missed opportunity.

Nowadays Mohieddine confirms that he opposed Nasser because he determined that the officers still couldn't continue to run the country without Naguib,[59] that even two years after the coup, in 1954, Naguib was still needed by the RCC. Because no other officer supported Naguib, and some of them, particularly Amer, could read street sentiment quite well, there is reason to believe that Mohieddine was motivated by a more selfish reason; perhaps he wanted to be prime minister in place of Nasser. But Mohieddine was not up to opposing Nasser, and after a few days the latter managed to dismiss and arrest all officers who had cooperated with Mohieddine, surround the rebellious units, and then place them under officers loyal to him. Khalid Mohieddine was placed under house arrest, then given a leave of absence and exiled to Europe. Ostensibly he represented the government in several European capitals. The exile of Khalid Mohieddine rather than a more violent fate reconfirms Nasser's opposition to the shedding of blood. In any other Arab country he would have been executed, or at least imprisoned.

After Mohieddine was out of the way, the rest of the Free Officers lost no time in publicizing the Naguib-Nahas contacts and exaggerating the threat they represented. This all but finished the general—not even Naguib's supporters among the Muslim Brotherhood could justify a return to the corrupt Wafd. But soon, in July 1954, the feud between Nasser and Naguib was rekindled by another policy disagreement. This happened when Nasser and British minister of state for foreign affairs Anthony Nutting signed an agreement in principle regarding "all outstanding issues between their two countries." The agreement that was to be finalized later promised the withdrawal of all the British forces in Egypt. While Naguib could not oppose the primary promise of the agreement, he did object to the articles that dealt with the Sudan and gave that country the right of self-determination. Naguib was half Sudanese and extremely popular in that country, and he thought that many of the officers would support him because they and most Egyptians believed the Sudan belonged to Egypt.

From July to the finalization of the evacuation agreement in October, the Muslim Brotherhood stepped up its campaign against Nasser. It continued to object to the articles granting the Sudan the right of self-determination, something which the RCC had accepted beginning in 1953, despite Naguib's protests. The Brotherhood certainly rejected the new treaty's stipulation that 1,100 British technicians be left behind as a nucleus for the return of British troops in case of an attack by the USSR against any part of the Middle East except Iran or Israel. Even today there are some Egyptians who accuse Nasser of giving up the Sudan in order to get an agreement on the Suez Canal that would enhance his popularity.[60] Of course, the Sudanese voted overwhelmingly for independence, and though a measure of cynicism may have been behind Nasser's move, he was right in thinking that evacuating the canal was uppermost in people's minds and that most people had no strong feelings regarding Egyptian unity with the Sudan. The whole issue was settled in his favor when the new Sudanese government came out for total "brotherly" cooperation with the Egyptian regime.

In October 1954 Egypt underwent another unplanned change. Many moves to reconcile Naguib and Nasser had been made between July and October, including an intercession by the visiting monarch of Saudi Arabia, King Saud. But the two found it impossible to work together after brief periods of peace, and each thought he would win over the other. Naguib did not appreciate the damage done to him by trying to cooperate with the Wafd and Nahas. On the other hand, Nasser's position was strengthened by his surgical removal of Khalid Mohieddine, by the simple fact that all his original comrades supported him and wanted Naguib removed, and by the growing organization and strength of the Liberation Rally. As very often happens in similar situations, the spark that led to a final confrontation between the two officers was supplied by an outsider who acted on the orders of a party not directly involved in the conflict.

On October 26, 1954, a Muslim Brother by the name of Mohamed Abdel Latif tried to assassinate Nasser while he was delivering a speech celebrating the signing of the evacuation agreement with Britain in a large hall in the Manshieh district of Alexandria. The Brotherhood had released pamphlets promising that the agreement "shall not pass."[61] Latif, a mere twenty-five feet away from Nasser, managed to fire eight shots, one of which wounded a guard. But he missed his target. Mayhem broke out, and the available audiotape of the incident has Nasser raising his voice above the din and authoritatively appealing to all "brothers and sisters" to stay calm. With a modicum of calm restored, Nasser, characteristically better at improvising than reading speeches, delivered one of his memorable lines. In his clear, distinctive, and attractive baritone voice he hooked into the veins of the audience and told them what they wanted to hear: "If Abdel Nasser dies then everyone of you is Abdel Nasser. . . . Each of you is Gamal Abdel Nasser. Gamal Abdel Nasser is of you and from you and he is willing to sacrifice his life for the nation." The hall roared with approval. Transported by his own words, Nasser raised his hands beside his head in the typical *baladi* or native style peculiar to the Said, and shook them backward and forward in a gesture of triumph. The assassination attempt began backfiring and playing into Nasser's hands a mere few seconds after it took place.

On Nasser's return to Cairo the biggest political crackdown in the history of Egypt began, and many of the thousands arrested suffered torture. It was a period of official terror that exceeded what had happened under Abdel Hadi. Seven hundred Muslim Brethren were rounded up during the first two days; 140 officers were dismissed from the service, and many of them were arrested.[62] A People's Court was created in early November and the mercurial Gamal Salem, appropriately elevated to deputy prime minister by Nasser, was made its president. It handled cases referred to it by special civil courts. In fact, the civil courts referred everything to Salem, who enjoyed his role and expanded the function of his court to include Communists arrested because of their opposition to the treaty well before the assassination attempt.

According to the People's Court's records, the atmosphere was not conducive to fair trials because the Muslim Brotherhood had planned to kill all members of the original RCC and dozens of officers who backed them. Some suspects were not represented by defense lawyers. Often the whole business descended to farce. The court files show statement following empty, unconvincing statement about a multitude of conspiracies to kill Nasser. Gamal Salem kept repeating the list of conspiracies, and leaned on the *er* at the end of Nasser, as if to emphasize its meaning of "victorious." But there was little doubt—and the behavior of the would-be assassin, who managed to escape for two days, proves it—that there had been an extensive conspiracy by people who were ready to die eliminating a socialist apostate. Eventually eight people were condemned to death, but the sentence of the Brotherhood's supreme guide, Hassan Hodeibi, was commuted. So was the sentence of the Brotherhood's leading ideologue, Sayyed Qutub. The remaining six people were executed, but one of the leading conspirators, original Free Officers member Abdel Munim Abdel Raouf, managed to escape. Like Khalid Mohieddine, Abdel Raouf had little power in the army or with his comrades. His departure was no more than an embarrassment.

The crackdown continued well into 1955, and what constituted a crime against "the revolution" was expanded to include membership in the United Revolutionary Front, the February 1953 open alliance of the Brotherhood, Communists, and Wafdists created to oppose the officers. The number of people who were detained during that period may have exceeded twenty thousand. There is little doubt that some, Muslim activists Mohamed Osman and Mustapha Sharaf among them, died under torture. Others were sent to what were later described as concentration camps, Abu Za'abal, Fayoum the Citadel, and Kharga,[63] the prisons that were expanded to cope with the new situation. When it came to the Muslim Brotherhood, Nasser showed none of the humanity and compromises that otherwise marked his regime.

The exact date of Naguib's removal is unknown, but it followed shortly after the assassination attempt. He was put under house arrest but never tried or sentenced. This time nobody in the army rose to defend him, and his street following of Muslim Brethren and Wafdists was already being hunted. The Nasser propaganda machine, using the facilities of the state and the Liberation Rally, went beyond accusing him of opposing land reform and abolishing the monarchy and began portraying him as a bumbling weakling whose young second wife (he had two) beat him up on a regular basis.[64] Of course, the Muslim Brotherhood was dissolved, and many of its leaders who survived the purge escaped overseas—to pro-Western countries that approved of the Brotherhood's Western-supported anti-Communism, mostly Jordan, Syria, and Saudi Arabia.

While Naguib had been discredited through his contacts with unacceptable reactionary groups, Nasser's street following was still too small to sustain his plans and secure him in office. This prompted him to use his new secret weapons, his unequaled mastery of speech making and his exclusive control of the state's media organs. He toured Egypt, ostensibly on behalf of the Liberation Rally, but in reality promoting his own personal standing.

He gave speech after speech and had the state radio carry them. All were long, well delivered, and convincing. "The glory and dignity of the people was above all else."

Just as important as what Nasser said was how he said it: he always sounded as if he were having a personal conversation with each member of his audience. He spoke to unknown listeners the same way he spoke to personal friends, and his audiences loved it.[65] Most Egyptians now thought Naguib the front man had fooled them. Nasser's personal efforts were augmented by the state media, which did everything from broadcasting songs written in his praise and sung by Um Kalsum, the leading singer in the land (*"Ya gamal ya mithal al watania,"* "Oh Gamal ultimate example of nationalism"), to producing thinly disguised plays denigrating his enemies. According to his associates, Nasser himself orchestrated this elaborate multilayered campaign.

In January 1955 the RCC appointed Nasser president, pending an election to the office. It was a major change of direction for someone who a mere year before had wanted the army to go back to its barracks, the very same man who had opposed his comrades and supported the reestablishment of parliamentary democracy. In fact, with his personal tours speechifying and promoting his decrees, the People's Court created to punish his enemies, and a most effective use of the state media, Nasser managed to create a dictatorial regime—at this early stage without knowing it.

Nasser defies being classified as a typical dictator, a brooding, secretive psychopath, or one who thrived on conflict. Still an adoring family man, he took time out from his sixteen-hour workdays to spend afternoons with his wife and children, the youngest named Abdel Hakim after Amer. He continued to live in the same modest house he had occupied when he was a colonel. Beyond his work and his family he played the occasional game of tennis, but he was never tempted by money or lavish living. Regardless of their status in life, he spoke to others with the utmost deference. Even the officers he dismissed from the army for being royalists or Muslim Brotherhood sympathizers continued to receive full salaries.[66] This pattern of contradictory behavior continued after he became popular enough and secure enough to win a free election. Calling for one was a chance he missed. By any historical yardstick, what existed in Egypt was something unique, a dictatorship without a dictator, or with a flawed dictator who still celebrated his association with the people.

# 3

# The Road to Suez

Nasser was pro-American, anti-Communist, against the corrupt monarchy and pashas, and opposed to political Islamic movements. But his admiration for America did not limit or diminish him. Unlike other Arab leaders of his time and later, he did not depend on America to exist. His natural, instinctive need to respond to the wishes of his people came ahead of all else, and made him popular. Until the end of 1955 and his rejection of America's invitation to join an anti-Communist regional alliance which held no interest for the Egyptians and the rest of the Arabs, reconciling his pro–United States inclinations with a populist attitude was relatively easy. Nasser's wish to remain independent of all alliances became an even bigger problem when he broke the Western monopoly on the supply of arms to the Arab world and bought arms from the Eastern Bloc.

Later, whether to follow his people or America became the strategic problem of his foreign policy, and it grew in importance after his references to "my people" and "our people" changed from Egyptian to Arab. When forced to make a choice, Nasser continued to accept the supremacy of the will of the people—even when what the people wanted was shallow and lacked reason. This acceptance of the popular will made him an enigma; outside governments, diplomats, and journalists could not understand why someone so worldly, able, and cautious would occasionally behave so recklessly. The contradiction between his diplomatic language and friendly relations with American diplomats and CIA officers on one hand, and his acceptance of his people's anti-Americanism on the other, was very near the surface.

Amazingly, the one major subject on which Nasser did not follow a clear populist policy was the important one of relations with Israel. He, Naguib, and a good number of his comrades believed peace was on the way at a time when the Egyptian people were most passionately opposed to Israel. But it was also true that Nasser contradicted his seeming moderation toward Israel when he published *Philosophy of the Revolution* in 1954. This booklet, which purported to give the leader of the Free Officers movement an ideology and which adopted Arab nationalism and placed it ahead of Egyptianism, contained a more confrontational Arab attitude toward Zionism. Now we know that it was written by the noted Egyptian journalist Mohamed Heikal, an ardent Arab nationalist. In it Nasser laid out what he considered Egypt's Arab identity and the obligations this entailed.

Nasser saw Egypt existing in and influencing three different but overlapping circles of political and cultural power: an Arab circle, an Islamic circle, and an African circle. The Arab circle was the most important one; it was more immediate and reflective of the thinking of the Egyptians. There was no separate Egyptian circle, none of the exclusively Egyptian nationalism embodied in the six-point program Nasser and his comrades had authored. *Philosophy of the Revolution* heralded a huge change of direction from an Egypt-first policy to Arab nationalism. Since this occurred well before any direct involvement in Arab affairs, it was clearly a case of modest ideology preceding action and not, as some allege, the other way around.

To the Nasser of *Philosophy of the Revolution,* leading the Arabs forward was Egypt's destiny. This, however, should be accepted as a personal belief of Nasser's. In the memoirs of Khalid Mohieddine, Abdel Latif Boghdadi, and Anwar Sadat, all written after Nasser's death and hence unencumbered by his presence (and the three authors represented different ideological tendencies within the new rulership of Egypt), there is nothing to suggest that other members of the Association of Free Officers agreed with Nasser's pan-Arab tilt and deviation from their original program. Their ambitions appear to have been local, limited to Egypt, and restrained, with special attachment to unity of ranks, work, and order. For the most part, Nasser's former comrades were busy becoming bureaucrats, coming to grips with their new ministerial or other high positions. Though diversity of opinion among members of the Association existed in abundance, Nasser's ideas prevailed. He was the leader of the officers' movement and eventually head of the government, and he had his way of dominating, regardless of the importance of the subject matter under consideration. He turned his positions into adopted policy acceptable by all. This reflected poorly on the competence of his comrades: Nasser's manipulations and strength of character reduced the rest of them to yes-men.

The change in direction from narrow Egyptian to broader Arab thinking immediately raises a number of questions. The first question is how a leader or state could assume an Arab position and lead the Arabs while accepting the principle of peace with Israel at the same time. On this Nasser was never clear; he left us with little that would help us reach a conclusion. Certainly there is nothing to resolve this contradiction in the accounts of his comrades and colleagues, Heikal included. He was never as direct and clear as when he (or Heikal) wrote his condemnation of Communism, *Communism As It Really Is,* early in 1953. This booklet was an explicit attack on Communism and "its evil consequences," and pleased the United States.

The second question concerns reconciling his ostensible commitment to democracy with his slow but deliberate movement toward controlling all aspects of Egyptian life. He either took all his comrades for granted or circumvented them even on such weighty matters. This was definitely true when he took control of the army through appointing Amer its commander in chief, something that should have rung alarm bells among fellow officers and which eventually came back to haunt him. Of course, there are dozens of subsidiary questions, such as the effect of this change of policy on Egypt's relations with the West and with the pro-West Arab regimes and whether Egypt could afford to lead the Arabs.

Nasser was strongly anti-Communist, but was he intrinsically anti-Israel? Was he pushed into his anti-Israel position by his pan-Arab ambitions or by the behavior of Israel itself? This is a question which still elicits heated debate on intellectual and street levels, and recent developments in the Middle East are likely to contribute to more discussion. According to Khalid Mohieddine,

"Nasser never closed the door on peace, he left it wide open. He was open to contact [by the Israelis] on the subject." Mohieddine was speaking of the early days and obviously making the point that Nasser always believed that peace with Israel was possible.[1] However, Dr. Huda Abdel Nasser, Nasser's daughter, rejects Mohieddine's statement and declares, "My father knew the Israelis did not want peace, so he decided it was impossible to try to make peace with Israel. The only time he accepted a peace proposal was when he wanted to expose the hypocrisy of Israel."[2] Hakim Abdel Nasser, Nasser's youngest son, provides a third, more complicated explanation which is somewhat supportive of his sister's position. He tells a story of former British minister of state for foreign affairs Anthony Nutting, the man who signed the agreement evacuating British forces from Suez, telling Israeli prime minister David Ben-Gurion that he had good news for him: Nasser was more concerned with raising the standard of living of the people of Egypt than in making war on Israel. According to Hakim Abdel, Ben-Gurion looked at Nutting and said, "You call that good news?"[3]

The story is meant to expose an Israel that had no intention of leaving Nasser alone to build a strong Egypt, a Ben-Gurion who was against any reform program that would turn an inward-looking Egypt into a threat. Considering Israel's inclination to support unpopular Arab leaders while rejecting the ones with a street following, this policy is probably the same today. For example, Israel always liked the Hashemites, the family of King Hussein, because they accommodated Israel. Unpopular and unacceptable to most of the people themselves, the Hashemites saw in Israel a natural ally against the development of democracy to replace their antiquated ways.

With the elements that produced the historical controversy over Nasser's true intentions toward Israel still in place, I find no better way to judge his attitude to peace than to examine the scattered contacts aimed at making peace between Egypt and Israel in the 1953–56 period. I say scattered because the contacts were occasional, and some did not go beyond transmitting some semi-serious ideas through an intermediary from an Israeli prime minister to Nasser. Ben-Gurion, committed as he was to direct negotiations between the Arabs and Israel (as opposed to involving third parties such as the United Nations), never tired of sending Nasser invitations to visit Tel Aviv. This is the kind of opening which becomes serious only if it is acted upon, and Ben-Gurion knew Nasser could never accept it and survive.

Moshe Sharett, Israel's second prime minister, though he never had Ben-Gurion's playfulness, was much more committed to initiating contacts with Nasser. He continually sent Egypt's new leader dry, formal, and sincere messages which eventually produced a response in the form of direct and indirect exchanges of views between the two sides. Most exchanges were improvised, taking place in unknown ways through different channels. However, there isn't enough material available on the subject beyond Mohieddine's encompassing statement about "keeping the door open" and authorizing Sadek to continue the contact with the Israelis.

One thing is certain: for most of the 1952–56 period, Nasser was preoccupied with his internal program and problems (abolishing the monarchy, land reform, and the creation of a bureaucracy from the old army officers) and later with wresting the presidency from Naguib's hands. Though he paid lip service to certain things such as liberty for all Arabs, there is no evidence of him doing anything about this advocacy until 1955 and the mostly diplomatic prelude to Suez, which included the creation by Britain of the anti-Communist Baghdad Pact, the results of the Bandung Conference, which saw Nasser join nonallied leaders such as Nehru, Tito, and Chou En-lai in opposing superpower hegemony, and the Czech arms deal, Nasser's purchase of weapons from the Communist bloc. Beyond setting an example for young army officers in other Arab countries (which were not short of history of army involvement in politics), he did nothing to influence events beyond Egypt's border.

I have reached an early conclusion that I will try to support. I believe that Israel forced Nasser to reinvigorate the Egyptian involvement in the Palestinian problem, inadvertently made Palestine of primary importance to Nasser and the Egyptians, and pushed the new Egyptian government into a totally anti-Israel position. Though not necessarily deliberately, when it comes to pressuring Arab leaders, Israel simply didn't and doesn't know when to stop. Israel has always misunderstood the dynamics of Arab society, the workings of Arab governments, and how many of its acts undermine moderate leadership in the Arab world.

In the case of Nasser, they pushed him so hard—mostly through their humiliating raids into Egypt and intelligence work inside Egypt—that he had no option but to respond, or lose the thing most precious to him, his standing with his people: his dignity. This is something the Israelis never understood because they never tried to understand it. And what made it easy for him to respond to Israel was the overwhelming anti-Israel feeling of the Egyptian people. More than most people who assume power through undemocratic means, Nasser's ideal was turning popular ideas into policy.

Nothing demonstrates how Israel forced Nasser to divert his energies toward an external problem instead of the demands inside Egypt better than the 1954–55 Israeli intelligence operation known as the Lavon Affair, and its subsidiary blunders, such as the famous raid on Gaza. Considerably more than an intelligence operation, the Lavon Affair was among the major events which profoundly changed the history of the Arab-Israeli conflict. In terms of its overall effects it compares with the Suez and 1967 wars, which is especially amazing considering that we still don't know all the people behind the affair and how it came about. Nevertheless, the limited material available gives a sense of the sinister atmosphere of Israeli politics, for whatever else the Lavon Affair was, it certainly was a successful operation to railroad a serving Israeli prime minister who wanted to make peace with the Arabs. It also exposes the disdain in which Israeli intelligence held the Arabs, especially if the Israelis truly believed that the operatives involved in the Lavon Affair would not be apprehended. Finally, the Lavon Affair confirms that Israel had influential, if not dominant, antipeace political clusters even in the early 1950s.

To be fully understood, the significance of the Lavon Affair has to be put in context. The border between the Gaza Strip and Egypt on one side and Israel on the other was never completely peaceful. How violent it was depended on one side's reaction to the other's misdeeds and the ability of Egypt to control refugee camp–bred Palestinian irregulars, the fedayeen or "sacrificers." The Israelis despised the people on "the other side of the fence." To the Israelis, even the regular Egyptian forces facing them were nothing more than a discredited army which they had defeated in 1948. But there were fedayeen who, with or without official Egyptian approval, sneaked into Israel to attack small targets. During Nasser's early days, the period of exclusively inward-looking policies and the belief that peace was on the way, the fedayeen had no official backing and in fact were often imprisoned for their activities. Yet Israel always retaliated for such attacks, whether or not they had official sanction; and it was the scale of the Israeli response, indeed often whether it was provoked, preemptive, or a gratuitous act of aggression by a militarily superior country, which revealed the Israeli state of mind. Of course, a disproportionate reaction meant that the fedayeen would hit again, the cycle of violence would repeat itself with familiar frequency, and more people would die and be injured. (This is not very different from what is happening in the West Bank and Gaza now.)

On August 28, 1953, an Israeli raiding party attacked Al Bureig refugee camp in the Gaza Strip, killing twenty people and wounding sixty-one more. Nasser limited his response to inner anger, merely protesting to the UN and repeating his appeal to the United States to supply Egypt with arms. This wasn't anything new: his efforts to buy arms from America, something which revealed his friendly feelings toward the country, had started soon after July 23, 1952.[4] But once again, America tarried. The CIA Cairo group (Copeland, Lakeland, and Mead among others), run mostly from a distance by Kermit "Kim" Roosevelt, favored selling Egypt arms, but the State Department stuck to the Tripartite Declaration of France, Britain, and the United States, which embargoed arms sales, and overruled the CIA group. When approached, the French repeated the American response. And Nasser's deep mistrust of Britain prevented his trying to buy arms from that country. So Egypt was not in a position to respond to the Israeli incursion even had it wanted to. This was still the case when the Israelis raided the village of Qibya in the West Bank in October 1953, again supposedly responding to a Palestinian fedayeen incursion, and killed sixty-six villagers. True, the raid was against territory under Jordan, but other Arabs felt the humiliation too. Like the rest of the Arab countries, Egypt condemned the attack but did nothing.

Finally, on November 2, 1953, Nasser received some good news from Israel. Hawkish prime minister David Ben-Gurion, the man behind Israel's policy of massive retaliation, announced his retirement and retreated to the Negev settlement of Sede Boker. He was succeeded by Moshe Sharett, Israel's first minister of foreign affairs and an accomplished diplomat, a linguist who spoke Arabic well and appreciated Arab ways and culture. Admirers called him "the Professor." The difference in character between Ben-Gurion and Sharett was visible; the older man was disheveled and uncomfortable in a suit, whereas Sharett was always impeccably attired and looked like a gentleman industrialist from the Midlands of England or the industrial heart of Germany. Many observers who knew him believed Sharett would lead Israel's Arab policy toward moderation, and with time, perhaps even peace.

The post of minister of defense, also held by Ben-Gurion when he was prime minister, went to Pinhas Lavon, an unpredictable protégé of Ben-Gurion who had always advocated a hard line against the Arabs.[5] This appointment reflected the divisions within the Israeli parliamentary system, based on proportional representation, rather than on any acceptance by Sharett of the hard-line Lavon policy. The amazing start of secret contacts between Israel and Egypt, Sharett and Nasser, began practically immediately after Sharett assumed office.[6] Professor Mordachai Bar-On, a former Israeli intelligence officer and diplomat, and Avi Shlaim, a highly acclaimed Israeli historian, have documented the momentous events of this period.

The original Israeli-Egyptian contacts took place through American diplomatic channels with some participation from the CIA. The earliest meetings were held in Washington, D.C. At first U.S. ambassador to Egypt Jefferson Caffrey is supposed to have acted as an intermediary, then there were other, unnamed diplomats, and then came direct meetings. In the Washington meetings, the Israeli side was represented by future president Chaim Herzog and diplomat Gideon Raphael; the Egyptians were represented by Colonel Abdel Hamid Ghaleb of the Egyptian embassy.[7] It is safe to assume that though they did not attend all the meetings, the Americans knew about the Washington ones. The background to the talks was auspicious: there were no major border incidents between the two countries during this period. Nasser managed to curb the fedayeen, so Sharett had no reason to retaliate, and, unlike the hawks, he did not initiate any raids. Goodwill was present on both sides.

We know nothing about these meetings beyond the general points: Egyptian insistence that the UN resolutions on the Arab-Israeli conflict form the basis for continued discourse, and Sharett's refusal to contemplate some of the things the resolutions demanded, such as the return of most of the refugees and ceding some land to the Arabs. There is no reliable record of what happened, even in Herzog's memoirs. But the contacts continued in Paris, and this reveals a commitment to dialogue on both sides. As stated before, some of the Paris meetings were held with the senior

RCC member Sarwat Okasha. This too is revealing. Either Nasser was acting on a correct presumption that the RCC supported a peaceful approach to the Israeli issue, or Nasser talked them into it. Either way, the RCC was in favor of negotiating a settlement to the Arab-Israeli conflict.

Eventually the main channels for what is known as the "secret negotiations" were first secretary of the Israeli embassy in Paris Shmuel Born, and briefly Ali Shawki, then Abdel Rahman Sadeq, of the Egyptian embassy.[8] Judging by the contents of letters exchanged without being signed between Nasser and Sharett, the two lost no time in getting down to discussing the hard issues which separated the two countries. Sharett wanted Nasser to lift the blockade of shipping to and from Israel through the Suez Canal and the Gulf of Aqaba; Nasser asked Israel to take back Palestinian refugees and, in a sign of his seriousness, began compromising regarding the number of refugees who should be repatriated. Though Sharett accepted the principle of compensating the Palestinian refugees, neither side was ready to go far enough in compromising. But the atmosphere of the negotiations was friendly, and Sadeq was known to have assured the Israelis that Nasser had no aggressive intentions towards them.

Professor Avi Shlaim rightly says that the contacts offered a modest degree of hope. My journalist father backs Shlaim's assertion and says that it was because of the "seriousness" of the negotiations that relations between Nasser and the mufti of Palestine (the head of the Arab Higher Committee and the Arafat of his day) deteriorated. The mufti, a militant, was totally opposed to Nasser's move. Unverified reports spoke of the mufti's joining forces with the Muslim Brotherhood in their opposition to Nasser's policy toward Israel. It is important to answer the question of whether these were not only secret but promising negotiations.

The answer is an unqualified yes. The negotiations represented something very serious—if only because the people involved reported directly to the heads of their governments and the mere act of meeting the other side represented a departure from the professed policy of at least the Egyptian government. To the Arabs, Egypt represented weight; it was the region's cultural center and the home of the Arab League. Its absence from Arab ranks would have ended the opposition of the Arab governments or, as happened under Sadat, weakened it irreparably. They had no plan to fight Israel, let alone defeat it, but they were not ready to make peace with it. The only leader to negotiate with Israel secretly before Nasser was King Abdullah of Jordan, and he paid for it with his life in 1951. The mufti's thinking was different: like Arafat, he wanted Arabs to arm the Palestinians to fight for their country and to support his leadership. His thinking was close to that of the Muslim Brotherhood. He certainly did not believe that Nasser should break ranks and negotiate a separate peace with Israel. He thought of Nasser's as the fallback position.

On the other side, many Israelis opposed negotiating peace with the leading Arab country at a time when Israel was young and its ethno-religious separateness from the rest of the region had not been solidly established. They believed that Israel needed more time for its national identity to gel, and saw peace as a dangerous step which contained in it the potential of Israel being submerged by a sea of Arabs. Taking this further, there was a danger to both the overall Arab position and Israel's Jewish identity if the negotiations succeeded. Unless one considers extremists within the country, as represented by the Muslim Brotherhood, being able to capitalize on anti-Israeli feeling, there was no danger to Egypt from within. Nasser was in a better position to continue the negotiations than Sharett. The question was not proffered at the time because it was and is impossible to judge the popularity of something secret.

What prompted the political hawks, David Ben-Gurion and Moshe Dayan, in Israel to oppose the secret peace negotiations was the moderate feelings toward the Arabs created by the Sharett government. The hawks decided to go beyond discrediting their own government; they decided to undermine Egypt's and Nasser's policies of moderation. Even at a time when it was finalizing a peaceful withdrawal agreement with Britain and in dialogue with the United States aimed at improving the level of security and intelligence cooperation between the two countries, the militant Israelis saw Egypt as a magnet for disaffected Arabs, an unsettling influence on the rest of the area that should be eliminated. This group of Israeli politicians believed that Britain would not sign an agreement with an unstable country, and the United States would refrain from allying itself with a shaky regime in Egypt. Moreover, by making Egypt an unsafe country, the hawks in Israel were administering a blow to Nasser's plans to attract foreign capital. He had already announced a number of measures of exempting foreign corporations from taxes and allowing them to gain majority control of companies in Egypt.

On the other side, the Arab countries had no idea negotiations were taking place, so there were no cries against Egypt breaking Arab solidarity. Here it should be remembered that the Arab countries usually followed Egypt, but the Egyptian public was not inclined to follow the other Arab governments. However, it merits repeating that in view of the involvement of someone of the stature of Okasha in the negotiations, either Nasser did consult his comrades and had many of them in his confidence, or he took their acceptance of his peace policy for granted. Since the memoirs of his comrades don't mention the issue, the latter looks more likely. Nasser's policy clearly shows that Palestine did not assume a primary position with him until later.

According to most accounts of the Lavon Affair, the leader of the Israeli hawks, David Ben-Gurion (and his followers), used his protégé, Defense Minister Pinhas Lavon, to undermine the Nasser and Sharett governments. As the story goes, Lavon, without consulting Prime Minister Sharett, appears to have activated an Israeli intelligence cell in Egypt.[9] Because Aman, Israel's military intelligence, is in charge of special operations, the activated cell, Unit 131, belonged to this organization and not to the infamous and perhaps more professional Mossad. Some members of the cell had been "sleepers" in Egypt since 1951. Others who were sent to join them arrived shortly before Operation Susannah, the intelligence code name for what they were about to start. The team began work in the spring of 1954.[10] Susannah operatives struck in early July, when Anglo-Egyptian negotiations regarding the replacement of the 1936 treaty by an agreement that would call for the evacuation of the troops along the Suez Canal were close to success. The United States and Egypt had cooperated on several security programs and were negotiating an intelligence-information-sharing agreement[11] and discussing a regional defense pact; the United States was trying to get Israel and the Arabs to agree on a scheme to share the waters of the Jordan River; and the Nasser-Sharett contacts, though they had not made much progress, still looked promising because both sides wanted to continue meeting and exploring the chances for peace. In fact, Nasser had expressed a desire to raise the level of contacts, something to which Sharett agreed—though nothing ever came of this.

Nowadays, most writers and analysts point out the amateurish behavior of members of the cell in their sabotage of cinemas,

American libraries, and post offices, and their plans to do the same to Western-owned establishments. But for Avrham Seidenberg, alias Paul Frank, all of the Israeli participants in Operation Susannah were arrested and tortured, and eventually confessed. One committed suicide, two were hanged, and the others were exchanged for thousands of Egyptian prisoners after the 1956 Suez War. Judged by what happened to members of Aman cell, Unit 131, Susannah was a failure. The list of mistakes attributed to the operatives can be summed up by the word incompetence. Judged by the human factor, the cost of agents "lost" to Israel, the operation failed. But if the operation's ultimate purpose was to get rid of Sharett and his policy of negotiating a peace agreement with Egypt and to undermine Nasser's relations with the United States, then Operation Susannah was a success. Moreover, the negotiations to share the waters of the Jordan, a pet project of President Eisenhower entrusted to his special envoy, Eric Johnston, came to an end partly because of the atmosphere created by Susannah and its consequences. The one thing Susannah failed to achieve was to stop the signing of the Anglo-Egyptian agreement, but then Unit 131 was not activated early enough to stop something which had been in the making for some time.

But more important, perhaps, just perhaps, all the amateurish behavior which violated the rules of the real spy world, like one person in Susannah knowing everything about all the rest, was deliberate. It is difficult to understand why Frank, the case officer of the operation and known to everyone in it, was not named in the confessions of the various people who were tortured, and managed to stay in Egypt for some time. Some argue that his cover as a German businessman was good, but others had similar covers, some deeper. According to her cover, Marcelle Ninio was an established travel agent; others were supposed to be Germans like Frank; and most had been in Egypt for some time.

To put it in the simplest terms possible, what Susannah started on July 4, 1954, was an incendiary campaign against British and American interests in Egypt. The first target, the American library in Cairo, was severely damaged. Susannah's various members then set fire to cinemas, post offices, and other libraries of the United States Information Agency (USIA) in Cairo and Alexandria. To the outside world, Egypt looked like an unstable country with an anti-Western population, a place one shouldn't even visit let alone invest in or cooperate with—exactly what the perpetrators wanted. According to General Abdel Fatah Riyadh, the man in charge of the forensic part of the investigation, one of the Israeli agents (Philip Nathonson) accidentally set himself on fire in front of the Rivoli Cinema in Alexandria. When he was apprehended and interrogated, he was found to carry an eyeglass case with a soft cleaning tissue on which were written the names and addresses of all of his colleagues. Later, under torture, he provided additional detailed information[12] which led to the discovery of microfilm, invisible ink, and radio transmitters. The remaining twelve members of the cell (minus Frank) were either manipulated toward certain arrest from the start or used after they were arrested by someone back in Jerusalem. There is no answer as to why the glasses case, containing a cleaning tissue with the list of operatives inscribed, and belonging to someone who accidentally set fire to himself, was discovered right away.

Israel has a history of always wanting to save the lives of its agents. It is difficult to conceive of an Israeli intelligence operation that called for the deliberate sacrifice of agents. However, it is well to remember that Susannah was not an ordinary intelligence operation. Among other things, there was a hurried air about the whole thing. The available evidence points to Lavon's involvement but not necessarily as the leading character in a plot. Among others, the late Moshe Dayan of Israeli military fame, one of the organizers of the operation, accused Lavon of misleading Sharett.[13] We still don't know whether Lavon authorized the operation in detail or whether he just gave it a general direction and left the rest to the professionals. Nor do we know who took the strategic decision to scuttle the negotiations aimed at reaching a peace agreement between Israel and Egypt. The odd nature of the operation and the mysterious (the details were not published) 1960 high court decision to absolve Lavon of overall responsibility for what happened in Egypt make reaching a definite conclusion difficult.

The odds as to who initiated Susannah are in favor of someone who was exasperated with the traditional Israeli way of making strategic decisions through changing government, someone capable of sending agents to their certain death to prompt Nasser to doubt Sharett's veracity, to terminate the secret negotiations, and to bring Egyptian-U.S. security and intelligence cooperation to an end. Nasser's conspiratorial mind was capable of attributing mysterious acts of sabotage to Israel, but the capture of Israeli spies meant he had to act, and in acting to explain the state of play between

Egypt and Israel. This meant there was pressure on Nasser to disclose that secret negotiations were taking place at a time when their chances of success had just ended and when such a disclosure would have lowered his standing in Egypt and the rest of the Arab world. It is no wonder that Nasser himself never deviated from thinking that the Lavon Affair's aim was to force him out of office.[14]

Surely the extensive list of targets and the unexplained laxness on the part of the Israeli agents made the apprehension of one of them likely. The list of targets, and the fact that the participants in Susannah knew about each other, must have been known to whoever controlled the operation. If not, then it was a case of allowing the agents to stumble on their own—and that too could have played into the hands of the instigator(s) back in Jerusalem. The demands for the release of the operatives by Sharett were a case of someone pleading for the lives of people who knowingly undertook to finish him politically. Another thing is clear: collectively the Sharett government was not responsible for Susannah. It was either a member of the government acting on his or her own, or an outsider important enough to overcome the legal barriers standing in the way. It had to be someone to whom a whole intelligence service would listen.

A fuming Nasser saw what he was intended to see: a conspiracy. Essentially, what Nasser believed is what mattered, whether or not it was true and whether or not it was an attempt to undermine him in favor of someone else. Even if Sharett himself was not involved, Nasser could not continue negotiations with a country which was divided over dealing with him. The investigation he ordered led to a trial of the captured Israeli spies, but he stopped the court short of exposing the reason behind Susannah: the secret peace negotiations. Nasser, already disappointed and undermined by America's refusal to supply him with arms, and skeptical enough about its policies toward Egypt to tell U.S. ambassador Henry Byroade that he was considering buying arms from the USSR, did not tell the Egyptian people that he was negotiating peace with Israel and sharing intelligence and security information with the U.S. government because he had nothing to show for either effort. To Nasser's propaganda machine, the world was black and white, and even during the secret negotiations he had been telling his people how perfidious the Israelis were, given the absence of concrete results. It was easier to follow the same line. He was trapped in a historical maxim which haunts most undemocratic regimes: having to settle for simple facts. The presence in Egypt of Israeli saboteurs who were apprehended and had to be punished made him turn down appeals for clemency for the Susannah operatives. The appeals were made openly by many Jewish organizations and politicians and in secret by the CIA's Kim Roosevelt among others. But these appeals came from people who did not fully appreciate what it meant for Nasser to lose his dignity, or even appear that way. In January 1955 he did execute the two Susannah members sentenced to death. He stopped all meetings with Sharett's representatives, because either he believed Sharett was conspiring against him or he knew that Sharett could not control the intelligence departments of the Israeli government. Sharett did not protest and was out of office soon after. Thus, in a sea of suspicion, the first attempt at an Israeli-Egyptian peace settlement ended.

In Israel itself, the affair made Sharett look weak and not up to the job of prime minister. He not only ordered an inquiry into what the press began calling the Lavon Affair, he tried to compensate for the people's loss of confidence in him by sending an Israeli ship, the *Bat Galim,* through the Suez Canal. The crew was arrested and the ship was denied passage, but Nasser released the crew to Israel after three months, almost simultaneous with the two executions. Although Nasser had given up on the Israeli government as a peace partner, he was still trying to maintain a good image with America and the West. In fact, Nasser's anti-Israeli propaganda was moderated, and the instructions for this came from Nasser personally. But in Israel people asked themselves how such a disaster as the Lavon Affair could take place in a democracy. Whatever the answers—and most of the ones given were unsatisfactory—the affair strengthened the hand of the antipeace group in Israel.

For blocking the Suez Canal and Aqaba Straits and making statements supporting Syria and Jordan against Israeli expansionist designs, Nasser was becoming a monster. The thought of Israeli citizens going to the gallows, regardless of the reason behind it, was a sure way to generate stronger anti-Nasser feelings. Lavon, professing ignorance about Susannah but unable to absolve himself, had to resign. After announcing his resignation, he accused Aman chief Binyamin Glibi of undermining him. His last act was to point an accusing finger at Ben-Gurion. Many in Israel agreed with him, but few were ready to do more, to expose the sinister existence in Israel of people who were above the law, even if they were among the country's founding fathers. Lavon exited on February 1955, two days after two members of the Susannah ring were executed in Egypt (another, Max Bennet, had already committed suicide). There was an international outcry against the executions. Jewish members of the British Parliament such as Maurice Orbach and American Jewish leaders who had tried to intervene with Nasser joined the protesters. Nasser did not budge; he was repairing the real and intended damage to his dignity.

Amazingly, Lavon was replaced as minister of defense by former prime minister David Ben-Gurion, the man thought by many to be the real moving spirit behind Susannah. Supposedly Ben-Gurion was helped along by another legendary Israeli, General Moshe Dayan, who rejoined the army from his first retirement and was renamed chief of staff. Ben-Gurion's stature as one of the founding fathers was so towering that he saw no need to consult Sharett on anything. A mere two weeks after he assumed office, on February 28, 1955, Ben-Gurion, without justifying it to the world except in the vaguest of terms and without consulting Sharett,[15] responded to the executions by ordering an attack on an Egyptian army post inside the Gaza Strip. Operation Black Arrow, as the attack was called, was led by Ariel Sharon, and as always when Sharon was in command the number of casualties was high. The Israelis left fifty-six Egyptian soldiers dead and dozens wounded—they were not taunting Nasser, they were humiliating him. Though he was devastated, Nasser had to swallow this humiliation. Once again he told the Americans of his need for arms, and once again the request fell on deaf ears. Unable to confront Israel on the field of battle, he opted to change policy and back raids by the fedayeen. It was the act of a desperate man.

For Nasser, it was a turning point. The decision to unleash the fedayeen guaranteed Israeli overreaction, and set Nasser on a collision course with Israel. Convinced that Israel had provided him with no room for maneuver, he would always claim that Israel did not seek peace with its neighbors. With or without Sharett, Israel had put an end to his plans to seek peace. Israel had betrayed him.

Nor did the final 1960 (Knesset) report on the Lavon Affair do anything to change his mind. To Nasser, the suggestions that some Israeli hawks had acted on their own meant that Israel was an unreliable peace partner. If unknown parties in Israel could undo a peace process, then there was no peaceful way out of the conflict. The November 1955 return of Ben-Gurion as minister of defense confirmed his worst fears. Among other things, Nasser knew that Ben-Gurion was close to Moshe Dayan. This meant that the Israeli army could return to raids to undo any political agreement it did not like. The Dayan penchant for overreaction is what we see in Sharon today.

In Israel, the demise of the government of Moshe Sharett, the one man who pursued peace with an endearing naive commitment, had been expected. The Americans, having played a role in starting the Israeli-Egyptian contacts, could have done something about assuaging Nasser's fears and stopping the Israelis reducing him to life without dignity. But the Americans did nothing, there was a marked increase in tension, and the Israelis dealt him one humiliating blow after another. In June 1955, Nasser's offer to demilitarize the frontier with Israel was rebuffed; in July both Sharett and Ben-Gurion threatened to fight to open the Gulf of Aqaba for Israeli shipping. Soon after, the Israeli right wing gained ground in the general election; and in August, Israel announced the purchase of French Mystère fighters. A short while later, an Israeli armored unit stormed an Egyptian army position in the Gaza Strip, and there was a fedayeen response, and a response to the response which left thirty-nine dead at Khan Yunis at the bottom of the Gaza Strip. Ben-Gurion behaved like a government within or above a government, but to Nasser, Sharett was still prime minister. Accepting that he couldn't match the Israelis blow for blow, on September 10 Nasser unilaterally demilitarized his side of the Egyptian-Israeli border. Something resembling an answer from Israel came from Ben-Gurion, who on October 22 summoned General Moshe Dayan back from Paris to plan a Sinai war. That Nasser couldn't even respond to this in an acceptable, popular way was the ultimate loss of dignity.

Nobody outside or inside Israel tried to save Sharett and his peace ambitions. Outsiders did not know what to do; the days of interfering in the internal affairs of Israel hadn't yet come. Inside Israel, Sharett had no loyal constituency in the Knesset, and he was too urbane and polished to command a street following. On November 2, 1955, a mere fifteen months after he took office and after months of watching Ben-Gurion create a warlike situation along the Israeli-Egyptian border without deferring to him, a totally broken Sharett agreed to relinquish the premiership and revert to being a nonpolitical foreign minister. In fact, Ben-Gurion did not want him in the government at all, and he was pushed out of his ceremonial functions in June 1956. He never spoke to Ben-Gurion again. On the very same day which witnessed Ben-Gurion's resumption of power, Israeli forces stormed Jebel al-Shaba and consolidated their grip on Al Auja Triangle in Sinai, the invasion gateway to the peninsula.

In Egypt, Nasser had bypassed the normal channels and had Colonel Salah Dessouki, normally attached to Minister of Interior Zakkaria Mohieddine, report to him directly on all aspects of the investigation into the Lavon Affair. As the facts became clear to him, Nasser's conspiratorial personality precluded believing that Sharett had known nothing of what happened. He saw a Sharett double cross and another blow to his dignity. But what most unsettled Nasser was what Susannah-Lavon did to his relations with the United States. A group of Egyptian intelligence officers planning to visit the United States to commence Egyptian-U.S. security and intelligence cooperation canceled its trip at America's request. In addition, Eisenhower's special adviser to the Middle East, Eric Johnston, the man who was trying to develop a regional equivalent of the Tennessee Valley Authority (for a dam, irrigation, and electricity production) was heading toward failure despite Nasser's and Sharett's support for the American plan to share the waters of the Jordan. The rising tension with Israel included Jordan and Syria, who found it difficult to agree on anything that accepted Israel as a permanent part of the Middle East. Also, the Israelis wanted a bigger share of the water than the Arab countries were willing to give. The two outstanding issues between Nasser and the United States, Egypt's request for arms and the financing of the Aswan High Dam, were temporarily frozen.

For Nasser, the American decision to stop cooperation on security and intelligence matters and to terminate the negotiations regarding the waters of the Jordan meant that the Americans had been waiting for an excuse to end both, that they had been cooperating with the Israelis all along.[16] In his mind, the conspiracy went beyond the Israeli government to include the Americans. So Operation Susannah achieved its goal of driving a wedge between Nasser and the United States. In addition to believing that Israel had no interest in peace, Nasser became very suspicious of the various schemes for cooperation with the United States presented to him by the CIA group in Cairo. Furthermore, Nasser refused to accept that Sharett would willingly include Ben-Gurion in his cabinet without there being close cooperation and amity between the two men. It is easy to see why an outsider would judge the operation by its effects on him and not by the bungling of individual operatives, what the Israelis used to judge its outcome. An outsider has difficulty equating the success or failure of the operation with the fate of what he considers dispensable operatives. To a non-Israeli, the evidence supports a conspiracy theory.

If the Lavon Affair confronted Nasser with the realities of dealing with Israel and how difficult attaining peace would be, then the creation of the Baghdad Pact shattered his belief that the Arab countries would place their relationships with each other ahead of the dependency of some of them on Western support to survive. Nasser thought that Western governments accepted or rejected Arab regimes depending on how subservient to the West these regimes were. Western plans for the Middle East had little to do with whether any regime was democratic or even mildly responsive to the wishes of its own people. On these points, nothing was more convincing to Nasser than the history of the Baghdad Pact, the anti-Communist alliance of Middle Eastern states which was formed in the early days of the cold war. Nasser couldn't get pro-Western Arab leaders or Western leaders to accept the simple premise that the Arabs were preoccupied with the Israeli threat rather than with a mostly imaginary Communist threat. It was a strange position for someone who detested Communism as much as he did.

The Western wish to include Egypt in a military alliance aimed at keeping the Soviets and Communism out of the Middle East was elevated to an official inquiry during the May 1953 meeting between U.S. secretary of state John Foster Dulles and Egyptian president Mohamed Naguib. Nothing binding emerged from this exploratory meeting by the first Western dignitary to visit Egypt; but, unlike the intrinsically antialliance Nasser, the conservative Egyptian president was not opposed to the idea. Serious American attempts to find charter members for the proposed pact started about a year later, by which time Nasser was setting Egypt's foreign policy. Nasser was intellectually and emotionally opposed to all alliances with outside powers. In fact, his opposition to Communists in the Middle East had more to do with the fact that they received their orders from an outside power, the USSR, than with ideology.[17] Furthermore, Egypt had been unsuccessfully trying to buy arms from the United States or France for nearly three years.[18] And in 1954 news had reached Nasser of a secret arms deal between France and Israel, the one leading to the delivery of the French Mystères.

The late Miles Copeland, a CIA operative and field officer who maintained contact with the Free Officers, told the writer that Nasser was so desperate for American arms that he once told CIA superagent Kim Roosevelt that all he needed was enough to use in a military parade. There is a ring of truth to this. Nasser needed to save face with his people, demonstrating to them that he had not blundered in his assessment of the United States. But Copeland also portrayed Nasser as being totally preoccupied with the arms problem after the February 1955 Gaza raid. Interestingly, Nasser still would not approach the British to buy arms lest he be accused of being subservient to the old occupier of Egypt, even after the French and Americans had given him the runaround.[19] There were totally different reasons for the American and French behavior. The United States wanted Egypt in the anti-Communist pact, and that was the price for supplying it with arms. The French, on the other hand, were concerned with Nasser's support for and training of Algerian rebels, which began almost immediately after the outbreak of the rebellion in that country in November 1954. In this case, Nasser most definitely misjudged the French reaction to his decision.

Neither France nor the United States invoked the articles of the Tripartite Declaration against the sales of arms to the region, because the United States had struck an arms deal with Iraq in mid-1954 in return for Iraq's acceptance of the alliance, and the French were negotiating an extension of their various deals with Israel. In return for stopping the sales to Israel, France wanted Nasser to stop his support for the Algerians. Like the United States and Britain, the French misjudged Nasser. His opposition to anything his people would not accept was total; he believed this was what differentiated him from the other regimes in the Arab Middle East and from the old ones in Egypt. He knew that his people supported the Algerian rebels. He needed the pro-Algerian Egyptian masses.

Early in 1954, Nasser told the United States that the only military pact he would consider joining was an Arab pact[20] and added that the Arab countries already had a mutual defense arrangement through the Arab League. Once again it was the voice of the people which determined his international policy. It works both ways. If an anti-Communist alliance was meaningless to him because the so-called Communist threat was remote, then surely it was of no concern to the average Egyptian. Whether he had already started thinking of following the wishes of the average anti-American Arab instead of the average Egyptian is unknown. But upon hearing that Iraqi prime minister Nuri Said was negotiating with the West to join the very same pact he had rejected, he dispatched Minister of National Guidance and RCC member Salah Salem to talk Iraq's elder statesman out of it. Salah Salem's mission was a failure; he was not up to dealing with the wily Nuri.

In September 1955, the shoe was on the other foot. Nuri Said, perennial prime minister of Iraq and the West's staunchest Arab supporter, journeyed to Cairo to convince Nasser of the wisdom of joining the pact, talking shamelessly of how the Arabs could not do without their British friends. The two men could not have been more different, politically and personally. Nasser's admiration of things Western had to do with America, its openness and its traditional support for nationalist movements. He loathed the colonial British and their patronizing ways. Nuri felt the opposite. He found the Americans naive, and their idealism offended his sense of historical continuity based on class. Nasser liked to meet face-to-face with the people, was an aficionado of folk music, ate native food, and had a sympathetic Egyptian demeanor which was reflected in a broad, infectious smile. Nuri, half Turkoman and half Kurdish, was an atrocious public speaker who hated people, drank whiskey, was more at home in London than in Baghdad, and wore suits tailored in London's Saville Row. Above all, it was the people factor which separated them. Nasser believed in them and took their thinking into account; Nuri was suspicious of everything and everyone the people liked.

The uneasy meeting added to the outstanding problems between Iraq and Egypt. From then on Nasser's list of objections to the alliance reflected his feelings toward Nuri, and Nuri never forgave the young man for terminating their meeting after less than an hour. Nasser resented Nuri's obvious subservience to everything

Western, and saw in him a man who represented a danger to the ideals of the July 23 revolution. Nasser's conspiratorial mind told him, most likely correctly, that Nuri was not above using his special relationship with the West to wrest Arab leadership from Egypt. The issue of who should lead the Arabs had bedeviled relations between the two countries for decades; this meeting made it worse.

Later, when the British replaced the Americans as the Western leaders of the pact, Nasser turned down a proposal that would have overcome the obstacle of Egypt's playing second fiddle to Iraq. The British proposed to include Egypt as the leader of the Arabs and suggested that Nasser join an alliance with Turkey—one assumes with Turkey's knowledge—that would make the two countries the founding members and magnet of the proposed alliance.[21] But Nasser's opposition to Arab alliances with outside powers was total. Dr. Huda Abdel Nasser offers the only reasonable explanation. She claims that her father was totally "opposed to alliances between strong and weak countries because they inevitably led to the strong country taking advantage of the situation and imposing its own agenda on the weak country."[22] This summation certainly describes Nasser's behavior.

On February 10, 1955, Anthony Eden, still British foreign secretary, made a stop in Cairo while on his way to Bangkok to attend a meeting of the Southeast Asia Treaty Organization, a Western-backed alliance. It was the only Nasser-Eden meeting, and there are many pictures of the two together when they met for dinner at the British embassy. Eden is in a dinner suit, tall, urbane, handsome, and accustomed to the camera; Nasser is in his colonel's military uniform (unusually, with a tie on), smiling perhaps too broadly and, in a gesture which must have been novel to Eden, clasping the foreign secretary's hand. The friendly, totally Arab gesture contained a message to any Egyptian who saw it. You hold hands with friendly equals, not with enemies or superiors. It certainly was a gesture of goodwill. The agreement to evacuate Suez had already been signed, and only Britain's wish for Egypt to join it in a defense pact was outstanding. This did not become a problem until later, when Eden made it one by acting as if following Britain were a requirement to which Egypt had to adhere. It was apparent to all who saw the two men together that reconciling the two social opposites' political attitudes would be impossible. Nor did the outward amity overcome the obvious differences in their understanding of what mattered in the Middle

East. (According to the journalist Mohamed Heikal and others, Eden sang the praises of the Bedouin in the manner of a romantic Orientalist, and Nasser could not understand why Eden thought the Bedouin were important.) But the first serious altercation between the two men was to take place later.

Literally on the eve of becoming prime minister, on April 5, 1955, Eden sent Nasser a secret letter pledging that Britain would stop trying to recruit Arab members besides Iraq to the Baghdad Pact in return for an Egyptian pledge to end the propaganda campaign against the alliance. Iraq had initialed the pact with Turkey on February 14, the signing ceremony was scheduled for May, and both Iran and Pakistan had made known that they would join Iraq and Turkey as soon as possible. The United States, originally the primary mover behind the alliance, did not even join the pact for fear of offending Saudi Arabia. The United States and Britain agreed that the latter should be the Western leader of the pact. The Saudi objection to the pact had less to do with rejecting an anti-Communist alliance and more to do with Iraq's position in the pact, since Hashemite Iraq and Saudi Arabia were run by two competing dynasties. In fact, Saudi Arabia's traditional morbid fear of the Hashemites of Iraq and Jordan and Western support for them would drive Saudi Arabia toward closer relations and a measure of cooperation with Egypt.

Eden's letter represents the first of many such rapprochements and marginal alliances in which Nasser was involved over the years. They all came undone because of basic differences in philosophy between Nasser and most Arab governments, the ones whose leaders did not believe in his form of populism. However, Nasser's brief political embrace of the backward and despotic Saudis, the people who represented everything he hated, does show Nasser at his most pragmatic. The champion of land reform allied himself with the world's most absolute feudal monarchy against a relatively progressive Arab country, Iraq, because it represented a challenge to both Egypt and Saudi Arabia. But this and other alliances with backward Arab countries had one thing in common: the support of the Egyptian people. In later years, Nasser would take these feelings of his Arab street constituency into account. Of course, in this case it was described as a natural alliance between brothers, which appealed to the streets of Cairo.

The reason Eden wanted a secret understanding with Nasser regarding his propaganda was because, using strong transmitters,

Radio Cairo's *Voice of the Arabs,* a Nasser-sponsored news program directed at the Arab people throughout the Middle East, had ended the British monopoly on propaganda in the Middle East. *Voice of the Arabs* commanded a huge following throughout the Arab world, much greater than that of British-sponsored competitor Near East Broadcasting, and Nasser was especially popular among educated Arabs, including Iraqis. Nasser's radio was nothing more than a special regional organ which specialized in giving the Arabs an Arab version of the news. Its very name, *Voice of the Arabs,* defined it. Practically all of its programs had martial music in the background, and its message was anticolonial and for the rights and dignity of the common Arab. The main editor and announcer of *Voice of the Arabs,* Ahmad Said, became one of the best-known public figures in the Arab Middle East. The message concerning the Baghdad Pact was stronger than usual: it called for the Iraqi people to rise against the pact and topple Nuri Said. According to *Voice of the Arabs,* the Baghdad Pact was nothing but colonialism in disguise. Why should the Arabs join an anti-Communist alliance when the Israeli enemy was regularly attacking positions in Gaza and the West Bank? It was an easy-to-understand message with a broad appeal.

Obviously, Eden was told that Nasser's anti–Baghdad Pact propaganda was successful. Eden's request that the propaganda be stopped was a major acknowledgment of, if not an outright concession to, Nasser's emerging pan-Arabism. It was an admission that Nasser's message was creating trouble for the West's friends, certainly those already in or inclined to join the Baghdad Pact. It is no exaggeration to say, as Egypt later claimed, that Eden had no intention of keeping his part of the bargain. However, his efforts to add Jordan and Lebanon to the Baghdad Pact continued after his promise, and he violated his undertaking and contributed to the Suez Affair through this particular act. Whether Eden meant to mislead Nasser is unknown, but that he eventually did was not even a secret. He never tried to make it one. Eden's attempts to expand the Arab membership of the pact were done in the open. Moreover, the British (to be followed by the Americans) then made friendly contacts with the Muslim Brotherhood, the only organization with enough street following to change Nasser's mind.[23] Although the Brotherhood supported all anti-Communist positions, and the British saw in it a counterweight to Nasser, the

Egyptian leader proved immovable. In judging the overall situation, what should be remembered is that Nasser had started a new phase in the history of the Middle East, one which openly called for opposing Western designs and indirect control of the region. Once this became apparent, the confrontation between the two sides was inevitable, and events occurred too fast for either side to control them.

Along with opposing the Baghdad Pact, Nasser had made another anticolonial decision, against France. He followed his 1954 decision to train the Algerians with another which provided them with some financial help. He dealt with the Front de Liberation Nationale (FLN), the nationalist movement seeking independence from France, as a sponsor. That Nasser's anticolonialism would prompt him to offer such a support is true, but also true is the fact that Ali Sabri, his main negotiator to purchase arms for the Egyptian army, had failed to get the French government to meet any of his requests for military hardware.[24] The two-year-old French rebuff to Nasser was followed by their decision to supply the Israelis with arms. The campaign against the Baghdad Pact and the support of the Algerian rebels meant that Nasser was challenging colonialism from the Atlantic to the Persian Gulf, his definition of the land of the Arabs. That was to become the core of his appeals to all Arabs. He and his propaganda organs (which cost him money badly needed for projects aimed at improving living conditions in Egypt) constantly spoke about the Arab lands stretching "from the ocean to the Gulf." He continually polished his speech making and found in it a tool to justify dangerous decisions. And the average Arab responded openly and positively to this speaker of an attractive middle Arabic everybody understood.

Did Nasser deliberately declare war against the British and French? Did he want to end their presence in or control of the Arab countries? If that is so, if it wasn't a case of slipping into a situation through the heat of rhetoric, then where did the rest of his comrades stand? The record of the period from the revolution until the end of 1955 documents the passionate involvement of Nasser's original comrades in all internal matters. All the original RCC members were promoted when Naguib formed the second postmonarchy cabinet after Maher resigned, and most of them were given added responsibilities when Nasser took over as prime minister and then ruler of the country. In meetings, RCC members debated land reform, the composition of the to-be-elected National Assembly, enticement to foreigners and wealthy Egyptians to invest in the country, a civilian versus military government, democracy versus dictatorship, and their relationships with the Muslim Brotherhood and the Communists. The records of the period expose the officers as well-meaning but naive men, each of whom threatened to resign several times when things did not go his way. Though Nasser's Arab position was made clear in *Philosophy of the Revolution*, none of his comrades appears to have felt as strongly on the subject, though those who belonged to the Brotherhood honored the concept of the Islamic *umma* (nation), and that saddled them with responsibilities in accordance with the teachings of the Koran.

So moving into the Arab sphere, assuming leadership of the Arab circle, was Nasser's decision, one which in all likelihood grew bigger than Nasser intended, and his colleagues were dragged along. The Egyptian intellectual Dr. Sherrif Hatatta speaks of Nasser "towering over mediocre men."[25] This is unfair: some of Nasser's colleagues (Zakkaria Mohieddine and Abdel Latif Boghdadi, for example) were extremely competent administrators who understood the problems their country faced. In addition, there was nothing substantially wrong with the Khalid Mohieddine commitment, nor was the one outsider Nasser listened to, Mohamed Heikal, lacking in vision or ideas. The truth is that Nasser towered above his colleagues not because they were mediocre, but because he was exceptionally gifted. As *Time* correspondent James Bell, a man who interviewed Nasser a number of times during his early days, said of him, "The man had it, and in droves; whatever it is that leadership required, he certainly had it."[26]

The primary event which changed Nasser and turned his tentative anticolonial steps into a regional policy which led to confrontation with Britain and France and supplanted his original Egypt-first policies was the Afro-Asian Bandung (Indonesia) Conference. It had already been scheduled for April 18–24, 1955, when Eden passed through Cairo. But everybody expected it to fail, so it was not included in the Eden-Nasser discussions. It turned out to be a triumph for the twenty-nine countries which attended, for it managed to adopt ten clear anticolonialist resolutions.[27] India's Nehru, Indonesia's Sukarno, Yugoslavia's Tito, Ghana's Nkrumah, and China's Chou En-lai were there; altogether, over half of mankind was represented. Also there and making his debut at an international conference was the tall, handsome, ever-smiling Nasser.

Nasser traveled to Bandung after Nehru and Tito paid him visits in Cairo. Both encouraged him to steer a neutral course in world affairs, and both advised him to be cautious. In Bandung, Nasser spent his time with the two men and China's Chou En-lai. Tito advised him not to trust anyone; Nehru counseled him to take his time and not to hurry in adopting a new policy. Chou admonished him for putting so much faith in America. Nasser was only thirty-seven years old, obviously groping for direction and short of international experience, but he was one of the stars of the conference, and though he listened more than he spoke, everybody took to him. And when he finally spoke, he gave a remarkable performance, an example of controlled passion. He returned to Egypt having intellectualized the idea that there was an alternative to his relationship with the United States—nonalignment between the Western and Soviet camps—and thinking of himself as a dignified world leader. This conference began the second stage of Nasser's career. Because most of the Middle East was directly or indirectly controlled by outside powers, he needed and celebrated nonalignment more than Nehru, Tito, and Sukarno did. The Middle East would never be the same again. The disenfranchised people of the region, already enamored with his words, began expecting action from him. As usual, he tried to respond to their demands.

What better way to dramatize the change in his persona than finally to obtain arms from a non-Western source. Acting on the advice of Chou En-lai, upon his return to Cairo he contacted the Soviet ambassador, Daniel Solod, and asked if the USSR would supply Egypt with arms. The answer was yes, but it was a major step and had to be finessed. In June, still bending to his intrinsic admiration for America and hoping for an American change of heart, Nasser told U.S. ambassador to Egypt Henry Byroade that he was considering buying arms from the USSR. Byroade did not believe him; he thought Nasser was bluffing.[28] To Egyptians in the know, this was the critical point, for whoever sold Nasser arms would become his friend.[29] With Israeli threats to open the Gulf of Aqaba for Israeli shipping by force as background, Nasser announced in September 1955 what had been known to Western intelligence sources for some time, an Egyptian-Czech arms deal. The USSR had nominated Czechoslovakia to front for the deal while Nasser finalized the arrangement to sell China Egypt's cotton to protect against a Western retaliation in the form of a boycott of Egyptian products.[30]

This was a huge gamble: the first contract to buy arms from the Communist bloc by a non-Communist country. It pleased the frustrated Arab people, weakened the Baghdad Pact and any alliance of Arab countries with the West, and undermined Western defense plans. It was a slap in the face to the West and its clients and a commitment to Palestine which pleased the Arab masses everywhere. Eden and the Foreign Office in London pointed the finger at the Americans and in September announced an initiative to solve the Arab-Israeli conflict. Too late, the United States sent emissaries, among them Eisenhower's personal friend and former treasury secretary Robert Anderson (a man who would have an important background role for some time to come), to ask Nasser to cancel the deal. Israel used the whole episode to draw closer to the West. There were pronouncements, disguised threats, secret offers of arms (by the CIA's Kim Roosevelt), and other inducements, but Nasser didn't budge. When the dust settled, the West and the world were confronted with a new Nasser, a Nasser loved by the Arab people for standing up to the West, a bigger-than-life man who was deriving a childish glee out of breaking the Western monopoly on the arms trade. For the West, unlike friend Nuri, Nasser became an evasive challenge. But the West still could not agree on what should be done about him.

Between October and December 1955, the results of the arms deal seemed to be snowballing. Secretary of State John Foster Dulles described the Egyptian-Czech arms deal as the "most dangerous development since Korea."[31] Israel, always available to capitalize on its enemy's preoccupation with other issues, stormed another position in Al Auja. Russia competed with the West in another field; aware of the negotiations concerning the building of the second stage of the Aswan High Dam, it made a spoiler's offer to finance it. Eden formalized his peace offensive to settle the Arab-Israeli problem on November 9, 1955, in a speech at the Guildhall. The United States, Britain, and the World Bank confirmed what had been in preparation for over a year, their own offer to finance all of the first stage of the Aswan High Dam ($400 million of $1.3 billion). Nobody else could have matched the offer, nobody else tried. An Israeli raid against Syria ended Eden's peace offensive and whatever chance there was of cooperation between

Syria, Jordan, and Israel to share the Jordan River waters. Chief of the Imperial General Staff General Sir Gerald Templer, this time in clear violation of the Eden-Nasser understanding regarding expanding the Baghdad Pact, visited Amman to push Jordan into joining the alliance. Pro-Nasser anti-British riots broke out in Jordan in opposition to this move. This forced King Hussein to declare that Jordan would not join the pact.

Soon Robert Anderson returned to the region to try to link the U.S. offer to help finance the Aswan High Dam with the Arab-Israeli conflict. His attempt to make the financing dependent on progress in resolving the conflict was a failure. Meanwhile Nasser was moving to fulfill one of the results of Bandung, recognizing Red China. To sell these various moves to the Arab people, his propaganda machine was growing bigger and bigger and doing more damage to the Western position in the Middle East. While he thought the Czech arms provided the means to protect himself, everybody else thought it meant an inevitable confrontation with Israel. Nasser must have known that, but once again he was responding to the voice of the people, in this case their desire to have a strong army capable of fighting Israel. Still, he did not act in a vacuum. For totally different, in some cases opposite, reasons, Israel, the United States, Britain, France, the USSR, and the other Arab countries wanted him to go to war.

# 4

# Give Them Dignity

Except for wanting to build the Aswan High Dam (and even that had a solidly international aspect), by the end of 1955 Nasser was occupied with fighting external battles. The Palestinian problem lurked in the background, but Nasser devoted most of his time to opposing the Baghdad Pact to stop Iraq's Nuri Said from using it to control the Middle East; he supported the Algerian rebels; made sure nothing stood in the way of realizing the arms deal with the Eastern Bloc; advocated what he, Tito, Nehru, and other nonaligned leaders described as "positive neutralism"; elevated Cairo to the undisputed anticolonial educational center for Arab and African students; and used his extensive propaganda machine to issue appeals to the Arab people to rid themselves of neocolonialism and its servants, their rulers.

All of these activities conformed to Nasser's large theme of searching for dignity. Certainly building the dam and reclaiming part of the desert, increasing Egypt's tillable land by one-third, would enhance the dignity of the fellahin: The dam had been a dream project for decades; Nasser made building it the most important and popular symbol of his regime. But there was little public support for the external issues. For most Egyptians, the Baghdad Pact was not a dignity campaign; they opposed it because Palestine came first. It only became a major one after Nasser identified it as nothing more than colonialism in disguise, a danger to Arab interests and dignity. Slowly and deliberately he spoke more as an Arab than as an Egyptian. It was a personal statement which ignored the opinions of his comrades and did not defer to the Egyptian people. Whenever he did this Nasser followed with a campaign promoting the idea he had adopted.

It was less difficult to adopt the cause of the Algerian rebels; Egyptians already sympathized with their fellow Arabs. Yet, it was a considerable step nevertheless, for it signaled an Egyptian commitment to Arab causes beyond Palestine. Like opposing the pact, taking an anti-French, pro-Algerian position was an avoidable, costly enterprise. But Nasser thought the price was worth it. Keeping the Arabs free came ahead of practical considerations. The same formula was used to attack the British presence in the Arabian Peninsula. Certainly, all these moves, in particular reassuming a leadership position on the Palestinian problem, had negative financial implications for Egypt. Again, to Nasser, it was an Arab calling which was not subject to economic considerations. He became identified with opposition to the Baghdad Pact, support for the independence of Algeria and southern Arabia, and the Palestinian problem. Alone Nasser stood against Britain, France, and Israel.

Inside Egypt the battle against Naguib had been won. But there was no way to defeat the Muslim Brotherhood, though thousands of its followers and dozens of its leaders, including chief ideologue Sayyed Qutub, were in prisons and camps built specially for political detainees. Trying to suppress the Brotherhood had begun in earnest with the attempt to assassinate Nasser, and it continued during Nasser's eighteen years in office. Unlike the Communist Party, and despite Nasser's use of Islam's leading institution of high learning, Al Azhar University, to discredit it, the Brotherhood never stopped functioning. In fact, the Brotherhood developed a regional structure and operated from other Arab countries. It was large enough and organized enough to become a magnet for regional and outside powers interested in influencing events in the Middle East.

In late 1955, the old Brotherhood-British contact was reactivated. Brotherhood delegates visited King Farouk in exile in Italy to explore possible cooperation against Nasser, possibly overthrowing him. Jordan gave the Brotherhood a home base and gave Brotherhood leaders diplomatic passports to facilitate their movements to organize against Nasser. Saudi Arabia provided the Brotherhood with cash. Even Western correspondents stationed in the Middle East in the 1950s praised the Brotherhood as zealously anti-Communist. Moreover, the United States was beginning to lean toward cooperating with Islamic fundamentalist groups, seeing them as a factor in creating a regional anti-Communist alliance of Muslim states.[1] Occasionally they were thought of as a possible replacement for Nasser, though America could never make a final decision on that.[2]

Meanwhile, Nasser's comrades in the government enjoyed their ascendancy to high office without worrying about much beyond hiring friends and expanding their power bases against one another. No corruption such as existed under Farouk resurfaced, but the old officers lived well and cared little for other things. There were occasional quarrels regarding individual spheres of influence, but Nasser had no problem controlling them. He continued to follow the same methods, prevailing on fellow officers through sheer strength of personality or by adopting policies and seeking their approval after the fact. Mostly he deferred to them after he and his government adopted policies and made these policies popular. Of course, the trusted Amer controlled the army. After the Brotherhood, the army was the second potential source of opposition. And Amer remained Nasser's source of information about the outside world. The ideas for the National Union (the successor to the Liberation Rally) and the National Assembly, the one-party quasi-parliamentary body that favored workers and peasants and eventually gave them 50 percent of the seats, were on Nasser's mind and often discussed with other RCC members, but the ideas had not yet been adopted. Overall, the original inclinations toward reestablishing democracy were fading because Nasser had decided that the country would revert to its former corrupt self and because he relished his status as spokesman for all the Arabs.

Most internal developments were to follow the publication of a new constitution and the holding of presidential elections, scheduled for June 1956. But by 1956 Nasser was already the leader among equals and everything was under his control. His old comrades continued to retreat into bureaucracy. This is why nobody else is identified with the Suez Crisis and the Suez War. The later collapse of the Anglo-French-Israeli conspiracy against Nasser begged for a hero, and there was no one else. Whatever changes took place in the personality of Nasser between 1952 and the end of 1955 were more political than personal. The only governmental system he could conceive of was a democracy supervised by the army, maintaining the army as his central constituency. But because he feared Islamic and Communist penetration of the army, he removed it from the spotlight and balanced its power by creating a specific populist image for himself. This was never openly articulated along the lines of *Philosophy of the Revolution* or *Communism As It Really Is*. It involved creating a personality cult for himself and marginalizing all his comrades except Amer.

In other words, Nasser set Amer and the army aside, but all other functions of the state came under him. His comrades acted for him, as ministers, assistants, deputies, representatives, and decorative figures. He looked the other way while some of them indulged themselves in minor corruption, something which he avoided. Even the talented Zakkaria Mohieddine was happy heading the security apparatus. And Salah Salem went further and had an open affair with Farouk's sister, the princess Fawzia.

Nasser took to wearing well-cut gray suits, and he loved neckties and had 250 of them, all striped and sober.[3] But he had no interest in money and worked an eighteen-hour day, and everybody rightly accepted him as a Mr. Clean. He kept in touch with world events by reading all the daily newspapers available to him, even foreign ones. At thirty-seven he still had a massive physical presence, but thanks to the occasional game of tennis, he had not gained any weight. He continued to live in the same modest house in Manshia, though he built an additional room, and he never felt comfortable working in a palace. He still ate very Egyptian dishes such as white cheese, fava beans, falafel, *tumiya*, and *mulukhiya*. Even his manner of greeting others was down to earth, and he raised his hands in a typical *baladi* gesture when returning a salutation. If we set aside his desire to control everything and his inability to delegate, his only vice had not changed; he smoked more than three packs of cigarettes a day. (He did change from the British-made Craven As to the American L&M brand.)

Unlike most fellow officers, Nasser kept his children in public school, but he returned home in the afternoon to play with them and share in what interested them and their daily experiences.[4] Tahiya, totally devoted to her five children, was not visible, and most Egyptians would not have recognized her walking down a street. It wasn't a case of religious seclusion, she just was not a public person. Often some of his old comrades would visit him at home to discuss state affairs and some would stay for an informal dinner, but she very seldom joined them. But the only one who came and went frequently and informally was Abdel Hakim Amer. He behaved like a member of the family. He and Nasser still played the occasional game of chess.

Within Egypt, discussing politics and the future of the country never stopped. People argued about democracy (or its absence), how the government treated its political enemies, and the state of the country's economy. Some wanted the army to go back to the barracks, but they were a small number of intellectuals with little political clout. The only threat to the regime came from the solidly entrenched Muslim Brotherhood. It always managed to penetrate the army and security system and still thought of using Naguib as a magnet for all the anti-Nasser forces. Many pashas and officials of the ancient regime were still in prison, but some were being released gradually because they did not represent a political threat. But there was a problem in releasing the several thousand Muslim Brethren and Communists. While Nasser did not know what to do about them, many of them suffered torture, and so did some of their innocent relations, including women.[5]

Nasser had obviously approved illegal imprisonment, but did he personally condone the use of torture? Was Nasser's internal security system similar to others in the Middle East, and did he depend on it to keep the Egyptians under control? My investigation into this matter reveals that what existed in Egypt was something quite different from what existed under the run-of-the-mill Middle Eastern dictatorship. All of Nasser's admirers and even his critics—Hisham Kassem, Sherrif Hatatta, and Mohamed Sayyed Ahmed among them, absolve Nasser of ordering torture. Hatatta and Ahmed were activists who spent years in Nasser's prisons and knew the workings of the system. Heikal, Dessouki, Ghaleb, Mohieddine, Hammroush, all deny and simply refuse to believe that Nasser knew of or condoned the mistreatment of prisoners, and suppose that he found out about it only later. All agree that it would have been out of character, that he was intrinsically against inhumane acts or any treatment which infringed on people's dignity.

But torture did take place. It was a case of a dictatorship producing and using dictatorial methods even though the head of state was popular enough not to need them. Nasser was so immensely popular after 1954 that he had no reason to use torture. Nasser much later discovered that torture was used without his approval, and this will be dealt with separately. He had unknowingly fathered many crimes and violated people's human rights and dignity. But it was the security system becoming semi-independent which was behind the torture. The system acted in Nasser's name without telling him what it was doing. Nasser had a morbid hatred of the Muslim Brotherhood, which he thought dangerous, narrow-minded, politically corrupt, and very often un-Islamic. Though it was extremely popular, Nasser imprisoned them without resort to due process of law, and torture, without his knowledge, followed naturally.

In the economic and social fields the situation was confused and unpromising. The three-year-old regime calling its program "Islamic socialism" was trying to mount a response to the Muslim Brotherhood. But Nasser and his comrades had no serious new economic plans beyond the colossal task of building the Aswan High Dam, implementing the land reform decrees, enacting a minimum-wage measure, and taxing the rich. Because of its anticapitalist policies, from the start the Egyptian government experienced serious problems attracting foreign capital to develop some basic industries—even after enacting laws allowing Western corporations majority control of Egyptian companies. Meanwhile there was a standoff between the old bourgeois class and the new government. They viewed each other with total mistrust, which precluded cooperation. So with extreme socialist or Communist measures, such as collective ownership and workers' ownership, unacceptable to Nasser, and the old bourgeosie and the industrial bloc (controlled by Bank Misr) owning most factories opposed to him and advising foreign companies not to trust him, it was difficult to give the economy direction. True, the feudal capitalist system that had run the economy was no more, but what replaced it was no more than a populist officer-run bureaucracy preoccupied with defining itself. Nasser grasped this predicament very early, and this understanding influenced his future policy of concentrating on some basic industries and insisting on public ownership of others.

With economic stagnation threatening the regime, finalizing the plans to obtain financing and start building the dam assumed both political and economic importance. Nasser was thinking of a new constitution for 1957. His election to the office of president was scheduled for June 1956, and at the same time the para-parliamentary bodies, the National Union and its National Assembly, would be created. None of these scheduled events excited the imagination of a people growing accustomed to hearing about the "achievements of the revolution" on a daily basis. And the dam was the revolution's major achievement. Even the social rights he was granting the people—the creation of teacher, student, peasant, worker, professional, and other associations—failed to capture their imagination. Nor did the creation of a youth organization with hundreds of thousands of members or the opening of much-needed vocational and technical schools.

So if, as many said at the time (and continue to say nowadays), the economic problems of Egypt were beyond solution and limited the evolution of an effective political system to express the policies of the revolution, then it stands to reason that any Egyptian head of state would have to create in other fields substitutes for internal triumphs. Throughout the twentieth century and under each of its rulers, Egypt always diverted attention from its internal problems by assuming a regional leadership role over the neighboring Arab and Muslim countries. Kings Fuad and Farouk did so, and before them the khedives. (So have Sadat and Mubarak after Nasser.) In reality Nasser's bid for regional leadership based on Arab nationalism was much more profound than what the rest attempted. It almost succeeded.

Nasser's involvement in regional Arab affairs was deep and deliberate. For the first time, the new 1956 constitution in preparation described Egypt as "part of the Arab nation." He not only followed in the footsteps of former leaders, including the various prime ministers and party leaders of the 1940s, but slipped easily into changing the character and identity of his country without deferring to anyone. He became *"Al Rayyes,"* the president of Egypt, in 1956; but the word also means "chief" or "leader," and that was how he was known to the Arabs for the rest of his life. Egyptian media organs did an excellent job of promoting the use of this word.

So by the end of 1955, with the prospects of speedy economic achievement and political development dimming, Nasser confronted the West and claimed the leadership of the Arab world. He knew too much history for this to have been anything but a deliberate act. Egypt's immediate past was full of examples of failed attempts to defy the West; even the humiliation of Farouk in 1942 was part of that legend. Nasser did not create new points of contention to justify his new posture but stayed with already accepted ones. He focused on the Baghdad Pact, the Czech arms deal, supporting the Algerian rebels, arming and training the Palestinian fedayeen, creating a nonaligned nations neutral bloc with Nehru and Tito, and trying to end the Western hegemony over other Arab countries. Because the United States had opposed the arms deal and the recognition of China, it too became one of the countries opposed to Nasser. Except from the Arab people, Nasser had no backing, not even from the USSR. (The USSR's *Who's Who* listed him as an American agent.[6]) The United States, Britain, and France had to decide whether Nasser was mad or dangerous or both. According to Mohamed Heikal, the inherent weakness of Egypt was behind Anthony Eden's famous later lament: "How can he do it? How can he?"[7]

The daily violence along the cease-fire line with Israel aside, the first clash after adopting this pan-Arab policy was between Nasser and Britain. Eden saw the Baghdad Pact as extending British influence in the Arab world. Britain controlled Iraq's and other Arab oil, and a British officer was commanding King Hussein's Jordanian army. Nasser knew that there were no Egyptian-British problems that had not been settled by the withdrawal agreement from Suez, which also covered the Sudan and would reach full implementation in June 1956. But Eden had broken the agreement between them on limiting Baghdad Pact membership, a truly regional question. Nasser considered General Templer's trip to Amman and British contacts with Lebanese president Camille Chamoun to be signs of a conspiracy against him. Furthermore, the famous picture of Eden and Nasser holding hands during the one meeting between them turned out to be a pretense. According to Nasser, Eden "behaved like a prince dealing with a vagabond."[8] Furthermore, Nuri of Iraq, Eden's chief friend and ally in the Middle East, was Nasser's number one enemy and chief competitor for Arab leadership. Now Nasser's propaganda machine called for the dissolution of the pact.

What Eden had feared most was happening. Nasser's message on Radio Cairo's *Voice of the Arabs* was successful. The Iraqi leader, arrogant and unpopular, had been saved by the British on several occasions in the 1930s and 1940s,[9] but he looked vulnerable now. British policy in the Middle East depended on Nuri. Jordan was too small and weak to lead, and Saudi Arabia was inward-looking and beholden to America. Nasser's loathing of the pact was a genuine expression of his opposition to outside alliances. His attacks on it were serious statements of policy in the form of exposés. *Voice of the Arabs* emphasized that Nuri was decorated by Britain, that he had ordered the Iraqi army not to help the Egyptians in 1948, and that he personally was guilty of eliminating political opponents in the 1930s, and it took issue with Nuri's treatment of such "clean" and anti–Baghdad Pact Iraqi politicians as Kamel Chederchi and Wafic Samarai. The support for the Iraqi politicians was the first example of Nasser depending on people within the enemy camp.

Radio Baghdad and the British Near East Broadcasting were short of material against Nasser. Nothing in Nasser's background was sensational enough to condemn him. His public and private lives were clean. In fact, when the Americans gave him what amounted to a $3 million bribe, he used it to build a radio tower which strengthened the signal of *Voice of the Arabs* radio.[10] His large prison camps were there and a stain on his regime, but members of the Muslim Brotherhood did not generate much sympathy. Unlike the Egyptian leader, the British and Iraqis had no sympathizers in the enemy camp. This prompted the British to raise the stakes, with Nuri obediently supporting them. They established contacts with the Muslim Brotherhood aimed at overthrowing him, conspired with Syrian dictator Adib Shaishakly to keep Syria out of Nasser's sphere of influence, and had General Ghazi Dhagastani, a highly respected former Iraqi chief of staff and a serving officer, develop reserve plans to overthrow the Syrian government and establish a pro–Baghdad Pact government in that country.[11]

Nasser's message had a ready Arab audience, and hundreds of people converted to his cause by the day; Nasser responded to the British challenge by increasing his broadcasts. He accused Britain of using people such as Nuri and King Hussein of Jordan in accordance with a policy of indirect colonialism. He began recruiting and sponsoring small groups of supporters, mostly opponents of all pro-Western regimes, throughout the Arab world. To liaise with followers or sympathizers Nasser used his press attachés in the various Arab countries. This was a curious tactic, aimed at winning the hearts of the Arabs and not at helping stage coups against governments. Had he wanted to overthrow governments he would probably have used military attachés. Some of these countries had a relatively free press, and Nasser's first step in establishing an organized popular base there was to bribe the local newspaper editors.

Beyond newspaper editors, the Nasser government bribed

opposition politicians, anti-Western elements, and believers in Arab unity. Hundreds of Iraqi, Syrian, Lebanese, Jordanian, and Palestinian politicians were on Nasser's payroll. Some of them were genuine in their support, while others were charlatans who lined their pockets and did nothing. Money needed for development within Egypt was being diverted to spreading Nasser's pan-Arab message to the Arab world. With time the Nasser government started thinking in bigger terms. It supported people who were vying for office and housed many of them in Cairo. To the dismay of the United States, trying its utmost to maintain friendly contact with him, his politics of convenience and accommodation meant that some of the people he paid were hard-core leftists.

While opposing Britain and its friends across the board, Nasser had no plan for what to do should one of these countries fall to his followers. *Voice of the Arabs* attacked Jordan and King Hussein mercilessly, but Nasser did not want to overthrow Hussein for fear of Israel occupying the West Bank.[12] Nor did he have a plan for replacing Nuri or turning Syria into a satellite state. What was uppermost on Nasser's mind in early 1956 was the Aswan High Dam and the original American offer. Nasser met with the chairman of the World Bank and got his backing for the project. He also met with French premier Guy Mollet to discuss Egypt's support for the Algerian rebels. A meeting with British foreign secretary Selwyn Lloyd was scheduled for March 1.

Even to Middle East experts, there was a definite, confusing contradiction in Nasser's behavior. One part of him, the man behind *Voice of the Arabs*, was calling Nuri "a traitor" and King Hussein "a midget" and the humiliating "son of a woman." This was his populist response to the Arab people and their feelings, totally undignified use of the language of street Arabs. The other part of Nasser was the statesman who was meeting with Eisenhower envoy Robert Anderson, Eugene Black of the World Bank, Guy Mollet of France, and Selwyn Lloyd of Britain. This split behavior, exaggerated in Nasser, was typical of many Arab leaders in the twentieth century. It was, and is, a reflection of the love-hate relationship between the Arabs and the West. It explains why Nasser held Eden's hand for the cameras after they had failed to agree on anything. Toward Britain in particular, Arab leaders have a love-hate relationship. They want to be listened to and treated as equals, and turn unreasonably emotional and negative when they are not. Nasser never believed that Britain would listen to him unless he shouted and kicked, in this case unless his followers in the Arab countries threatened the policies and interests of Britain. But he also believed in the British sense of fair play. The British response to this dual attitude was equally wrong. Instead of advocating real dialogue, they expected total subservience.

On March 1, 1956, while he was meeting with British foreign secretary Selwyn Lloyd, Nasser received the news that King Hussein had dismissed General Sir John Baggot Glubb as chief of staff of the Jordanian army. Wrongly assuming Lloyd knew what was happening, Nasser congratulated him on showing restraint and not making an issue out of the dismissal. Glubb's removal had been demanded by Nasser. In firing him Hussein seemed to be bending to the will of the pro-Nasser people of Jordan. In fact, he did it because Glubb had patronized him and had refused to take Hussein seriously. Glubb, a narrow-minded Bible-thumper, always behaved as if he were the uncrowned king of Jordan. As it were, Nasser and Lloyd were meeting to negotiate a cessation in the war of words. The following day, when Eden finally got the news that Glubb had been fired, relations between the two countries fell apart. Eden blamed Nasser for Glubb's end and vowed to destroy him.[13] Glubb himself returned to London to declare that Britain was being "chased out of the Middle East by words."[14] So the first break between Egypt and the leading participant in the Suez War occurred in March 1956, over a development which pleased Nasser but was not of his making.

Several attempts were made to remedy the situation, but the overriding animosity between Eden and Nasser prevailed and the conflict was totally personalized. This, however, was far from being the end of the line between the two countries. Britain and Egypt dealt with each other in accordance with diplomatic norms until later in 1956, when circumstances created an opportunity for a vengeful Eden to try to replace Nasser by joining a conspiracy. The Suez War was the result of a convergence of the interests of Israel, France, and Britain against Nasser. None of the conspirators alone had a big enough reason to start a war with Egypt, but they merged their reasons to justify a war. As we will see, the war was the work of a committee acting in secrecy and haste. The planning suffered from lack of open agreement as to what to do about Nasser. It was a conspiracy and it had its shortcomings.

Nasser's unyielding verbal attacks on British interests and protégés looked as if they were inspired by the USSR. This was how

Eden, Nuri, and King Hussein saw things. But this was not true; Nasser's attitude toward Communism was still the same as when he wrote *Communism As It Really Is,* and the Communist bloc had no influence on Egypt. The arms deal served the purposes of Egypt and the USSR in unbalancing the Western position in the Middle East, but there was little else beyond that except for official visits which produced little of substance. Not only was the Communist Party in Egypt illegal, but Nasser simply did not want to enlarge the relationship with the USSR. In terms of ideology, he was willing to borrow from the Communist model without copying it. He altered whatever Communist ideas he liked to fit the circumstances of Egypt and the Arab world.

Nasser's confrontation with Israel which culminated in the 1956 Suez crisis had its origins in the Lavon Affair. Not only did Ben-Gurion and the militants eliminate Sharett and stifle the movement toward peace in its infancy, they embarked on a policy of massive retaliation. In August 1955, Israeli army units stormed several Egyptian positions in the Gaza Strip, ten days later they killed thirty-nine people in the town of Khan Yunis, and Israel attacked again soon after Nasser's September 20 unilateral demilitarization of the border. By March 1956 this had been followed by four major attacks against Egypt and a very serious one against Syria. By April 1956 Egypt, unable to do anything militarily significant, had relaunched another fedayeen campaign, and this time it was relatively successful. Of course, the Israeli response was disproportionate.

As usual, the Israeli attacks against an Arab country unified the Arab people. In this case the humiliation of the Arabs prompted many of them to support Nasser in his Arab persona. There was no one else on the Arab stage. But there was more to what was happening between Egypt and Israel than military raids and fedayeen incursions. Ben-Gurion, the author of the massive-retaliation policy,[15] was among the founding fathers of Israel who refused to define the borders of the Jewish state. By implication, Israel kept open the option of acquiring more Arab land. As the Gaza Strip and Sinai were never part of Israel's expansion plans, occupying the lands of the West Bank, Jordan, or Syria, or all of them, was more of an option. Nasser assumed the role of protector of Jordan and Syria.

Israel's occupying the most holy places in Jerusalem and sources of water would have forced Egypt to meet its treaty obligations to help the other Arab countries. Nasser's assumption of his Arab identity reconfirmed Egypt's commitment. This is what made Ben-Gurion's preoccupation with the largest Arab country so total. Ben-Gurion saw Egypt as representing a unified Arab mass and leading an Arab ring around Israel. Sharett told the writer Kennett Love that his erstwhile comrade wanted war with Egypt to intercept Arab cooperation and military coordination.[16] A third reason for Israel's wanting to remove Nasser was his rising star in the international arena. Though his friends came from countries which had never supported Israel—Yugoslavia, India, and Indonesia—Bandung and what followed it created a world figure, something Israel, realistically or otherwise, found threatening.

Early in 1956, the United States finally woke up to the disastrous potential of an Israeli-Egyptian conflict and initiated Project Alpha. The secret project had President Eisenhower behind it, and his friend and later secretary of the treasury Robert Anderson was chosen to mediate between Ben-Gurion and Nasser. It was a stillborn attempt at achieving peace. Anderson, a folksy Texas millionaire, failed to impress either side and offended Nasser by linking the aid for building the Aswan High Dam to Nasser's willingness to settle the Palestinian problem. The conspirator in Nasser thought he was being blackmailed, particularly when the Cairo CIA group replaced Anderson and took over Alpha.

Nasser had not been responsible for the increasing tension between Israel and Egypt. Israel flaunted its military superiority, and Ben-Gurion manifested no inclinations toward moderation. Giving the fedayeen a free hand and reconfirming the commitment to Syria and Jordan was all Nasser could do. Swallowing his pride, he sent a reduced list of the arms Egypt needed to U.S. ambassador Henry Byroade. There was no answer. Meanwhile the Arab pressure on him to use his army to respond to Israel was so great that it almost threatened his claim to Arab leadership. Still, he refused to send the army to certain defeat and admitted that he had no plan to liberate Palestine.[17] According to Byroade, Nasser had no wish to fight Israel.[18] His army began to receive some arms from the $330 million deal with Czechoslavakia in early 1956, but generally it was ill-equipped and lacked training, and Nasser knew it. Israel, however, had regularly received arms from France and had mastered them, and its army was better trained and better led.

In a way, the Arab refusal to join the Western-backed Baghdad

Pact had played into Israel's hands; the pact could no longer be used to protect some Arab countries from Israel. Moreover, Sharett's demise meant Israel was united and single-minded. Ben-Gurion and his cohorts rightly believed that subduing or even eliminating Nasser would end a lot of problems. Syria and Jordan would become easy prey to the Israeli expansionist plan, all fedayeen activity against Israel would cease, and a new Egyptian leader might open the Suez Canal to Israeli shipping.

According to available evidence, the first French-Israeli meeting to discuss "Nasser's future" took place in June 1955.[19] There was nothing mysterious about the French trying to pressure Nasser into abandoning the Algerian cause. Nasser was the backbone of the Algerian rebels, and to a lesser degree supported other anticolonialist movements in Africa. The French were willing to bargain, perhaps sell him arms, as late as March 1956, when Nasser met with French foreign minister Antoine Pineau and launched an ill-fated peace offensive. But Nasser couldn't go through with it; he never compromised on opposing colonialism and championing Arab liberation movements. That Nasser chose to meet with the French "to negotiate" was a publicity stunt. He was unwilling to accede to any of their demands, but he wanted to know their position.

So the problems between Nasser and Britain, Nasser and France, and Nasser and Israel were separate but interlinked. Nasser's refusal to enter into any alliance with outside forces clashed with the British desire to maintain some kind of control over the Arab Middle East. Because of British dominance, France had no interest in the Baghdad Pact. Israel also viewed the alliance with misgivings and feared that the Baghdad Pact might be turned against it. Israel was concerned with the consequences of the arms deal and Nasser's new Arab policy, and saw Nasser's rising star in the international arena as menacing. The European powers did not share Israel's concern about a new Arab alliance and believed that Israel would win any regional war in the foreseeable future.

The three anti-Nasser countries had one thing in common: they opposed any Arab leader who had a street following and who would, or could, unite the Arabs. Israel's repeated attacks against Nasser's armed forces were aimed at denying him hero status. He had to react to the actions of Britain, France, and Israel or lose his still-young popularity with the Arab people. He kept the attack on the Baghdad Pact at a maniacal pitch, increased his support for the Algerians, and gave the Palestinian fedayeen more arms. The situation was similar to what had happened before—even the players were the same—but it was on a considerably larger scale.

There was no immediate reason for Nasser to quarrel with Britain after it gave up on his joining the Baghdad Pact. The issue was the right of other Arab countries to join the Baghdad Pact; in other words, Britain and Egypt were competing to lead the Arabs. The same was true for his problem with France. For most Egyptians, the Algerian problem, unlike the Palestinian issue, was remote, and the question of support for the Algerian rebels did not preoccupy them. Nasser's adoption of the Algerian problem was part of his effort to create his Arab-leadership persona. It was Nasser who made the Algerian cause popular with the Arabs and gave the Algerians airtime and money. In this case he was not responding to the feelings of the people. In exclusively Egyptian terms, he could have got away with offering the rebels no or less support. Of course, he would have bargained, using the issue of Algerian rights to gain something for Egypt. Here too, Nasser behaved as an Arab leader.

Nasser's adoption of a new position vis-à-vis Israel was forced on him by the other side. The tangible evidence for his desire to opt out of the Palestinian problem includes the reduction in the 1953–55 Egyptian defense budget, his participation in the secret negotiations with Sharett, his unilateral demilitarization of his side of the border, and the fact that he repeatedly received American and UN emissaries who sought to mediate between him and Israel. In fact, even though most exchanges amounted to very little indeed, contacts between Nasser and Ben-Gurion in the form of oral messages never stopped. It was Nasser's frustration with Israel's determination to have it exclusively its own way and the scale of Israeli incursions that made him want to buy arms from the West and later, under pressure, to seek military hardware from the Eastern Bloc.

The arms deal signaled a change in Egyptian-American relations. America had overlooked Nasser's support for the Algerian rebels, thought his appeals to the Arab people against their leaders were superseded by his anti-Communism, accepted his anti-Israeli position as a normal one for an Egyptian leader, and was not disturbed by his mild socialism. But though Nasser had considered buying Soviet arms before, the Bandung Conference and

Chou En-lai paved the way for the September 1955 arms deal. The United States, still listening to the Cairo CIA, wisely refrained from judging the deal as a hostile act. Relations with Egypt continued as before, but the offer to help finance the Aswan High Dam was thrown in doubt in November 1955 by the Secretary of State Dulles. That is when Washington decided that the arms deal as part of a personal policy by Nasser to promote Nasser threatened the Western position in the whole Middle East. And the United States doubted that Nasser wanted the Middle East for himself alone. The United States was wrong.

U.S. secretary of state John Foster Dulles considered the policy of "positive neutralism" adopted at Bandung nothing short of evil.[20] The Americans had expected the vague two-word phrase which originated in Bandung to fall into disuse soon after the conference ended. But it didn't, and political parties, writers, and the average Arab began using the phrase after Nasser repeated it in his speeches. His radio stations began using it, though some of his own diplomats had no idea what he had in mind.[21] Because Yugoslavia's adoption of positive neutralism did not threaten its neighbors and India's and China's commitment to it was superficial, it was Egypt which bore the brunt of American anger. However small or large the danger, Nasser wanted the Arab world to follow him instead of the West, and this was giving the USSR a chance to break out of its encirclement. Dulles believed that leapfrogging over pro-West countries such as Iran and Turkey created a USSR threat to Western oil interests.

Throughout the Middle East, "positive neutralism" soon became the rhetorical weapon of Nasser's followers and agents. The press offices at Egyptian embassies were expanded. Nasser's message was adopted by mercenary Arab journalists. Millions of Nasser's pictures with captions referring to positive neutralism were printed and distributed. In addition, a huge number of Nasser followers and members of political parties that advocated Arab nationalism accepted him as the leading advocate of Arab interests and offered their services freely. Anti-West writers and ambitious army officers in every Arab country memorized and recited his speeches and slogans, but like him they were not pro-Communist. There was nothing in the arsenals of Britain, France, or Israel that could match Nasser's Arab speech making. But as usually happens with propaganda campaigns, the message got completely out of hand, and ended up promising considerably more than the leadership could deliver.

Jordan's King Hussein, President Chamoun of Lebanon, and Nuri Said of Iraq were called "agents" and "slaves." There were top-of-the-chart songs about Algeria and Palestine, such as "I Am from Algeria." Accusing King Hussein of being a CIA agent was easier than accepting the counteraccusation that Nasser was a tool of Communism. There was no shortage of sordid stories about Chamoun's personal life. Of course, there were the devastating attacks on Nuri Said, fourteen-time prime minister of Iraq, a man who never did anything contrary to the wishes of Britain, the country that had created him. Finally, almost a year after Bandung and after the failure of Project Alpha, the United States joined the countries clamoring to subdue Nasser. Secretary Dulles dispatched Kermit Roosevelt, the leader of the Cairo CIA group, to discuss the arms deal with Nasser. But it was too late, and Roosevelt had nothing concrete to offer.[22]

Soon after, Robert Anderson tried again, and Herbert Hoover Jr., an assistant secretary of state, made his own halfhearted try. But once again the Americans tied everything to solving the Palestinian problem in a way unacceptable to the Arabs.[23] American diplomacy was marked by linkage: linking an offer to build the dam to reexamining the arms deal, linking everything to a settlement of the Palestinian problem. To Nasser, linkage smelled of conspiracy—the other side always wanted more. Meanwhile, Israel was, as ever, poised to strike at Egypt, Britain withdrew its troops from Suez on June 13, 1956, and stood by the Baghdad Pact, the French were looking for a way to punish Nasser for his Algerian policies, and the USSR was trying to endear itself to Egypt by offering to build the dam and participate in other economic development projects.

The last thing this delicate situation needed was for someone to upset the balance by introducing a new element onto the scene. But in May 1956, Nasser did exactly that: he gave diplomatic recognition to Red China, an act that inevitably alienated the United States. It was not a mad or purely provocative act; he wanted a guaranteed source of arms just in case the West and the Soviet bloc agreed on an embargo, something Nikita Khrushchev had proposed to Eisenhower a few weeks before. Nasser followed this by reaching an accord on the implementation of some articles of the overall agreement with the Suez Canal Company on May 30. By receiving Soviet foreign minister Dimitri Shipelov for the second time a month later, Nasser was definitely provoking the United States, which did not accept Nasser's seemingly endless balancing act between the West and the Communist bloc. Using economic aid as an instrument of policy, it decided to punish Nasser by stopping the food aid program. Senators and congressmen called for even more concrete action against him.

On July 19, 1956, Secretary of State Dulles withdrew the offer to build the Aswan High Dam, citing Egypt's heavy financial commitment because of the arms deal and what was bluntly described as "the weakness of the Egyptian economy." While there was no known consultation with Britain regarding the announcement, the Eden government had known this might happen. Eden had been party to making the original offer and, except for the exact date, had been kept apprised of the likelihood of withdrawing it.[24] The dam project had been under constant review since the failure of the Anderson and Hoover missions to promote linkage. A Foreign Office memorandum about keeping Nasser guessing regarding confirmation of the offer to build the dam, and countering his propaganda, said, "Many of these measures will be taken in conjunction with the United States."[25]

In fact, the manner of the withdrawal was aimed at Nasser personally. Unlike Britain and France, which for some time had seen him as a menace and advocated a colonial solution—military action—American had, until his actions were deemed helpful to the USSR, viewed Nasser, for almost two years, as "controllable." This had meant that he was not a threat to the flow of oil and a tool of the USSR. But after the Baghdad Pact, the arms deal, the dismissal of Glubb, and the freeing of the fedayeen, the recognition of China was too much for Washington. Dulles resorted to his Christian anti-Communism and thought the time to cut the Egyptian leader down to size had come. Nasser was away from home attending a nonaligned nations' conference at the Yugoslav island of Brijuni, and the announcement of the cancellation was made without the proper diplomatic notice.

The direct Dulles slur against the Egyptian economy ignored the nature of Nasser. Either the CIA group still near to Nasser had failed all along to advise Washington of the importance of dignity to Nasser, or Washington had dismissed its reports as a superficial analysis of the Arab mind-set. The plan to build the dam and the difference this would make to Egypt had been daily on the front pages of Egyptian newspapers and the lead items on radio news bulletins. Every Egyptian and Arab knew that the dam would increase the country's cultivatable land by one-third—by 8 million *fedans* (nearly an acre).[26] It would be bigger than the Hoover Dam in the United States (365 feet high, two-thirds of a mile thick, and two and a quarter miles long) and would create an artificial lake bigger than Lake Mead. In fact, building the Aswan High Dam with Western money (U.S., World Bank, British) was one of the pillars of Nasser's positive neutralism, and the Soviets, despite public statements, had not made a definite offer. Nasser had depended on the West for the dam project, the cornerstone of his economic program, and thought that it balanced the arms deal with the other side and showed him as completely neutral.

Nasser returned to Egypt in a hurry from Brijuni. Despite the many signs that the United States and Britain had had second thoughts regarding the project for months, the move had caught him in the wrong place and totally unprepared. Still a believer in America's goodwill, he had not thought America would withdraw the offer. In Brijuni, Tito and Nehru advised caution, and he used the small time during his return flight to Cairo to reassess his position. When Britain followed the United States a day later and withdrew its part of the offer, Nasser, still believing in a diplomatic way out with the United States, wanted the World Bank to do the financing on its own. Obviously turning to the Soviets and growing more dependent on them was something he didn't want. But Chairman Eugene Black of the World Bank turned him down.[27] This was a major blow; now he believed that the United States had declared economic war on him. That was his assessment as conveyed to the small groups of people with whom he met to discuss the crisis.[28] But he refused to assume any part of the blame.

After instructing his finance minister, Abdel Kader al-Kaissouny, to transfer Egyptian reserve funds to Switzerland, Nasser concentrated on three possible courses of action.[29] All of them involved paying the West back for the damage done to his prestige and realizing money to build the dam. The options were nationalizing the Suez canal, nationalizing 50 percent of the canal, or threatening to nationalize it.[30] Clearly the canal was the focus of his attention as a source of income for building the dam and for underwriting Egypt's economic development, but also as a remedy for the historical damage done to the Egyptian people and Nasser's psyche and pride. He decided in favor of full nationalization.

On July 24, 1956, Nasser the populist crowd pleaser took over from Nasser the deliberate leader. He used the occasion of the inauguration of a gas pipeline from Suez to Cairo to lash out at the West.

He made an open promise that the "high dam will be built." Then he resorted to improvising and told the West to "go choke on your fury."[31] The refrain was broadcast repeatedly on *Voice of the Arabs*. For the first time in the twentieth century an Arab leader had openly challenged all of the West. Although almost every Arab sympathized with and supported him, on their minds was the question "What next?" Many were apprehensive and doubted whether he would get away with it. But they bought radios to keep them in touch, some using their savings, and the local mosques were packed daily. The sermons were anti-West and orchestrated.

Between the "choke on your fury" speech and July 26, Nasser devoted himself to planning his final official response to the United States and Britain, and the world waited. There was no escaping it—the canal was the only Egyptian asset and revenue earner worth anything. After making the strategic decision to nationalize, he reverted to his conspiratorial ways. Keeping his relationship with the people, his psychological lifeline, in mind, he decided to turn what he was planning into another blow against imperialism. Even the civilian members of his cabinet, including Kaissouny and the diplomat Mahmoud Fawzi, were not told of his thinking or his plan.[32] His chief confidant on his secret scheme was one Colonel Mohamed Younis, an engineer and Nasser's classmate at military college.

Nasser met with Younis alone. Younis listened to Nasser with utter astonishment. The plan was all prepared in Nasser's mind, but he needed Younis as a field commander. There was no alternative to physically occupying the offices of the Suez Canal Company, then announcing the canal's nationalization and confronting the world with a fait accompli. Younis and Nasser estimated that they required a mere thirty men to succeed, with others available for support. The takeover would be carried out the night of July 26, during a Nasser speech commemorating the fourth anniversary of King Farouk's abdication. It was also exactly one month after his election to the office of president of Egypt. The venue was Mohamed Ali Square in Alexandria, the very same spot where a member of the Muslim Brotherhood had tried to shoot him twenty months before. Foreign diplomats expected something dramatic, but they had learned not to predict Nasser's moves.

Nasser and Younis agreed that the physical occupation of the Suez Canal Company offices would commence when Nasser mentioned in his broadcast speech the name of Ferdinand-Marie de

Lesseps, the French engineer who had become a symbol of imperialism and exploitation. Younis's men, strategically located in the cities of Port Said, Suez, and Ismailia, would act in groups of five on instructions contained in envelopes given them shortly before. The instructions were detailed, included a warning against any use of force, and wished the participants Godspeed. The name of the operation was on the envelopes: *Izza wa Karama,* Glory and Dignity.

The speech is one the Arab people still remember. There was no prepared text; Nasser depended on notes on the back of an envelope. He started slowly, speaking in a plain, clear style, a variation of *baladi* Arabic, avoiding dialect but without going classical. He did this for half an hour without getting to the point—it was a preamble made up of a list of Western crimes against Egypt. There was nothing new in them, but Nasser was pitching his accusations higher and higher, giving them added emphasis, and the expectations of the listener were lifted. Then he reviewed the dam project and contacts with the United States and made fun of the American diplomats who had tried to pressure him into concessions. Then came the reward; he spoke as if recalling every grain of hatred conjured in his racial memory by the name de Lesseps. "De Lesseps, de Lesseps," he hissed loudly to millions of Egyptians and other Arabs listening to him. Younis, acting alone, had succeeded in having the envelopes distributed and was now helping officers carry out the orders.

Of course, to Nasser it was a day of *Izza wa Karama,* built around his personal decision and planning.[33] After repeating the signal to Younis several times, he finally told his audience that fellow Egyptians were occupying the company's offices at that very moment. The company was being reclaimed "in the name of the people." The hundreds of thousands of people cheering him in Alexandria lapsed momentarily into silence. But repetition did the job; they finally understood him. They went delirious with shouts of *"Kuwayyis ewi,"* or Well done. Then he repeated his last four sentences. The level of response grew higher and people turned to each other, hugged, cried, and said, *"Mabrouk,"* Congratulations. Nasser himself was overwhelmed by his own words. When he claimed the canal "in the name of the people" he shook with laughter that was intended to be mocking but was so nervous and uncontrolled that he could hardly speak. He looked like a person laughing at his own joke; but he finally recovered, and the supreme speaker was once again in total control. Even Egyptian journalists stood on chairs and waved their white handkerchiefs. It was Nasser's answer to "What next?" and with that, the Arab masses, historically lovers of showmanship, took him to their hearts more than ever before.

Arabs throughout the world listened attentively, and thousands ran into the streets shouting slogans of support. From North Africa to the Arabian Gulf, people built bonfires while others shot their guns in the air in celebration. Nasser had achieved his first pan-Arab triumph and become a hero when he broke the Western monopoly on the supply of arms, but this was bigger. Soon his pictures were to be found in the tents of the Yemen, the souks of Marrakesh, and the posh villas of Syria. There had never been a precedent to what was happening; an Arab, using the word as a weapon and the relatively modern technology of radio, was battling the West and winning. He was giving Arabs a sense of being which had been denied them for most of the twentieth century.

Only Nuri Said, in London to avoid the Baghdad he hated, thought differently. He sought a meeting with Prime Minister Anthony Eden and gave him his famous counsel; "Hit him, hit him hard, and hit him now."[34] The clash between the old Middle East and the new Middle East was in full swing. The old Middle East was still under sheikhs, emirs, kings, presidents, and strongmen beholden to the West; the new one consisted of ordinary people who followed Nasser's leadership. Meanwhile, Nasser issued clear instructions that nothing was to mar the passage of international shipping through the canal. Rightly, he was enjoying his moment of triumph and was determined not to provide his enemies with excuses to attack him.

What followed the act of nationalization exposed the real thinking of the participants in what came to be known as the Suez Crisis. Every country involved in the dam debacle began justifying its actions and blaming the others for the gathering crisis. Nasser's nationalization was immediately rejected by France and Britain, the owners of the Suez Canal Company. But it was President Eisenhower of the United States who saw the magnitude of the problem clearly and acted swiftly and in the open. Two days after Nasser's nationalization speech he dispatched Assistant Secretary of State Robert Murphey to London. Although Murphey's mission was to be evenhanded and prevent war, Eisenhower very much wanted Britain to listen to him and, to appease the fuming Eden, took the step of freezing Egyptian assets in his country.[35]

In London, the political and media pressure on Eden to respond forcefully to Nasser was mounting. Eden, having suffered the firing of Glubb and the failure of the Baghdad Pact to attract other Arab countries, had already decided that the world was too small for him and Nasser. He sought and obtained a cabinet decision in favor of the use of force against Nasser a mere twenty-four hours after the Nasser speech. On July 31, he told Eisenhower that he was considering an immediate military attack on Egypt.[36] The old general rejected the idea and advocated caution. Beyond promises not to allow the nationalization to pass and calling Nasser names in press conferences and newspapers, the French did very little in the open. They just continued the secret meetings with Israel that had started in mid-1955 in response to Nasser's Algerian policy. Meanwhile, the Israelis, except for an occasional skirmish, fell ominously silent.

Nasser's *Voice of the Arabs* attacked Britain, France, and Israel without reservation, and won the propaganda war. Nasser's preoccupation was with Britain. To him, it was Great Britain that mattered and would inevitably become the main decision maker for what would follow. Like Eden, Nasser believed that Britain had to act; but, without offering specific proposals, he still believed in a diplomatic way out. Nasser devoted considerable time to anticipating Britain's next move, even studying British decrees nationalizing companies after World War II. Meanwhile, the USSR made its pro-Nasser position clear. The Americans were in the middle: they opposed military action but were reluctant to abandon their allies. Only the United Nations was in a position to meditate the dispute. Noting that, Nasser decided for direct contact with Secretary-General Dag Hammarskjöld.

The concession agreement granting the Suez Canal Company the right to operate the canal and to guide the ships running through it was scheduled to expire in 1968. But it was an agreement between the Egyptian-registered Suez Canal Company and Egypt, not a treaty between two sovereign bodies. The company was subject to Egyptian law. International law was not applicable.[37] Moreover, even the Constantinople Convention of 1888, the ultimate source of judgment on maritime disputes, appeared to favor Egypt and support its right to nationalize the company, though there was a question regarding blocking the passage of goods. Egypt's legal right to nationalize the canal was never in question.[38] This is why the British government balked at the

American suggestion that it should go to the International Court.[39]

The problem was between two ways of thinking: Eden's belief that Egypt lacked the skill to operate the canal and Nasser's confidence that the Egyptians, by themselves, were capable of running the canal well and without disrupting international trade. He refused to accept any part of Eden's allegation. It was *The Times* of London of July 28, two days after the takeover, that led the attack on Egyptian competence and questioned "Egyptian skills." The French government and press were not far behind. The British Labour party's opposition under Hugh Gaitskell felt the same way. This was also the position of the British press until the weekly *Observer* broke ranks nearly a month later and opposed any use of force against Egypt. In Egypt, Nasser, behaving presidentially if not regally, was on the attack. He gave speeches urging the people to prepare for "the battle," issued directives to put the armed forces on maximum alert, chaired the cabinet and committees to discuss the finances of the country, created organizations to trade with the Eastern Bloc, paraded through the streets full of cheering crowds, and attended mosque prayers. On several occasions he lost his voice to laryngitis.

Eden eventually found himself foundering. The massive support he had immediately after Nasser acted dwindled with every passing day. Mohamed Younis and the Egyptians were indeed proving themselves equal to the task. Eden had taken an Egyptian failure to run the canal for granted; he had no other excuse to justify his rejection of the nationalization decree. Younis became the second hero of Suez. Nasser, totally secure in his position, had no problem heaping praise on Younis. According to those who knew him, Nasser believed the story of Suez had just begun.

Given the atmosphere of the crisis—the diplomatic moves, the background to diplomatic offers, the missions, rejections, and preparations for war—it is easy to understand why Suez turned into a catastrophe. The dispute was new, unique. The legality of Nasser's action was immaterial. To Eden, it was a historic challenge to Britain by a former colony, by a colonel in the army of a former colony. This made Eden see it as a personal confrontation. Eden's Britain thought it was the guardian of Western interests in the Middle East, and Eden saw himself as the Western leader in charge of this guardianship. Eden's Britain was not prepared for Nasser's action.

Not even American disapproval could disabuse Eden of wanting to use this imaginary guardianship to oppose Nasser. To him, the prime minister of Great Britain was not to be challenged by an upstart; the social and psychological legacies of colonialism were against that. It was later claimed that poor health contributed to his bad judgment, but the evidence to support this excuse is not convincing.[40]

According to the insider account of Anthony Nutting, who resigned as minister of state for foreign affairs in protest over the handling of the crisis, Eden was hardly ever in control of himself on the subject of Nasser. At one point he reacted to the mention of Nasser's name by saying, "I want him destroyed, I want him removed." When reminded of the consequences of invading Egypt without having a replacement for Nasser, he surrendered to more unreason: "I don't give a damn if there is chaos in Egypt."[41] Even Eden's wife joined the fray and protested, "How dare this Egyptian challenge Anthony?" The *London Daily Mirror* backed the Edens' somewhat racist attitude by comparing Nasser to Hitler, and opposition leader Hugh Gaitskell concurred.[42] The *Daily Telegraph,* according to Mohamed Heikal, elevated Nasser's action to conspiracy and attacked his master plan (to control the Middle East). The British Near East Broadcasting settled for Nasser being "a barking dictator" whose action was a betrayal of Egypt. French premier Guy Mollet, not to be outdone, spoke of forcing Nasser to disgorge what he had swallowed, and the French press, in a reference to the revolution in Kenya, spoke of a Mau Mau along Suez.

Because the Suez Crisis became a propaganda war at the highest level, Nasser personally took charge of the propaganda machinery of the Egyptian state.[43] It was he, with relish and with Heikal's help, who directed the verbal attacks against Britain and kept the attacks against the United States relatively controlled. In fact, Nasser informed the world of his policy through speeches and the announcements on *Voice of the Arabs*. Nasser correctly assumed that Eden was trying to get rid of him personally whereas America was essentially anti-Communist and had overreacted to the arms deal and the recognition of China. The British were "exploiters," certainly "arrogant" and above all "colonialists" who lived off the "blood and sacrifices" of other people. "Colonialism was dead, dead and finished." The number of the Egyptian workers who died building the canal was repeated and exaggerated. "The canal is Egyptian and will stay Egyptian," he declared in a taped speech. France received equal treatment but not equal time, considerably less than the British. And Israel was nothing more than "a poisoned dagger implanted in the heart of the Arab nation." He made fun of America and spoke of American attempts to twist his arm, and he mentioned certain diplomats by name, but he never accused America of criminality. He just protested against its naïve ways. According to an unpublished thesis on his speeches by May Oueidah of the American University of Beirut, *honor, glory, dignity,* and *pride* were his pet words.[44] Of course, there was the constant reference to Allah and the taken-for-granted fact that He was on the side of the believers.

But Nasser eventually discovered that he needed more than his own words. The passage of time, which proved his point regarding Egypt's ability to run the canal, also revealed the unbridgeable gap between him and Eden. The inevitability of war dawned on him, and he realized that an invasion could not be stopped. This is why he created an armed people's militia. He went as far as to draw up plans for in-depth resistance to an invasion army. But to him the hopelessness of the situation did not matter; it was a case of right and wrong, and Egypt was right. He expressed belief in the people of the world and accepted them as judges. He believed that Egypt and the Arabs depended on him and wouldn't want him to back down. The support he received worldwide was not military or economic, but it was important to his developing sense of self-righteousness. He spoke of world public opinion and accorded it importance before others did. According to all his comrades who are still with us, he actually thought there was something new at work in the world. Nevertheless, Nasser was marching into battle knowing he would lose. Deliberately he tried to occupy the moral high ground. He did believe that his defeat would lead to an anti-colonial war throughout the Middle East. By staying the course, he was threatening to pull the temple down, just like Samson.

Indeed, in the battle for the Arab street, it was an unequal contest, with Nasser way ahead. Nasser gave voice to the historical frustration of the Arabs. The average Arab waited for Nasser's radio speeches like a groupie. He had become an icon and an incomparable speaker. Cinematic footage of his speeches was used later, and he was as good as he was on radio plus being a handsome star. The Egyptian press offices which had distributed his pictures in the past stopped doing it; now his pictures were made available by local printers throughout the Arab world. There was no way for the British, French, Israelis, or even the Americans to match the emotion of the songs which were written during the Suez Crisis. First came "Allah Akhbar" ("God Is Infinitely Greater"), then "We Shall Fight," and finally the open call to arms, "It Has Been Too Long, Oh My Arms." When the British bombed *Voice of the Arabs* off the air, Jordan and Syria filled the gap and broadcast on behalf of Egypt. Practically all the official media of the Arab governments lined up behind Egypt. Their people demanded it.

The only success the British propaganda machine achieved was to entice the Muslim Brotherhood to direct broadcasts against Nasser from Cyprus and to accuse him of dragging Egypt "into an abyss."[45] This was the one thing Nasser feared most; he was convinced that Eden would use the Brotherhood's network within Egypt to try to carry out a coup against him.[46] But the nationalization of the canal was so popular that even the Muslim Brotherhood suffered because it opposed it. No move against Nasser from any source was made. Later the pro-Nasser Arab employees of British Broadcasting in Cyprus walked out in protest against London's policies, and the station, which was financed by the Foreign Office and was not part of the BBC, and which had been renamed from Near East Broadcasting shortly before, had to run a reduced schedule.

It was sometime during this period that Nasser, only thirty-eight, was diagnosed with diabetes. If that had any effect on him then, it certainly did not show in the cinematic footage of the time, nor had any of his old comrades interviewed by me noticed anything in person. Some did find out, but the subject was not for discussion. One assumes he was advised to reduce his work schedule, but he did not. The way Nasser behaved during the early days of the Suez Crisis was a serial of the one-day performance of July 23, 1952. Not only was he everywhere, but this time he was wearing a suit, looking somewhat older but with a manly step and spring in his legs and overall an enhanced, more mature and trustworthy physical presence. He never rushed or seemed to walk fast. When speaking, he sounded as if he were making an important point to a friend. One could say that he was attempting the most difficult sales job in the world, selling intangibles dredged up from a distant past, the glorious pages of Arab history, which he brought to life by the sheer power of his personality. Short on gestures, most of the time he spoke with his hands clasped behind him and depended on his voice, his remarkable ability to project, which added meanings to words. There are pictures of him brooding while waiting to speak, but none where he looks unhappy behind the microphone. Facing the people, meeting them, obviously endowed him with energy and good humor. Regardless of the hour, he responded to his audience and came to life. He was never too tired to improvise. And there is no record of him practicing even one speech.

What lay behind Nasser's appeal to the Egyptians and Arabs was not understood in the West. In 1956, Nasser filled a historical void in the lives of all Arabs who had been waiting for things to change since World War I. By action and word Nasser hooked into their minds and hearts, the only Arab leader ever to do that. He, the man from nowhere, represented hope, and the hope became the gospel of daydreamers. For the first time in the twentieth century the Arab people were deliriously in love with one of their leaders. It was the more remarkable because Nasser was realistic in what he promised the Arabs. He had nothing material to give them and always spoke of the struggle and difficult road ahead. In fact, what he had to offer was no more than a vague promise to reclaim Arab honor. The bond between Nasser and the Arab people that materialized in 1956 was not tangible, having to do with regaining Arab dignity and honor by defying the West. This is why it was impossible for the West to understand or accept what Nasser represented.

During the Suez Crisis the average Arab had a lot to ponder. Would the West, in one combination or another, eliminate Nasser and set the clock back? Were the obvious policy differences between the United States and Britain and France real or a smoke screen? Were the British and French thinking of reoccupying the Middle East, supporting the Muslim Brotherhood to assume power, or a combination of the two? Where did Israel fit into the picture?

Eden was the anti-Nasser Western leader who mobilized first. Operation Musketeer, the code name for the invasion of Egypt, was put in the hands of General Sir Hugh Stockwell. The general's planning was hampered by the absence of a specific purpose for the operation. Diplomatically and inside Britain it was impossible for Eden to acknowledge that he wanted Nasser removed. Even without that acknowledgment, the British ambassador to Egypt, Sir Humphrey Trevelyan, and Eisenhower believed Eden's rigid stand was contributing to an increase in Nasser's prestige and popularity.[47] Moreover, Eden made clear that force would be used if negotiations failed, without being clear as to the aim of any negotiations. Conversely, Nasser accepted the possibility of an Israeli, Israeli-French, or British attack, but he never believed that Britain would join Israel in a conspiracy against the Arabs.[48] Not only did he believe Britain was above that, but he also tried to gain time and to avoid any pretext for starting a war. When the British and French insisted on paying the passage fees to the old company, Nasser instructed his people to let the ships through.[49]

For three months after the nationalization, until the Suez invasion of October 31, 1956, the world watched endless tries at open diplomacy, and there were secret negotiations as well. Following his visit to Eden to try to prevent war, Secretary of State Dulles pressured Britain into holding an international conference of canal users as a first step, the first London conference. To make this palatable to Britain and France, he had prevailed on President Eisenhower to join their allies in freezing Egyptian assets. He followed this by supporting the dispatch to Egypt as head of an international mission Australian prime minister Robert Menzies, who presented Nasser with the already adopted resolutions of the conference. It was a waste of time. Menzies, though representing eighteen nations, did not go to negotiate but to present the conference's resolutions.[50] More British than the British, Menzies patronized Nasser, and his mission was a dismal failure. He inflamed passions further by criticizing Nasser upon his return to London. On September 10 the second London conference of canal users opened with American support, but there were problems defining who was entitled to attend, and Egypt boycotted the meetings. Nasser wanted all users present, while Britain was selective. Eden, hoping to entice the United States into joining Britain and France in a single policy against Egypt, postponed the invasion plans and shifted them from Alexandria to Port Said. He accepted Dulles's thin proposal to create a permanent Suez Canal Users Association (SCUA) to oversee the running of the waterway. When Egypt flatly turned down the SCUA and Eden thought this was an excuse to invade, Dulles disowned the association to avoid being accused of collusion. By September 15 the British and French, doing what they were preaching against, tried to paralyze traffic in the canal by pulling out all European pilots on contract to the old company. Incredibly, Younis kept the traffic moving, with the help of some Greek, West German, and Russian pilots who refused to follow their governments. Egypt proved it could more than cope, and traffic actually increased. The British and French suffered a substantial loss of face, especially when Dulles openly declared that the SCUA was not going "to shoot its way through the Canal." Any chance of a united Western approach to the crisis disappeared.[51]

Then Britain and France backtracked and presented a resolution to the UN Security Council, although the USSR vetoed it. There was an Egyptian counter-resolution to the Security Council, which Britain and France vetoed. In fact, the United Nations was so paralyzed that Secretary-General Dag Hammarskjöld threatened to resign. Only the United States clung to any hope that an international solution might be found, and this hope originated with their representatives in Cairo. Meanwhile, the USSR was facing a minor uprising in Poland and a full-fledged rebellion in Hungary. Russian leader Nikita Khrushchev advised Nasser that under no circumstances would the Soviet Union go to war over the Suez issue. This was not unexpected by Nasser, and his reenergized contacts with the Eastern Bloc continued. The USSR's vague offer to help to build the dam was still alive.

Despite Khrushchev's statement that the USSR would not fight for the canal because that would lead to a third world war, a warning was issued to Eden and Mollet by the USSR's prime minister, Field Marshal Nikolay Bulganin. It was followed by news of Communist volunteers organizing to go to Egypt. There is no reason to think that Nasser took any of this seriously. But the maneuvers did help maintain his standing with his people. Meanwhile he appealed against the intransigence of Britain and France to the only power in the world capable of helping him, the United States of America.[52] The Americans were flabbergasted and advised him not to expect them to oppose their allies openly, but indicated some willingness to provide nonmilitary help.

The diplomatic efforts continued in a vacuum. Neither Eden nor Nasser would budge. The British prime minister, mentally reverting to times past, was convinced of the need to replace Nasser but had no plan to do it. Simultaneously, Nasser saw in what he was doing a dangerous defeat for Eden that might backfire. The British prime minister was already isolated, depending solely on an inner cabinet group. His obsession with Nasser was so morbid that his staff and colleagues spoke of his illness and surgery, the removal of an ulcer and a stone, as the only "adequate explanation."[53] Unable to attack Nasser alone for financial and moral reasons and with time running out, he settled for the only opportunity to remove Nasser that presented itself. He joined the conspiracy of Israel and France, well after he had turned down a similar offer from Mollet on July 27.[54] Amazingly, he warned Israel that Britain would support Jordan if retaliatory raids such as those carried out against the West Bank villages of Qalqilya and Samu continued. While no exact record exists of the number and nature of the meetings between Israel and France during this period, there is little doubt that the French were in constant contact with people such as Moshe Dayan and Shimon Peres deputizing for Ben-Gurion.[55] There were several meetings between the two sides in September.[56] As early as the first week in September Prime Minister Ben-Gurion had assured the French of his "cooperation," but he was still demanding written guarantees of support from Eden before proceeding. And it is now a matter of record that Moshe Dayan and other Israeli officers supervised the shipment to their country of French arms for the Sinai campaign well before Britain joined the conspiracy. However, what remains unknown is whether the actual decision by Eden to enter into secret conspiracy with France and Israel to attack Egypt and possibly replace Nasser took place in late September or in mid-October. Walter Monckton's resignation as defense minister over Eden's war seems to suggest a September date. The visit of French emissaries to Eden on October 14 and Eden's and Foreign Secretary Selwyn Lloyd's visit to Paris on the sixteenth were, by the looks of it, to finalize plans. The Israelis, having insisted that they would not proceed without the total backing of the British, were now satisfied. On October 22 Patrick Dean, the secretary-general of the Foreign Office, had the thankless task of signing what has since become known as the Sevres Protocol, the actual three-way agreement between Israel, France, and Britain. Lloyd was there but Eden was not. There were three copies. The Eden copy is missing.

In September 1956, regional and international developments provided a smoke screen for the conspirators. The USSR found itself bogged down in fighting against Hungarian nationalists. The Americans advised their nationals to leave the Middle East, inadvertently confirming that the crisis was leading to war. The Israelis ordered UN observers ousted from their major post in Al Auja on the edge of Sinai. Nobody even protested. Ben-Gurion received assurances that the British would destroy the Egyptian air force on the ground before Egypt could mount a response against Israeli cities. The British and Israelis, replying to messages from President Eisenhower, misled the Americans regarding their plans. Invasion orders that took into consideration Israeli involvement were issued to British and French forces. Nationalists beholden to Nasser won a parliamentary election in Jordan, and King Hussein tried to appease his pro-Nasser population by joining a military alliance with Syria and Egypt. The movements of the American Sixth Fleet and units of the Soviet navy in the eastern Mediterranean went on unabated. All efforts to bring the two sides together failed. On October 29, as required by the collusion agreement, Israeli paratroopers were dropped near the Mitla Pass in the middle of Sinai. It was the beginning of Operation Musketeer, as the British and French knew it, and Operation Khadesh, as the Israelis called it. Hours later, with the French air force protecting Israeli skies, the Israeli air force mounted dozens of attacks against Egypt proper. To Britain and France it was time to speak of a military threat to the canal, the phony pretext for intervening in the fighting. Nasser ordered the Egyptian army, most of which had been withdrawn during the crisis, to go back into Sinai. On October 30 Britain and France issued an ultimatum to the combatants to withdraw ten miles away from the canal. In essence, this would have meant the Egyptians withdrawing thirty miles and the Israelis advancing sixty miles. The Israelis accepted the ultimatum; the Egyptians did not.

In the United Nations, Britain and France intercepted all efforts to stop the attack on Egypt. On October 31, witnessing the merciless aerial attack on all parts of Egypt by the Royal Air Force and aware that his army would be unable to stop an invasion, Nasser personally took over the command of the battle. His first order, coordinated with the two countries involved, was for Egyptian air force planes to go to the Sudan and Saudi Arabia to avoid destruction.

For unknown reasons, Nasser refused to wear his military uniform, perhaps because he was only a colonel. Having had time to reconsider, Nasser ordered Sinai to be reevacuated. Then he telephoned King Hussein and president Shukri Kuwatly of Syria to ask them to stay out of the fighting. When Hussein objected and argued in favor of joining the fray, Nasser told him that it was a three-way conspiracy, named the countries involved, and openly lamented British participation. He asked Hussein "to save his army from destruction."[57] He followed that by issuing orders to block the canal, and he supervised their implementation. Altogether forty-seven ships were sunk in the waterway.[58] According to Mohamed Heikal, it was at this point that Nasser gave an interview to the London *Times*'s James Morris in which he restated his simple purpose: "We want to build the dam; we want to build our pyramid." Commanding all aspects of the battle and in complete control of everything while on the move, Nasser summoned Abdel Hakim Amer and Salah Salem to see him in the city of Port Said. He berated them mercilessly in front of several comrades. News had reached him that they had suffered something akin to nervous breakdowns and had been heard advocating surrender.[59] Broken and near tears, Amer shamelessly repeated his call to surrender in the presence of his friend. "Nobody is going to surrender," Mahmoud Hammroush remembers Nasser saying. "Nobody is going to surrender or escape and everybody is going to fight. Pull yourself together, Hakim. The whole army will be converted into a guerrilla force and pulled deep into Egypt, and let them fight us there. Your behavior is unmanly; the first shots have hardly been fired. Not only have I taken direct command of the army, I don't want you people issuing any orders. There is no countermanding my orders. Don't you understand they are trying to destroy the army, that it is a three-way conspiracy? If you can't do any better than mope like old women then you will be arrested and tried."

It certainly was not Amer who stood by him through the difficult hours of the Suez War. The stalwarts were original RCC members Abdel Latif Boghdadi and Zakkaria Mohieddine, and the diplomat Mahmoud Fawzi. Boghdadi was put in charge of organizing the resistance along the canal. Mohieddine became Nasser's alter ego, making sure all his orders were obeyed. Fawzi was an outstanding representative at the UN. Since it was an invasion of Egyptian soil, invoking Churchillian maxims came naturally to Nasser, who vowed to fight for every inch of Egypt. Local militias were being trained to back up the army. Of course, people by the tens of thousands were fleeing the canal area toward Cairo, but there were young people heading for the canal to fight, and the trucks carrying both escapees and volunteers were decorated with Nasser's pictures. Yet, it is remarkable to remember that there was no breakdown in order during this period. People left their houses open, but even thieves were lifted by a rare nationalist spirit inspired from above and did not take advantage of the situation.

The only two strategic decisions were to abandon Sinai and to block the canal. Nasser made both. The withdrawal was not a model military operation, and many officers panicked and abandoned their units. Egyptian soldiers fought bravely even inside Sinai and held the line for a week, but they were poorly led. On several occasions Nasser personally had to give fighting units detailed withdrawal orders. The blocking of the canal was a different matter. Nasser approved the plan, and received the reports on the sinkings one by one. During a tour of the canal area before the British and French paratroop drop, he decided that his place was with the troops along the canal. But he later thought better of it. Meanwhile, with the Israelis still locked in bitter combat in many places in Sinai, the British and French incessantly bombed the Egyptian army, military airfields, and other facilities. The Egyptians fought alone because Nasser, honorably fearing that the British and French would destroy everything in their way, turned down new Syrian and Jordanian offers of help.

Syrian workers destroyed three pumping stations of the Iraqi Petroleum Company, which carried oil to the Mediterranean; Saudi Arabia embargoed the shipment of oil to Britain and France; and other Arab countries suffered internal stresses but took diplomatic actions against Britain and France. Pro-Egypt, pro-Nasser rioting erupted from the Atlantic to the Gulf. Back in Baghdad, Nuri watched developments with unconcealed apprehension. According to his nephew and former member of the Iraqi cabinet Jamil Abdel Wahab, when Nuri received the news about a landing along the canal he turned utterly pale. "What are they doing landing there? They've got to get him in Cairo. We can't survive this, we will pay for this." On November 5 British paratroops began landing at Port Said, and the French at Port Fuad. The UN was so crippled by vetoes that it could decide on nothing, and more or less stopped functioning. It was President Eisenhower of the United States who tilted the scales when he unambiguously called for immediate Israeli, British, and French withdrawal from Egyptian territory.

Israeli mopping-up operations continued after a UN cease-fire resolution was accepted on November 7. The Israelis continued to harass stranded units of the Egyptian army and left many of them without food and water. The British and French some twenty miles down the canal stopped in their tracks and faced the danger of Egyptian irregulars.

The immediate reaction to the invasion was simple: practically the whole world sided with Nasser. Everybody saw his survival as a victory for Egypt. Nasser thought otherwise. He knew that Eisenhower had saved him. He felt defeated "by my own army" and wished the army had acquitted itself better.[60] But something beyond the realities of battlefield conditions was happening to Arab-Western relations.

Nasser had stopped "them." Nasser had depended on unknown, untried factors called Arab support and world public opinion and used them to deny France, Britain, and Israel victory. Sinai was occupied, but the canal was still Egyptian. There were UN resolutions that accepted the canal's Egyptian identity and called for clearing it. The British and French forces withdrew from Egypt in December 1956, under the supervision of the United Nations. On April 8, 1957, the Suez Canal was reopened, a month after Israel's withdrawal. Nasser's victory was complete. Al Rayyes Gamal Abdel Nasser had achieved a miracle. The notion of world public opinion took hold. Colonialism was a thing of the past.

The Israelis have little concern for their international reputation, but the whole Suez War was a huge blow to Britain's and France's prestige and international standing. Operation Musketeer had cost them fifty casualties altogether, the Israelis less than two hundred, and the Egyptians two thousand. For Nasser, success did not depend on winning; it depended on surviving. To the Arabs, he was still there, a defiant, living symbol of their hopes, will, and desire. Nobody thought that he had won the war, but every Arab knew that he had fought in their name. Moreover, he behaved with impeccable dignity before, during, and after the battle.

# 5

# The Dark at the End of the Tunnel

The resignation of British prime minister Anthony Eden on January 9, 1957, ostensibly for health reasons, confirmed Nasser's victory. There was no gloating in Cairo; the news was reported with little comment. The British and French evacuation of the Suez Canal area in December had been the occasion for celebrations and speeches. The canal itself was cleared of sunken ships and reopened on April 8, another occasion for celebrating victory against the invaders. Even the Israelis eventually ran out of delaying excuses and left Egypt on May 8, 1957, and with that the tripartite invasion came to an end. There were formalities, like compensating the shareholders of the canal company and other subsidiary issues, which had to be addressed later. But the canal was Egyptian.

Two background developments nagged at Nasser and augured poorly for the future. One was the creation of the United Nations Emergency Force (UNEF) to police the Egyptian side of the Israeli-Egyptian border. The moving spirit and author of the UN resolution creating UNEF was Canadian minister of foreign affairs Lester Pearson, whose efforts toward achieving a Middle East peace won him the Nobel Peace Prize. The multinational force was intended to guard both sides of the Israeli-Egyptian border. But Israel refused to accept any troops on its side of the border, and after long negotiations between UN secretary-general Dag Hammarskjöld and Nasser, all of UNEF ended up on the Egyptian side. Nasser had no intention of ceding any of Egypt's rights to control its territory, and from the beginning it was understood that the UNEF presence was at the discretion of Egypt. But there was an oral agreement with Hammarskjöld regarding ending fedayeen activity.[1] Hammarskjöld was a man Nasser trusted, and the understandings between them reflected the two men's ability to work together. Nasser saw more of Hammarskjöld than any other world statesman except Tito. This is why relations between Nasser and the UN deteriorated after the death of Hammarskjöld in 1961. There was nothing resembling those good relations with the new secretary-general, U Thant.

Most Arabs were so euphoric over Nasser's canal victory that the creation of UNEF either was ignored or escaped them altogether. Within Egypt itself, Nasser managed to usurp whatever was left of the will of the people and that of his comrades. There was no resistance to his assumption of a very special status—like other dictators, he absorbed everything into himself. The army, under the loyal Amer, had legitimized the regime. Immediately after the Suez War, Nasser personalized the regime. His former comrades, even when he appointed them prime minster like Ali Sabri in 1957 or speaker of the National Assembly like Anwar Sadat the same year, receded further into the background.

Nasser's direct relationship with the people, his popularity, reduced the importance of all other posts except his. But he made a point of keeping his old comrades with him. He saw no need to eliminate any of them and tried to perpetuate their presence as if it mattered while making sure that it did not. He certainly spent considerable time talking them out of their frequent threats to resign. These threats seldom amounted to anything until the early 1960s, when Boghdadi and others did indeed resign over his tilt toward the USSR and adoption of socialist policies.

However, unlike other military groups who took over Middle Eastern governments, Nasser and his colleagues never completely turned on each other or used violence to eliminate colleagues and stop them from competing with them. In this case, there was no competition as to who was boss. Among other reasons, Nasser did not feel that any of them could compete with him, certainly not when it came to his standing with the people. But he was still cautious, and the Youth Organization, though made up of supporters, was limited to two hundred thousand members, not large enough to represent a potential danger to the state or become independent of it. The peasants and workers associations were handled the same way. The 1957 takeover by the state of private economic functions went almost unopposed. Many historians and journalists attribute the absence of conflict at the top to Nasser's personality. His leading biographers and other writers, such as Jean Lacouture, Anthony Nutting, Desmond Stewart, and Nejla Abu Izzidine, see another reason for the relatively peaceful running of the state; they claim that Nasser was essentially a pacifist.[2]

Pacifist or not, with the exception of Amer, Nasser was never familiar with his old comrades. Although some of them visited him at home, he kept a distance from them, and surprisingly, they accepted it. They revered him because of his unique standing and position with the people and because there were no hidden weaknesses in the man while there was much to admire. Power did not corrupt him. He was tolerant of human weakness and never spoke of the shortcomings of others. There were patterns to his behavior, for example having American friends (Roosevelt, Lakeland, and James Eichelberger of the CIA among others) with whom he thought he could discourse. His forgiving attitude accounts for why Amer and Salah Salem were never punished for their shameful behavior during the invasion of the canal, and why Amer's offer of resignation was turned down. Nasser pretended that he had never heard of their wish to surrender. Even Salem's affair with Princess Fawzia, King Farouk's sister, though frowned upon by the home-loving Nasser, was overlooked.

The field marshal, Amer, continued to occupy a unique position. He was Nasser's main source of information about happenings in the outside world and of his successes and failures. That Nasser looked the other way and dismissed stories of Amer's womanizing, drinking, hashish smoking, and unmilitary behavior is testimony to their close friendship. When several of the original RCC members made an issue of Amer's bad influence on the army and unfitness for command, Nasser backed Amer on all but minor points.[3] In fact, he often placed personal loyalty ahead of competence in a way which inhibited his wish to have a strong government.

After the Suez War, Boghdadi was appointed general administrator for reconstruction of the canal area and performed admirably. Zakkaria Mohieddine's authority over the security system was expanded, and he became Nasser's Mr. Reliable. Abdel Munim Amin became known as being pro-American, while Ali Sabri was supposedly pro-Soviet. The others were shunted from one ministry to another and involved themselves in small acts of corruption which ultimately weakened them, while Nasser looked the other way. In fact, his honesty was almost tactile; according to historian Keith Whitlock, "There was a blanket of morality in which he sought to shroud himself."[4]

Outside Egypt some Arab leaders and intellectuals viewed the deployment of UNEF with misgivings. They feared it might mean a de facto Egyptian peace with Israel. And, in fact, though he no longer believed peace was on the way, Nasser did exchange some secret messages with the Israelis through Hammarskjöld.[5] Ben-Gurion, using Hammarskjöld and others, never tired of inviting Nasser to meet him either secretly or openly; Nasser's final response was to question whether he would be allowed back home after accepting such a meeting. He firmly believed that the Arab people were solidly against Israel and on occasion cited the example of King Abdullah of Jordan, who was gunned down for conducting secret negotiations with the Zionist state.

But the Arab people did not know about his limited secret contacts with Israel, and Nasser had become a bigger-than-life character. Most were sure that there must be a good reason behind permitting UNEF to operate. Nuri's regime did try its utmost to use the deployment against Nasser, but that failed if only because Iraq itself was not trying to do battle with the Israelis. Some fedayeen, including one Yasser Arafat, already suspected of belonging to the Muslim Brotherhood, found the strictures placed on them by Nasser so confining that they moved to places like Kuwait. Even in Kuwait Arafat was pro-Brotherhood and anti-Nasser. Others tried to operate without authorization from the Egyptians and were "hounded, jailed and interrogated."[6] The only official armed Palestinian presence was a battalion attached to the Egyptian army. Among the people who saw danger to the Arab cause by the deployment of UNEF was the then leader of the Palestinians and the Arafat of his day, the mufti of Palestine, Hajj Amin al-Husseini, the man to whom Nasser had offered his services in 1948. He did ask Nasser about the consequences of the UNEF deployment but got no answer. It was an insult the mufti would not forget.

The other reality that the average Arab missed but that

changed the character of events in the Middle East was the January 1957 adoption by the United States of the Eisenhower Doctrine. This development came after a thorough examination by the Eisenhower administration of U.S.-Egyptian relations and the determination that American security interests and Nasser's nationalism, Egyptian or Arab, were irreconcilable. Adopting the Eisenhower Doctrine was a deliberate move to replace Britain in the Middle East and to isolate and reduce Nasser. It followed a brief period during which the Americans considered supporting King Saud of Saudi Arabia as a counterweight to Nasser,[7] an idea eventually dismissed by its author, President Eisenhower. This was followed by Operation Omega, a confused CIA caper aimed at either winning Nasser or eliminating him. That too failed, and this was when the Eisenhower Doctrine emerged.

The doctrine represented a pledge by the United States to protect the countries of the Middle East against Communism and its "agents." President Camille Chamoun of Lebanon, ever so dismissive of the Arab people and what was unacceptable to the Lebanese, was the first Arab leader to adhere to the American doctrine. He was followed by Saud of Saudi Arabia, Nuri of Iraq, and Hussein of Jordan. All of them saw in the doctrine an attempt to control Nasser's appeal to the Arab people and to protect them against it.

Still preoccupied with the Baghdad Pact, Nasser had no problem in allying himself with pro-West but anti–Baghdad Pact Saudi Arabia. Once again opposing the alliance came first. Still, America's move to replace Britain and France as the guardian of Western interests throughout the Middle East left Nasser uncertain as to whether he was considered a Communist agent and thus included in the aims of the doctrine. True, according to the doctrine, U.S. interference depended on an invitation by a country threatened by the Communist danger, but there was no shortage of Arab leaders who would claim Nasser was an agent of international Communism. Hussein of Jordan and Chamoun of Lebanon were willing. Because nobody could clarify things for him, Nasser suspended all secret contacts with the Cairo CIA and would no longer meet Eisenhower's emissaries. There was more to America's distinct coolness to Nasser and his equally frigid response to the Eisenhower Doctrine. A full-fledged CIA study of the man described him as "vain, suspicious, confident, resilient, courageous, a risk-taker and obstinate."[8] Clearly he qualified as an agent of Communism.

The Eisenhower Doctrine was followed by open U.S. support for Islamic groups,[9] and this effort was far-reaching enough to include the creation of anti-Nasser Islamic cells in eastern Saudi Arabia, near the oil fields.[10] Other Islamic groups flourished in Pakistan and eventually fathered smaller, more militant ones in Afghanistan. This time the only way out for Nasser was to move closer to the USSR. But Nasser was very clear on what this amity meant. He was willing to become a client of the USSR, to work with them, but not as a satellite, and he was always against the Egyptian Communist Party.[11] Outwardly it looked as if the American support for Egyptian, not Arab, nationalism that began in 1952 had come to an end. In fact this was not the case, and it was Nasser more than any world leader who played out a love-hate relationship with America and thereby invited the U.S. to assume Britain's old role in the area. True, relations with the USSR were good enough that there was no longer any need to use Czechoslovakia as a front. But the same man who had broken the Western monopoly on the supply of arms was fond of things American, including watching American films every week. His favorite was *It's a Wonderful Life,* a sentimental all-American story made by Frank Capra.[12]

America's entry into the Middle East on a grand scale found the British promoting the idea of killing Nasser,[13] an idea presented to the CIA in London through intelligence officer George Young. The American thinking had not gone that far, and with the Americans opposing the idea, the British backed out of the scheme. Later (but only briefly) the CIA funded a Muslim Brotherhood office in Geneva, the Islamic Center, which was entrusted with the planning of Nasser's assassination, code-named Operation Sipony.[14] According to former CIA regional director James Critchfield, Kamal Adham, head of Saudi intelligence and the late King Faisal's brother-in-law, was a key player in this operation. Operation Sipony was aborted at the last minute because the decision on how to assassinate Nasser kept changing. On one occasion the protagonist was arrested, a second would-be assassin failed, and the third gave up.[15] When the Islamists could not do it, the CIA considered cooperating with British intelligence to carry out a coup. But, unlike the CIA, the State Department was opposed to organizing coups.[16]

There is something strange about the attempts to kill Nasser, which according to Mohamed Heikal were "too many to count."[17] Stephen Dorril's solid history of MI6 lists no fewer than ten British plans to kill Al Rayyes, and two French ones. They were supposed to have started in February 1956 and gone on into the early 1960s. They included using his doctor, and later the recruiting of officers. Of course, there was the usual resort to old-fashioned methods, such as loading his can of shaving lotion with explosives and a cigarette packet that would fire a poisoned dart into his heart, not to speak of putting something lethal into his coffee.

Nasser himself spoke of an attempt against him involving the payment of £160,000.[18] The French appear to have tried by using a hit man from on top of a building. Even Secretary of State John Foster Dulles misinterpreted an innocent statement by Eisenhower which amounted to "Something must be done about him." Dulles acted with the CIA chief, his brother Allen, to eliminate Nasser. Dulles later discovered that Eisenhower was not sanctioning the killing of Nasser, just silencing him. Eisenhower had said, "Can't we finish this?"[19] What is odd is that none of these attempts succeeded. Nasser continued to mingle with crowds, go to mosques, and parade in the backseat of a convertible car.

The first confrontation between the United States and Egypt after the declaration of the Eisenhower Doctrine involved Jordan. The U.S. stand against Arab unity or cooperation schemes among Arab states was strategic, and Jordan was needed to keep the Arabs divided. Jordan had slipped from Western control during the Suez Crisis, in October 1956, when a pro-Nasser coalition won the elections and Suleiman Nabulsi became prime minister. Responding to an offer from Saudi Arabia, Syria, and Egypt to replace the British subsidy, Jordan terminated the 1948 alliance with Britain in March 1957.[20] But the Arab countries failed to deliver, and Hussein, his treasury empty, decided to change direction yet again and use the coolness in U.S.-Nasser relations to establish a position with America. Unable to challenge Nasser openly, he sought a way out with the help of the CIA. Together they concocted a plot against the freely elected government of Jordan. Using the Bedouin of his army, Hussein announced the discovery of a coup against him, arrested and dismissed Nabulsi, army chief of staff Ali Abu Nawar, and dozens of army officers and politicians. A state of emergency was declared.

Hussein claimed that the two men had plotted against him with Nasser's knowledge and backing. What they were plotting in a country they already ran was never articulated, but the young king implied that he personally was the target of the plot, that

Nasser wanted him replaced. Hussein described Nasser's behavior as perfidy and recalled his support for Nasser during the Suez War. Though there was evidence that most of the accused if not all had been framed, the Western press accepted Hussein's story at face value. It reported a coup attempt that never was. The real coup was what Hussein did, which was planned by the CIA, using Bedouin troops loyal to the monarchy and carried out by Hussein against his own government. Of course, the CIA was happy to help and put Hussein on a salary,[21] and in the background there was an American offer to provide Jordan with a financial subsidy of $50 million per year in return for King Hussein's open support for the United States' regional policy. Hussein became a CIA salaried employee.

The Jordanian situation represented a confrontation in microcosm between the pro- and anti-Nasser forces in the Middle East. Naturally Iraq was ready to help Jordan, but Iraq's ties to the Baghdad Pact meant that the stationing of troops in Jordan carried the potential of Baghdad Pact troops being used against Israel, something the Israelis feared. So the CIA prevailed on Saudi Arabia to dispatch troops to help Hussein. King Saud had opposed Nasser's 1955 socialism, criticized Nasser's unilateral nationalization action, then supported Nasser during the war, but eventually resented Nasser's references to the oil as if it were his; now Saud dispatched four thousand troops to Jordan. It was a totally Arab gesture against Nasser. Contrary to Saudi claims, the troops were of no use against the Israelis. Of course, Jordan received expressions of support from Lebanon and Yemen. It was the usual business of the governments being against Nasser while the people, powerless and unorganized, were for him.

Except for attacking Hussein on the radio and accusing him of being "a tool of the imperialists" or "a descendant of traitors," Nasser's hands were tied. Israel had for some time made it known that it would respond to Hussein's overthrow by pro-Nasser Jordanians or other militants by occupying the West Bank. From the beginning Nasser had accepted the Israeli threat at face value and would not challenge it. At one point he told news correspondents Wilton Wynn and Harry Ellis that he didn't want Hussein toppled because the consequences would be too dire. His inability to help a takeover in Jordan became a source of comfort for the Western powers and an embarrassment to Nasser's Arab supporters. But even without the Israeli threat, Nasser had no plan for Jordan and was in no financial or logistical position to implement one anyway. The election of Nabulsi had been a victory for Nasser, indeed a democratic victory free from official interference, tantamount to a plebiscite on his brand of Arab nationalism and his positive neutralism. But he had not thought how to use Nabulsi beyond pointing out his nationalist credentials. Nasser opted for inaction when he knew that there was no way for King Hussein to share power with a government whose leader was beholden to Nasser. Nor was Hussein about to abdicate. A confrontation between the two sides was inevitable.

Conceivably Nasser could have turned Jordan into a satellite of Egypt for a few months, but Egypt had not been prepared for that. Disaster would have followed. For the same reason, the utter unpreparedness of the pro-Nasser forces to follow their election success with something concrete, annexing Jordan was not feasible. For Nasser, the leader of the Arabs who was calling for unity and government by the people, losing Jordan or not responding to the wishes of the Jordanian people was not an option either, particularly losing it because of an Israeli threat. Jordan was needed for any future military confrontation with Israel, and Nasser was obliged to support the Jordanian elements loyal to him and to save Jordan from being a buffer state shielding Israel. It was a confused picture: Nasser needed Jordan, but didn't know how to hold on to it or turn it into an ally without Israeli interference. In the middle of this impossible situation, Nasser continued to appeal to the Jordanians and to claim their loyalty. In fact he was able to undermine the various Jordanian governments through the disruptive action of his followers; but neither he nor his followers were capable of creating a government that could stand up to Israel.

Nasser accepted defeat in Jordan without going to battle. His Jordanian followers were not up to the task of confronting King Hussein. Israel was behind the monarch, while the pro-Nasser Jordanians didn't know what they were supposed to create. There were no instructions from Nasser to his followers after Nabulsi's election. The consequences were a major setback for Nasser and his brand of Arab nationalism. The pro-Nasser Arabs were accustomed to winning and could not reconcile themselves to being paralyzed. The United States stepped in to provide Jordan with financial aid, and the CIA, in the person of agent James Russell Barracks, slowly and methodically weeded out pro-Nasser elements from the Jordanian government and army. Nasser's first defeat in the Arab arena was administered by America, his new opponent. Suddenly there were limits to what Nasser could do. The use of CIA money against him was effective.

Because he was not in a position to annex Arab countries or run them as tributaries, Nasser had to lower his and his followers' expectations. In this case that meant retreating from the open call for unity advocated by the Syria-based Ba'ath Party, the Arab Nationalist Movement, and other parties. The unity between Arab countries he preached, vague to begin with, became more so with time. His message was anticolonial, against Arab leaders who followed the West unquestioningly; it supported the Arabs in their attempts to control their own oil and promised the restoration of dignity to the common man. But most of the call for unity was implicit, because he spoke of the Arabs collectively. He did not speak of the rights of Syria, Jordan, Egypt; he spoke of the rights of the Arabs, and his listeners understood that to mean that the Jordanians, Syrians, Egyptians, and the rest were one. This general formula won the hearts of the Arab people because it reflected their feelings. They believed in Nasser and expected him to live up to his promise to free them from the Western imperialists and the kings, emirs, and sheikhs who acted as deputy sheriffs for the West, and to unite them.

So the challenge to the West was clear, and the major Western powers lined up against Nasser. If we accept the documented fact that Nasser was never enamored of the USSR, the Communist Parties, or their designs for the Middle East, then what we have is a popular leader who was at odds with both East and West. Indeed his attachment to positive neutralism did mean occupying the middle ground, something America refused to accept and the USSR did not understand.[22] While this and his failure to use his popularity effectively suggested that he was vulnerable, the facts tell a different story. Financing the Aswan High Dam did preoccupy him. For that he received $300 million and technical support from the USSR. Moreover, the USSR did replace the military hardware destroyed in the 1956 war. Simultaneously, America, aware of Nasser's anti-Communist tendencies, never stopped trying to reclaim him. Assuming the leadership of the Arabs without giving it definite direction, Nasser still played the two sides against each other. But eventually both sides became tired of being manipulated.

Nasser was much more stung by the defeat of his backers in Jordan than the world realized. He recognized the coup as part of an American plot, a conspiracy. To halt the momentum of his movement, as the Hussein coup in Jordan did, was to cripple it and pave the way for further failures. Nasser thrived on success, and Jordan, two-thirds Palestinian and heavily committed to his cause, could have been held by his feckless followers if only he had tried to lead them. Failure in Jordan reduced the chances of succeeding elsewhere. He simply had no plan for any of the Arab countries, beyond wanting, almost needing, the loyalty of their people. Considering that some of them were literally foreign to him, such as the Omanis and Yemenis, one could state that Nasser was in love with the idea of Arab unity without knowing how to implement it. Perhaps all he wanted was to be the most popular Arab leader since Mohamed.

Luckily for Nasser, this failure was not appreciated by the Arab people, who accepted the conspiracy theory, and it made little dent in his popularity. Yet, he was not capable of changing his ways and continued to depend on disparate, unorganized groups who had no plan either, nor any appreciation or ideas as to what should be achieved under his leadership. Nasser himself was happy being the hero of the Arabs everywhere, but without claiming the position and admitting to thoughts of empire. The average Arab had hoped that he would extend his Suez success. Only America saw an opportunity in Nasser's popularity; the Americans tried to convince him to use it to make peace with Israel,[23] which only a popular leader could do. When Nasser refused to act on the American suggestion, the United States prevailed on Jordan, Lebanon, and Syria to give refuge to the Muslim Brotherhood and on Saudi Arabia to give the Brotherhood money. Once secret, these facts about the Brotherhood were revealed in a television interview by the son of one of their supreme guides, Said Ramadan.[24] In fact, for thirty years the Brotherhood was the only legal political party in Jordan, and for most of this time it was the beneficiary of U.S. support. (Some of the militant Islamic groups operating in Jordan today go back to that period.)

The Arab people on whom Nasser depended came from all walks of life. There were intellectuals who believed in Arab unity, peasants who felt their governments abused them, workers who wanted to share in the wealth of their countries, businessmen and specialists such as Saudi minister of petroleum Abdallah Tariki who thought the West was stealing the oil wealth, and the run-of-the-mill people who felt that their rights were denied them but refused to accept that religion or religious political parties were the way out of their predicament. The teachings of the Brotherhood fell on deaf ears because Nasser was a practicing, pious Muslim, but he was an Arab politically. The Arab people accepted his credentials and rejected the Western-sponsored militants. Except for the king of Saudi Arabia, Nasser's competitors were pro-West secularists. On the other hand, the Brotherhood espoused the concept of *al umma*, or the nation of Islam, which is larger than the Arab nation. To the U.S.-sponsored Brotherhood, the bases of governance were the Koran, Sharia law, and the teachings of the Prophet. Here again Nasser was caught between two divergent forces without belonging to either. The West ostensibly had no position regarding a secular versus a religious state, and supported fundamentalist Saudi Arabia and secular Iraq as well as the Brotherhood. For nearly a century the Arabs had lost the right to decide the fate of their countries. The Arabs were on an implicit search for dignity before Nasser, but he articulated their grievance and made it popular. Until Nasser, they believed no Arab leader could stand up to the West and survive, and pointed to the fate of King Ghazi of Iraq, who was murdered because of his opposition to Britain, and how the rest of the Hashemite family paid a heavy price for wanting to unite the Arabs after the First World War and were not accepted until they changed political direction. In reality the West was opposed to Arab unity while promoting the Islamic movement because the latter was anti-Communist.

Of course there were some problems of immediate concern to all Arabs, and some that affected one country more than the others. In Jordan the Palestinians followed Nasser because they believed that he was the only Arab leader capable of standing up to the Israelis. To them, Nasser's Soviet arms deal, which broke the Western monopoly on this trade, symbolized triumph over the West. Also, they believed that but for the participation of Britain and France, his army would have acquitted itself better in the Suez War. Many original Jordanians (non-politicians) also believed in this. There were unity clubs, Arab youth clubs, and many secret civilian formations, together with an impressive number of military ones whose members were officers offering their allegiance to Nasser. But they were nothing but loose organizations and made up of *mu'aidain*, or "backers." Some of them undoubtedly took money from the Egyptian embassy in Amman, and used some of it to raise demonstrations whenever they were instructed to while pocketing the rest. Others were committed people who believed in Nasser's message of freedom, socialism, and unity and were willing to do anything to advance it. But overall, they did not represent a cohesive, self-perpetuating action group, and Egyptian intelligence, the organization which ran them, did nothing to organize them. Egyptian intelligence spent tens of millions of pounds on its followers throughout the Arab Middle East, so the Nasserites did have sufficient funds. What they did not have was the will; that, only Nasser could provide.

In regard to money, Nasser's supporters were no better than his enemies. Nasser always referred to the people who occasionally came out in support of Nuri and Hussein as *"al murtazaka,"* the mercenaries. But he followed the same formula unnecessarily. His popularity would have been enough. Nasser started bribing or investing in known charlatans during the plebiscite in the Sudan, where the practice actually backfired.[25] But obviously—and this is true of undemocratic systems, which cannot admit failure—the lesson had not been learned. Some of the people Nasser backed in Lebanon were known gangsters who could always depend on toughs of the country, traditionally the harbor boys, to march in support of the cause. The situation in Lebanon was more complex and also more revealing than in Jordan. Beirut was the press center for the whole Middle East; most of its dailies and weeklies were regional. They were run by talented people and had a great deal of influence. Knowing that they needed the support of the Lebanese press, Nasser's followers, unable to think of something imaginative, advised him to buy it. The press attaché at the Egyptian embassy in Beirut, Anwar al-Jamal, had a high percentage of Lebanese journalists on his payroll, including some at major dailies such as *Al Anwar* and *Al Youm*. The countries opposed to Nasser responded by financing their own newspapers and magazines, including the prestigious *Al Hayat*. Very few publications in Lebanon remained independent. When the CIA entered the fray, the role of Beirut as a center for the free press and as a refuge for the political exiles of the Middle East came to an end. Nothing but advocacy publishing took place, even when people too big to be handled by a press attaché trekked to Cairo and audiences with Al Rayyes before getting their envelopes.

It was the same story with Lebanese politicians. They were salaried, and were paid more to guarantee their followers. Some actually bought a following after they received their retainer from Cairo. Again, while there were genuine followers or supporters, such as the highly principled socialist Kamal Jumblat, there were also mercenaries and others of dubious character. Among the most impressive of the organizations which supported Nasser was the Arab Nationalist Movement (ANM), a highly successful political cluster which originated at the American University of Beirut, spread to most of the Arab countries, and advocated a war against what it called "the reactionary regimes." One of its slogans was "The road to Tel Aviv is through Riyadh." Among the leaders of the ANM was the Palestinian George Habbash, later the leader of the Palestine Liberation Front and a committed socialist who viewed with unease the activities of some of Nasser's followers.

The golden age of Nasser, 1955–58, found him unable to harness the power of the people who followed him. Whatever Arab nationalist organizations there were in Jordan, Lebanon, Syria, Iraq, and the Arabian Peninsula—the ANM, Nejed al-Fatat, the Front for the Liberation of the Arabian Peninsula, and to a certain degree the Ba'ath, which operated in a number of countries—had existed before Nasser. When he finally adopted his Arab persona, old and new believers in Arab unity shared his ideology and occasionally merged or cooperated with Nasser followers, but without forming a specific group. Though he did try to use the effective ANM against the Brotherhood, the great majority of Nasser's followers were never organized in any permanent structure like the Brotherhood's established parties, clubs, and other action groups. His followers were lower on the social scale and called themselves "Nasserites," despite his objection to the label.[26] But only loosely could they be termed "followers"; very seldom were they educated enough or disciplined enough to be an effective instrument of anybody. They called themselves Nasserites because until him they had no label and to suggest greater closeness with their idol. He preferred the simpler Arab nationalist label.

But then he really did not want a political movement, even if it assumed the right name and was created by him. That is why he had problems with the ANM from the start: they did not share his willingness to compromise except later, and even then, they broke with him after only three years. An organized political movement such as the ANM had a clear political program that its members had to follow. After three years of operating under his aegis, the

ANM parted company with Nasser over ideology. The ANM leadership was made up of doctrinaire people opposed to any compromise with the existing pro-West regimes. When Nasser opted for a measure of accommodation with Saudi Arabia and Jordan, the Arab nationalists broke with him and went their own way. He thought he should decide when to oppose or befriend other Arab regimes. Having a political movement meant deferring to it, but as a leader or undisputed chief of the party, he was not willing to do that. There was little ideology involved in this, just Nasser's appreciation of realpolitik. Yet there were certain issues regarding which he would not compromise. They included the dignity of the common man, an instinctive rejection of interference by outside powers in the Middle East, a refusal to mix religion and politics, and the issue of slavery. He communicated with the people in the most natural way of any Arab leader of the twentieth century—in many ways he was one of them—but, aside from the above mentioned issues of principle, he always backed away from dictating to other Arab countries. Yes, he actually avoided giving advice to fellow Arab governments, except, understandably, to Jordan and Syria during the 1956 crisis, when preaching to their people. There is no escaping the conclusion that Nasser represented an odd type of dictator. He manifested a need to be loved, or followed because he was loved, which most other dictators do not have. His dictatorial ways were a mixture of populism and a need to be accepted as a man of principle.

Either he naively wanted consensus among the Arab people, wanted the street and souk people to march unquestioningly behind him and ignore their governments (or perhaps force their leaders to march behind him with them); or he believed that he was a leader destined to win against lesser enemies, the unpopular pro-West clutch of kings, emirs, and sheikhs. It would have been very difficult to adopt a political program that encompassed and justified his feelings toward Nuri and his on and off cooperation with the House of Saud. He would automatically have condemned himself. Appealing to the people provided him with many ways to escape judgment of his performance and his promises, the vague ideals that he espoused (e.g., "Arab oil for the Arabs") without any specific plans to realize them. He shared the mood of the people without being held to account by them.

Furthermore, he used the absence of a political structure

behind him to excuse some activities by his followers. According to Mohamed Heikal, Nasser was fond of saying that he could control the actions of people whom he had chosen but had no way of controlling those who chose him.[27] This attractive but unsound justification of what his followers did meant that he lacked the means and organization to control millions of his followers. Nasser was the prisoner of the ordinary Arabs as much as he was their leader. His success or failure depended on them. There was no blame to allocate, just the one to share. In fact, adopting the broad political teachings of a man who placed honor above all (and he did tell British ambassador Sir Humphrey Trevelyan not to try to threaten him "like Farouk") is hardly the equivalent of subscribing to a doctrine or political philosophy. If we accept that he won the battle to restore, in whatever form, the dignity of the Arabs, then maintaining it must have been a problem. He had to keep winning against West and East. Both were doing everything possible for the control of the Middle East.

For a while after Suez and the major defeat in Jordan, Nasser reverted to his old efforts in the internal field. The confiscation and nationalization of British and French assets begun with the Suez Crisis were expanded to include tobacco, cement, pharmaceutical, and phosphate industries. In all cases compensation was paid, though the way it was determined was somewhat arbitrary. Because the previous opening to outside investment and the offering of tax incentives had yielded no results, Nasser nationalized more companies, and in 1957 made them part of the economic development organization. The state took over in many areas, but he still stopped short of total governmental control—what he needed to carry out his program—and two-thirds of the economy remained in private hands. Yet this effort did achieve a measure of success.[28] Agricultural production increased, and investment in industrialization, aided by generous tax breaks covering the granting of oil-prospecting concessions, kept rising. The Helwan steelworks were on their way to becoming the country's largest enterprise. They were not as efficient as their European counterparts, but they provided the country with product and employed tens of thousands of people. Above all, there was the unfinished business of the Aswan High Dam and his decision to cooperate with the USSR to build it.

The Liberation Rally was abolished, and the National Union was created in mid-1957 to replace it. The National Assembly was to be the national representative body. This move allowed Nasser to sideline Gamal Salem and Anwar Sadat, who had run the Liberation Rally; he always used these changes to relieve people of their duties, however temporarily. The idealist in Nasser expected half of the National Assembly's members to be workers and peasants, but this did not happen, mostly because of lack of interest by both peasants and workers. To correct this, Nasser had to hold another election, this time a doctored one that guaranteed the desired outcome. The new National Assembly included representatives of student groups, women's organizations, and trade associations. It was obvious that this was no more than an improvised quasi-parliamentary structure, an imposed parliamentary system. But Nasser did indeed want it to work; he favored debate on domestic issues, including students' rights, women's rights, and the potential for unionization, and measures to break the hold of the local notables on the agriculture of the Said.

His actions included the prohibition of employment for children under twelve, the provision of clinical care, the distribution of free food, and the control of employment practices.[29] He had given these government-sponsored syndicates social and economic rights, and the National Assembly was his way of trying to give them political rights. But his attempts to grant the people political freedom from above failed, essentially because he stopped the various organizations from working out their own programs and planned their agenda for them. Furthermore, he still carried out the occasional arbitrary crackdown against the Muslim Brotherhood or, as in April 1957, the Communists. Whether he would have behaved differently in the absence of the ever dangerous Brotherhood is something we will never know. His preoccupation with the Islamic danger did warp his judgment.

The democratic cooperative society Nasser dreamed of never materialized. For the National Assembly, he was always careful in selecting the speaker, and he manipulated people like Ali Sabri and Anwar Sadat, encouraging them to compete with each other. By towering over them and refusing to assume a dictatorial military persona and by dissolving the RCC and making its old members act as individuals, he stopped Egypt from becoming a militarized society.[30] So, neither democratic nor military, Egypt essentially became a military-bureaucratic society. Both the strength and the weakness of the military-bureaucracy were in the fact that it was not self-perpetuating. It could be done and undone at the pleasure of the executive branch of government, in this case the office of the president. All that Nasser had to do was to displace one of his old comrades and the department he ran would certainly change character.

Of course, his almost overshadowed 1956 elevation to president coincided with the adoption of a new constitution, albeit a temporary one. It was a meaningless document in terms of advancing democracy because it invested vast discretionary powers in the office of the president, promised a measure of democracy which came from above and hence was not democratic, and was not permanent. The country was being run by an officer class of people who became bureaucrats learning on the job. They constituted the new bureaucracy, which was no better than the old one.

Yet, Nasser, when committed to a scheme that did not need the help of others to carry it out, did manage to introduce some much-needed reform. In a way, he was the only person brave enough to propose strategic changes. He was committed to most of them more than to his old comrades, and, as with agricultural reform, he carried them out more intelligently. In the judicial area, Nasser's pragmatism and refusal to allow religion a direct say in governance showed very early. This time he scored against the country's conservative institutionalised Islamic tendencies. He secularized the religious courts, which used the Koran for legal analogy and guidance, making them part of the civil courts. He also began the steps which culminated years later in giving women equal rights.

As expected, the Muslim Brotherhood objected, describing the decree secularizing the courts as un-Islamic, and opposing equal rights for women. Enacting anything anti-Islamic was the last thing on Nasser's mind; though there was an absence of dogma in his approach and his actions changed in accordance with circumstances, he never deviated from wanting a form of Islamized modernity. This came under attack from the Brotherhood in the form of the book *Signposts Along the Way*, written by the ideologue Sayyed Qutub. Written while the author was in prison, it was reprinted six times and described the Nasser government as a second Jahiliya, the age of ignorance that historically preceded Islam.[31] In essence, ignorance, according to Sayyed Qutub, was the opposite of being Islamic.

Nasser followed the decisions on the Islamic courts and women by making education compulsory, and the number of students at all levels of education kept climbing by leaps and bounds. This was even more dramatic in technical and vocational schools, where the number of students enrolled from 1952 to 1957 increased by an average 40 percent per year. He went further and pressured the religious leaders (ulemas) of Al Azhar into accepting modernity by including the sciences in their syllabus. It was a major step, the first attempt to reform Al Azhar in centuries. Of course, Nasser used Al Azhar against the Brotherhood. He manipulated its ulemas and challenged the Brotherhood's Islamic legitimacy.

Initially, Nasser tried to confine his efforts to Egypt, but after the Suez Crisis, he was tied to the whole Arab Middle East. He had moved quickly but incrementally to assume his Arab persona; but suddenly, after the crisis, becoming a modern Arab was his primary motivation. "His ideas were more Arab than Egyptian," says Mohamed Fayyeq, a former high official of his regime. Adopting an Arab position distanced him from domestic Egyptian problems. The demands of being leader of the Arabs were great, and he ignored some pressing Egyptian problems such as family planning, exhausted the resources of his country chasing the dream of unifying the Arabs,[32] and alienated practically all of the Arab heads of state at the same time. He even put the question of leading the Arabs ahead of the Palestinian problem and separated the two.[33] Not only did dealing with regional Arab questions come first, the problem of Palestine was put on the back burner. As such, the confrontation with Israel changed. He limited it geographically and stopped it from being the sole regional issue. On the other hand, the competition with Israel spread to Africa, where Nasser's anticolonial credentials were pitted against Israeli technology. It is well to note that in Africa, Israel could count on the support of the Brotherhood against Nasser.[34] Competing in Africa and other issues meant ignoring the Palestinians in favor of the larger picture; Nasser did indeed keep the fedayeen on a tight leash, and he turned down all the mufti's requests for reactivating a Palestinian entity. Nasser was never comfortable with the mufti, and the mutual suspicion of the two men never abated.

However important the skirmishes with the mufti and with Israel in Africa, Nasser needed to compensate for the Jordanian defeat. His Arab credentials were at stake, and Nuri and King Hussein, along with the CIA, were trying to subvert the pro-Nasser government in Syria. When that did not work, Turkish troops massed along the Syrian border and Turkey accused Syria of harboring Communists. The first response to the Turkish threat came from the mercurial King Saud, who, though supporting Jordan against Nasser, decided to announce his support of Arab Syria against Turkey. In August 1957, Nasser, faced with a loss of face he could hardly afford, outdid Saud by landing four thousand troops in the Syrian port of Latakia. The troops would have been of little use against Turkey's huge army, and the USSR, though ostensibly with Egypt, was opposed to regional muscle flexing, but the gesture worked. Nasser reclaimed some of his lost prestige, particularly with the Syrian people. He put an end to Iraqi ambitions to annex Syria, which had been a subject of discussion since World War I.

In fact, Nasser's response to Syria was the culmination of the military alliance between the two countries which had started in 1955. Even then, the Syrians were for closer cooperation, perhaps even union, with Egypt. But, showing he didn't intend to act on the vague calls to unity in his speeches, Nasser had turned them down. He settled for wanting closer commercial ties, hardly a substitute. But the Jordanian failure had left him with no choice but to act, and his grand gesture of sending troops guaranteed him a say in the future of Syria. In the end he assumed a commitment from which the Syrian people would refuse to absolve him, and the results would come to haunt him and to determine Arab history for the foreseeable future. Instead of symbolic gestures, Nasser needed to accept union with Syria.

Israel, aware of his widespread and growing popularity among the Arabs, decided to use its intelligence services to oppose him throughout the Middle East. The whole region became an arena for Nasser's and Israel's intelligence operatives, with an occasional appearance by the CIA. Many of the Bedouin officers of Jordan's army, who owed their positions to King Hussein's patronage, worked with the Mossad. Beirut acted as an information souk where people bought and sold their wares. There was something dangerous in competing so openly for control of the Middle East. Israel and Egypt infiltrated every palace, ministry, and intelligence service in the area. The contest certainly undermined the rest of the countries of the region, which couldn't compete with the two major players. On occasions, what was at stake was whether or not a country was truly independent, as when the CIA bribed the president and several former prime ministers in Lebanon.[35] Even the death of a manager of a Beirut discotheque, Caves du Roy, produced evidence that the man had been a triple agent for Israel, Egypt, and the CIA—and had possibly worked for the KGB too. According to a Lebanese security officer, the nightclub manager had been eliminated by Nasserites. Whether the killing was sanctioned by Cairo was never known. Even the head of Lebanese security, Farid Chehab, was to admit that he helped the British and Israelis out of hatred for Nasser. The ethnic head (the ranking local agent) of the CIA station in Beirut accused Nasser of plotting to eliminate Christianity from the Middle East. Nasser was under attack.

While Nasser professed to be repelled by the idea of creating an Arab empire, the master of collective emotions behaved as if creating, building, or melding such an empire was uppermost on his mind. According to him the Arab world was "the land where Arabic is spoken,"[36] and that was larger than what the rest of the world accepted. Certainly he never deviated from addressing "the Arabs from the Atlantic to the Gulf," a massive geographic entity considerably larger than the United States. The Arabs were his "brothers and sisters." "The Arab nation" was one and indivisible. There were problems as well as opportunities which were, however, uniquely Arab. Of course that magnet for nationalist forces, oil, came into play, and "Arab oil for the Arabs" was an inevitable slogan. This was a source of annoyance to the Saudis and other oil-rich countries, who thought the oil was theirs alone. In fact, the "Arab oil for the Arabs" slogan is the clearest indication that Nasser's ambitions covered the whole Arab world regardless of its size and character. After all, Egypt had not begun to pump oil, so Nasser was deputizing for the countries that had.

Nasser not only focused on the average Arabs, he tried to build a direct connection with them that bypassed their leaders. He was successful, and listening to him the Arabs felt as one. Beyond his speeches and the appeal to the masses, he did try to establish a direct link with local leaders, through his embassies and sometimes directly through his intelligence service in Cairo. The creation of pro-Nasser cells throughout the Arab world was coordinated by Zakkaria Mohieddine, the very same man who had organized the coup of July 23, 1952. But Nasser's followers in Syria, Iraq, Jordan, Lebanon, and Saudi Arabia did not take direction from Cairo, because Cairo lacked the personnel to impose direction; instead, they followed their own interpretation of what might please Al Rayyes. Among the Nasser followers who arrogated to themselves the right to interpret Nasser's thoughts were professional politicians, such as former premier Saeb Salam of Lebanon; others whose loyalty to him was a protest against the leaders of their country, such as Saudi oil minister Abdallah Tariki; and professional soldiers who were following their own ambitions and often violating their oath of loyalty, such as Ali Abu Nawar of Jordan.

Nasser's lame excuse of not being able to control those who followed him ignores the simple fact that he made no attempt to control them, or even give them guidance. Besides, how does one control the masses and indeed the heads of mass movements after they are told that their leaders are traitors? The strength of the accusation suggests that he wanted something done about what he considered a political crime. That most of the Arab leaders were corrupt and deserved to be overthrown was probably true; but Nasser, even though he always hesitated when the opportunity presented itself, claimed the right to do it. There was no way to tell Abu Nawar that he wasn't fit to lead Jordan, and Tariki, a founder of OPEC, eventually went too far when Saudi Arabia was not ready for change. But Nasser never used or tried to use either to control Jordan or Saudi Arabia.

Nasser was in a position to destroy, or at least unbalance, what existed. To understand this, one has to accept the importance of the word to the Arabs, the fact that it is as philosophy was to the Greeks. But despite the *Daily Telegraph* allegation, he actually had no master plan to control the Arab world, or to run it indirectly. He could convert people to his cause by the use of the word, and the word was their source of hope, but he stopped there. Beyond hope and the essential personal dignity, he had nothing else to offer. He did not last long enough to suffer the consequences of not delivering on simple promises, not quite. Yet, there isn't a single serious instance of him disowning or reprimanding people because of their behavior. For example, Nabulsi of Jordan was indeed a man of honor, but the behavior of the untalented and meddling Abu Nawar offended everybody in Jordan. Saeb Salam was a master politician, but Nasser got himself in trouble in Lebanon by recruiting and using a braggart, Adnan al-Hakim. He wanted the support of everyone, even the shallowest of men; psychologically he needed it. He was never in the business of accepting and rejecting people, he was in the business of charming them, for whatever else they became after that, they were his and his alone. As with former members of the RCC, not using them did not mean that he didn't want them there. He wanted to retain the option of resorting to what his followers were capable of doing. His emergence, what he expressed more boldly than even Tito and Nehru, and his making of Egypt a solidly Arab country were among the most important regional developments of the twentieth century. But at his most subversive, in 1956 and 1957, when he had the chance to become the leading Arab revolutionary leader of all time, he failed. At best he was a nationalist and not a revolutionary leader.

He failed to have a revolutionary program that would harness the energy of the millions of people who believed in him, to give them clear constructive direction, to institutionalize the modern Arab nationalism he advocated, and to tell the world what he wanted. There was no strategy to his vision, to achieve his dream and the dream of his Arab millions, though there were aims. Whether this was a personal shortcoming, a statesmanlike stand, or the result of the unceasing pressures against him after Suez by outside powers, the United States in particular, it is a key to following his career after he became leader of the Arabs. Perhaps Nasser's failure to follow a truly revolutionary path, as opposed to a nationalist path, was a trait that had been with him all along. Says Mohamed Heikal in praise of his old boss, "He hated the idea of violence, of blood." Dozens of other writers from both East and West concur. This moderation was and is an admirable human trait, but not suitable for people wanting to control and run the Arab Middle East.

He was peerless, even before Suez. The writers Richard Johns and David Holden, authors of *The House of Saud,* described his visit to Riyadh, Saudi Arabia, early in 1956: "Tens of thousands rushed forward cheering wildly, breaking the police barrier, desperate to touch the God-like figure." He certainly represented an Arab attitude, and expressed it in elegant language. Nasser himself became the symbol of Arab suffering from historical injury, the face of a people dead set against their imposed rulers, determined to have their say. He made his mark on them by words and deeds. He kept Jordan at the boiling point. The Palestinian refugees there took their direction from him, and even most of Jordan's army officers were loyal to him. Any quarrel with Hussein split the country between the majority Nasser loyalists and the British-trained Bedouin soldiers who followed the monarchy. Very often, after bloody confrontations, such as when Britain's General Templer visited Amman, the country looked like a battleground. But contrary to the image the Western press created at the time, the king was the more likely winner of their on-and-off contest. Nasser stopped short of sanctioning the shedding of blood, while Hussein did not shy from it or from imprisoning hundreds of people.

Nasser cast a shadow across Lebanon and claimed a number of its politicians as followers. Objecting to this and seeing in Nasser a danger to the whole Middle East, President Camille Chamoun accepted the Eisenhower Doctrine and refused to follow the rest of the Arabs suspending diplomatic relations with the aggressors. Chamoun was a perverse character who spoke regularly and falsely of Nasser's threat to Christianity when no such danger existed, and when thinking people realized Islamism as we know it today was the long-term danger. Nasser never forgave him for that and eventually made him pay dearly for his mistake, and Chamoun was never again acceptable to the majority of the Lebanese people. After Suez, Beirut taxi drivers would turn their radios full blast in front of posh Beirut hotels such as the St. Georges when Nasser spoke, so that everybody would listen to him. In cafés in the Basta district of Beirut, usually noisy venues for backgammon players, everything would come to a standstill whenever Nasser spoke. He gave the traditional leaders and monarchists of Iraq sleepless nights worrying about his ever increasing number of followers. The Iraqi police, tired of confiscating his pictures, allowed people to hang them, and they became a fixture in every hut, shop, and store. He so overshadowed the thinking of the Syrians that political parties and leaders competed as to who was closer to him. In reality he was closest to the Ba'ath Party, a pan-Arab entity which had existed since 1946, but which had a different order of priorities, placing unity and freedom ahead of socialism.

He penetrated the closed kingdom of Saudi Arabia and became an idol to many of its diverse people. In 1955 there was a pro-Nasser uprising among the Saudi troops stationed at Taif.[37] It was put down bloodily—the pro-Nasser officers were beheaded. But the brutality did not stop other officers from trying the same thing in Dhahran in 1956. Also in 1956, there was a strike by over fifteen thousand Aramco workers, who shouted pro-Nasser slogans. A number of them were beaten to death[38] and others disappeared, never to be seen again. In the middle 1950s his relationship with King Saud changed on an almost regular basis: Saud had been an ally; then he objected to Nasser's arbitrary way in nationalizing the canal; then he signed a military alliance with him again and allowed the Egyptian air force to take refuge in his country. Of course, the CIA had its own interpretation of the Eisenhower Doctrine and early in 1957 gave Saud money to oppose Nasser.[39] It is true that Saud was elated by American support. But here again there is no evidence that Nasser tried to intercept any of the efforts to destabilize others undertaken in his name, either before or after the fact. But the obvious shortcomings have to be balanced by the wholesomeness and justice of Nasser's calling for freeing the slaves in Saudi Arabia. He did this on a regular basis, mostly on radio. It was another goal from which he never deviated and which he pursued relentlessly until it became a fact. It was a noble commitment.[40]

In Yemen, Nasser was the most popular leader in the country. His picture was pinned to the sides of tents. Of course his support for the Aden-based Popular Front for Liberating Arabia did not go unnoticed. Similar things were happening in North Africa and within what we now call the United Arab Emirates, then still British protectorates. Superficially, it looks as if Glubb had been right and Nasser was chasing the West out of the Middle East with words. This is not true; Nasser did not create the call for unity and Arab cooperation, he joined it. It was a role looking for a hero, and he became that hero. But it was his personality which endowed the hero with his specific qualities, what would eventually contribute to his success or failure. Certainly his masterful use of the word did nothing but help him.

If one believed in the right of the various Arab countries to shake off foreign control and become truly independent, then Nasser could undoubtedly be faulted for not having a program to give content to his words. But it merits examining whether he was ever allowed enough time and space to develop such a program. The West had a vested interest in the future of every Arab country in the Middle East and was not ready to cede these countries to Nasser, to allow them to become his tributaries or part of his sphere of influence. Strategically Nasser was right in realizing that Suez was the end of colonialism as it had been known, but it also was the beginning of the American era in the Middle East. With their anticolonial background, the Americans never tried to run the Middle East directly, but they certainly tried to run the people who ran the Middle East, the kings, emirs, sheikhs, and occasionally presidents who behaved like deputy sheriffs for America. It was easier for Nasser to attack the record of Britain and France than to fight against the money America was willing to spend opposing him.

The issue was joined after the promulgation of the Eisenhower Doctrine. America assumed responsibility for Western interests through its undertaking to oppose direct and indirect Communist penetration of the Arab Middle East. The American formula was open-ended. There was nothing new in opposing direct Communist penetration of the area—it had always been taken for granted that the United States would oppose it the way it had opposed the Communists who had tried to take over in Greece. However, there was a lot of room for interpreting "indirect" penetration and defining the people who fronted for the USSR, and whether that meant, or included, Nasser. With UNEF in place guarding the Sinai-Israeli border and the Strait of Tiran, there was little prospect of an Arab-Israeli confrontation. Still, maintaining a quiet balance between the Arabs and Israel was among the aims of the doctrine, as was protecting the source of oil. It is quite possible that the United States intended to use the doctrine selectively and kept things vague by design. At one point it looked as if Syria might become a point of contention for having followed Egypt and signed its own arms deal with the Eastern Bloc in 1956. Nothing overt happened, but Iraq did try to organize a coup in Syria aimed at installing in Damascus a pro-West government opposed to Nasser.[41] Because of his preoccupation with the Baghdad Pact and with Syria neurotically with him at all times, the country uppermost on Nasser's mind was Iraq. The country had several political parties, among them the Ba'ath and the National Democrats, both of which were committed to a brand of Arab nationalism advocating the unity of the Arabs in one big country. Iraq also had a sizable underground Communist Party and an officer class that had a history of interfering in politics. The royal family, installed by the British in 1921, was not popular, nor indeed was Nuri with his Baghdad Pact. A police state more extensive in form and reach than Egypt's was in existence, but people listened to the calls of *Voice of the Arabs* to overthrow the monarchy and liberate themselves. Nasser was the hero for a whole new generation. His speeches were memorized and recited, his pictures were reproduced secretly, and, though nothing came of it because the war did not last long, tens of thousands had gone to the Egyptian

Nasser as an earnest young cadet in the mid-1930s. Later he returned to the military academy as an instructor. *Dar Al Hilal*

The Free Officers Association was founded and led by Nasser. A collection of young unknowns, they used General Mohamed Naguib *(bottom right)* as a "respectable" front man. *Hassan Diab*

Nasser *(right)* and Naguib: Nasser and his front man in 1953. A year later Nasser ousted the popular soldier from office and became the undisputed *rayyes* (chief) of Egypt. *Al Ahram*

Nasser and his family. Three generations of Nassers. His father, Abdel Hussein Nasser, is on the far right. The children are daughters Huda (with headband) and Mona and son Khalid. Nasser's brother Izz al-Arab is standing behind him. *Al Ahram*

Nasser's wife, Tahiya Nasser *(right)*, paying a courtesy call on a Burmese delegation visiting Cairo. A highly educated woman who spoke English and French fluently, she shunned the limelight. *Al Ahram*

Personal habits: Focusing on his wife, Tahiya. Photography, chess, and American films were Nasser's only pastimes. *Al Akhbar, 1960*

Palestine, 1948. Egyptian army officers display weapons captured from the Israelis in Faluga in the Negev. Nasser is at left in jodhpurs. *Dar Al Hilal*

Abdel Hakim Amer was Nasser's closest friend among the officers who overthrew King Farouk in 1952, but they became bitter rivals after the 1967 war. *Al Ahram*

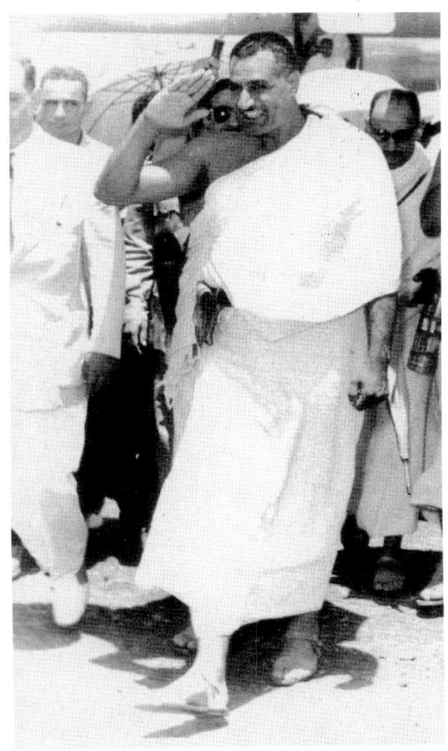

The observant Muslim. An observant Muslim who made the hajj to Mecca in 1954, Nasser opposed the idea of political Islam. *Al Akhbar*

Bandung, 1955. The Mufti of Jerusalem *(foreground),* Imam Mohamed al-Badr of Yemen (wearing dark glasses), Nasser, and King Faisal of Saudi Arabia (with hand on chin) meet in Bandung, Indonesia, in 1955. *Dar Al Hilal*

In 1956, leaders of the neutral block, Nasser, Nehru, and Tito *(foreground, left to right),* conferred on Brioni Island, Yugoslavia. *Mohamed Yusef*

Nasser capturing the attention of his armed forces. The most charismatic Arab leader since the Prophet Mohamed speaking to War College graduates in 1957. *Al Ahram*

Only Nasser was popular enough to trust army officers and mingle with them freely. *Al Ahram*

Watching maneuvers with army officers in the early 1960s. Nasser stopped wearing a military uniform in 1957. *Al Ahram*

Arab unity. Presidents Gamal Abdel Nasser of Egypt and Shukri al-Kuwatly of Syria signing the protocols creating the United Arab Republic in February 1958. *Dar Al Hilal*

Land reform gave title deeds to *fellahin*. Nasser's anti-establishment land reform program was among his few successes. *Al Akhbar*

Nasser with foreign dignitaries. Nasser welcoming President Tito of Yugoslavia *(right foreground)* to Egypt in 1958. Tito and UN Secretary General Dag Hammarskjöld were Nasser's closest foreign friends. *Al Ahram*

With Khrushchev *(second from left)* in Moscow, 1958. Later he addressed the Soviet Presidium and received a three-minute standing ovation. *Al Akhbar*

Britain and the USSR stopped the march of Arab nationalism by supporting Nasser's enemy, Iraqi strongman General Abdel Karim *(seated at center)*. *Al Akhbar*

After a rocky start, Nasser and King Hussein of Jordan became close friends. *Akhbar Alyom*

Nasser in Syria. With the two loyalists who contributed measurably to the breakup of the UAR, Syrian colonel Abdel Hamid Saraj *(at Nasser's left)* and Abdel Hakim Amer. *Al Akhbar*

With Castro in New York in 1960, when both addressed the UN General Assembly. *Al Akhbar*

The aftermath of war. Viewing the east bank of the Suez Canal after the 1967 defeat. *Al Ahram*

Field Marshal Abdel Hakim Amer *(center)* was blamed for Egypt's defeat in 1967. To Nasser, he was still the person "I loved most." *Al Ahram*

Nasser and Arab leaders. Arab League meeting in 1969 in Cairo. Despite appearances, Nasser and Arafat (with kaffiyeh) never liked each other. *Dar Al Hilal*

With Arab leaders. Meeting the press with King Hussein of Jordan *(seated at center),* and a member of Kuwait's royal family during the September 1970 heads-of-state conference in Cairo. (The author believes he is the unrecognizable figure on the lower left side of the picture.) *Al Ahram*

The Arabs are orphaned. Four million mourners walked in Nasser's funeral. *Al Akhbar*

Tahiya Nasser, hands clasped, visits her husband's shrine in 1970 with her three sons and two daughters. *Al Ahram*

embassy to volunteer to fight in the Suez War. The Iraqis, for decades suffering from a sense of frustration that drove them into periodic violent upheavals against their government, expected Nasser, their hero, to do something to save them. But neither he nor they knew how this act would reveal itself.

There were two approaches to Nasser by Iraqis asking for support in their efforts to change the government of their country. The first came from the ranks of the army. A group from the military called the Free Officers, modeled on his own movement, wanted Nasser to support them the moment they declared an antimonarchy, anti-West rebellion. The Free Officers were led by Brigadier Abdel Karim Kassem, an Iraqi officer with an impeccable record; and they went as far as asking for air cover in case of a coup.[42] The request was relayed to Nasser, who turned the officers down. Perhaps he decided against helping them because doing so would challenge the Eisenhower Doctrine and lead to a confrontation which he wanted to avoid. He certainly took the doctrine seriously. Or perhaps he did not know enough about the officers and did not want to be involved in a failure. There is also the more likely possibility that he did not really approve of soldiers in politics, despite his personal background. Whatever the reason, it is obvious Nasser was not an Arab revolutionary pursuing Arab unity regardless of the consequences. Whatever his aim, he did subscribe to certain principles, and they included reluctance to sponsor coups d'état. We are back to Nasser being unable to define his goals and to follow that definition with open eyes until it was realized through his millions of followers. In this case, his refusal to help the Iraqi officers was to have a profound influence on future Iraqi-Egyptian relations and the history of the Middle East.

On the other hand, Nasser offered open support to a political opponent of Nuri's, Sadiq Shanshal of Iraq's National Democrats.[43] The combination of turning Kassem down and supporting Shanshal does reveal an inclination toward cooperating with politicians rather than with armies and their officers. Even in Egypt, the stewardship of Amer helped keep the army safe for the regime and also distanced it from politics. It went further than that: the very popular Amer "bribed" Egyptian army officers by not subjecting them to the rigors of army life and by allowing them to line their pockets. Whether Nasser's preference for civilians over soldiers was part of a broader thinking about the potential success of his subversive activity in the mid-1950s is something we do not know. But, once again, it is hard to believe that he had no plan for the countries whose regimes he was explicitly undermining and trying to replace. Bluntly stated, it is inconceivable that Nuri's overthrow was advocated, as it was on *Voice of the Arabs*, without any thinking about what kind of regime or individual leader might replace him.

The real test of Nasser's advocacy for Arab unity was to come from Syria, for years an unstable country coveted by Iraq but with pro-Nasser inclinations. From 1949 on, Syria had suffered one coup d'etat after another. There were British-sponsored army moves aimed at merging the country with the Hashemites of Iraq. Against that there were the American attempts to control the country through its army and keep it independent because America's main allies in the Middle East, Israel and Saudi Arabia, opposed the creation of a big and powerful country. In fact, neither the British nor the Americans had a coherent policy. Had they seen beyond controlling the somewhat neurotic country, they would have been able to implement their plans and change the history of the Arab world.

Syria's first military leader, Colonel Husni Zaim, took power with CIA help in March 1949. He was a pompous, monocled, and ignorant fool who lasted a mere seven months before being overthrown and killed by another colonel, Sami Hinnawi. The unfortunate Hinnawi, assumed to be pro-British and hence pro-Iraq, was overthrown by the CIA after three months. His replacement, Colonel Adib Shaishakly, lasted almost four years but was under constant threat. Though Syria was a country that was willing to disappear into a new, larger Arab formation, an Arab unity scheme, the behavior of Britain and America was worse than what Western colonialism had sanctioned in the past. Britain and the United States confirmed a Western willingness to kill, subvert, destabilize, misrepresent, forge alliances with villains, use assassins, and bribe dozens of politicians, then attribute the results to Syria's immaturity and an Arab inability to deal with the idea of a nation-state. From the time of his conversion to Arabism, Nasser had watched the Syrian scene with dismay. He believed the West was after Syria to keep it from uniting with another Arab country; after all, it was the home of Arab nationalism, or so it claimed.

Beginning in 1957, Syria looked as if it might become a Communist satellite. It had a highly organized Communist Party with an impressive leader who had been elected to parliament, Khalid Baghdash. The country, anti-West at the best of times, was experiencing a pro-USSR, pro-Communist period. Unlike Egypt, it did not have a leader who could befriend the Eastern Bloc yet maintain its independent Arab identity. Moreover, the most impressive Syrian bourgeois politician of his time, Khalid Azm, made common cause with the Communists, the anti-Western and pan-Arabist Ba'ath Party, and the Communist chief of staff of the Syrian army, General Afif Bizri, against any attempts to "subvert" the country into accepting U.S. hegemony. Nasser had already demonstrated his commitment to Syria by taking the considerable symbolic step of dispatching troops to help against the danger of a Turkish invasion. Now he saw Syria threatened from more than one direction. The presence of Bizri troubled him; not wanting Communists in the governments of the Arab countries was gospel to him. When Nasser told a visiting Syrian delegation which included President Shukri Kuwatly and Prime Minister Azm that Syria should have some political housecleaning, both men countered by insisting that only total political union with Egypt would save Syria from Communism or chaos. Nasser turned them down. He insisted that political union would take a minimum of five years to prepare.[44]

A while later, another Syrian delegation visited Nasser to press upon him the idea of complete unity between Egypt and Syria. This time the delegation included the Communist Bizri. Nasser told them to consider a solution short of total union. Thinking that Nasser would continue to advocate a form of federal union and would continue to oppose the idea of immediate total union between the two countries, Bizri, wanting the negotiations to fail, stood solidly behind the latter. The trap Bizri set for Nasser backfired when the latter, now more afraid of a Communist takeover of the country than of anything else, agreed on a total merger.[45] The United Arab Republic (UAR) came into being on February 1, 1958, and the decision was ratified by a national plebiscite on February 22. Very soon after, Nasser dismissed Bizri and carried out a crackdown against the Communist Party of Syria.

Noting its nature, the United States accepted the union, but the USSR objected to Nasser's behavior. Iraq announced that it was merging with Jordan to create yet another larger Arab country, the Arab Federation. The Iraqi-Jordanian move was a protective one aimed at satisfying their unity-seeking people. Most members of the old RCC were against the union, especially Zakkaria

Mohieddine, but their opinions had ceased to matter. It was Nasser's position as leader of the Arabs that dictated his direction. His original refusal of the Syrian offer and support for something less than total union betray considerable misgivings on his part. It wasn't only a case of the whole enterprise being fraught with danger; he feared that the cause of unity would be damaged by failure.[46]

The outcomes of the UAR and the Arab Federation will be described in future chapters. However, any discussion of Arab unity as an idea, as expressed by the UAR or the Arab Federation, belongs here. To Arabs from all walks of life a measure of Arab unity had indeed been realized by the creation of the UAR, but it was not the Arab unity that had been a dream since at least the First World War. As an expression of the Arabs' shared language and history and hope, though it was only a substitute for the real thing, the Arab people still wanted it. When Nasser traveled to Damascus one month after the UAR was announced, people from all over the Middle East came to greet and cheer him. They mistook what he had done for a lasting Arab cohesion that would restore their glory to them.

Intellectuals compared the union to what had happened in Germany and Italy a century before. The fellah and the laborer thought it would improve their lot. Many members of the middle class accepted the UAR as the nucleus of a larger country to come, a country that would offer them more than did its parts. Nasser had advocated unity, but even he realized that the Arabs were not ready for it. Being ready for it meant long-term planning or becoming a revolutionary. Becoming a revolutionary meant throwing caution to the wind, something Nasser the conservative, ardent nationalist never did. He opted for unity when it was forced on him, and then he became its only symbol.

The Arab Federation was no more than a last-minute fabrication to keep Nasser from claiming the rest of the Arab world. Even Nuri Said wanted unity, but he thought the future of any Arab unity was in cooperating with the West. Other Arab countries felt threatened by it. For the first time ever, the British and Americans did not intercept an Arab unity scheme. The takeover of Syria relieved them of having to do something about it. The Soviet Union rejected the nationalistic ideas embodied in creating the UAR but was relieved that a potential confrontation with the West had been avoided. Things came together much more easily than anybody had expected.

What happened was very simple. Nasser, forever unprepared to live up to his calls for Arab unity, was caught by the need to save Syria. As a matter of principle he could not but accept Syria's offer. However, accepting this noble idea, supported as it was by the Arab people, without years of preparation meant that it was likely to fail. Even with sound planning, the danger of failing was big; the differences between the two countries were enormous. What Nasser originally asked for, five years of planning and trial, was justified. The ultimate aim of the Arabs, unity, was implemented as if it were a simple issue with no consequences. Eventually Nasser was proved right in his trepidations; it was the idea of Arab unity itself that suffered and was discarded because the idea was confused with the way it had been realized. Arab unity never recovered from the disaster of the UAR. The top believer in Arab unity in the past few centuries put his relationship with the Arab people ahead of common sense. In the process, Gamal Abdel Nasser destroyed the dream of Arab unity.

# 6

## And I Shall Divide Your Araby into Two

The U.S. government, though still doubtful about Nasser's intentions in late 1957, gave up the idea of promoting King Saud as a leader of the Arabs at the same time. That policy was so halfhearted that it revealed the shallowness of American Middle East policy, and it disappeared without leaving much of a trace. Even His Majesty didn't seem to take it seriously, nor did Iraq's Nuri Said and the most ardent of America's friends. Moreover, Saud renewed the American lease on the Dhahran air base, accepted the Eisenhower Doctrine, and abandoned the idea of forming a national tanker company in partnership with the Greek magnate Aristotle Onassis to compete with American oil companies. Hardly a consistent man of vision, Saud couldn't decide whether to follow Nasser as the new Saladin and liberator of the Arabs or to condemn him as a meddler who should devote himself to Egypt and its many problems. Saud himself suffered from this dichotomy, and his foreign and regional policies were marked by frequent changes in direction, often on the advice of advisers with commercial and other ulterior motives.

In 1955 Saud had received a two-hundred-man Egyptian military mission to train his army. Early in 1956, he joined Egypt and Syria in a military alliance against the Baghdad Pact. During the

Suez Crisis and War, he openly supported Nasser to the extent of housing Egyptian aircraft fleeing the attacks of Britain, France, and Israel, and later he imposed an embargo on the shipment of oil to France, Britain, and Germany. This was followed by an invitation to Nasser to visit the capital of the desert kingdom, which the latter readily accepted. His presence produced the largest demonstration in the history of Riyadh. The implications of the popularity of the Egyptian leader did not escape Saud, who suddenly reversed policy in late 1957. Saud arrested hundreds of pro-Nasser supporters in his country, then dispatched troops to Jordan to back King Hussein against the Egyptian leader. Also, immediately after Suez, with equal lack of preparation, and with seemingly sudden awareness of Nasser's immense popularity as a result of his arms deal and the crisis over the Aswan dam, he joined the Americans in opposing Nasser's regional schemes and in trying to intercept his attempt to impose his will over other Arab states. Saud's shifts of direction took place against the background of a feud with his more talented brother and heir apparent, Prince Faisal, which was forcing him into rethinking some of his policies.

Saud and his brother were openly vying for control of Saudi Arabia in a way which demanded the attention of all parties interested in the future of the Middle East, including the two contenders for regional leadership, Nasser and America. Faisal was as calculating as Saud was spontaneous. Faisal adopted religion as a dogma with which to combat Arab nationalism in general and the Nasser variety in particular. He sought and got America's support for Muslim fundamentalism, at the time distinguished by its opposition to godless Communism and other leftist ideologies. Cleverly he emphasized how Saud's spendthrift ways had turned Saudi Arabia into a debtor, opposed any normalization of relations with the USSR, and portrayed Nasser as a power-hungry apostate. Saud, already heavily dependent on America, couldn't think of responding to his brother's challenge except through becoming more pro-American. Despite the damage this might do to the country and its traditional structure, this suited the Americans. A weak Saudi Arabia more dependent on oil income was preferable to a strong one with its own foreign policy.

Because of his personal qualities and the potency of using Muslim fundamentalism against what America had decided was the Nasser menace, Faisal came out way ahead. After some hesitation, and well before the final decision to force Saud to step down,

America threw its weight behind Faisal, and there was a tacit agreement on the use of religion against Nasser, which eventually became a joint policy. Both sides supported the anti-Nasser Muslim Brotherhood and emphasized the Communist threat to Islam and the Arab world. America could not join Faisal in equating Communism with Zionism for fear of offending Israelis and Jews, but it looked the other way while he derived benefit from this absurd association. Naturally the tribes, in their own way the most conservative social clusters, were financed, and accepted this ideological line. Countries with common relations to both, Jordan and Pakistan, benefited from this turn of events.

The dispatch in 1957 of Saudi troops to help King Hussein was the first manifestation of the new anti-Nasser policy under Saud, and of course Faisal, still foreign minister, gave the move his support. It was easy for Nasser to deflect this, which he did by painting Hussein as the tool of the tools of America; but there remained some remnants of anti-Communism among the faithful.

Soon after, Saud decided his ultimate salvation lay in trying to eliminate Nasser rather than trying to stop him politically. Although he and his advisers lacked experience, a Saud-sponsored, full-fledged, stupid attempt was made to assassinate Nasser immediately after the UAR came into being in February 1958. Nasser had been expected to travel to Damascus to celebrate the union, and he did so in secret on February 24, 1958. Incredibly, it was his first trip to Syria. He had become the country's president without seeing it. He was accompanied by Amer, Abdel Latif Boghdadi, and Anwar Sadat. For the average Syrian this visit by Al Rayyes to the Syrian Province, as the country became known, was a complete surprise.

For a week, the atmosphere in Damascus resembled a carnival; crowds in the tens of thousands roamed the streets singing old songs and new ones written to welcome their president and the hero of Arabism. Every Syrian town worth its name sent a delegation to Damascus to join in the festivities, and so did most of the cities in Lebanon. Towns that didn't have banners caught up with the rest and designed ones. There were placards greeting Abu Khalid ("father of Khalid") and Al Rayyes on the tens of buses that made the trip. Crowds of people would gather in the square in front of the Diafa Palace until Al Rayyes, always in a suit and looking very tidy, came out and spoke to them. I was in Damascus as a young reporter; along with thousands of others, I stood across the street and watched the Hospitality Palace ("hospitality" is *diafa* in

Arabic), where Nasser greeted some visitors from the north of Syria who had waited for hours. Their voices rose; their arms went up in the air in gestures of greeting or folk dance; their joy showed in the glow in their faces, which looked transformed by an inner light. They acted as if they had just seen a messiah. Then Nasser motioned for them to stop, and they did, and he spoke to them slowly, in a voice of reason and intimacy that told them he loved them too.

For better or for worse, the modern Arab nation, indeed every Arab who believes in his roots, will never see the likes of this moment again. After hundreds of years of separateness, the Arabs were united again, and Nasser was the symbol of this unity. For reasons which transcended whatever doubt the critics of the union had publicized, the creation of the UAR had given Damascus a chance to relive its old glory. One couldn't be there without thinking of the Damascus of old.

In the halls of power, things were hardly at a standstill. Nuri was trying, despite British objections, to realize Iraqi's major regional claim and annex Kuwait to the new Arab Federation to compensate for the loss of Syria to Nasser. This did not mean a cessation in Nuri's plotting to pry Syria loose from Nasser and have it join the Arab Federation of Iraq and Jordan and create the much discussed and British-approved Fertile Crescent of nations, a much more natural and geographically cohesive landmass whose people had more in common than the Egyptians and Syrians. But things were moving Nasser's rather than Nuri's way, and Imam Ahmad of Yemen dispatched Crown Prince Badr to Damascus with an offer to join the UAR in an entity to be called the United Arab States. Again there was no way for Nasser to say no, but what he finally accepted was a loose federal union rather than total integration, Syrian style.

President Camille Chamoun of Lebanon, an ally of Nuri's and King Hussein's, was already conspiring with the CIA's Wilbur Crane Eveland to undermine all pro-Nasser political leaders in his country. But in what was the least competent move, and the most likely to backfire, onetime Nasser ally Saud involved himself in an amateurish plot to assassinate Al Rayyes and terminate the Egyptian-Syrian union. Lacking a security or intelligence service and without anyone who would advise him properly, Saud relied on his chief financial adviser to use the only thing the Saudis understood: money. With relations between him and his brother Faisal at an all-time low (there is every reason to believe Faisal was kept in the dark), the affair represented a late attempt by Saud to reestablish his paramountcy within his country.

Saud had followed the creation of the UAR and watched the enthusiasm it generated among all Arabs, and this badly planned move reflected his belated unease over the future of a Middle East functioning in the shadow of the new strong country with a charismatic leader and Communist backers. While Nasser's major opponent, America, had made it plain that it opposed Nasser's overall schemes, it also knew that Nasser was saving Syria from Communism, something that the American-sponsored coups of the early 1950s could not do. America had no option but to grant the Egyptian leader its grudging approval. This would suggest that Saud's plans for Syria did not include the United States. The naïveté of the conspiracy suggests that it was a purely Saudi endeavor conceived by Saud and his advisers. In fact, the ample evidence now available names royal adviser Yusuf Yassin, a Syrian diplomat for hire and so-called expert on Syria who had made his fortune in Saudi Arabia, as the "brain" behind the plot.

What prompted Yassin to go for broke is unknown. Either he mistakenly thought America would be impelled to provide Saud with help after the fact, or he was misled by individual CIA agents who had been known to give American policy a highly personal interpretation or to act on their own. It certainly was a step too far for the usually conservative Saudis, though fear of Communism by the House of Saud was genuine. Accepting the formula of like attracting like in human affairs, one assumes, and the facts of the case support it, that Yassin was no more clever than his royal mentor.

The actual plot was very simple. Operating on orders from their commander, Syrian jet fighters were to shoot down Nasser's plane over Syrian airspace as it flew back to Cairo from Damascus. Yassin, who later claimed that he was prompted into action by a strong anti-Communism and belief in Islamic principles, managed to establish contact with Colonel Abdel Hamid Saraj, officially the head of the Syrian security service, but probably the most powerful among the pro-Nasser Syrians. Saraj was such a devotee of Nasser he was known to blush in the presence of his idol.[1] Mistaking Saraj for a Muslim believer, Yassin couched his murder plan in religious dogma and presented the USSR as godless and its backing for Nasser as a threat to Islam. Of course, His Majesty King

Saud was willing to reward the perpetrators of the noble act. Yassin and Saraj agreed that only the head of security (named the Deuxième Bureau after its French counterpart) was capable of issuing this kind of order to the commander of the air force.

Amazingly, this offer was repeated to Saraj by a local CIA officer, who also emphasised the pro-Muslim nature of what was being contemplated.[2] It is obvious that some American field operatives did not agree with their government's acceptance of the union and that at least one of them held or was given the erroneous view that Saraj was an observing Muslim. Saraj, a master conspirator and an extremely able security chief known to the Syrians as the "Red Sultan," pretended to accept their offer. He asked Yassin to make him a check for £2 million as a down payment. He pretended to need money to pay several would-be helpers. The check was arranged in no time at all. But none of this explains the involvement of the CIA, or at least one of its local officers. Because no official documents have surfaced to explain this contradiction or expose American double-dealing, one is reduced to thinking that it was a rogue CIA operation.

The Red Sultan, behaving like an obedient schoolboy having done his homework, gave the check and recordings of his conversations with Yassin to Nasser. Al Rayyes had not allowed the atmosphere of the festivities to preclude a possible attempt on his life, but he had thought Nuri would be behind it. In fact, Nasser thought Nuri would still try to disrupt the Damascus celebrations, but he thought the attempt would be more elaborate, because Nuri coordinated everything with London. The American involvement never ceased to puzzle him, but the natural conspirator did not dismiss it outright.

Soon after this attempt, Britain, the United States, and, according to Mohamed Heikal, also France tried to remove Nasser. But whether these were actual plots or expressions of desire which never materialized into actual attempts on Nasser's life is not known. There was no doubting the reality of the Saudi debacle, however, and Al Rayyes was extremely pleased with his protégé. Nasser's dependence on Saraj, already heavy, increased, and with time he entrusted him with enough power to run Syria. On March 4, 1958, Nasser, one of the great natural publicists of the twentieth century, stood on the balcony of the Diafa Palace and waved a copy of the Saudi check in the air. In his own inimitable style, he managed to reduce the story to the level of the audience of tens of thousands watching him. They understood him, and the shouts against the agents of imperialism, what he called the "syndicate of monarchs," were deafening. The cheers for the hero of the moment were louder—one could hardly hear the hundreds who offered to sacrifice themselves in his place. The hero of the moment was indeed lucky in his Arab enemies, who were divided between the thoroughly hated Nuri and the disastrously incompetent Saud.

Of course the UAR radio stations in Cairo and Damascus would not leave the story alone. It was, according to both of them, the alarm bell "which should wake up the Arabs to the dangers surrounding them. Allah be with you and glory to the Arabs." Once again Nasser did not address the Arab people's huge social, economic, or political problems or the other problems facing the UAR, how to make the new state work and how to move forward with the now accepted Arab unity. The problem he shared with them was the conspiracy against the Arabs, the outside forces trying to stifle Arab nationalism. He said nothing about what they could do to give substance to momentum to unity, to make it an effective force in their lives, but a great deal about protecting that which had been achieved. As usual, Nasser was reacting rather than acting. The provisional constitution of the UAR was to be announced the following day, but in his pronouncements, what the constitution contained and promised paled in comparison with outside dangers. In fact, the whole Saud stupidity was a godsend. Nasser was always better at fighting the shadowy agents of reaction and ignorance, the ones behind all real and imagined hurdles, conspiracies, and setbacks, than at promoting something concrete. If Nasser needed something dramatic with which to leave the people of Syria, then Saud had given him an escape route.

Saud himself was finished. His brothers were mortified by the crassness of it all. Even that uneducated lot knew cash and not checks are used in assassination and similar conspiracies. Besides, many of them did not condone interfering in other countries' affairs and resorting to violence. They saw involvement in such schemes as opening the doors for others to try to subvert Saudi Arabia. In a few days, the senior members of the House of Saud convened the family council and asked Saud to cede all power to Crown Prince Faisal. Saud initially demurred, but there was no support for him, so he finally had to comply. He did not abdicate, as the family had no experience in that; he just surrendered control to his more able brother and became a figurehead. Faisal, constant in his rejection of nationalism and advocacy of Islam, never deviated from being anti-Nasser. Godless Communism and its supporters were his enemies because they were the enemies of Islam.

To gain support among the Arabs, Faisal's appeal incorporated familiar pet hates. "Communism and Zionism are the same" became the cornerstone of his anti-Nasser policy. Nobody took this ideological absurdity seriously, but his support for the Muslim Brotherhood, other Muslim groups, and religious teaching institutions throughout the world was successful. Later he went further afield and built bridges with anti-Communist Muslim countries such as Iran and Turkey. And as indicated before, Saudi money was spent sponsoring Muslim groups in Africa, on many occasions in cooperation with the Israelis, who had a vested interest in limiting Nasser's influence on the continent. Modern Islamic fundamentalism began with King Faisal, with solid American support. It was created to fight the enemies of Allah, at the time Nasser and the Soviet Union; but as we have seen, this movement has turned into a monster of its own.

A day after Nasser diverted the attention of his people to the Saud conspiracy and stated that "the agents of imperialism" would never stop their "absurd attempts to redivide the Arab world," he followed the announcement of a new provisional constitution by proclaiming the creation of a six-hundred person National Assembly and the disbanding of all political parties. Egypt was to have four hundred members and Syria two hundred. Half of them were to be appointed by the president, with two hundred coming from the Egyptian National Union and one hundred from the old Syrian parliament. The new cabinet comprised thirty-four positions, twenty Egyptians and fourteen Syrians, but each province got two vice presidents (Boghdadi and Amer for Egypt and Akram Hourani and Sabri Assali for Syria). Saraj was appointed minister of interior for Syria, in essence Nasser's security chief for the country.

The Ba'ath Party was represented in the cabinet and through Vice President Hourani, but Ba'athists, though party to the union negotiations which had created the UAR, were still taken aback that the dissolution decree included them. Instead of being recognized as the first promoters of unity (in their slogan the word *unity* comes ahead of *freedom* and *socialism*), they became its first victims. In a sign of the times, among the very few things that Nasser suggested during his stay in Damascus was that members of the government refrain from drinking alcoholic beverages in public.[3] Evidently he did not know of Amer's drinking and other transgressions.

Interestingly, Nasser flew from Damascus to Moscow to discuss bilateral relations, a "routine" visit that had been delayed from the month before. During one of the meetings with Khrushchev an old subject once again arose which explains the nature of the relationship between the two nations. The official Soviet translator told Nasser that Khrushchev thought that despite the ban on all parties, the Syrian Communists should be allowed to function freely. In answering, Nasser did not mince his words. He described what Khrushchev demanded as an internal matter which was not a subject for discussion with outsiders.[4] To him, Syrian Communists were no different than any other Syrians and the USSR should accept that. Khrushchev, taken aback, blamed the flare-up on the translator and denied that he had meant to interfere in the internal affairs of the new country. Neither man wanted to turn this into a problem between their two countries.

There was no way for Lebanon to escape the consequences of the creation of the UAR. A somewhat autonomous part of Syria under the Ottoman Empire, Lebanon became an independent country when colonial France redrew its borders to underscore its Christian identity and fortify the dominance of the Maronite Catholics. Syria had never accepted this, had insisted that Lebanon was part of Syria and that what the French had designed was an illegal, imposed creation, and had refused to exchange ambassadors with the new country. As such, relations between the two countries were always tentative and subject to interpretation. The Lebanese, fearing closeness with the rest of the Middle East might reduce their independence and Christian identity, depended on the West for support against any menace from Syria.

Though it was the only functioning democracy in the Arab world, the Lebanon of 1958 was an extension of what the French had designed. It had a shared power structure in accordance with an agreement known as the National Pact. Unwritten and essentially unenforceable, the pact stipulated that the president of Lebanon be a Maronite, the prime minister a Sunni Muslim, the minister of defense a Druze, the speaker of parliament a Shia

Muslim, and so on down the line. Adhering simultaneously to this division of power and the principles of democracy was difficult at the best of times. Injecting a new element into this delicate equation was likely to result in more stress than the system could handle. This is what happened when Lebanese president Camille Chamoun decided to invoke the Eisenhower Doctrine, ostensibly to protect his country against what he claimed was a Communist-UAR combined threat.

Both Chamoun and the United States knew better. Nasser did not covet Lebanon and always thought of it as a special situation, and he never cooperated with the USSR against any Arab country. In fact, the Beirut CIA office and the embassy were divided as to whether such a threat existed. Most accepted that Nasser's plans did not include Lebanon. Of course, the existence or absence of a threat could not be judged without reference to the articles of the Eisenhower Doctrine, which were conveniently vague. A Chamoun friend[5] and senior CIA representative who reported directly to the White House and the National Security Council, Wilbur Crane Eveland, "led an anti-Nasser orchestra."[6] Eveland, though he had dubious credentials and suffered from alcoholism, managed to get his point of view heard.

Whatever the background, a major confrontation between Nasser and America over Lebanon was in the making. It did not come about because the UAR was identified as a front or ally for the Communists, it came about because the interests of the UAR and the United States were not reconcilable. The United States did not act against the creation of the UAR, because America too believed a Communist danger to Syria existed. But the emergence of the UAR as a regional power meant an inevitable clash with America. Nasser wrongly believed that the two countries could coexist and always hoped for better relations between them. But the differences of opinion over Palestine, oil, regional hegemony, Arab unity, and relations with the USSR stood in the way. While still accepting that he was anti-Communist, the United States no longer believed he could stop the USSR from attaining a strong position in the Middle East. The United States believed the USSR was using Nasser, while Nasser wanted to use both sides.

The Lebanese resort to the Eisenhower Doctrine was transmitted to the Americans secretly by Foreign Minister Charles Malik.[7] Skirmishes, mostly unarmed, between government forces and followers of pro-Nasser politicians Kamal Jumblat and Saeb Salam had broken out throughout Lebanon in April 1958, one month after the UAR came into being. As usual, the trouble began in protests against the government, in this case over the alleged murder by the government of a pro-Communist Christian newspaper editor who had been part of an anti-Chamoun coalition. The government responded by claiming that the unrest was a Communist plot hatched in Damascus and aimed at nothing less than undermining the separateness of Lebanon. The fact that the authorities in Damascus, acting on Nasser's orders, were carrying out a crackdown against the Communists did not seem to matter. The protests in Lebanon intensified and turned into riots all over the country, and the riots escalated into organized armed clashes which produced armed enclaves controlled by local militias, both in the major cities and in the mountains. The escalation of the conflict was organic; each side tested the other by raising the stakes. By late May the country was in a state of civil war.

There was an accepted tradition among the Arab governments that inter-Arab disputes should be referred to the Arab League, and Chamoun and Malik wanted to avoid accusations of violating this tradition. The Lebanese complaint to the Arab League was a model of simplicity: it accused the UAR of gross interference in its internal affairs and attempting to subvert a sister country. This charge was backed by lists showing that arms were being smuggled into the country from Syria and accusations that undercover Syrian army officers were behind some of the major incidents of rebellion. The Arab League debate which followed foreshadowed worse things to come. While some countries supported Lebanon, most refused to condemn the UAR. On balance, Lebanon was rebuffed, and this left the door wide open for Lebanon to resort to the UN, seek American help, or both. Chamoun determined that there existed an American obligation to help him against what he considered the evil of Communism and its followers. A look at how he came to this position is necessary.

The Lebanese constitution stipulates that a president can be elected to one six-year term. The only way for a president to be elected twice is to skip a term, then run again. Chamoun a tall, handsome, and arrogant Anglophile, wanted to renew his term in office by amending the constitution and running for the presidency twice in a row. As the president is elected by parliament, the Chamber of Deputies, he began his efforts by rigging the parliamentary election by gerrymandering and the use of bribery. The result was overwhelmingly in his and his supporters' favor. In the process, many a Lebanese political leader opposed to Chamoun, including Druze leader Jumblat and Sunni former prime minister Salam, lost their parliamentary seats. It was scandalous, a violation of the spirit and fact of Lebanese democracy, and it stood against the essences which made governing the country possible. But Chamoun would not be deterred.

Chamoun expanded his accusation. To him, Nasser took his orders from the USSR, and Chamoun's Lebanese opponents took their orders from Nasser. Furthermore, this was no ordinary situation; what was at stake was Christianity in the Middle East. To Chamoun, Nasser's movement was nothing but an alliance between radical anti-West Islam and Communism. Chamoun's foreign minister Charles Malik, a man who eventually became a raving lunatic avoided by everyone while roaming the streets and shouting in defense of Christianity, was the architect of this self-contradictory accusation. With the conflict inside Lebanon spreading and the date for the presidential election approaching, Chamoun was pressuring the pro-Nasser forces. Nasser had to respond, not necessarily to protect his followers, but because the reelection of Chamoun would mean the use of Lebanon as a base of operations against him in Syria, something which was already beginning to happen.

This time it was not a case of controlling his followers, it was a case of wanting his followers to win a war by proxy. Nasser never contemplated annexing or directly controlling Lebanon, but for obvious reasons, he could not trust Chamoun. Nasser had to support his followers. The arrogant Chamoun, who actually thought of himself as Nasser's equal in the Middle East stakes, had to be stopped. The Lebanese situation was surrendered to the Red Sultan, Saraj. He took complete control of it and lost no time in providing support for the pro-Nasser factions, everything from money, to light arms, to officers who would train them. But Nasser was not the only party forced into taking a position. The United States, while it had not decided in favor of applying the Eisenhower Doctrine, could not allow Chamoun to sink. The proxies were leading their sponsors.

Inside Lebanon the civil war formalized the division of the country into Christian and Muslim halves. Chamoun's support came mainly from the Christian population, while most of the pro-Nasser elements were Muslims. The sectarian division had always been in place, but Chamoun solidified it and made it considerably worse, and what he provoked in 1958 laid the foundation for the bloody civil war which consumed Lebanon in the 1970s. Mercifully, two people intervened in 1958 to keep this from becoming a final split: Maronite patriarch Butros Maouchi and army chief of staff Fuad Chehab. Both loyal Maronites, they opposed Chamoun's selfish designs and acted to stop the country from disintegrating, Maouchi by coming out against a second term for Chamoun, and Chehab by refusing to use the army to support Chamoun and keeping it neutral. Yet, even when undermined at home, Chamoun and Malik decided to lodge a complaint in May 1958 with the UN Security Council. The complaint alleged massive infiltration of men and matériel from Syria into Lebanon.

A UN inspectors team headed by the Uruguayan Galo Plazo came to Lebanon to investigate. Lebanon and Syria are separated by mountainous terrain, which was difficult to monitor, and the time was short; but the UN officers still produced a report which caused considerable consternation on the Chamoun side. They refused to accept the "massive infiltration" description. The situation was not covered by the Eisenhower Doctrine, and the Americans who believed in that prevailed. Chamoun's phony resort to the doctrine to justify seeking a second term seemed to founder. But he never gave up. Chamoun thought that the United States would follow him because being anti-Communist was all it cared about.

The period from the creation of the UAR to the Iraqi coup d'état of July 14, 1958, probably saw the highest level of intelligence activity in the history of the Middle East. Beirut was teaming with CIA, KGB, and UAR operatives, and of course it was the age of superspy Kim Philby and the many operatives the French had left behind. King Hussein received CIA money to cause Nasser trouble in Syria (by resorting to terror—explosions and public disturbances), but he pocketed the money, pretended that an aide had cheated him, and did nothing.[8] The Iraqis never tired of sending agents to Syria for the same purpose. The appointment of a former army chief of staff, Ghazi Dhagastani, to oversee efforts against Syria attests to their importance. The American Friends of the Middle East (AFME), a CIA front organization, opened offices throughout the region. *Newsweek* magazine joined the stampede, with foreign editor Harry Kern using the overseas offices as CIA cover. Kim Philby was in Beirut to represent the *Observer* and the

*Economist*. Iran under the shah was just beginning to feel the effects of oil wealth; it began recruiting spies and, allied with Iraq in the Baghdad Pact, began working against Communist infiltration of the Middle East. Even Saudi Arabia, which had always provided financial support to Bedouin tribes in many parts of the Middle East, increased its subsidies to those in Syria with the hope of using them against Nasser. The CIA recruited Syrian politicians whom they hoped to use when Syria reverted to its singular self.[9] Of course, Chamoun was demanding CIA money incessantly.

The tension which followed the creation of the UAR was palpable. Syria was certainly the object of most anti-Nasser designs and plots, some of them involving millions of dollars in bribes distributed in cash. Nasser owned the street, the people loved him, but the governments of the Middle East were solidly against him, and there was some opposition by minorities. There was also Nasser's budding feud with Khrushchev regarding the relationship between nationalism and Communism. Cleverly, Nasser tried to use U.S. fears of the USSR's success to stop the Americans from opposing him completely, and the United States did not know what to do. In addition to Tito and Nehru, the one international relationship he had was with UN secretary-general Dag Hammarskjöld, and he still tried to use this channel to ease out of the Arab-Israeli conflict.

Sometime in the middle of 1958, the leader of the Palestinians, the mufti, left Egypt huffily to reside permanently in Beirut after he had determined that Nasser's contacts with Hammarskjöld regarding a peace settlement were serious. Very little is known about the peace overtures during this period, but there is reason to believe they were genuine, and it appears that Nasser was very keen on finding an opening. To the mufti, it was a betrayal, but there was little he could do because of Nasser's standing in the Arab world.[10] In fact, the ultranationalist mufti refused to go public with his protest against Nasser's plans. Later he would join forces with those opposed to Nasser, Iraqi leader Abdel Karim Kassem in particular. So Nasser was under attack from the pro-West Arab right, promoters of their own leadership positions, and also by the Islamist militants. The only pro-Nasser entity-partner in the Middle East could hardly have been less important: Yemen. Suddenly, on July 14, 1958, the picture changed.

The coup d'état against the Iraqi monarchy had implications as serious as those of the Cuban missile crisis. Once again Nasser was visiting Tito in Yugoslavia. Instead of returning to Cairo, he followed his instinct and Tito's advice and flew secretly to the Soviet Union, all the while staying in touch with developments. Not only were King Faisal of Iraq, the regent, Abul Illah and other members of the royal family killed right away; except for Nuri, most politicians had been rounded up, and commanders of most army units switched allegiance to the rebels. It was the one coup in the history of the Middle East that came as a complete surprise to everybody and where there was no connection between the leaders of the coup and outside forces. The leader of the coup was none other than Brigadier Abdel Karim Kassem, the very same officer who had contacted the Nasser government asking for help two years before. He was assisted in his efforts by Colonel Abdel Salam Aref and Iraq's Free Officers, most of whom were admirers of Nasser and wanted to unite with the UAR. Aref was a Nasser follower, and he personally led the assault on the royal palace of Kasr al-Zuhour.

The army units which carried out the coup were on their way to Jordan to bolster its anti-Israeli defenses as part of the Arab Federation. This is what permitted them to carry ammunition, which for security reasons they usually didn't. Aref's brigade led the way into Baghdad while Kassem held back in case the initial attack did not succeed. Then Kassem would have led another attack by a superior force. As it was, the attackers faced practically no resistance, and the all-important first communiqué to the Iraqi people was broadcast by Aref early in the morning. Aref told a stunned Middle East that the royal family had "suffered what it deserved," then appealed to the Iraqi people to apprehend Nuri. Nationalist songs followed, and hundreds of thousands of people poured into the streets, wildly cheering and welcoming their officer brothers. But the pictures the people were carrying were those of Nasser. Nobody knew the leader of the coup, but everybody knew Nasser as the leader of the Arabs and wanted Iraq to join the UAR.

Two days later Nuri was caught dressed as a woman. When a mob tried to arrest him, he faced them with a small six-shooter. They disarmed him, killed him, dragged his body through the street, buried him, then disinterred him and ran over his body with their cars until there was nothing left of him. Nasser's victory was complete; his most serious enemy and the West's most important friend in the Middle East was out of the way. The Iraqi army had joined the rebels immediately, and nobody had tried to defend Nuri and the monarchy. Yet, the lesson of what happened escaped the West altogether. The road for Nasser and his Arab nationalism was wide open. Or was it?

Like Iraq's neighbors throughout the area, the first thing Nasser did on hearing the news of the coup was to issue orders from Yugoslavia putting the forces of the UAR on maximum alert. But he also ordered Special Forces and air force units to the Syrian-Iraqi border.[11] He followed that by extending recognition to the new government in Baghdad and stating that "any attack on Iraq was tantamount to an attack on the UAR, in accordance with the security agreement of the Arab League." On July 15, U.S. Marines landed in Lebanon, and on July 16, British Special Forces landed in Jordan. Whether this was in response to the Eisenhower Doctrine or an overall expression of policy to save Western allies Chamoun and King Hussein is irrelevant; after the coup they amounted to the same thing. However, there is little doubt that both countries would have fallen to pro-Nasser forces without the American and British presence. It was reoccupation, a commitment to underpin the states created after the First World War, or to continue to maintain them as indirect colonies.

Meanwhile, Nasser and his entourage, which included Heikal, had gone to Moscow from Yugoslavia for emergency meetings with Khrushchev. Nasser, the UAR president, requested a clear statement of position regarding Iraq from the USSR. He was told that the USSR would not get involved in any confrontation with the West over Iraq.[12] When Nasser expressed his displeasure, the Soviets issued a limited statement on July 18: "The USSR cannot ignore the military moves taking place near the Soviet Union." Later the Soviet leaders announced that their navy would conduct maneuvers near the Turkish-Syrian border and offered diplomatic recognition to the new Iraqi republic. Clearly, Khrushchev was trying both to discourage Nasser from striking further afield and to avoid a confrontation with the West. Moreover, the USSR a few days later refused to supply the new Iraqi regime with much-needed small arms.[13] The USSR, like everyone else, thought the Iraqi coup had been organized by Nasser and refused to share in policies dictated by the Egyptian leader.

Both the U.S. forces in Lebanon and the British in Jordan consolidated their positions, though the neutral Lebanese army would not cooperate with the U.S. troops. Everybody agreed that the landings were a springboard to invade Iraq and return it to the Western fold. The American force in Lebanon, augmented by ten thousand additional marines, was commanded by Admiral James Holloway of the Sixth Fleet. A day after the landing of the forces, the admiral chose to leak to the famous American broadcaster John Chancellor the news that his forces were equipped with nuclear rockets.[14] Holloway expected Chancellor to violate what he described as an "off-the-record" conversation and there is every reason to suspect that he was issuing a threat. As it was, Chancellor refused to be used; he did not violate the admiral's trust. The parties concerned with the Iraqi situation, in the dark because little was known about coup leader Kassem, were trying to determine their next move.

The United States and Britain needed to answer strategic question of whether Iraq's inevitable withdrawal from the Baghdad Pact and possible joining of the UAR constituted grounds to invade the country. Western powers had put no obstacles in the way of Syria joining Nasser because he was saving it from the Communist threat. It was a point more acceptable to the Americans than to the Brits, who continued to oppose Nasser's Arab unity schemes. In fact, there were differences of opinion between the United States and Britain about the type of threat to the region that Iraq could represent. Consistently, the United States was preoccupied with the Communist threat to the region and watched the development of relations between Iraq and the USSR. On the other hand, Britain was adamant that Iraq would never go Communist because Arabs were not an ideological people by nature. Also from the start, Britain decided that Nasser was the source of danger to British and American interests. The British believed that Iraqi adherence to the UAR would create an unstoppable avalanche that would force most Arab states into Nasser's orbit. Certainly pro-Nasser clubs existed in Saudi Arabia and Kuwait. The British believed stopping Nasser from controlling Middle Eastern oil came ahead of all else. Early developments, though vague, seemed enough to justify the positions of both countries.

On July 18, Nasser surprised the world and flew into Damascus from Moscow on his way to Cairo. Everybody who knew he had gone to the USSR had expected him to land in Baghdad. But in one of the most important developments of the late 1950s, one which helped shape the Middle East and will continue to form its future, Kassem refused to grant Nasser permission to land in Baghdad. He described Nasser's request to visit the Iraqi capital as untimely.[15] It must have been a stunning rebuff for Nasser. The number two man in the Iraqi coup and Nasser's leading advocate among the Iraqi Free Officers, Colonel Abdel Salam Aref, traveled to Damascus to meet the UAR president. Aref, reflecting his own inclinations but with tacit approval from Kassem, who was trying to gain time, spoke openly of the likelihood of Iraq joining the UAR. However, the overriding issue among all the parties concerned with Iraq's future was avoiding a Middle East war.

The behavior of Kassem during the early days of his government was puzzling, and there is a great deal to it which remains unknown. Kassem, an Arabized Kurd, was an odd outsider, an intense, unmarried man with a thin voice and no charisma. His success in overthrowing the monarchy was followed by huge demonstrations of support throughout Iraq, but the name the crowds chanted was that of Nasser. Moreover, his comrades in arms, the Iraqi Revolutionary Command Council, were Nasser followers in favor of joining the UAR. Only the Iraqi Communist Party supported Kassem, but neither that nor his obvious ambition to become Iraq's supreme leader are enough to explain the animosity he had for Nasser. Perhaps he never forgave Nasser for refusing to meet or even encourage him and his comrades two years before the coup. Or—and this would not be a surprise—Western intelligence sources provided Kassem with information about Nasser's relationship with the CIA.

While there is no solid evidence to support this, it is axiomatic that the United States and Britain were satisfied regarding the intentions of the new Iraq government, above all that it would refrain from affecting the flow of oil or joining the UAR. However, there is no accepted story as to how these assurances were transmitted to a bloodthirsty government that had killed its country's king and the rest of the royal family. In 1995, Iraqi Ba'ath leaders Hani Faqiqi and Abdel Satar Douri, participants in the events of July 1958, told me that coup leader Abdel Karim Kassem had sought and arranged a meeting with British ambassador Sir Michael Wright hours after taking over control of Baghdad. According to their story, Kassem assured Wright that he would not join the UAR or interfere with the flow of oil and that Iraq's leaving the Baghdad Pact would not be precipitate. Both politicians were adamant that this was the reason behind the West's cancellation of the plans to invade Iraq. Furthermore, the rest of Kassem's comrades, also operating under the umbrella of Free Officers and elevating themselves to a Revolutionary Command Council, are believed to have found out about the Kassem-Wright deal, and opposed it to the extent of creating a splinter among the original group only days after the Iraqi army took over the country.

There is more than rumor to this story. The British had invested considerable money and effort creating individual Arab identities to defeat the larger Arab one. They wanted the Iraqis to be Iraqi, the Syrians Syrian, and so on. They believed the Iraqis would never play second fiddle to the Egyptians and promoted separateness through these prejudices. The only form of Arab unity the British would countenance came in three large blocks, one comprising Egypt and the lands of the Nile, a second made up of the Fertile Crescent (Syria, Iraq, Jordan, and Palestine), and a third lumping the Arabs of the desert together and creating a country out of the Arabian Peninsula. Of course, Britain supported the League of Arab States, which was created to provide a channel for cooperation between their countries that would vitiate the demands for real unity.

Abdel Latif Boghdadi's *Diaries* speaks of a deliberate American attempt to ease the tension through small acts, among them accepting that no outside power was involved in the Iraqi coup and convincing Chamoun not to seek a second presidential term in Lebanon.[16] Lebanon then elected General Fuad Chehab as its new president, and the conflict between the pro- and anti-Nasser elements in Lebanon ended after a meeting between Nasser and Chehab at Chtourah on the Syrian-Lebanese border. Obviously Chamoun's personality and his belief in a totally Christian Lebanon had exaggerated the danger to the Christians. In fact, Nasser never wanted Lebanon as part of any unity scheme, only that it not be used as a base against him. There was no reason for Lebanon and the UAR to feud. After his meeting with Chehab, Nasser immediately issued orders to Saraj in Damascus to cease supplying their partisans in Lebanon with money and light arms. The Americans also went ahead and set themselves a deadline for withdrawing from the area, October 1958, and resumed providing the UAR with grain and other commodities under favorable terms in accordance with the rules of the aid programs. The United States and Britain decided against inflaming the situation and were encouraged to do that by the behavior of the new Iraqi leadership on oil. Moreover, there were no signs that Kassem was enamored with playing a junior partner to Nasser. The issue of Iraq was put on hold.

The successful American attempt at easing tension had begun shortly after the landing in Lebanon by American marines, and Nasser had responded positively. What Nasser needed to explain to the Arab people was what the Iraqi coup meant for his brand of Arab nationalism. The usual call to higher Arab ambitions of freedom, socialism, and unity were always ahead of the realities on the ground. The rhetoric was his link with the people, but now things were changing. Even though he was taken aback by the refusal of Kassem to receive him in Baghdad, Nuri was gone, and he still got satisfaction from meeting Aref and was waiting to see whether his protégé could hold the line against Kassem. Nasser knew that a new statement explaining the new regional realities was needed.

In his statement Nasser incorporated a highly personal interpretation of the latest developments. The people had grown accustomed to hearing policy questions directly from him, and on this occasion he would be more explicit. He spoke in front of a huge crowd a day after his arrival in Damascus, and once again much of the speech was improvised and did not follow Heikal's written text. Some people expected an announcement of an immediate merger with Iraq, while others thought a later date would be better. Nobody knew what he had in mind. It was one of the most important speeches he ever gave. Without knowing it, the listeners were hearing Nasser at his very best as a speaker while being told, albeit subtly, that his Arab nationalism caravan had come to a halt.

May Oueidah's accomplished thesis on Nasser's speaking style reveals how Nasser manipulated his audiences. In this speech, he brilliantly adopted "a clever use of the triplets as a kind of invitation for Iraq to join the double unity (UAR) and make it a triple unity."[17] He carried the theme further, successfully bridged the different sounds of Egyptian, Syrian, and Iraqi Arabic, and rose to a semiclassical level without losing or boring his audience. He then clearly stated that Arab nationalism was "emerging from behind its ramparts." Slowly he began raising the stakes, again improvising but with the utmost deliberateness. "The holy march, on which the Arab nation insists, will carry us forward from one victory to another." Here the audience had not only joined him but was egging him on, and he responded by repeating landmark sentences time and again. *He is committed to an Arab unity which will move forward; Iraq is a step on the way.* He was improvising again, and his improvisation soared above and beyond anything he had ever said in the past. He incorporated his call for unity into a larger framework, which became his statement of policy: "My brothers, the flag of freedom which flies over Baghdad today will fly over Amman and Riyadh. Yes, the flag of freedom which flies over Cairo, Damascus, and Baghdad today will fly over the rest of the Middle East . . . Yes, the Arab flag of freedom . . ." For the first time, Nasser was opting for full union, even if it was unattainable and Baghdad was out of reach.

To Western ears the repetitiveness would sound as if he were making an overstatement. But it is the Arabs' way of asserting themselves and making themselves more understood, the speaker following a cultural tradition without which he might not be believed. It is the measure of how much and where to repeat and emphasize, which comes from reciting the Koran, which the speaker has to decide and which is the key to success or failure. Nasser always decided what to emphasize, what to repeat, by gauging his audience's reaction to his words. He was a master at reading his audience, and the mastery did not stop with his live speeches; later he decided what speeches were to be repeated on radio, and how many times. In the case of the speech in Damascus, it was repeated a number of times because it was the high point of modern Arab nationalism. It expressed the hopes, aspirations, and dreams of generations. Most Arabs thought they were marching behind Nasser toward certain unity. The Arab nation from the Atlantic to the Gulf was never more within sight than at that moment. Fundamentally the Arabs wanted Nasser to achieve the quest which had eluded others. They thought Arab unity was only a matter of time, and not years but months. After all, he had Egypt, Syria, and (as far as they knew) Iraq behind him. But about the Kassem rebuff, or why there was no declaration of union with Iraq, there was not a word.

And he still had no plan; he could not explain where Iraq fitted in the overall scheme of things. He did not know. He had to resort to more spacious and essentially empty generalities. "Arab nationalism belongs to itself and to God"; vague, but he still "lifted their spirits."[18] For the first time in his life he tried to lead the Arab people toward a specific aim, which is what they wanted. They needed to be led because they were without the social fabric that would bind them into a collective will. They could not act on their own and turn dreams into realities. What had been missing in

Nasser's relationship with his people was exposed; without him as an expression of Arab frustration and the consequent search for dignity, there was no modern Arab nationalism. Diluting the call for immediate Arab unity, it was the high point of his career. After that his calls for unity never had the same ring of truth to them. But the high point of his career came and went without most Arabs noticing it. It was the prospect of failure, having nothing concrete to say about Iraq, which pushed him into making what he knew was a feeble bid.

Nasser eventually began addressing himself to Syria in the fall of 1958, soon after the change of government in Iraq. To oversee "developments in Syria" he formed a tripartite committee made up of Ba'athists Akram Hourani and Salah Bitar and his old RCC colleague Zakkaria Mohieddine. The inclusion of Mohieddine, the leading opponent of unity with Syria, was curious. There is no way to explain it except that Nasser was trying to neutralize opposition to the idea of the UAR with his old group. In fact, by moving Hourani and Bitar to Cairo, Nasser was doing the same thing, in this case neutralizing people who had their own ideas about how Syria should be run within the UAR. Incredibly, he put Syria under Abdel Hamid Saraj, the security chief who had blocked King Saud's plan to assassinate Al Rayyes, without consulting anybody about it. With this simple act, Nasser gratuitously reduced Syria to a police state. Arab nationalism became the name for another dictatorship. He had no idea that the people's love for him as the leader of the Arabs was conditional. Elevating a brutal thug to the position of governor of Syria violated the unwritten bond between Nasser and the rest of the Arabs. Sadly, there was no one capable of telling Nasser this simple truth.

Saraj began his new career by imprisoning a few hundred Communists, forcing General Bizri out of office, and driving Communist leader Khalid Baghdash into exile. Nasser supported Saraj in all these efforts. He accepted Saraj's allegations that the Communists were opponents of Arab unity and were always conspiring against it in countries beyond Iraq. Believing that, Nasser went ahead and conducted another crackdown against the Communists in Egypt. The anti-Communist moves left the USSR seething with anger. To Moscow, acceptance of Nasser's independent policies did not allow for a totally anti-Communist policy in the UAR. But Moscow knew that it was Communist support for Kassem that had instigated the crisis.

But in his position as Nasser's supremo in the economic field, agriculture in particular, Saraj was lacking. Pushing forward the creation of a small industrial base was beyond him, so efforts in that area failed. Pleasing Al Rayyes by applying the laws of agricultural reform that were used in Egypt was catastrophic. Conditions in Syria were different, and there was room for innovative thinking. This did not happen, and when some landholders objected to the decrees, Saraj reverted to form and imprisoned some of them. Of course, Nasser depended on Saraj for his assessments of the situation. Nasser was totally committed to enacting new laws because, to him, they produced similar results and that was what he wanted for Egypt and Syria. This approach was simplistic enough to be idiotic.

Saraj also became involved in the all-important area of appointing military commanders. The Syrian army reacted against his appointing Egyptian officers to high posts that should have gone to local officers. Only four months after the creation of the UAR, Syrian army officers were protesting their relegation to secondary positions.[19] The Syrian ministers in Cairo were also without any influence and felt that their postings amounted to exile. Thus, the four sources of power in Syria—the Ba'ath Party, the Communist Party, the landholders, and the army—were uneasy about Nasser's Syrian policy from the very beginning. They had nothing in common with one another, but their rejection of his policies made things difficult for him. He was still popular, but his supporters were not organized into a cohesive force that would help him implement his policies.

Nasser's belated attempt to change the way Syria was being run by Saraj consisted of appointing his close friend, Abdel Hakim Amer, governor-general. There is little doubt that coming in December 1959, it was a panic appointment. Nasser's awareness that things were not working in Syria drove him to substitute friendship for substance and depend on his closest associate. The move backfired. Ba'athist ministers Mustapha Hamdoun and Abdel Ghani Kannout resigned in protest. A day later, Ba'ath Party founder Michel Aflaq resigned from the central government, and he was followed by Akram Hourani and then Salah Bitar. All of them had complaints regarding the policy being adopted in Syria, the treatment of the Syrians as upstarts by Egyptian associates, and what they considered the insulting appointment of Abdel Hakim Amer as Syria's absolute ruler. A meeting between Nasser and the protesting Ba'ath Party produced a confrontation without resolving anything. When Syrian minister Ahmad Abdel Karim argued heatedly with Nasser, the latter could not do better than state, "I am the elected president of the people; anyone who doesn't accept my authority can exit [*yemshi*]." Nasser was confirming that the UAR was already falling apart.

In no time at all, and without much happening in the open, the UAR and Kassem's Iraqi regime were at each other's throats. The struggle for Arab primacy between the two had been inevitable. Abdel Salam Aref and Nasser had agreed on Iraq joining the UAR when they met in Damascus on July 19. Nasser knew that Kassem had neither approved nor been a party to this agreement. In fact, Kassem moved very fast to marginalize Aref and stop him from playing the role Nasser had played with Naguib. The feud between the two leaders of the Iraqi coup climaxed in a power struggle which Kassem won and which ended with the exile of Aref as ambassador to Germany. It was a classic Nasser mismanagement of a situation in an Arab country; he supported followers without understanding their standing in their country. As with Abu Nawar in Jordan, Nasser was backing the wrong man, someone who was not up to his or Iraqi expectations.

But Aref was not alone in asking for unity with the UAR, and Nasser was still popular with the Iraqi people. Both the Ba'ath Party and the National Democrats continued to advocate unity, and most of the original group of officers who had overthrown the monarchy were for Nasser. But instead of allowing his followers to determine the course of events in Iraq, Nasser confused the situation by smuggling in agents from Syria to undermine the Iraqi regime. The man behind this activity, which was extensive enough to include saboteurs, was none other than Saraj. At this juncture, Nasser's Arab nationalist policy consisted of Amer running Syria and Saraj running the Iraqi desk. The situation which was beginning to unfold went beyond the UAR unraveling; Arab nationalism was losing its identity.

However ill-advised Nasser's Iraqi policy, it still put Kassem under considerable pressure. To counter Nasser's popularity he increased his reliance on the well-organized Communist Party. Kassem went further and created the Communist-backed Popular Resistance, a paramilitary organization with extrajudicial powers to investigate and arrest enemies of the revolution.[20] Bands of members of this force roamed the streets of Iraqi cities, arresting people and then torturing them. Aref was arrested, tried, and sentenced to death upon his unannounced return from Europe.

Other officers were subjected to indignities. A People's Court originally created to try the monarchists switched direction and began trying Arab nationalists. The president of the court, Fadhil Abbas Mahdawi, a glib vulgarian, used the trials to wage verbal war against Nasser and to accuse him of being a coward who hid behind "the skirts of UNEF."

By the beginning of 1959, Iraq was in the grip of a terror campaign which was reshaping the political structure of the Middle East. Nasser condemned the Communists and declared that he would not allow them to control an Arab country. Khrushchev countered by accusing him of being a reactionary nationalist. The United States expressed its fear regarding a Communist takeover in Iraq.[21] Britain continued to disagree and identify Nasser and his Arab nationalism as the source of danger to Iraq and Western interests. The USSR and Britain made strange bedfellows and supported Kassem against Nasser, the former because he favored the local Communist Party. Relations between the United States and Nasser improved because both sides were acting against the Communist threat in Iraq. Noting the deterioration of public order and safety, senior Iraqi army officers put out feelers to Nasser to ascertain his attitude toward any attempt by them to stage an anti-Kassem coup. Nasser was receptive.[22]

On March 8, 1959, an anti-Kassem rebellion broke out in the northern Iraqi city of Mosul. Its leader had been a member of the Iraqi RCC, but one of its minor and least imposing figures. In fact, Colonel Abdel Rahman al-Shawaf was known as an impetuous figure in search of glory. The real leader of the planned coup, Colonel Rifa'at Haj Sirri, did not have time to organize. Shawaf, in touch with the UAR authorities for some time, preempted Haj Sirri and started the uprising on his own.[23] It all began with the army attacking the Communist-front organization the Peace Partisans, one hundred thousand of whom had converged on the city of Mosul for an ostensibly leftist antiarmy festival. Kamel Kazanji, the Partisans' leader and a known Communist, was killed by Shawaf personally. The Peace Partisans responded by attacking some army units and inducing some soldiers to join them. A day later it looked as if every strain of Iraqi society had decided to express itself through avenging historical grievances.

Soon soldiers rebelled against their officers; Kurdish tribesmen attacked Sunni landowners; the People's Militia—a Kassem-founded paramilitary gendarmerie—attacked and ransacked the posh parts of the city; Kurds and Turkomans battled openly; Sunni tribes invaded the villages of Shia tribes; the Peace Partisans formed roving death squads; Christians switched sides practically by the day, depending on their perception of who might win, and thousands trekked to Mosul to support their co-religionists or ethnic kin. The Communists were the most cohesive group, and there is little doubt that they had anticipated the explosion of emotions which resulted from their behavior. While this kind of leaderless mayhem spread from the city to its surroundings and the oil city of Kirkuk, Shawaf was unable to generate the support he needed to control enough of the army and prevail over the pro-Kassem elements.

Shawaf lacked air cover, the one radio station he controlled gave a very weak signal, and he was in Mosul and not where things happened, in Baghdad. In the capital, Sirri and company were caught unprepared and decided not to move against Kassem. Using his Communist-led air force, the Communist Party, and the Popular Resistance effectively, Kassem took four days to regain control of the city. Shawaf was killed by some of his own subordinates after they switched sides. The number of people killed exceeded two thousand, with many times that number injured.[24] Encouraged by their Mosul success, the People's Militia, another name for the Popular Resistance, increased their harassment of non-Communists in other cities, according to *Time* magazine.[25] Suddenly, the Communist threat to Iraq became very real. All depended on whether Kassem threw his weight behind them.

Saraj had tried his utmost to keep going what has become known as the Mosul Rebellion. He had been alerted to the uprising by Iraqi officers well before it started, and his agents roamed northern Iraq looking for would-be Nasser supporters to arm. Camouflaged army trucks were entering Syria carrying ammunition and matériel for the Mosul rebels. He tried to bolster the weak radio station which broadcast from Mosul with a transmitter located in Syria, but without much success. Of course, his own radio stations aired the declarations of the anti-Kassem rebels without examining them, and Radio Damascus followed suit. He opened the Syrian door for all the wounded and escapees. Finally, when things looked bleak, Nasser did consider the dispatch of UAR troops to Iraq, but decided against it.[26] To Nasser there could be no movement forward for Arab Nationalism without controlling Iraq. The march toward unity should not assume a different way. This meant killing Kassem or overthrowing his regime before the Iraqi general became an accepted component of the Middle East's political landscape.

Nasser was in Syria hosting Yugoslav leader Marshal Tito when the Mosul Rebellion began. During the remainder of Tito's stay and later Nasser was presented with misleading facts which made him think the rebellion would succeed. His advisers, including Saraj and Amer, insisted that Shawaf was winning and that the end of Kassem was near. Kassem's loyalists gained the upper hand for the opposite reason; they overestimated the strength of his forces. Nasser, not for the last time, had decided against direct interference that would include the use of the UAR's armed forces. There would be no direct military effort against an Arab country, in this case Iraq. His army was ready, popular Iraqi officers Sirri and Nadim Tabakjalli controlled units that would have come to his side, most of the Iraqi people still adored him; but he still refused to shed Arab blood. In the years ahead, he was to dispense with the maxim "Arabs don't fight Arabs," but only under duress.

Nasser returned to Cairo a disappointed man, certainly a defeated one. The homecoming speech celebrated the triumph of Arab nationalism, but once again without delivering the reward of victory, Iraq. The confrontation with Kassem became personal and bitter. To Nasser, Kassem was an unworthy man who depended on the USSR and Britain to stop the march of Arab nationalism. Of course, there was also Kassem's dependence on the local Communists. The awareness that Nasser's popularity with the Iraqi people was not enough to overthrow Kassem was a surprise. Nasser, as would become apparent in the future, underestimated the strength of local loyalties. There was no way to move forward without resorting to violence, to resort to another Mosul, or to try to eliminate Kassem. To his credit, Nasser refused to do this. On occasion he even withheld support from anti-Kassem Iraqi Army officers.

The statistics out of Mosul disturbed Nasser, and he blamed the Communists. To him Arabs would not fight and kill Arabs the way they had without the influence of the alien Communist ideology. His anti-Communism deepened by the day, and there was another crackdown against the local Egyptian party. Even an old comrade, original RCC member Khalid Mohieddine, then an editor of *Al Masa'* newspaper, was accused by Nasser of supporting Kassem and the Communists and unceremoniously fired. Nasser's anger against the local Communist Parties found him accusing them of treason. Uncharacteristically angry while delivering speeches, he repeated that he would not tolerate the existence of a Communist regime in Iraq, or any part of the Arab world. It was a clear warning to the USSR and the clearest statement that he thought the Middle East belonged to him and his brand of Arab nationalism. Khrushchev responded by accusing Nasser of being a hotheaded young man, and drew a distinction between UAR-USSR cooperation and their ideological differences.

Obviously Mosul was also a defeat for anti-Kassem America, which watched as the Communists saved Kassem in Mosul and gained greater control of the various government departments of Iraq. Allen Dulles told a Senate committee that "Iraq is now the most dangerous spot on earth."[27] He followed his warning by appointing James Critchfield, one of the CIA's top experts on Communist infiltration, to run his field operations in the Middle East.

Critchfield admits that he knew very little about the Middle East, but his brief was "to stop Communism in Iraq."[28] The United States would cooperate with others, Nasser in particular, to combat Communism in the region. Having established contacts with the Muslim Brotherhood, which opposed Nasser and his UAR, the Americans apparently made a strategic shift. Slowly the common aims of the two sides, Nasser and the CIA, drew them together. How explicit this cooperation was is not known, but the United States did restore the food aid program, and certainly communications between the two sides became easy. But removing Kassem was to prove a difficult task. Among other things, there was always the danger of the Communist Party replacing him. The Iraqi Communists themselves were contemplating such a move.

In dealing with Iraq and other Arab countries, Nasser was hampered by how little he knew about them. Sadly, he still relied on loyalists who very often knew less than he did or had their own agendas. The Iraqi army officers who had been members of the original group which overthrew the monarchy were committed Arab nationalists and in a position to undermine Kassem and revert to their original intention of adhering to the UAR. However, communication between them and the UAR was never easy, and they did not think the UAR people listened to them but to people like Saraj. A major point of difference between the two sides was the Iraqi officers' wish to start an immediate war with Israel. The Ba'ath Party had a relatively effective apparatus in Iraq, but Nasser was trying to diminish its importance and so avoided working with Ba'athists. But the rest of the Iraqis upon whom Nasser depended in his struggle with Kassem were a totally unfit and unreliable lot. Among them were businessmen, tribal leaders, and even impostors who saw in the situation a way to make money—and they did. Precious money was wasted backing the wrong people because Nasser did not know who was who among Kassem's opponents. But Nasser didn't just support the wrong people, he lost good people who became disaffected because of the bungling of his intelligence and propaganda apparatuses. Nasser lacked Arab talent, which was a grave shortcoming.

The situation got even worse when Iraq decided to use its media to respond to UAR propaganda and attack Nasser. While other opponents had used their media to attack Nasser, this was the most organized confrontation of its kind, and like *Voice of the Arabs,* Kassem's radio had a ready audience of leftists and Communists. It began using the People's Court proceedings, which were aired, as a forum against Nasser. Colonel Mahdawi, the head of the court and Kassem's first cousin, turned out to be a wordsmith extraordinaire, and his way with words matched Nasser's top broadcasters. He had begun by putting the royalists on trial immediately after the July coup, and now he turned his attention to the pro-Nasser conspirators against Kassem, including Nasser's protégé and the man who had killed the royal family, Abdel Salam Aref. Mahdawi compared Nasser to Museilmah al-Kazab (Museilmah the Liar, a legendary Arab twister of the truth). When other departments of Radio Baghdad resorted to invective, there was no shortage of material. To recall Nasser's humble background and shame him among certain social groups—the Iraqi establishment in particular—the radio broadcast a song about a postman *("Will boustagia yeshtikou min kutr marseeli").* Politically, Mahdawi accused Nasser of using UNEF to avoid war with Israel. Of course, Nasser's treatment of the Communists and Muslim Brotherhood was not forgotten. Nor were Nasser's close advisers spared. Amer became "Al Musheer al-Fatteer," the Nerd Field Marshal, and there was no shortage of stories about the criminal behavior of the (Syrian) secret police of Saraj. It is no exaggeration to say that the people of the Middle East listened to such programs instead of listening to comedy shows. *Al radh,* harlotry, was the order of the day, and Mahdawi, though talented, was a vulgar street Arab. How Nasser, a father of five well-brought-up children and a model husband, allowed things to sink to this level is baffling. But little doubt exists that the problem between him and Kassem had become a clash of personalities.

Nasser saw Kassem as an upstart and felt that it was he, Nasser, who had paved the way for the revolutionary movement in the Arab world and made Kassem's success possible. On the other hand, Kassem looked down on Nasser's Arab nationalism and socialism and wanted more drastic measures in both areas and closer relations with the USSR. Nasser was playing a game of power politics while Kassem came close to a total alliance with the USSR. To the Iraqi leader only an alliance with the Soviet bloc would help the Arabs regain Palestine. Dealing with America, as Nasser did, was hopeless.

Both Nasser and Kassem sacrificed a lot of principle in the fight. Nasser drew close to America though he did not trust that country, after it had let him down over the Aswan dam deal and the arms deal. Kassem, unable to rely on the Arab nationalists, depended on and supported the local Communists as a counterweight to them and in the process created the People's Militia. (Also called the Popular Resistance). This feud was the low point of Arab politics in the twentieth century. Practically all the important Arab leaders got involved and were exposed as lacking substance, not only in resorting to invective and subordinating principle to expedience, but in terms of the bitterness manifested by each side against the other, considering what was at stake. Statesmanship was in short supply.

While committed to the unity of Iraq as one nation, Nasser even put out feelers to the Kurds to help him against Kassem. He offered them more of a say in the future of Iraq than Kassem was willing to offer them. Kassem appealed to Syrian army officers to rise against their Egyptian counterparts, the ones preferred by Nasser. King Hussein was following the advice of his resident CIA officer and publicity specialist, John Fistere, who was also advising him regarding how to wage a media campaign against Nasser. Again the situation in Syria appears to have been Nasser's weakest point. Saudi Arabia's short but unhappy experience in inter-Arab politics forced it to withdraw into its traditional isolation, but not without financing Muslim groups against godless Communism and its followers (Nasser). Moreover, this was a period of turmoil in the desert kingdom which saw a number of attempts at reforming the government. And the mufti of Palestine, whose penchant for conspiracy fit him like his religious garb, moved out of Cairo permanently and gave his support to Kassem against Nasser. He believed, not without evidence, that Nasser was seeking a peace settlement with Israel through Hammarskjöld.[29] The mufti not only had informers who had penetrated the Egyptian army and security services, he shared his misgivings about Nasser's Israeli policy with other Arab and Muslim countries.

However one assesses the results of the confrontation between Nasser and Kassem and the accompanying divisions in the Arab camp, it is definitely true that Kassem's successful stance against Nasser resulted in a loss of momentum for Arab nationalism, and this exposed Syria to innumerable plots by parties opposed to Nasser and the UAR. Syrians opposed to the union pointed out the secondary role played by the Syrians in the running of their own country. Pro-West elements, though weak, criticized the agricultural reform program and the damage it was doing to Syrian agriculture. Rightly they pointed out the difference between the two countries, and that Syria had space and a different landowner-tenant relationship. Syrian army officers resented being subordinated to Egyptian officers, whom they accused of being less competent than they were. Syrian Bedouin tribes received money from Saudi Arabia to stop them from being loyal to Nasser. A small minority of people who always promoted a monarchist Syria worked with King Hussein to bring about the dissolution of the UAR. The USSR had no option but to continue supporting the Syrian Communist Party against Nasser. The CIA supported schemes to weaken the UAR lest it become a danger to its major allies in the Middle East, Israel, and Saudi Arabia. The mufti opposed Nasser because he believed an Arab world under Nasser would mean the Egyptian leader had the final say in settling the problem with Israel, something that would marginalize him. Even the Ba'ath Party came out against Nasser because they saw no future for political parties under him. The Ba'ath was for the union, but its intellectuals advocated a multiparty system made up of believers in Araby and not in a single-party Soviet-style regime.

Late in 1959, Nasser blamed the resignations of the Syrian members of the UAR cabinet on the West and Kassem. In the course of doing it, he absolved Amer and Saraj from contributing to any of the problems that plagued the Northern Province.

The Nasser response to the complaints whirling around him was out of character. He not only made no effort to make the old Syrians stay, he did not replace them with other Syrians. Instead, he made matters worse by giving Abdel Hakim Amer presidential powers in Syria. This was a mistake on more than one level, and it showed that Nasser was out of touch. Amer knew nothing about

Syria and was not the studious type who would apply himself to solving its problems with diligence. Furthermore, his history in Egypt, particularly his performance during the Suez crisis, did not guarantee him a good reception. Amazingly, this mistake was followed by another. After the elections to the National Union, Nasser promoted Saraj to replace Amer. Saraj was given the title of chairman of the executive committee of the Northern Province. Saraj resorted to what he knew best. Syria became a police state. Not only was Syria turned into the junior member of the UAR, but its people were denied equal rights with their fellow Egyptians.

The UAR, which Saddam Hussein later called "the Nasser experiment," was a failure in two ways.[30] The strength of regionalism, supported as it was by the United States and the West, energized the anti-Nasser forces throughout the Arab world. And Egyptian colonialism replaced what existed before as Nasser adopted the methods of a police state.

# 7

# Search for an Honorable Exit

Gamal Abdel Nasser, astute, instinctive, and with a rare natural ability to sense and judge his surroundings, was probably the only one among the Egyptian and Arab leadership who saw the 1958–60 period as the beginning of the end of his Arab nationalism. He became convinced that unity among the Arab states was not possible. What led him to this dramatic conclusion escaped the diarists of the period, people such as Heikal, Sadat, Boghdadi, Khalid Mohieddine, Hammroush, and others. Lack of intelligence and intellect exempted Nasser's trustees and close associates Saraj and Amer. Nobody expected them to show any understanding. Perhaps Dr. Mahmoud Fawzi and Zakkaria Mohieddine, both able men who became prime ministers later, shared Nasser's inner fears, but neither ever articulated them. Both were the silent, loyal types.

It was not a case of a mad dictator realizing and acting on the consequences later, but of a brilliant though soft manipulator of men and mover of masses having to confront an insoluble problem. What failed him, what drove him to this conclusion, was the sudden, devastating awareness that what he depended on most, the loyalty of the people, wasn't worth a great deal. Certainly, it wasn't enough to provide him with the backing he needed to pursue his quest. The awareness of failure showed in the ungentlemanly shrillness and street Arab name-calling with which he attacked Kassem. He no longer occupied the high ground; after confusing the educated Arabs, he addressed himself to the lowest common denominator, the uneducated Arab who revered him and did not know any better. And it was this type of follower who failed Nasser, leading him to his conclusion.

Nasser's attacks on the Soviet Union were prompted by the Soviets' friendship with Kassem. His bold accusation that they wanted to control the Middle East, at a time when he was heavily dependent on them for arms and financial aid, was another indication that the gambler in him had taken over. Pressure always exposed the worst in him, and in this case the pressure came from within. It dealt with the death of his grand dream, and he could not share it with anyone. Reports of meetings show him less than patient with old colleagues, unavailable to them and uncharacteristically dismissive of their opinions. The amity which had characterized the relationship between him and his original comrades had gone. The crackdowns against Muslim fundamentalists and Communists were harsher than in the past, and the numbers of people he imprisoned at a time ran into the hundreds. These weren't the actions of a leader not knowing what was happening, but the behavior of someone unable to control his inner anger or share his predicament with others.

And Nasser was groping for a way out, constantly trying to develop a governmental system that would ease his burden, allow him to work fewer than eighteen hours a day. Miraculously, the one area which did not suffer his decline into a lesser man was his home life. He was still the loving father and husband who flourished when with his family. Even when diabetes and arteriosclerosis were causing him constant pain, family film footage of the time shows him taking a singular joy in playing football with his sons. He still spent his afternoons with them, and to them there were no signs that things were unwell. His close relationship with his wife, Tahiya, was rock-solid. There are hints here and there that Tahiya had been his confidante during his days in the army and that she did participate in dangerous missions on his behalf. If true, all this came to an end after his marriage and the arrival of the five children. Tahiya devoted herself to creating a happy atmosphere for her husband, and making him happy represented her exclusive concern.

What confronted Nasser regionally and inside Egypt, what changed him and left him feeling betrayed, was what he always wanted to avoid. In August 1959 he wrote an article for *Life* magazine outlining his Egyptian and Arab ambitions. Unsurprisingly, freedom from outside influences was uppermost in his mind. With the British withdrawal from Egypt and Suez, and the creation of the UAR, as monumental achievements, and involved as he was in a vicious feud with Kassem, what he wanted most was for the Arab world to decide its own fate.

It is true that he expected the Arabs (to him meaning all Arabic-speaking people) to opt for freedom and unity, and he never doubted they would—until Mosul. His rejection of outside influences was a natural extension of his assessment of what the Arabs wanted. Both Western influence and what the Soviets offered were rejected totally. *"Bilad al-Arab lil Arab,"* or "The Arab countries are for the Arabs," was his slogan. Years later he was to restate what he had written in *Life* and repeat it to his adviser Mohamed Heikal: "We don't need custodians."[1] Whatever changes and turns he underwent in dealing with Arab leaders and the Arab countries was an inter-Arab game. His commitment was to Araby. He would rather have been a slave in the House of Saud than a deputy master under the British in Iraq. His analysis of British and Russian actions in Iraq was correct.

The other problems which preoccupied him were new and specifically Egyptian. He didn't feel comfortable addressing the problems of Syria, because they were new to him. That Syrian landowners differed from their Egyptian counterparts was something that did not escape him, but how to cope with the differences did. But he was candid in discussing what he knew, Egypt's social and economic maladies. "We have enough [problems] for a whole generation," he admitted to Heikal. Nor was he unaware of what remedies were required or what his government could do. Population growth of over 2.5 percent was very much on his mind, but he was comforted by figures showing a GNP growth of 4.5 percent. He proposed no solutions for controlling the increase in population, probably because he feared Islamic reaction, but it obviously disturbed him. To underscore the success of the regime, he proudly spoke of the growth of industry in Egypt, the increase in the production of textiles, the fourfold rise in steel production, the electrification program, and the making of radios and even assembling of trucks. But he had nothing to show for conditions in

Syria. Toward the new province he behaved much like a student who had not done his homework. Even the abundance of land which made some of his reforms unnecessary was new to him.

As during the earliest days of the revolution, he was for the army returning to the barracks; and if he did not support taking it out of politics, he advocated a transitional period of an army-controlled government, after which democracy would be restored, or introduced in steps. But though he continued to try, neither happened, or came close to being achieved. All his colleagues in the RCC opposed any return to any form of civilian government, and they wanted to retain power as representatives of the armed forces. Amer especially wanted the army in politics, to enhance his personal position. Because Nasser put a distance between the government and the army and because Amer had nothing to offer except being a field marshal created by the original coup, Amer turned the armed forces into his exclusive sphere of influence. Nasser's preoccupation with running the rest of the government allowed Amer to act without restraint. Suddenly Nasser's closest associate became his competitor.

Slowly and deliberately, the Egyptian high command was becoming made up of Amer's cronies, officers more loyal to the fun-loving field marshal than to Nasser or the state. Their lack of soldierly qualities—in fact, being rather fat—became their trademark. Amer controlled their promotions and positions. They spent much of their time in the Gazira Club, the former playground of the pashas. They were allowed to make money by awarding contracts. They certainly paid little or no attention to their regular military duties. Nasser behaved as if he didn't want to know.

Nasser became a reluctant dictator overseeing a clutch of also-rans who lived in his shadow. His dictatorial ways didn't consist of eliminating old comrades, but of refusing to control them and having them accept their personal relationship with him as a way of retaining their freedom. Later, in the absence of competition, he became sole leader of Egypt. Later still, and mostly because of circumstances, he became leader of the Arabs, the darling of the people who took him to their heart and never considered a replacement for him. He towered above his colleagues, depended on his standing with the common man, and ignored all else. This gave fellow officers a great deal of room within which to operate. Power corrupted him by making him believe there would be no corruption while he was around and while he set an example for personal behavior. He believed his own word that a clean government reflected the behavior of a clean leader, and he was clean.

To him his position was unassailable. It crystallized his belief in Arab nationalism as a cleansing force which automatically rid the Arabs of corrupt leadership, and it pushed him into international entanglements which he could not win. He came to believe what he had advocated in *Philosophy of the Revolution*, that the role of the leader of the Arabs was there for the taking. Inevitably, because he fulfilled the role of the incorruptible leader, he saw himself as Allah-sent. This belief prompted him to allow Heikal to call him the "pious president." This growing pride showed clearly during his 1960 trip to the United Nations and his meetings with world leaders such as Eisenhower and Khrushchev. In New York, every move he made suggested that he considered himself a world leader worthy of their company. His Bandung days were a thing of the past, part of the training of a novice. Of course a pious, self-righteous president could make no mistakes—he was above criticism. It was during the very same year, 1960, that he nationalized the Egyptian press and reduced it to his personal mouthpiece. To him there was nothing to fear from merging his own person with the image of a president when the same president was above reproach.

The brooding Egyptian fellah from Beni Mur with modest ambitions was replaced by a brooding modern-day Saladin who, unlike his historical model, was fighting unwinnable battles. The big prize, uniting the Arabs in one big, strong country, was gone. It was the threat of creating such a country which gave him stature; and it was the emptiness of this threat, the fact that he couldn't even pursue the prize, which haunted him. After 1959, even his speech making lacked zest. His speeches became long and repetitive, and that palpable inner energy which the people had felt was gone. Yet whatever it is in life which propels dictators to pursue their march of folly got hold of him. He knew that the mysterious link between him and the Arab people was not enough, that the Mosul Rebellion proved it. He realized that he did not have what was needed. Whatever backing the Arab people gave him did not represent a force he could use to overcome the other forces facing him. The support of the Arabs was ephemeral, not solidly based. In the words of one of his favorite diplomats, Tahseen Beshir, there were no Arab people whose commitment to Araby came ahead of their belief in family and tribe. To Beshir the Arabs were nothing but "tribes with flags."[2] This analysis of the Arab social condition is as pertinent today as it was forty years ago.

This realization is why Nasser never mentioned his relationship with the people directly, not even in conversation with his closest associates. But his behavior, particularly during the unity talks with Syria and Iraq in 1963, showed how he had changed. He elevated and praised the Arab people, kept feeding them the notions of glory and dignity, dredged up their glorious past to shake them out of their historical slumber. At best this use of rhetoric was a calculated risk. For a backward people, words were enough to keep them happy, but words could not turn them into a social force which gave his ambitions content. And he had already used what tangibles were available to him, the arms deal and the Aswan High Dam project (the first phase of this project was slated for completion in 1961). He succeeded in using both, and they stand as monuments to his achievements, but he had little else to offer. Having begun building the dam in 1958 and used the arms deal to inflict a diplomatic defeat on the West, he was left with a house made of words. His source of power was his promise to the Arabs to achieve Arab unity, which was beyond attaining. He understood the meaning and significance of what had happened in Mosul.

Others didn't understand, however, and it was the word which still bound him to the uneducated Arab of Cairo, Damascus, Alexandria, and other city crowds. In fact, many thought the Iraqi rebellion and what followed it, Mosul included, was the second stage of his career and the height of his success. They assumed that his failure came later, after he discovered that the Arabs accepted the concept of unity more than its realities. This was not so. His strength, the fact that he was the vocal embodiment of Arab unity hopes, unattainable after Mosul, came first. Publicly, Nasser never linked his failure with what happened in Mosul, but there were people near to him who felt the connection. Some rightly refused to believe that Kassem was holding the line against him without the support of outside powers and that every passing day confirmed this and eroded Nasser's position. He had to move forward or lose, but Kassem and the British brought Nasser's and Arab ambitions to a standstill.

Sooner or later Nasser had to test whether the power of the

people who followed his word was enough to realize his articulated ambitions. When promise followed promise without reversing the defeat at Mosul or producing something tangible, things became untenable. Mosul was an early but defining defeat. Nasser never recovered from it. Kassem eliminated most of Nasser's high-placed followers and got away with it. The people were in love with slogans, the word of Nasser, but the ambition was beyond realization. Nasser depended on the people and they on him, but neither had anything to offer the other.

"From the Atlantic to the Gulf" was Nasser's territory. People spoke Arabic there, and it had the potential to be one big country, larger than the United States. Before Kassem, Britain, and the USSR blocked his way, turning all the states that made up this land into one country was Nasser's dream. It was still a dream during his brief years of glory, 1954–58; but it was a shadow of a dream after his failure to win Iraq. The dream had to reside in somebody from Beni Mur, a simple Arab who expressed it in the name of the people rather than on behalf of the establishment. Anybody less Egyptian and Arab wouldn't have dared have such a dream. Except for his intrinsic Arabness, he was no different from the people with an Arab nationalist message who had preceded him, including the ones who rose against Turkey in 1917.

In his attachment to the land and people and his belief in the rightness of their cause Nasser resembles today's fundamentalists and their dreams in a disturbing way. Speak to them about what their people want: dignity and glory are central to their answer. This is not the place to explain it, but the Arab conquest of the land which followed Mohamed was based on belief, a dream of divinity and the glory of dying for a just cause. This was the dream Nasser represented. He was the most absolute expression of the Arab quest for glory—and he failed. The much discussed absence of social cohesion would suggest that today's Muslim fundamentalists will face the same fate. *Inshallah.*

That testing point for Nasser's dream came very early in Syria, immediately after Kassem's coup in Iraq. It occurred a mere six to seven years after Nasser transformed the Arab scene, turning the docile believers into a militant threat, historically a short time indeed. The celebrations of Syrian-Egyptian unity were dizzying, full of the enchantment of folk songs, dance, and music—mostly made for the occasion. Yet very little happened to advance UAR-Iraqi unity. And Nasser had needed a committed crowd to save him in March 1959, during the Mosul Rebellion. The test was his attempt to stage an anti-Kassem coup in Iraq and incorporate Iraq into the UAR and, like Mohamed, lead the Muslim horde from one victory to another. Invoking what he and Araby stood for, he appealed to the Iraqis to rise against Kassem, the divider. The appeals failed. Each group and each tribe, the Iraqis included, followed what it had learned from its past, without heeding his words. His talk of intercepting a Communist danger and removing a divider of the Arab nation fell on deaf ears. Regionalism as promoted and protected by the British triumphed. It wasn't that people didn't love Nasser and his words; there simply wasn't enough commitment to overcome what really existed as an Arab society. Called upon to march behind Nasser, the Arabs discovered more reasons not to do it than to restore a glorious past. As in their behavior with Lawrence and the legendary Ibn Saud, the basically Bedouin Arabs wanted up-front payment, and the promise of more. In this case, they wanted protection for what they had. Arab individual genius, the inherent selfishness of being a member of the tribe, was stronger than the attraction of the colors of the flag of the son of Beni Mur.

Nasser easily grasped what had happened. The question was, What next? His followers were no different from the rabble that had followed Lawrence of Arabia half a century before, the Arab nationalists of 1917 who had no nationalist commitment. Their attention span was short and they suffered selective amnesia which rendered them impossible to lead. The question facing Nasser was the same one asked by the Arabs after the arms deal and the Suez Crisis. In this case too, the masses thought he had defeated the West by wresting Iraq from Western control, and he needed to add to his momentum. He continued to work eighteen-hour days without finding an answer and without finding the people who would assist him in his task. He was alone.

"People who live the way I do, do not last long," he is supposed to have told his confidant Mohamed Heikal. Meanwhile diabetes, high blood pressure, and arteriosclerosis, progressive as they are, were taking a greater toll. There is little evidence of how bad his physical condition was—even members of his family did not know.[3] (His frequent heart attacks, which would have finished a lesser man, became known only after his death.) He was in no physical condition to pursue his old theories of establishing a functioning democracy. And since he had no plan and no solid base on which to build one, no government or governmental systems he could use to start one, and no talented people on whom to rely, the easy way out would have been to resign. But he did not opt for the easy way out. He never tired of trying. His ego kept him from taking this drastic step.

He stayed, keeping what he had. Even knowing how fickle they were, he had nothing behind him except the Arab people. Failure to capture Iraq reduced his relationship with them to dust. Suddenly his love for the Arab people turned into disrespect, and they began to tire of his long speeches and the promises they contained. Dealing with Arab leaders became easier than ever before. A Nasser settling for something less than a revolution by the people was more acceptable to them. They could even go through a trial of a unity of purpose, instead of total union or unity of class, which was interpreted differently by different leaders. Nasser decided in favor of a common Arab purpose (freedom from outside control, liberation of Palestine, and control of the oil). It was a major strategic move which, in order to have any chance of success, had to involve other Arab governments. What the new picture lacked was a believer in the people and the complement, a people who believed in the convoluted concept of unity of purpose. Only with such a populist groundswell would the Arab leaders have to deal with Nasser as the *primus inter pares* of Arab politics. It did not happen; every leader saw to it that his people were more attached to local conditions than to what Nasser and Arab nationalism had to offer.

The other leaders' ability to use local considerations and conditions to overcome the appeal of Nasser's larger vision was aided by the West, the United States and Britain in particular. Nasser's Arab Nationalism was anchored in solid history, but it collided with reality on the ground and its less romantic day-to-day influence on the life of the average Arab. In Lebanon, Nasser's Christian supporters were being buried in an Islamic sea that would deny them their Christian identity. The Jordanians, though lacking a long history, feared being reduced to nothing more than a minor tribe. The Iraqis needed something that accommodated their ethnic and religious divisions. The Kurds, for example, would matter less in one large Arab country than in Iraq. The Syrians rejected all things that denied them a leading position, because they considered themselves more Arab than the rest. In the case of Saudi Arabia, it was fear of sharing their oil wealth with the poor Arabs of Egypt, Syria, and Jordan.

This made it easy for anti-Nasser local leaders to oppose the idea of one Arab state stretching from the Atlantic Ocean to the Gulf. In all cases, especially Jordan, the West was willing to provide economic aid to the "separatists," thus underscoring the shortcomings of what Nasser represented. The romanticism of Arab nationalism was no match for the "tribalism" of most Arabs. Besides its being a better way to face the Israelis, Nasser failed to articulate the benefits of Arab nationalism. Outwardly the pull of Arab nationalism was so strong that it precluded admitting a stronger local attachment. So many Arabs found themselves promoting Arab nationalism in public and working against it in secret—with the West and the local leaders outbidding Nasser in buying people's loyalty. Nasser offered an intangible—glory; but local leaders and the West offered money.

A long list of local, regional, and international problems faced Nasser after the creation of the United Arab Republic. Some were old, others were new; many had been minor but had grown serious with time; and others were a combination of old problems and new ones which resulted from the union, and for which he had found no solution. King Saud was ousted by his brother Faisal, and Nasser had to face the challenge of a Faisal-CIA-Muslim alliance aimed at destroying him and ending his Arab nationalism. King Hussein had survived all attempts to silence him and formed a de facto anti-Nasser alliance with Israel, and Hussein himself began to meet with the Israelis in May 1963.[4] The Jewish state could use Hussein as a buffer against fellow Arabs when all Nasser wanted was to remove him or turn him into a follower. Kassem was proving a hard nut to crack. Iraqi opposition to Nasser had deep roots in the country's religious and ethnic makeup, and represented the first popular challenge to his inter-Arab primacy. The mufti of Palestine, the Arafat of his time, was accusing Nasser of hiding behind UNEF, the UN body separating Egypt and Israel, and of wanting to settle the Palestine problem without deferring to the Palestinians. The mufti was looking for ways to expose the hypocrisy of the Egyptian leader, and this included supporting Kassem, a budding PLO, and whoever was opposed to a settlement with Israel. Lebanon remained uneasy about Nasser's desire to control it as the gateway to and commercial center of the Middle East. The pan-Arabist Ba'ath Party, having forced union with Syria on Nasser, was suffering from second thoughts and wanted Nasser to change his ways, abandon the idea of a one-party system, and cede a measure of power to local political organizations. Instead of being his followers, the Ba'ath wanted to be his partners.

Simultaneously, the United States was beginning to doubt the wisdom of having allowed the UAR to come into being. Many thought the United States should have opposed all ideas of Arab unity because they threatened Israel and Saudi Arabia. Not only was the UAR capable of becoming a magnet for other Arab countries and forming a larger union, it was in direct conflict with U.S. interests. For example, both countries wanted to control the strategic Yemen. John Kennedy had been elected president, and he and Nasser, though they never met, were the same age, exchanged letters, and liked each other. But this was not enough to overcome the built-in conflicts of interests over oil and the Arab-Israeli problem. They were the two issues where Nasser could have done something, but he knew that his rhetoric contained promises beyond achievement, that he couldn't settle with Israel while promising the Arab people eventual victory over the Zionist entity. The USSR was dismayed by his anti-Communism, his imprisonment of local Communists, and his refusal to draw closer to them. His vehemence against everything Communist was astonishing. The USSR rightly felt that Nasser was using it in his own game of power politics. Nasser's avowal that he would never allow Iraq to fall under Communism was seen as serving America.[5] Radio Sofia, among the radio stations of the Communist bloc that had an Arab audience, lost no time in accusing him of being an American agent. The public attacks between Nasser and Khrushchev reached a very low level of name-calling, though the relationship was saved eventually by the presence of the common Western enemy and their mutual desire to drive the United States out of the Middle East. The French were still hatching plots against Nasser for his support for the Algerian rebels.

Above all, it was the British who had it right. They never ceased to view Nasser as a danger to Western regional interests, oil and hegemony, and wanted him reduced to size or eliminated. To the British, Nasser was a menace, a meddler who relied on the Arab street for support. However misguided their handling of the Suez Crisis had been, the British strategic judgment of the man never varied. The British did not believe in Arab popular movements and had always opposed Arab nationalist ones. The British believed the Arab people would let Nasser down in Iraq before he made that discovery—and of course the British did everything they could to support the Arabs continuing to be a rabble. They convinced themselves that rabble do not create empires, or part of them. The British had no faith in the Arab people or any schemes aimed at uniting them unless the leaders of these schemes produced entities which would come under direct British control.

The third set of problems with which Nasser had to contend were purely Arab or internal Egyptian ones. Syria, or the union with Syria, was not working. Saraj was a hated security man whose presence reduced Nasser's popularity. In particular, the all-important merchant class hated Amer, who did not understand Syria's problems and proved totally unable to cope with them. His Egyptian ways and easy manner were alien to the earnest Syrians, and his lifestyle, including his womanizing, offended them. His appointment of Egyptian bureaucrats to run things Syrian when there were suitable Syrians to do the job pleased no one. It is baffling that Nasser would choose both Saraj and Amer for their loyalty and place that ahead of their talents (or lack thereof). He couldn't see through either, and the damage from both was considerable.

Fear, what dictators suffer from most, determined his choice of the two incompetents. He needed people loyal to him. Zakkaria Mohieddine, Boghdadi, Ali Sabri, and others had greater talent, but they were their own men and spoke their own minds. Nasser settled for true mediocrities when better men, possible replacements for his leadership, were available. It went further; he couldn't believe the crimes of which they were accused. It is doubtful that people informed him of the degree of torture taking place in prisons run by Saraj, and Amer's happy ways had produced good results for him in the past. He thought Amer's personality would overcome all the obstacles in his way. In view of the fact that he always believed Amer's assessment of the army's readiness to battle Israel (always wildly exaggerated), this should come as no surprise.

The Muslim Brotherhood, with Saudi support, became a bigger thorn in Nasser's side. Not a month passed without a new attempt to assassinate him. They did it both on their own and also with British and occasionally American cooperation. According to the historian Stephen Dorril, everything was tried to kill Nasser, including poison, nerve gas, the mixing of pills in his coffee, and the usual dispatching of hit squads trained especially for the purpose. Like Castro he was lucky, and very much like Castro he benefited from the ineptness of the would-be assassins.

With exceptions, Nasser's following among non-Egyptian Arabs was made up of a collection of feckless fools who were best making cheering crowds. He couldn't tell one Iraqi from another, so he missed out on some good ones who wanted to help him and the cause. The Yemenis were total strangers. He saw them as aliens, funny little men with colorful daggers. The Lebanese wanted his money and nothing else. And even the Saudis, including members of the royal family, misled him because he knew so little about them and where they belonged in the extended family. The Syrians typically never tired of lecturing him on who they were and what Arab nationalism meant. Of course, there were always self-righteous Palestinians who viewed him as a symbol to be used by them to solidify the belief in Palestine and anti-Zionism. In addition to the Muslim Brotherhood, there were believers in traditional ways and freedom-loving intellectuals. His followers were the real representatives of the people, the Syrian village headman, the Lebanese harbor chief, the Iraqi without roots or background, and others who made a profession out of being Nasserites. They were the ones who could organize a shouting crowd. But he never melded them into a political body he could rely on and use against the more sophisticated and organized forces arrayed against him.

Even nature got into the act against him. For three years Syria suffered from one of the worst droughts in its history.[6] The National Union in Egypt was proving to be a failure because nobody thought it would function properly while Nasser was alive and while he continued to gather power in his hands, impose his will, and decide everything. The National Assembly, the parliament of the National Union, was of no use; while Nasser was there, nobody was interested in becoming a member. In the end most members were appointed.

Amer, to Nasser's surprise, was successfully using the army as a center of power to compete with his erstwhile friend. A likable man, Amer became ambitious and turned the upper command of the armed forces into a club. Most of Amer's generals lacked military credentials. Nasser appears to have been aware of this, but he did not want a strong army which threatened his position, generals who used their rank menacingly. Meanwhile, all attempts to import Titoism failed because Yugoslavia was a completely different place with some expertise only in industries that Egypt couldn't match.

The policy and public failures occurred while Nasser was suffering bouts of severe diabetes and heart attacks. He was in constant pain but never showed it. He took the occasional week of rest, but I know of no single person, members of his family or visiting dignitaries, who ever heard him complain about the pain racking him. However wrong his strategic decision to depend on the Arab people, it was one he believed in, near and dear to his heart. It was his lifeline.

In the face of these huge political problems, Nasser determined to revert to one of his original ideas: using Egypt to create a pseudodemocratic system. Any test of the idea's potential would have to happen in Egypt. It was the country he knew most and where he could depend on the docility of old comrades, however weak and ineffective they were. In his mind Egypt was also the country he could turn into an example that would attract other Arab countries. Egypt could compensate for failures elsewhere. He was not abandoning his Arab dream, though he knew it had essentially failed; he was trying to be realistic by making Egypt a model that would attract the rest. He wanted Egypt to lead by example, by becoming the leading country in an Arab grouping. Also, feckless as they were, a return to Egypt was what some of his comrades wanted. They had little taste for the rest of the Arab world.

Nasser's efforts to make Egypt a model began with Al Azhar. The pressure of the Muslim Brotherhood was real, and he needed a substitute, a preemptive, alternate source of Islamic guidance. Al Azhar, as we have seen, had been outside of modernization for centuries. It had not moved forward an inch. Beyond prevailing on the ulemas to introduce a syllabus of the sciences and change the existing teaching program to include teachings based on moderate Koranic interpretations, Nasser wanted the oldest Islamic institution of learning in the world to lead. Without being explicit or coercive about it, he wanted Al Azhar to act as a church hierarchy whose word would supersede what the Brotherhood and Saudi Arabia promoted. Because Sunni Islam never had a hierarchy, he tried to use the past.

With the utmost deliberateness, Nasser leaned on Al Azhar to borrow from the old teachings of Mohamed Abdu, the modernizing nineteenth-century cleric. This was an attempt to fuse Islam and socialism, creating, as he thought, a wider appeal through integrating both. Whatever ideology he wanted to follow had to be homegrown, as was the name "Islamic socialism." To Nasser, whatever ideas were to be implemented had to come from the Islamic-Arab heritage, and nobody was more qualified to propagate such ideas than Al Azhar.

He conceived of the merger of Islamic and Communist thought as a second Arab revolution, something deeper than the simple corrective measures which followed the coup of 1952. It was a real attempt to enfranchise the underprivileged. This showed best in the statistics about education mentioned earlier, but there was also a qualitative difference. Even village schools adopted his new program.

With Nasser's guidance, Al Azhar's changes in the syllabus filtered through to lower levels of education, and evolution as a scientific principle became acceptable subject matter. Some mixed coeducational schools appeared, women's rights were spoken of openly, and divorce laws were amended in line with the merger of the religious courts into the civil ones. But perhaps the most far-reaching change was the fatwa commanding the readmission to mainstream Islam of the Shia, Alawais, and Druze. They had been considered heretics and idolaters for hundreds of years, but Nasser put an end to this for once and all. While endearing himself to the majority Shia of Iraq and undermining Kassem might have played a part in this decision, there is no doubting the liberalism of the man in this regard. Throughout his life, Nasser manifested an attractive lack of prejudice which found him respecting and paying homage to Jews, Christians, and members of other Islamic sects. Outward manifestations of piety affected him openly.

Nasser's moves didn't stop there. Desperate for help in toppling Kassem, Nasser established lines of communication with the independence-seeking Kurds of Iraq. This was a very serious step indeed for the promoter of Arab unity. It did not endear him to many Iraqis, and it underscored his cynicism to many other Arabs. But as in selecting the wrong followers, Nasser's decision to give a measure of support to the Iraqi Kurdish leader Mullah Mustapha Barazani was no more than backing a feudal landlord about whom he knew very little. Another point of principle was being sacrificed, through innocence, ignorance, or both.

Al Rayyes was thrashing away aimlessly, desperately trying to please. As can be seen through everything he did in response to Kassem, he was a man so obsessed by the Iraqi leader that he formed an alliance with America to overthrow him. Old believers in Arab unity such as the Ba'athists and Arab nationalists viewed his actions with fear and dismay. To many of them, he began to show signs of insensitivity to what he preached, what dictators show under stress. His attitude toward Kassem could have been reduced to one sentence: The man who halted the march of Arab nationalism had to go.

Yet, even then, he was too popular for believers in Arab nationalism to argue with him publicly. Except for Ba'athist Akram Hourani, a man he had made a vice president of the UAR, nobody made open accusations against Nasser. Hourani's allegations, especially the ones accusing Nasser of ignoring Palestine, were dismissed as sour grapes. The disagreements over his serious compromises, the suspicions of the mufti and others that he was conducting secret negotiations with Hammarskjöld to make peace with Israel, were never made public. Whatever was happening was another of Nasser's above-discussion secrets. Yet, much like Arafat today, he was indeed the only Arab capable of making peace with Israel. Had he made that decision, I have no doubt that the people would have followed him. The remaining Arab leaders did not measure up to him, and wouldn't have dared try. Only Nasser could combine the words *peace* and *dignity* and get away with it.

But in the early 1960s Nasser was looking mainly to remedy the problems of Egypt. Nasser's inward-looking policy coincided with a U.S. wish for him to do the same. Coupled with the natural empathy he and Kennedy had for each other and his open opposition to Communist penetration of the Arab world, this produced one of the most trouble-free periods of U.S.-Egyptian relations on record. The United States was concerned with his regional meddling, but not with Nasser's internal politics, and once again began providing Egypt with grain and other commodities on easy terms. The Americans had been looking for a Muslim Billy Graham, and suddenly Nasser himself assumed that role.[7] He opted for a moderate socialist Islam, though it took a great deal to merge socialist goals and Islamic beliefs, and that was acceptable to the United States. The use of Al Azhar was something of which they wholeheartedly approved. Furthermore, Nasser's public spats with Khrushchev confirmed to the United States that Nasser was his own man and that his brand of Islam was probably a more effective antidote to Communism than Faisal's confused policies, the uneducated equating of Communism and Zionism.

Nevertheless, the Americans, though pleased to save Syria from the threat of Communism, still suspected Nasser was not totally reliable, and so did not abandon their plans for an anti-Soviet Muslim alliance. Faisal of Saudi Arabia and the shah of Iran continued to plan an Islamic conference as a counterweight to Nasser's Arab nationalism. And the Americans started leaning toward the British position, which precluded Arab adoption of foreign ideology as a substitute for traditional ways. The liberal Americans who designed their country's policy after the Second World War, the opponents of British and French colonialism, now accepted the old-fashioned ideas which originated in London. It was an American admission of failure. The United States had no objections to anything that would stop, or temper, Nasser's regional meddling. But they thought that it would come as a result of an American policy aimed at "living with Nasser."

The test of how much Nasser had changed was on the way. In June 1961 Kassem—following other Iraqi leaders of earlier in the century, Nuri among them—threatened the use of force and laid claim to Kuwait. He feared the British offer of independence to the sheikhdom might end the Iraqi claim to the oil-rich patch forever. A contingent of about 1,500 Royal Marines landed in Kuwait to protect the country against the Iraqi threat—the Iraqi army had moved to the border. Kassem, unprepared except for a war of words, stopped short of embarking on a military adventure. Because the government which followed his in 1963 accepted a Kuwaiti cash offer to refrain from invading Kuwait, there is reason to believe a ransom was all Kassem had in mind. Iraqi blackmail of Kuwait goes back centuries.

However, it was Nasser who administered the riposte to the Iraqis. Pretending that he wanted to keep the British out of an Arab conflict and using the inherent appeal of "an Arab solution," he prevailed on members of the Arab League to form an Arab force to replace the British. With Egyptians in the lead, Arab forces landed in Kuwait and protected that country against Kassem. The foremost advocate of Arab unity changed position and played an antiunion role. The feelings of the Iraqi people, united as they were in wanting Kuwait as part of their country, were ignored. With that, Nasser ceded his position as the advocate of Arab unity. But once again, his control of the press in Egypt and other countries protected him. It created the background justification for his anti-Kassem policy. The United States was so enamored with what he was doing, Assistant Secretary of State William Rountree openly declared that Nasser was a man with whom the Americans could work. The Arab people were never told the truth, only Nasser's version of it.

Of course, Nasser coined a new phrase to replace his old ones: *"Wihdat al hadaf,"* "unity of purpose," rather than *"Wihdat al saf,"* "unity of ranks." He adopted the unity of purpose slogan as a new banner. But any chance of this succeeding and ending his predicament was very small indeed. For example, in 1962 he broke diplomatic relations with Jordan and Saudi Arabia because neither would leave him alone. Both were determined to capitalize on his hour of weakness.

On September 28, 1961, Syrian army units rose against the UAR, took Syria out of the union, and reclaimed it as independent. Amer's headquarters was surrounded by Syrian commando units, and he was escorted to the Damascus airport and put on a plane to Cairo. The other culprit, Saraj, having been appointed a vice president of the UAR, either was already in Cairo or made his way there in haste. As Middle East coups go, it was not an impressive affair. Most army units around Damascus had a difficult time making up their mind whether to support or oppose the coup, while most of the army in the north stayed loyal to Nasser and fought to save the union. Estimates of the number of people who died trying to keep Syria loyal to Nasser vary, but run as high as five hundred.[8] Unlike the army, Ba'athist leaders, Akram Hourani and Salah Bitar among them, came out in favor of the coup.

Nasser's immediate reaction was to oppose the breakup by force, and Egyptian Special Forces were dropped around the Syrian port of Latakia. But, once again, Nasser subscribed to the maxim of Arab never fighting fellow Arab, and he ordered the Egyptian forces withdrawn after forty-eight hours. That he had been willing to commit Egyptian troops to fight an Iraqi army invading Kuwait was all but forgotten. In this case it was easier and more statesmanlike to take the high ground, and, not for the first time, his behavior was seen as virtuous. His publicity machine made the most out of it, and the average Arab accepted his claim.

In a speech to the Arab nation he admitted many of the mistakes that had been made and refused to condemn the secessionists. He went further and accepted personal responsibility for what had happened. Simultaneously, he recommitted himself to Arab nationalism and described events as nothing more than a setback. To him, not even an event of this magnitude would halt the march of Arab unity. He rose above the occasion.

Privately, however, Nasser suffered something resembling a nervous breakdown. People who saw him soon after the breakup spoke of his health deteriorating considerably. He smoked more, was less communicative, and brooded. But he did not blame or punish anybody, and even Amer's efforts were praised. To close friends such as Mohamed Heikal he confided that the breakup of the UAR was the product of a conspiracy. He even alleged that Kassem knew all about the intended coup well before it happened. And Kassem was not the only suspect: Nasser pointed a finger at the Saudis, the Jordanians, and the rest of the Arab governments. Though he never said it, to him the breakup was the culmination of Mosul. These accusations notwithstanding, he continued to believe that a special relationship existed between him and the Syrian people and that it would one day express itself and punish the conspirators.

In October 1961, Nasser finally reacted to the Syrian departure and, turning inward, embarked on a major nationalization program in Egypt. He had convinced himself that total adoption of socialism was the answer to his problems, that a stricter application of Soviet-style government would have protected him against what had happened. He saw in his new approach a second revolution, a completion of what he had started in 1952. Early in 1962 he began toying with the idea of the UAR following a "Charter for National Action." This was under consideration sometime before the breakup of the UAR, but it was to be adopted by Egypt later. It was no more than another of his exploratory ideas, his constant attempt to develop a representative system of government that would relieve him of some of his duties and create a true Arab state. Youth groups, socialist study institutes, laws regarding the acquisition of wealth, and even agricultural cooperatives were created. With them came greater oppression. Thousands more Muslim fundamentalists were imprisoned, though the regime itself admitted that no more than fifty officers had belonged to the Muslim Brotherhood—considerably less than what would be needed to stage a coup.[9] Yet, upon hearing that officer Rushdi Khalil had died under torture, Nasser demanded an investigation and condemned any revolution that would do this to its children.[10]

The Charter for National Action was no more than an outline of what a Nasserite Arab was supposed to be, elementary in nature and thinking. With the Ba'athists, Communists, and other Syrian groups still clamoring for a new union where the political parties would be represented, the charter's appeal was limited to the Nasser rabble, the people who insisted on calling themselves Nasserites. Of course, the old National Union was brought back to life and renamed the Arab Socialist Union, but nobody took it seriously; nor for that matter did anybody take the other ideas of introducing democracy seriously. Arguments about how the Syrians and Egyptians had failed during the three and a half years of unity were a game being played in a vacuum. The fact that the two countries had parted company was an indication of failure, and now Nasser and the Ba'ath were allocating the blame for who would go down in history as having betrayed the Arabs. As long as Nasser was alive and well and capable of overwhelming the people around him, the chances of creating a democratic or semidemocratic system had little chance of success. Some of his old colleagues were servile. Sadat was jokingly referred to as "Colonel yes-yes."[11] It was said that Nasser could always depend on three votes, his and two from Sadat.

Unlike Egypt, Syria was diverse, vocal, enamored with dignity, and fractious. Syria wanted to be more rather than less Arab and socialist. The Ba'athists in particular saw themselves as the leaders of modern Arab nationalism and the guardians of the rights of the common man. In fact, it was Egyptian Arabism which was in trouble. Neither Nasser's old comrades nor the average Egyptian was enamored with what Syria produced for them. Even as Nasser was becoming aware that Arab nationalism had failed, he was already lamenting having gone along and united with the Syrians. If managing Egypt was difficult, running Syria was a nightmare. Only months after the 1958 union, Akram Hourani, a vice president of the UAR and leader of the Ba'ath Party, openly accused Nasser of selling out on Palestine.[12] Nasser's lack of preparedness to run Syria went beyond Saraj and Amer; it involved not knowing the place—"not knowing," according to a then common saying, "that Syria was willing to fight to the last Egyptian soldier."

Nasser's muted reaction to the Syrian action didn't last long. To close friends he admitted that cooperating with Jordan and Saudi Arabia, *"Wihdat al saf,"* had been a huge mistake because the two countries had never stopped conspiring with the West against him. His bitter refrain was given momentum by the efforts of King Faisal to capitalize on Nasser's weakness and build an Islamic alliance. Faisal called for holding an "International Islamic Conference" made up of the Arab countries, Turkey, Iran, and Pakistan. This new alliance was to replace Nasser's Arab nationalism with a pact based on religion. In this case, Faisal began by depending on Pakistan, the poorest of the countries involved, because it was willing to provide Saudi Arabia with military protection in return for financial aid. It was a return to what Nuri Said of Iraq had advocated years before, an anti-Communist collection of nations which had Islam as a common base.

In August 1962, the divisions in Arab ranks were so deep that there was an attempt at reconciliation under the auspices of the Arab League. A meeting was scheduled for the small town of Chtourah on the Syrian-Lebanese border. Topping the agenda was an Egyptian compliant against the slander campaign being waged against it by the Syrian government. The Syrian government, suffering from internal pressures by the substantial Nasser following, countered by demanding an end to Egyptian interference in its internal affairs. Eventually the whole discussion centered on Egypt's authority, exercised through Egyptian secretary-general Abdel Khalik Hassouna, to dismiss the head of the League's office to boycott Israel. Syria claimed that Hassouna never acted except on Nasser's orders. When neither side would compromise, the meeting broke up in acrimony. Nasser pulled out his delegation and declared that he would act on his own.

Acting on his own meant addressing himself to developing a governmental system for Egypt. Of course the basis for this was to be the Charter for National Action, the Arab Socialist Union, and the National Assembly. There were attempts to work from the ground up by creating village cooperatives and social centers, and to a limited degree this worked. But Nasser wanted more, something like an executive committee of the Arab Socialist Union to lead the country, instead of a president. He went as far as to suggest the creation of a presidential council, and that he would run the country through being the chairman of this council and of the Arab Socialist Union. But nobody would allow him to resign. However, the various moves adopted by him did mean that the government had taken over everything. He was in the middle of a successful Soviet-style five-year plan. Yet, the already mentioned incident of the officer Rushdi Kahlil having been tortured to death came close to making him resign. He had no explanation for it. He refused to accept it as a subsidiary result of a government that was not held accountable for its actions.

The tilt toward a Soviet-type system brought about the only major ideological split among the original members of the RCC. Tired of Nasser's turns and changes, many wanted him president for life, something which he rejected. On the other side, Amer wanted guarantees that he would be the regime's second man. Abdel Latif Boghdadi and Hussein al-Shafai, utterly opposed to extreme socialist measures, objected to the adoption of the new system and resigned. Boghdadi saw in Nasser's behavior a loss of direction and wanted closer relations with the United States rather than the USSR. Amer's sole concern was his position.

Nasser's fortunes unexpectedly changed on September 26, 1962, when there was a coup in Yemen. It was carried out by Colonel Abdallah Sallal against Imam Mohamed al-Badr. Sallal was pro-Nasser and supported his schemes. Yemen had been since 1958 part of the United Arab States, with Egypt and Syria, but the whole union had gone dormant. The first news was that the imam had been killed, but it later became clear that he had survived the attempt on his life and managed to flee from the ruins of the Bashar Palace to the country, where he was protected by his Zeidi co-religionists. Unlike the cities, the Yemeni countryside was Zeidi and committed to the royal family. That aside, Nasser could not ignore the opportunity and its potential of threatening Saudi Arabia and Faisal. Sallal was recognized immediately by Egypt, and Nasser made clear that his emergence was a sign Arab nationalism was far from dead.

In a remarkable show of sympathy with forward-looking regimes, the United States recognized the new Yemen Arab Republic less than two months after the coup, on December 19. This caused considerable unease in Saudi Arabia. Kennedy's motives had always been suspect to the Saudis, and for him to support Nasser against a traditional ally represented a direct threat to the balance of power in the region. Once again, it was the British who identified Nasser as the main threat to the whole Arabian Peninsula. Almost immediately, they formulated plans to help the imam start a military campaign against Sallal and managed to turn the whole thing into a city-versus-country confrontation. But the threat of a U.S.-USSR showdown loomed. Nasser found himself in the uncomfortable position of supporting the Marxist Front for the Liberation of the Arabian Peninsula and the equally radical Union of Sons of the Arabian Peninsula. Without restraint placed on the situation by the British, the chance of an American-Soviet war by proxy was very real.

A very strange armed struggle developed. The British, using former Special Air Services (SAS) officers such as David Sterling, Bernard Mills, and John Cooper, acted as advisers to the imam. Still occupying neighboring Aden, the British had a vested interest in helping the moderate imam and his people. They used the Yemeni mountain tribes effectively and quickly came close to defeating the rebel Yemenis and their Egyptian supporters. Nasser responded by adding to the small contingent of Egyptian troops he had previously sent to help Sallal hold the cities. Saudi Arabia and Jordan backed the imam, and the Saudis financed the British efforts lavishly. Furthermore, without the knowledge of the Kennedy administration, the CIA joined forces with the British and Saudis against its own government. The American decision was made secretly by the CIA's James Critchfield with the help of Kamal Adham, head of Saudi intelligence, King Faisal's brother-in-law and a moving force behind the Islamic movement.[13] Of course Amer made daily predictions of Egyptian victory.

The whole Yemen affair immediately took on serious implications when in October 1962 a number of Saudi pilots defected and joined Nasser. They were joined by the Jordanian chief of air force staff. There were divisions among the House of Saud regarding their policy toward Yemen, but the anti-Nasser wing prevailed. Tribesmen from throughout the Arabian Peninsula were recruited to fight against the apostate Nasser, and they knew their territory well. Some Yemenis switched sides, supporting Nasser during the day and turning against his forces at night. It was a war for which he was not prepared, and unusually, most of his old colleagues questioned the wisdom of continuing it. But it was his old friend Robinson who assured him time and again that victory was near. The incompetent field marshal misled his boss every step of the way. Foolishly he sought glory for himself by becoming the hero of a war.

Considering that the Yemeni coup had followed the formation within the Saudi royal family of a pro-Nasser clique opposed to their government's anti-Nasser activities, it looked as if Nasser was recovering much lost ground. In August 1962, Prince Tallal bin Abdel Aziz, onetime Saudi minister of finance and King Faisal's half brother, used Beirut to announce the formation of the pro-Nasser movement of the Free Princes. The purpose of the movement was to oppose Faisal's Islamic policies, support Arab nationalism, and win Yemen. While those who joined the Free Princes from the ranks of the family were minor figures, Princes Abdul Muhsin, Mussad, and Abdel Rahman, it was a pro-Nasser move of serious implications and it reflected Nasser's popularity in the desert kingdom. In the background was Minister of Petroleum Abdallah Tariki, a cofounder of OPEC, who followed oil policies dictated by Cairo and not by Faisal. A Nasserite through and through, he was too popular to be dismissed by the king.

In addition to these developments there was the victory against France by the Algerian rebels. It was a victory for Nasser and his movement. But it is well to remember that unlike the Saudis, Nasser was fighting on unknown territory. After being asked to send more troops to support Sallal, he supposedly asked U.S. ambassador to Egypt John Badeau to brief him on conditions in Yemen.[14] The Egyptian leader knew nothing about the divisions between the pro-monarchist Zeidis and their Shafi opponents, or about the mountainous terrain. Before 1963 was over, Egypt had committed to the Yemeni war more than twenty thousand of its best soldiers.

When Nasser's forces failed to achieve victory, he resorted to using poison gas.[15] Kennedy, until then hoping for a negotiated settlement, ordered the U.S. Air Force to provide the Saudis with air cover. Nasser reacted by once again attacking parts of Saudi Arabia, Najran Province in particular. Suddenly what both sides feared most, a U.S.-USSR confrontation, became a possibility. The Arab countries rushed to mediate and to contain the conflict. Between late 1962 and the end of the war with Israel in 1967, there were no less than eight conferences and meetings between Nasser and Faisal. There were the Erkwat, Haradh, and Alexandria conferences; the Taif, Jeddah, and other agreements; secret agreements involving Kennedy; and a call for a referendum. The war ebbed and flowed. In the words of an unknown American diplomat, Yemen was Nasser's Vietnam; he was ill-served by his generals and dragged in bit by bit. The war there sapped his resources and diverted his attention away from Israel. Once again he had listened to Amer against the advice of others. Once again, he demonstrated a devastating lack of judgment regarding personal friends. It was a colossal failure and showed a flaw in Nasser very few suspected. Once committed, as in his personal war against Kassem, he lost all peripheral vision.

Meanwhile Nasser was affording the Free Princes unlimited support. They used Cairo to promote Arab unity, to call for nationalizing oil or using it against the West, to promote pro-Nasser strikes in Saudi Arabia, to create many political groups to support the effort in Yemen, and to publicize the keeping of slaves by the Saudi monarchy. The Saudis hit back by sponsoring several attempts by the Muslim Brotherhood to assassinate Nasser, including some in 1962 which used Egyptian army officers. In February 1964 Prince Tallal made up with his family and returned to Riyadh. The CIA had a hand in it. The fire in the Arabian Peninsula was put down. Nasser was left mired in Yemen, unable to win or extract himself. Important as that was, the real battle for Araby was already in progress. After Arab nationalist coups in both countries, Nasser had a second chance to capture and control Syria and Iraq. He chose not to act. Deep down in his heart, he knew that what had happened in Damascus following the Iraqi coup in 1958 accurately reflected the truth of Arab nationalism as it existed. This time, his rejection of what he had advocated was public. It was his final decision on the subject, and the saddest conclusion to the prospects of modern Araby.

On February 8, 1963, there was a bloody and successful coup against Abdel Karim Kassem. It is important to describe it thus because the identity of the people who carried it out is subject to question. To the world it looked as if units of the Iraqi army rebelled against the Iraqi strongman in the name of Arab nationalism. It took more than twenty-four hours of bloody street fighting to achieve supremacy over him and his supporters. He was eventually captured, put through a sham trial at the television station, and executed, and his bullet-riddled body was shown on Iraqi TV to convince his followers to cease resistance. Even by gruesome Iraqi standards it was a hideous performance. What was to follow, though, was worse. Members of the Iraqi National Guard, a paramilitary formation created by the anti-Kassem forces, took the law into their hands and began a campaign to eliminate Kassem's followers, supposedly Communists and fellow travelers who had treated Arab nationalists badly. The first to go was air force commander Colonel Jallal Awkati, an admitted Communist, who was gunned down in the presence of his young daughter. With his departure a small-time adventurer by the name of Munther Mandawi took over the air force and went to work, bombing Kassem's ministry of defense headquarters into rubble. The whole air force eventually joined the rebels.

To his lasting credit, Kassem refused an offer to help from the Communists to resist and protect him. Hundreds of thousands of Communists and fellow travelers had marched from the poor people's quarters to offer their support. But he decided to avoid a civil war. When Kassem eventually surrendered, he was refused the honor of keeping his military insignia and side arm, handcuffed, and rushed to the TV station. Together with a small number of supporters, he was abused along the way. After a perfunctory trial, he and his followers, his cousin Colonel Fadhil Abbas Mahdawi of the People's Court included, were executed on the spot. It was a shameless performance, except for Kassem's utterly gentlemanly behavior throughout. He accepted the principle of being tried in an open court and refused to answer questions otherwise. He spoke passionately of building housing for the poor, of equipping the army and forming all-Palestinian units to train to fight in their country. He had very little to say about Nasser, he ignored him. Well after his execution, it was discovered that Kassem's salary had been donated to an orphanage and that he had slept on a regular army cot next to his office. Except for his opposition to Nasser there was not a great deal for which to criticize in him.

The charge against Kassem was of conspiring against Arab nationalism and unity, and executing many army officers who supported it and considered Nasser their leader. All this was true. Among those executed were Colonels Nadim Tabakjalli and Rifa'at Haj Sirri, men revered by their troops and indeed committed followers of Nasser. Common knowledge had it that the coup was led by General Ahmad Hassan al-Bakr, a Ba'athist who had also been involved in the 1958 coup, and indeed he was the field commander. However, the rebels called on the pro-Nasser Abdel Salam Aref and made him their leader and president. He was the very same man who had been second to Kassem in the 1958 overthrow of the monarchy and the one who had wanted union with Syria and Iraq in a larger UAR. Abdel Salam Aref was not the cleverest of men, though a believer in Nasser. The rest of the rebels were, like Bakr, Ba'athists, who never managed to get a hold on things until

Saddam Hussein came to power after their second coup in 1968. It looked as if Nasser had exacted his Mosul revenge. Above all, there was reason for him to punish the people who had supported Kassem against Arab unity, the Communists and fellow travelers. The USSR held its breath. Their ally in the international arena was utterly opposed to Communists, and it was Communists who had won Mosul for Kassem by giving him enough popular support to halt the march of Nasser's Arab nationalism. Moreover, with the Communists out of the way, Nasser might finally claim Iraq. But, very much like Kassem, Nasser knew that the Communists represented a large segment of Iraq's population. He couldn't be rid of them without dividing Iraq forever. Like it or not, they had made their point. The Iraqis had rejected his unity scheme. A takeover in Iraq would mean occupying Iraq by force. Nasser refused to do that. He wanted to be summoned to Iraq to run it. Otherwise, Iraq would become a bigger problem for him than Syria had been. He went with his original assessment, giving up the idea of acquiring Iraq and settling for trying to turn it into a tributary country.

Alas, the facts of the February 8, 1963, coup differed from their appearance. It was neither a Nasser coup nor an Arab nationalist one. It was one of the most elaborate CIA operations in the history of the Middle East, and an operation so badly conceived that its results continue to haunt Iraq to this day. The operation was organized and carried out by one William Lakeland, an attaché at the U.S. embassy in Baghdad, a former attaché in Cairo, and a specialist in clandestine operations. He put together a collection of anti-Kassem army officers, elements of the Ba'ath Party in Iraq, fellow Ba'athists in Syria, and an assortment of people who genuinely feared a Communist takeover of the country. Their diversity did not diminish their determination to eradicate the Communist threat to Iraq.

Lists of Kassem supporters to be executed were prepared well beforehand, and even featured some who had resigned from their Communist Party positions and were no longer members. The lists were given to the Ba'athist thugs of the National Guard with the simple order to eliminate them. The leaders who carried out the murder campaign had received the lists from William Lakeland and the CIA. What to do with them was unambiguous. The orders to kill Kassem's supporters were carried out, and the defenseless victims perished individually and in groups. Estimates of the number of people who were murdered vary, but I personally managed to gather a list of over eight hundred people. They were former members of the cabinet, doctors, lawyers, professors, journalists, and ordinary workers. None of them was ever tried. The list, mostly put together by CIA agent William McHale, was followed methodically; the knock on the door, the shine of metal in the dark, then the final shot. Even Nasser al-Hani, a former Iraq ambassador to Lebanon made foreign minister immediately after the Ba'athist coup, was murdered two months later when his loyalties became suspect. In Cairo Nasser made no move to stop the carnage, claiming he had no control over what was happening.

In fact, Nasser had sold out completely. Having conspired unsuccessfully against Kassem for years, he had reached an agreement with the CIA whereby the Agency would rid Iraq of Kassem, and in return, Nasser promised to cede control of Iraq to the CIA. The Egyptian contact with the CIA was one Taha Yahya. Among his duties was recruiting young anti-Communist Iraqis living in Egypt. Among them was a young exile by the name of Saddam Hussein. There is reason to believe that Saddam contributed to the elimination list while in Cairo. Two months later, after he returned to Baghdad, he became a torturer in detainee camps. It was the likes of Saddam who cleansed Iraq from Communism for the CIA. And he did this with the blessing of the head of the Ba'ath Party, Michel Aflaq, and the knowledge of Nasser's intelligence—perhaps Nasser himself. Whether Nasser knew of Saddam matters very little, but that he sold out on Iraq alters his image in the eyes of history.

No other Arab leader in modern Arab history has involved himself in a conspiracy of blood of this magnitude. In 1958 Nasser lost Iraq over Mosul, and he suffered the psychological wounds which went with the loss. In 1963, he willingly gave up Iraq because his ego could not bear continued personal defeat by Kassem. Nasser's loathing of bloodshed was reduced to an abstraction. There is no evidence that the shedding of Muslim Brotherhood and Communist blood gave him sleepless nights. Both had cooperated with Kassem against him.

With Aref as a figurehead president, everybody expected an eventual Egyptian-Iraqi union. But the Ba'athists, stung by their treatment in Syria and now in control of the new government, were not ready for an immediate merger on Nasser's terms. The party was also split between a right and a left wing, guaranteeing there would be no repeat of the Syrian debacle. Nasser watched what was happening in Baghdad with care and had second thoughts, a reconfirmation of what he had already suspected. However, events were given impetus by another coup in Syria, exactly one month after the Iraqi one and more ideologically inclined. The Syrian Ba'athists' commitment to unity was total, but conditional on Nasser implementing some democratic measures.

The Iraqis began to quarrel soon after their assumption of power. Nasser had no idea which side to support. The Ba'ath wanted control, while Aref, relying on his past reputation and relationship with Nasser, wanted an Arab nationalist movement beholden to Nasser. Both factions began feuding over the spoils, with the Ba'ath insisting on controlling the army under Bakr. The one job refused by members of both sides was that of head of security (Jihaz Hunein). When nobody accepted it, the twenty-six-year-old Saddam claimed it and became the agency's head. The master organizer lost no time in making it the most effective instrument of government. Soon Jihaz Hunein had a branch in every Iraqi town and village, and through those branches controlled the Ba'ath Party, its apparatus, and the rest of Iraq. It was Saddam's first official position, but he would parlay that into directorships of the peasants, workers, and veterans organizations and the directorates of oil workers and the militias. In no time, he controlled more of Iraq than any man alive—including Bakr, a second cousin who had relied on Saddam because of their kinship. In fact, two years after the takeover, Bakr had been reduced to a figurehead and Saddam was Iraq's supremo.

The Iraqi and Syrian branches of the Ba'ath lost no time in establishing contact and deciding to petition Nasser to re-create the UAR. Large delegations from both countries descended on Cairo for that purpose early in March 1963. The negotiations toward forming a new union began on March 14 and lasted for two and a half weeks. There was no plan by any side, no model blueprint or a program. Nasser presided over the proceedings. The Syrian Ba'ath was represented by founders Michel Aflaq and Salah Bitar, who had supported the secession of Syria in 1961. The Iraqi delegation was headed by Ali Saleh Sa'adi, a leftist with very few inhibitions and less method. The record of the unity meetings is available, and it proves, if such were needed, that Nasser was indeed the leader of the Arabs during the 1950s and 1960s. Without doubt he was the leader of the leaders of the Arabs.

Nasser was addressed as "Mr. President" or "Excellency" by

those present, while he called all of them by their first name. Unlike them he had done a great deal of preparatory work, and that meant studying the American federal system and the various experiments in the USSR. He had done his homework; nothing in the constitutional history of these countries escaped him. Furthermore, he had gone into the history of the UAR in detail, mistakes included. Sparing no word or gesture, he berated the Iraqi and Syrian attendees mercilessly, accused them of being phony nationalists, and made fun of their constant change of direction. None of them answered him; none of them dared. They settled for being sheepish and apologetic.

After reducing them to humble followers, he launched into a detailed, well-conceived plan for unity. He favored a federal system which began with a merger of defense and foreign policy. He stipulated a short four-year term for the president and rejected the idea of president for life. All other moves toward unity were to be taken in steps. Legislative councils were to oversee the functions of the state. Everything was to begin between Egypt and Syria, for even the disasters of the past experience had lessons they could learn and apply. Implementation was to be delayed, perhaps for years, with nothing taking place at once. Of course, with Egypt and Syria, and later when Iraq was included, the system was to allow for the necessary representation of peasants and workers. Nasser made a point of including that.

Feigning ignorance, he attacked the connection of some members of the Iraqi Ba'ath with the CIA and mentioned William Lakeland by name. He admitted that he had known him when the latter was an attaché in Egypt, and said that Lakeland was most untrustworthy. At one point, staring directly at the Iraqis, he accused them of being an American creation, the offspring of an ill-conceived Arab empire idea developed by Lakeland and his colleagues. That the CIA had given the new Iraqi regime light arms to fight the Kurds in return for the Ba'athists giving the CIA modern Russian tanks and planes to study was something he knew all about. Nasser distinguished between the types of cooperation he had had with the Americans and the total surrender to the CIA by the Iraqis. One thing was clear: Nasser no longer believed in the idea of an Arab empire. He didn't even believe in a union that would survive the internal stresses of regionalism. He now believed that Britain had succeeded in dividing the Arab world and that overcoming these divisions had become impossible.

Bitterly he changed subjects and spoke of the political past of the UAR and other attempts at unity. He spoke of the humiliation of being ejected from Syria and made clear that nothing similar would ever be allowed to happen again. Gamal Abdel Nasser was hardly a toy to be used and discarded by the empty intellectuals of Arab unity. He was a teacher lecturing his students, above all educating Ba'ath leader Aflaq in the meaning of unity and its responsibilities. Speaking from notes for hours, he left them no room to protest. He preempted all their arguments. Essentially, the speech was a simple statement: *I, Gamal Abdel Nasser, am the leader of the Arabs and without me you are nothing. Either take what I have to offer you or leave and never return.*

It was not a show or a testimony for the history books. He made no objection to the new flag of the proposed federation carrying three stars for the three countries, but he stubbornly refused to agree to anything but what was done slowly, methodically, what was guaranteed to succeed and so protect him against future humiliations. But had he given up on Arab unity? Was he willing to admit it? Had he reached the point of admitting what he had accepted after 1958, that Arab unity was impossible to achieve? Moreover, did he even believe in the unity of purpose he so promoted? His handling of the whole unity negotiations suggests that he had given up at least publicly. He agreed to many minor points and to meet with the Syrians and Iraqis again, but he never did. Things were left hanging. There was no follow-up. There was a new Nasser who still towered over other Arab leaders, but belief in the common Arab cause, his cause, had evaporated. He continued to fight in Yemen to keep the Saudis at bay, helped African independence movements, even got special satisfaction out of Kennedy winning his debate with Nixon, but something had gone missing. He was not a dreamer anymore. Mosul and Syria's defection had produced a bitter man.

According to Heikal, Hammroush, and others, Nasser thought of oil as a curse rather than a blessing. He believed that it divided the Arabs between rich and poor and increased the West's interest in the region. He had grown tired of Egypt's intellectuals and their demands for democracy—he even imprisoned the writer Louis Awad for protesting too much. Though his relations with Kennedy were good, he had also given up on reaching a lasting détente with America. The constant attempts by the Muslim Brotherhood to kill him had taken their toll, and he depended on the security people more than he wanted. In addition, Syria, the new PLO, Jordan, and others were criticizing him for not leading the Arabs against Israel. His health deteriorated badly; in particular, he suffered from arteriosclerosis's painful effects. Home with Tahiya was bliss, but nothing else was working. Even Amer was causing him trouble. What had elevated Nasser to his unassailable position, the unique qualities of leadership he possessed, drove him further away from the people. He could not deliver on his explicit and implicit promises to them. Distancing himself from the people was as painful as realizing Arab nationalism was not attainable.

Relief from the results of Syria's defection and not being able to stop the war in Yemen came from unexpected sources. The war in Yemen was going mostly badly, and he resorted to using chemical weapons and so destroyed his international image. The Palestinian problem reappeared in a way he could not ignore. Late in 1963, the Israelis began to divert the rivers of the Jordan to irrigate the Negev. King Hussein of Jordan, Nasser's on and off enemy and the man who "confused him,"[16] called on Nasser to take military moves to stop Israel. There was no way out of this for Nasser except to call a meeting of heads of states of the Arab League. He had hoped for an American intercession, but Kennedy's murder in November 1963 put an end to that. According to his youngest son, Hakim Abdel, Kennedy's death was the one thing that drove Nasser into deep depression. "For days he looked as if he was about to mope."[17] Nevertheless, the Arab League meeting took place in January 1964, after the pro-Zionist Lyndon Johnson, who was dismissive of the Arabs and their problems, had become president.

As had happened constantly since the Suez Crisis, once again Nasser was forced to change direction and devote his time to regional problems. On occasion for a month or two, the National Action Pact, the Arab Socialist Union, the National Assembly, imposing civilian control on Amer, creating a new Revolutionary Command Council, creating a working judicial system, and even creating a presidential council instead of an office of the president were all set aside while Nasser reentered the regional arena to compete with Lyndon Johnson. He borrowed ideas from Tito and the USSR, strengthened the land reform program, created co-ops, and improvised constantly, but he made no progress. Beyond completing the first stage of the Aswan High Dam with a lot of fanfare in which the USSR participated, there was nothing new. The domestic situation was bad. Ali Sabri was made prime minister, but Amer never stopped scheming and trying to circumvent his chief competitor, the pro-American Zakkaria Mohieddine, who replaced Sabri as prime minister. But even that was not enough for Johnson. The death of Kennedy devastated U.S.-Egyptian relations. The good atmosphere and attempts at bridge building were no more; Lyndon Baines Johnson viewed Nasser with disdain, and Nasser detested him.

Never free to concentrate on Egypt after the Suez Crisis, Nasser became once again the prisoner of his own declared ambitions. No attention was paid by adversaries to his change of direction, the new adoption of unity of purpose. He was down, and the United States wanted him there. Yemen, Islamic movements, Saudi Arabia, and Iran were used against him. But more injurious was the use of fellow Arabs who accused him of forsaking the Arab dream. In a way he knew they were right and wanted out, but there was no way for him to get out and continue to be Nasser. It was in the 1963–65 period that Gamal Abdel Nasser became a shadow of his old self. The onetime leader of the Arabs who had accepted the possibility of the battle for Arab unity became aware that he was losing the Arab street. The people were no longer responding to his word, but his word was all he had. He spoke, spoke and promised, but there was no glitter.

From 1962 to 1967, Nasser concentrated on his Soviet-style five-year plan. Early on he received support from Kennedy and his representative, Dr. Edward Mason. Things went well, with increases in industrial and agricultural production. Politically he appointed Abdel Latif Boghdadi and Ahmad Hussein vice presidents to balance Amer's army presence. Then he reverted to the idea of a presidential council with him as its chief. Here he confronted Amer, who, as first vice president, demanded veto powers. Nasser stood his ground, made himself commander in chief of the army, and relegated Amer to second in command. There was something akin to a revolt by young officers who supported Amer, but it was put down. In 1962 when Boghdadi resigned in protest over Nasser's adoption of socialist schemes, other members of the original RCC went further and objected to Nasser's view that a "second revolution" was needed.

But while Nasser turned his attention to Egypt, Amer continued to conspire against him. Amer did not want to replace Nasser, but he wanted to be his equal through control of the army. Instead of building the army, Amer devoted himself to building a state within a state based on a vicious security apparatus. It operated independently, and it looked as if Nasser was completely out of touch. The government, nominally, was still for the people, but it was not by the people. The people who ran things were Amer and, with the security system under him, Salah Nasr. The Committee for the Liquidation of Feudalism, operating under Amer, opened the door for widespread corruption. Hashish parties became the order of the day, along with having affairs with film stars. When Nasser finally became aware of these things it was too late. The regional problems were converging on him and he had no one to help him. In the critical years of 1964 and 1965 Nasser stood alone. Only his past standing saved him and Egypt from total collapse.

# 8

# Leader of the Arabs

Nasser never managed to distance himself from the Palestinian problem and concentrate on Egypt's internal problems with the reforms that he wanted to implement. One could say that the Palestinian problem imposed itself on him. Having to deal with it was part of being the leader of the Arabs. Beginning with the arms deal with Czechoslovakia, the nationalization of the Suez Canal, and the 1956 tripartite attack on Egypt and its consequences, the undisputed leader of the Arabs was Gamal Abdel Nasser. But well before Nasser had appeared on the scene, all the way back to the 1920s, Arab leadership had concentrated on Palestine. In the late 1950s and the 1960s even Nasser's enemies accepted his primary position and held him responsible for the confrontation with Israel. Although all Arab governments competed for the soul of the Palestinians, accepting him as the overall leader was an indirect admission of his standing with the Arab people and Egypt's leadership of the Arab world.

Nonetheless, Syria, the Palestine Liberation Organization (PLO), Saudi Arabia, and even Iraq reserved the right to act independently and expected Nasser to deal with the consequences of their actions. This was particularly true of the Syrians and the PLO, the two entities which shared common borders with Israel—the

Syrians directly, and the PLO through using Syria, Lebanon, and Jordan. The rest of the Arab governments had their own excuses for doing little against Israel except in the diplomatic field and chose to sit on the sidelines. To maintain his position of leadership, Nasser had no option but to accept the responsibility of being the leader of a divided house, an extension of his belief that "imperialism divided the Arabs."

In January 1964, the Arab League, responding to a call from Nasser, held its first summit conference in Cairo. The purpose of this meeting of heads of state was to produce a common Arab position against Israel's plans to divert the waters of the Jordan River to irrigate the Negev. Syria and the PLO, Yasser Arafat's Fatah organization and the largest of the Palestinian paramilitary groupings, were reacting to the Israeli diversion efforts in ways that could lead to war. The Syrians skirmished with the Israelis on a regular basis, and Fatah—still independent, and not a member of the PLO—having moved out of Kuwait and headquartered in Damascus in 1961, followed a policy of infiltrating Israel and attacking Israeli installations. The Israelis, unfazed, responded disproportionately; occasionally they used their air force against the Syrian army, and once they attacked and destroyed a minor Syrian water-diversion scheme, threatening an all-out war.

Nasser, aware that he was expected to lead any confrontation with Israel and doing everything not to be trapped into a war for which he was not prepared, decided to hold a summit meeting to share the responsibility with the other Arab states. He was reorganizing his armed forces, but the Egyptian army was no match for the Israelis, and Nasser knew it. His attempts to discourage the Syrians and Fatah from provoking the Israelis went as far as admitting that he had no plan to liberate Palestine. Rather than dwell on his army's lack of readiness—and the armies of his critics were no better—he attributed the whole disastrous situation to the lack of unity among the Arabs.[1] But Syria and the Palestinians refused to heed his warnings. So adamant were the Fatah people in their confrontational policies that they were suspected of acting on behalf of one of the Arab governments with an interest in undermining Nasser, in this case the Syrian or Kuwaiti governments. Whether Fatah had an explicit alliance with the Arab governments remains unknown to this day, but there was an anti-Nasser unity of purpose.

The summit produced declarations that promised "all methods" would be used to intercept Israel's water-diversion plans. But what precisely the Arabs might do if Israel continued with its attempt to divert most of the water from the Jordan, and from smaller rivers in the no-man's-land between Israel and Syria, was never explained. In fact, the only concrete result of the summit was the decision to create an entity to represent the Palestinians. The Arab Higher Committee, the mufti's organization that had purported to do this, had ceased to function after 1956. In May 1964, the decisions made in Cairo were implemented, and the PLO, without Fatah's participation, was confirmed by the Arab States as an umbrella organization of Palestinian political groupings at a conference held in the Ambassador Hotel in Jerusalem. Both the PLO and Fatah put liberating Palestine on top of their agenda, a challenge to Nasser. He had put unity among the Arabs as his first aim.

The PLO was the brainchild of Nasser and the strongest indication yet that he was willing to cede or share his responsibility and leadership position to avoid a war with Israel. Even Amer's inflated estimates of the strength of the Egyptian army failed to convince him that his armed forces were a match for the Israelis. Nasser's support for the Palestinian entity was aimed at satisfying the Palestinians' wish for a voice in Arab councils while keeping them under control.[2] The way Nasser controlled the Palestinians in Gaza, his refusal to allow them to stage raids against Israel from areas under Egyptian administration, was a model for what he wanted, and further proof that he did not want confrontation with Israel. Occasional raiding parties managed to infiltrate Israel, but he refused to allow the Palestinians in Gaza to establish military training camps except under strict Egyptian control. This policy of limiting the Palestinians' ability to infiltrate Israel had been adopted by him from the beginning and was what led Arafat and a handful of Palestinian comrades to leave Egypt to create Fatah and begin operating out of Kuwait in 1958.

Nasser nominated Ahmad Shukeiri as the PLO's first chairman. The rest of the Arab governments accepted Nasser's nominee because they too were reluctant to grant the Palestinians more than a token symbol of independence. This is how and why Ahmad Shukeiri, a brainless braggart who had been a diplomat for hire, became head of the PLO. Fatah, whose eventual chairman, Yasser Arafat, was imprisoned by Nasser in 1954 for being a member or an associate of the Muslim Brotherhood, refused to join the PLO. Operating out of Damascus after about five years in

Kuwait, and working closely with the Syrian government, Fatah rejected any control of the Palestinians by fellow Arabs. Not only did the Fatah leadership insist on maintaining its independence and freedom of action; many of its leaders believed that if armed and supported, the Palestinians could defeat the Israelis. They believed that "violence is the only way" and that "liberating Palestine can only come through the barrel of a gun."[3] Here it must be recalled that Arafat and his comrades were old-fashioned unworldly Arabs who probably believed what they preached. The list of Fatah's original founders doesn't contain the name of anyone sophisticated enough to understand that conquering Israel was beyond their capabilities.

So the PLO was a child of the Arab establishment and not a revolutionary organization, and Fatah operated in a similar fashion, depending on Arab financial support for survival. Thus reliant on Arab governments, the two competing Palestinian entities had to observe certain rules and restrictions. Nevertheless, Fatah maintained an independent stance toward Nasser and the Arab Nationalist Movement (ANM), the established claimants to the leadership of the Palestinian cause. While the world thought of Nasser as the staunchest anti-Israeli Arab leader, Fatah operated on the basis that he was not to be trusted, that he had already made up his mind to make peace with Israel. The mufti was suspected by the pan-Arabists of influencing the Fatah attitude toward Nasser and of using Fatah to give the Palestinians the right to determine their own future.

The other Arab governments that supported the creation of the PLO had no problem backing Fatah. In fact, a divided Palestinian camp was easier to control, and the financial dependency of Fatah and the PLO made the organizations easier to handle. Fatah—whose Arabic acronym in reverse, *Harakat Tahrir Falastin*, means "conquest" or "new dawn"—stood for the same basic ideas as the PLO, although Fatah and its leaders, mostly right-wing former members of the Muslim Brotherhood, followed a line closer to that of the conservative Arab states. Arafat and the other leaders of Fatah used money they received to gain greater support among the Palestinians, now grown weary of the policies of the rest of the Arabs, the ineffective Arab League in particular.

Fatah's determination not to be controlled by a Nasserite Egypt or through the Arab League was a direct challenge to Nasser's leadership of the Arabs. Though he knew this, Nasser dismissed

Fatah's ability to challenge the status quo. But the old conflict between advocates of the Palestinians assuming responsibility for their own affairs and the rest of the Arabs, who wanted to control them, now became a bigger issue. Coming only a few years after his break with the mufti and his destructive quarrel with Kassem, the dispute found Nasser in the uncomfortable position of opposing armed action against Israel. In contrast, Kassem had actually trained and supported special Palestinian military units, the Palestine Liberation Army, before his overthrow, and had even proposed the formation of a Palestinian government in exile. The Syrians acted militantly on their own. The conservative Arab governments, Jordan and Saudi Arabia in particular, were having their own problems with Nasser. In other words, despite supporting the Nasser-inspired creation of the PLO, everybody opposed Nasser.

Afraid that military training for the Palestinians would lead to trouble, Nasser refused to budge. He thought that a trained Palestinian force would inevitably want to do something that would provoke Israel. But Fatah did not need him, for it had direct contacts with Kuwait, Saudi Arabia, and other oil-producing countries. And in addition to receiving financial support from the Arab countries, it collected money from the Palestinians working there. The financial support it received gave it independence from regional political movements and made it dependent on the traditional regimes for future support. As far back as 1959 Fatah had published the weekly *Phillistunana* (Our Palestine) and distributed it to Palestinians throughout the Middle East. Fatah represented a greater challenge to Nasser than he realized, and its establishment of military training camps in the West Bank and Gaza, its recruitment, and its other programs added to its luster.

Moreover, Fatah succeeded in exaggerating the results of its infiltration campaign. This broadened its popular base. The Palestinians were hungry for anything resembling action against Israel. It received backing from most Palestinians at the expense of the pro-Nasser movements such as the ANM and other, Damascus-based Palestinian groupings. Shortly after the creation of the PLO, Fatah became so popular that the pro-Nasser organizations, the ANM included, had no choice but to adopt positions and methods similar to the ones promoted by Fatah.[4] After considerable hesitation the pro-Nasser ANM also began sending infiltrators into Israel. Nasser's position against infiltration was left without Palestinian support. The presence of fifty thousand Egyptian troops in

Yemen precluded a simultaneous challenge to Israel. Nor did the Saudis, Nasser's opponents in the Yemen war, offer him a way out of the conflict. The Saudis refused to consider the negative effects their anti-Nasser position had on the Arab camp. Their concern was their backyard, Yemen, and they could see that Nasser was hemorrhaging. That suited them. (However, attempts to find a solution to the war in Yemen never stopped, and there were agreements and truces, especially in 1965 with the Taif and Jidda agreements and the Haradah conference.)

The May 1964 Jerusalem meeting to promote the PLO confirmed the election of Ahmad Shukeiri as chairman, and this was accompanied by the usual rhetoric. Fatah was represented at the Jerusalem meeting by Abu Jihad, one of its founders and eventually Arafat's second in command. But Fatah limited itself to the role of an observer and did not participate in the discussions or accept the PLO as the sole representative of the Palestinians. In fact, its refusal to abide by the decisions of the PLO was made clear, and it made a great deal out of its intention to keep up the pressure on Israel, regardless of the consequences. Nor was Fatah impressed by the creation of a parliamentary body, the Palestine National Council, or the greater support for the Palestine Liberation Army. In fact, Fatah attacked Nasser indirectly by heaping scorn on Shukeiri and his antiquated ways. The Arafat group went further than denying PLO hegemony: Fatah actively sought to undermine the new entity through its contacts with King Faisal of Saudi Arabia. The then Saudi minister of oil, Ahmad Zakki Yamani, had helped make this link, and Yamani himself became the middleman between Fatah and the Saudi government.[5] A strong relationship with Saudi Arabia suited both sides. Combined with the quagmire in Yemen, this automatically diminished Nasser's ability to afford the PLO greater backing and created strains on the Egyptian economy.

The Fatah challenge to Nasser over who was in charge of the Palestinian problem was considerably more serious than he realized, and the timing of this challenge guaranteed it support from other Arab countries. Beyond the obvious differences on strategy, a small circle of Palestinians that included the mufti and Yasser Arafat believed that Nasser was ready to negotiate a peace agreement with Israel.[6] Supposedly he had been converted to this position by UN secretary-general Dag Hammarskjöld, who had the distinction of seeing Nasser more times than any other world leader. Whether there was a secret understanding between Nasser and Hammarskjöld to make peace has never been established. Nowadays many people in the Arab world and many experts on Arab affairs believe that Sadat's Camp David peace agreement with Israel began with a Nasser-Hammarskjöld secret agreement. According to those who believe that such an agreement existed, Sadat had known about the secret Nasser position, and Sadat's efforts were nothing more than a continuation of what Nasser had started.

In fact, the test of what the Arabs should do regarding Israel had reached a climax in March 1965, when Tunisian president Habib Bourguiba called on the Arabs to bring the conflict to an end in accordance with the original UN resolutions. Bourguiba made this proposal on several occasions. The most memorable was in 1965 when he was visiting Jordan. Violent demonstrations against Bourguiba broke out throughout the Arab world, and the Tunisian president was accused of treason. Whatever plans Nasser had to settle the Palestinian problem, if they indeed existed, came to a sudden end. The reaction to Bourguiba's proposal meant that he could not negotiate peace with Israel and survive. Even in Egypt the Muslim Brotherhood managed to stage huge demonstrations against any peace overtures. Nasser was trapped. Unlike Sadat, he had a constituency to respond to. His followers expected militancy from him, and he was not ready or willing to undertake any unpopular move toward Israel and alienate most of the Arabs. Unlike Nasser, Sadat never captured the imagination of the Arabs. In making peace with Israel, he had no popular following and nothing to lose.

Meanwhile, though Israel knew that Nasser had no connection with what the Syrians and PLO were doing, the Israelis still thought of him and his Arab nationalism as a bigger danger to them than the rest of the Arabs combined. Hemmed into this untenable position by both sides, Nasser decided to freeze his position vis-à-vis Israel, which meant maintaining a state of inaction, including refusing to allow the Palestinians to conduct raids against Israel from the Egyptian-controlled Gaza Strip. He opted for maintaining the status quo while hoping that the Israelis would avoid overreacting to Syria's and Fatah's activities and dragging the whole Middle East into another war. Strangely, Nasser often depended on the good behavior of his enemies to save him. The earliest example of this dependence was his belief that Britain would never resort to war over Suez.

The PLO under Shukeiri was feckless and corrupt and more decorative than combative. It created the Palestine Liberation Army and was successful in publicizing the fact and making documentary films about it, but did little else. Fatah had chosen to go its own way, and the ANM had followed suit while advocating a truly revolutionary line that called for the overthrow of the Arab governments as a first step toward total war against Israel; but the Shukeiri organization had no clear-cut policy of its own. Considerable vagueness surrounded its position on harassing the Israelis. In fact, its existence was symbolic. The Palestinians were allowed to speak for themselves (under Arab supervision), but the PLO posed no threat to Israel. Even its one achievement was questionable: the Palestine Liberation Army was small and of dubious quality.

Nor were the PLO and Fatah anti-West. The ANM was, but the PLO's and Fatah's dependence on the oil-rich countries meant that they were beholden to their pro-West sponsors. Fatah, dependent on pro-West governments for funds and the use of their territory, was nationalist rather than a revolutionary movement. Kuwait would not have backed a revolutionary or radical movement. Tellingly, it refrained from attacking Western interests anywhere in the Arab world at a time when it could have. With time, Arafat and Shukeiri devoted most of their efforts toward getting Arab financial support. The truly anti-West organization was the ANM—which, unlike Fatah, was not allowed to operate in most Arab countries. That was understandable considering the call of its leader, George Habbash, for the overthrow of the pro-West Arab governments. Simultaneously Nasser thought that his alliance with the ANM would protect him against accusations of being soft toward Israel. His was a totally contradictory Arab position.

In the early 1960s, there was no viable threat to Israel. Nasser was preoccupied with Yemen, his Vietnam, and no danger to Israel could exist without Egypt. The Kennedy administration had sympathized with the Nasser position, and the American president had tried his utmost to help Nasser extricate himself from Yemen. Kennedy believed that Nasser was more dangerous when under pressure. Kennedy's recognition of republican Yemen soon after the monarchy was overthrown amounted to a notice that America would support the forward-looking regimes in the region. For three years, Kennedy and Nasser conducted a personal correspondence in which they discussed everything in the Middle East.[7] The Nasser-Kennedy correspondence signaled an American interest in finding a solution for the problems of the Middle East, including the Arab-Israeli conflict. Of course, it also exposed the difficulty of achieving this. Their letters were open and frank, so much so that it caused consternation among such traditionally pro-West, anti-Nasser Arabs as Lebanese president Camille Chamoun, King Hussein of Jordan, and King Faisal of Saudi Arabia. In addition, Nasser himself accepted the exchange of letters as a healthy development that promised to give him what he had always wanted, an understanding with the United States on the fate of the Arab world. Such an understanding would have had to involve a Nasser-America alliance, and Nasser took to revealing the contents of some of the letters selectively. This is why Nasser's son Hakim says that Kennedy's death was the one occasion that saddened his father for weeks.

The friendly, or semifriendly, relations with Egypt which existed under Kennedy came to an end under Johnson. The new American administration reversed course and saw Nasser as a threat to U.S. regional interests. Furthermore, Johnson resented Nasser's support for the anti-American Congolese rebels and his opposition to the American position on Vietnam. As usual, but wrongly, Nasser was in the habit of trying to react to every American move. By 1966 Nasser's reactions had taken on a strident anti-American tone. Of course, this did nothing to change America's Middle East policy, but it pleased the USSR, another country whose relations with the United States were hitting rock bottom.

In the Middle East, the Fatah and Syrian skirmishing and infiltrating efforts were small and mostly unsuccessful. The Fatah political program, naive and superficial, called for the establishment of a multiethnic state of Muslims, Jews, and Christians in Palestine, something the Israelis readily rejected. In 1963, King Hussein, then in control of the West Bank, started having secret meetings with Israeli diplomats to keep anti-Israeli activity from the West Bank under control.[8] Against King Hussein's wishes, Fatah was using Jordan to infiltrate Israel, and the Jordanian monarch was trying to control the situation and avoid Israeli retaliation. Of course, Hussein transferred the blame to Nasser whenever things went wrong, and accused Nasser of encouraging the infiltrators.

Now Heikal claims that Nasser failed to condemn Hussein over his contacts with Israel for a simple reason: Nasser didn't know about them. This is most unlikely; the meetings were frequent and known to many people, including some pro-Nasser officers of the Jordanian army who would certainly have reported them to the Egyptian government. In all likelihood, Nasser did not want to make his already uneasy relationship with Hussein worse, and feared that Israel might react to efforts to censure Hussein by occupying the West Bank. Khalid al-Hassan, one of the founders of Fatah, admits that his organization tried to entangle "the Arab armies in a war with Israel." Indeed this was central to Fatah's policy; their wish to control Palestinian affairs was accompanied by efforts to keep Arab governments involved.[9] In addition, Kamal Adham, King Hussein's brother-in-law and head of Saudi security and intelligence, was busy creating an Islamic bloc against Nasser's Arab nationalism, what Nuri Said of Iraq had wanted to do years before.

Once again the Saudis had America's, Fatah's, and the PLO's full support. King Hussein was also participating in American-backed anti-Nasser activity, which included allowing the Muslim Brotherhood to use Jordan as a base for its activities against the Egyptian leader. In Syria, the anti-Nasser efforts were carried out directly by the CIA. According to senior CIA operative William Crane Eveland, the agency funded anti-Nasser efforts in Syria and Lebanon at a cost of over $100 million.[10] Unlike the State Department, the CIA could change direction without having to explain itself or offer justification. Its earliest efforts against Nasser began in the 1950s, when it used Aramco's Government Relations Department to create Islamic cells in eastern Saudi Arabia.[11] Incredibly, the CIA never tried to undermine him through character assassination; they too found that the man had no vices.[12] Even faraway Morocco was opposing Nasser and deporting Egyptian teachers who followed his Arab nationalist line. Newly independent Algeria, tired after years of civil war, had no stomach for combat. Lyndon Johnson was in the White House, and his relations with Nasser were so bad that he rejected all attempts by the Egyptian president to mend them. The United States eventually cut off aid to Egypt in 1965. Soon after, the USSR stepped in and offered to replace the wheat America used to give Egypt. The goodwill of the Kennedy years was now history. By the time 1966 arrived, U.S.-Egyptian relations had turned into a war of words, and Nasser's strident position was enough for Johnson to try to pay him back.

Nasser stood alone; Egypt had a serious financial crisis, wanted no confrontation with anybody, and was desperate to settle the Yemeni war. Nasser's standing with the Arab people was secure, but, having decided that popular support did not afford him enough strength against his Arab enemies, he stopped using his effective radio broadcasts to undermine them. In fact, the situation was now the reverse; with America's help Faisal of Saudi Arabia was leading an Islamic anti-Nasser coalition.[13] He had already tried to chip at the popularity of Nasser's Arab nationalism through the creation of a World Muslim League. The league was so important that its secretary-general, Mohamed Sabbah, was a minister in the Saudi cabinet. Pakistani troops were invited to Saudi Arabia to help protect the oil fields. Clearly Nasser was now in conflict with Israel, America, and Islam at the same time.

Looking back, it appears as if the Johnson years were the golden era of American support for Islamic movements. Until then the United States had afforded them some intermittent support. Under Johnson, the arrangement was formalized, and the support the Islamists received was predetermined and aimed at specific targets or situations. Indeed the Johnson administration had no limit on support for this short-sighted policy and refused the counsel of those who saw the Islamic threat lurking behind it.

Meanwhile the rest of the Arab countries showed no inclination to do anything about Palestine beyond providing financial support to the PLO and Fatah. The Iraqis did very little to help the Palestinians. They offered military training to a few hundred Palestinians and hid behind geography, the fact that Iraq had no common border with Israel. But even this limited help was short-lived—they stopped training the Palestinians when the latter refused to take orders from them. The Saudis and others had no armies to speak of and were satisfied with the PLO's assuming responsibility for the Arab-Israeli conflict. Each Arab country had its own reasons for distancing itself from the problem of Palestine. The implication of all this was obvious. By ceding the fate of the Palestinians to the PLO, the Arab countries were absolving themselves of this responsibility. It was at this point that the conflict became a Palestinian-Israeli affair rather than an Arab-Israeli one.

For some Palestinians, Arafat included, this was a way of creating a distinct Palestinian identity and the positions of leadership which accompanied it. For Nasser, the narrowing of the struggle into one between Palestinians and Israelis was a major setback which strengthened his belief that Arab unity was unattainable. What better example of Arab disunity than having the stricken Palestinians opt for being Palestinian rather than Arab? To Nasser, Israel was safe without a united Arab front. Nasser was bitter because the Palestinians were knowingly contributing to the failure of Arab nationalism and supporting Faisal at a time when he was creating the Islamic alliance to undermine Nasser. Considering that two members of the alliance, Iran and Turkey, had good relations with Israel, it is logical to conclude that Fatah and Arafat were placing their particular interests ahead of Palestinian interests. This was not the first time that Arafat, taking a leaf out of the mufti's book, had done that. Nothing that would infringe on his leadership position was ever acceptable. He wanted a state where he would be president. The size, structure, or nature of the state didn't matter to him. Nasser watched this with dismay. He began looking for a way out of his problems with his fellow Arabs.

After Kennedy there was a lack of understanding by America of Nasser's position and his comparative moderation. Johnson had neither the background nor the inclination to accept Nasser as the leader of the Arabs. Having been leader of the Senate, Johnson was aware of the strength of the pro-Israel lobby, and he manifested no desire to do anything but accommodate it. The friendly correspondence which marked the Nasser-Kennedy relationship would have been alien to Johnson. This shift showed in CIA activity in the whole Arab world. The Agency went as far as supporting the Syrian wing of the Ba'ath Party, which opposed the Egyptian-Iraqi-Syrian unity schemes.[14] The Agency cooperated with all the intelligence departments of the countries which opposed Nasser. Among others, the already mentioned Kamal Adham had total American support. In Jordan, the CIA supported Brigadier Radi Abdallah, the military aide to King Hussein. Jordanian intelligence provided the Israeli intelligence agency Mossad with a window on Arab politics. According to Mohamed Heikal, the Agency was involved in the breakup of the UAR, and its efforts in support of the breakup cost $12 million.[15]

All Nasser had was Arab popular support. His relationship with the USSR had been tarnished by his anti-Communism, and his position as one of the leaders of the nonaligned world meant very little and cost Egypt a lot of money. Not only did hundreds of African students attend Egyptian universities at the expense of Egypt, Radio Cairo spent more hours preaching politics to the Africans than did the Voice of America. Naturally, Nasser's propaganda machine devoted more time broadcasting to the Arab people than was normal. In many places Nasser was confronting ad hoc alliances of conservative Arab regimes, Islamic fundamentalists, Israel, the United States, and the Communists at the same time. This was certainly true of his efforts in Nigeria and other West African countries. The odds were stacked against him, and how he expected to win against them is baffling.

Battling against superior odds marked the period from 1961 and the breakup of the UAR to the end of his life, even after the 1967 war with Israel. All three areas outside Egypt in which he was involved became battlegrounds. The Arab countries, sponsored by the West—Saudi Arabia, Jordan, and the rest—were trying to undermine him, most seriously by their accusation that he was hiding behind UNEF, the UN force which was placed on the Egyptian side of the border with Israel. The Saudis led the way. But the Jordanians were not far behind; operating under the supervision of a CIA propaganda specialist by the name of John Fistere, they taunted him constantly. He was accused of being a "paper tiger," a braggart hiding behind a UN shield. The Jordanians also invented story after story of Nasser conspiring to kill King Hussein by trying to poison him, shoot down his plane, or replace his nose drops with acid. The press in the West accepted these fabrications at face value. The obvious fact that Nasser had a considerable following in the Jordanian army and could have organized an anti-Hussein coup without much difficulty was ignored. To the American, British, and European publics, and members of the U.S. Congress, Nasser was—despite considerable evidence that an understanding with the West was uppermost on his mind—the Saddam Hussein of his day. Newspapers called him an upstart and accused him of being a front for the USSR. Lady Eden's "that Egyptian" was recalled, as was French premier Guy Mollet's comparison to Hitler.[16] And as with Saddam, the royalist regimes used the Nasser threat to enhance their standing with the West. Nasser's shortcomings were exaggerated, while those of the Saudi and Jordanian regimes were totally overlooked.

Seasoned Middle East observers realized the danger inherent

in supporting militant Islamic groups, but nobody was willing to accept their point of view. King Faisal's use of Yemen to weaken Nasser was obvious, but here too all the blame was directed at Nasser. The criticism of Nasser's acceptance of UNEF was unqualified, even though UNEF's removal would have led to war. In the West his relationship with the United States under Johnson had deteriorated badly, and members of Congress and others continued to call for punishing Nasser for having good relations with the Soviet bloc. Even in Europe most countries opposed him and wished for a replacement. His Communist friends in the Eastern Bloc were cool toward him because they thought he was essentially pro-West and pro-United States. His relations with them depended on their willingness to supply him with arms. They resented the way he treated the local Communists. The USSR never forgave him for siding with the United States in its efforts to overthrow the relatively pro-Soviet regime in Iraq, and was aware of his correspondence with Kennedy and of the imprisonment of thousands of Communists in Syria and Egypt—not to speak of their elimination in Iraq. Internationally, the only support he had was from his friend Tito of Yugoslavia, and that was minor in terms of its effectiveness, since Tito had little to offer beyond advice. In 1964, Nasser—still committed to resisting the interference of outside powers in the Middle East—managed to hold the second nonaligned-nations conference in Cairo. It was an empty gesture which produced nothing, an attempt to replicate Bandung and the glory days of positive neutralism.

Aware of his isolation and inability to solve any of the major problems facing him, Nasser focused on implementing some internal reforms. According to his comrade Abdel Latif Boghdadi, Nasser's new reform program was modeled after the USSR. After years of resistance to adopting the ways of outsiders, he had no option but to try to copy another tired system. Landowners were limited to fifty acres instead of one hundred, and people with high incomes had to pay a special tax. This began with people earning ten thousand Egyptian pounds, a low amount even by Egyptian standards. Belatedly, he began to worry about Amer's inability to train and modernize the army, and the state within a state which Amer had created. Aided by Salah Nasr, the head of security, the field marshal had turned the army and security apparatus into a separate fiefdom loyal to him personally and not to Nasser or the state. Army and security officers were controlled by Amer and

Nasr through corrupt ways, and some were blackmailed into anti-Nasser positions. The Amer-Nasr clique stopped at nothing, not even involvement in the drug trade.[17]

Nasser was the last to know that Egypt had become two countries; the one known to the outside world, which he represented, and another, utterly unwholesome one under Amer and his cronies. Beyond representing a betrayal of Nasser, Amer's ambition denied Nasser the benefit of knowing about developments within the country and the army. Comrades from 1952 and before still thought the relationship between the two men was solid, so they refrained from telling Nasser of many of the things they knew. Most Egyptians, however, did hear about the Amer clique's raucous parties, hashish smoking, and forcing themselves on the starlets of the Egyptian cinema.

As unbelievable as it seems, the world of parties and clubs in which Amer lived was unknown to Nasser. His attachment to his family produced an unworldly man who knew nothing of the fun life Amer led. To Egyptian diplomat Tahseen Beshir, the Middle East is unlikely to produce his equal in "cleanliness" for a long time. Beshir tells how Nasser, when he decided to buy apartments for his two daughters, Huda and Mona, had no idea of the cost of apartments in Cairo. When his aides discovered what he had allocated for this purpose—and it was all he had—they secretly made a collection to augment it and help him. According to Beshir, Nasser never knew of this and he died still thinking that he had at least managed to buy his daughters apartments from his meager savings. Even today, there is something unusual and attractive about the way his sons and daughters live. Unlike the Sadat family, they have no need for official protection, and the sources of the little money they have are easy to identify.

The army officers loyal to Amer, the unsoldierly lot responsible for Egyptian military disasters, even had a group that called itself the Free Officers. Supposedly, they modeled themselves after the original Free Officers. But Amer's Free Officers had no political ambitions beyond considering themselves above the law. They certainly thought very little of military discipline or of training their troops in using the equipment acquired from the USSR. Nasser, isolated and bereft of anyone who would tell him the truth, was the last to know about this.[18] His sensitivity against interference by outsiders in Egyptian affairs stopped the Soviets from telling what they knew through their advisers in Cairo.

When all his worst suspicions, gathered in bits and pieces from his old comrades, proved true, he immediately appointed himself commander in chief of the armed forces and made Amer his deputy. Though it allowed the problem to continue, it was a courageous move. By 1963 the loyalty of many army officers to Amer was so deep that going further than this could have provoked a coup d'état. In fact, this may have been why honest officers chose not to speak against Amer. Beshir explains Nasser's ignorance in terms of Nasser spending all his spare time with his family. Sherrif Hatatta, an Egyptian writer imprisoned by Nasser, agrees. In fact, all the interviewees for this book agree. They explain Amer's success by describing him as a sympathetic person. According to Beshir, "He was loaded with charm."

Without any Arab backers, with his relations with the West in tatters, and with lack of trust between him and the USSR limiting that relationship, Nasser was left with a dangerous internal problem which suited the Amer-Nasr axis. The Amer threat was a problem that he had to face.

Acting against his closest friend pained him, but his remedy was only half of what was required. Amer was too popular with the army to be removed outright or assigned to another position. Nasser had to settle for confirming his primacy over Amer by making himself commander in chief and thus confirming his supremacy as leader of Egypt. His total dependence on Amer to keep him in touch with developments within the country reduced him to a man operating within a vacuum. This occurred at a time when the people were suffering serious economic hardships because of Yemen and Nasser's determination to provide help to nationalist movements in the Middle East and Africa. His efforts to create a democracy through the Arab Socialist Union and the National Assembly were moribund. They were well down on the list of his priorities.

The only truly organized part of the regime was the army, the original central constituency of the regime, which was still under Amer's control. According to Boghdadi, Nasser did once again try to resurrect the Arab Socialist Union and the National Assembly and use them as stepping-stones toward democratic development. He wanted to use them to solidify his popular base, one with which his followers identified. This amounted to an admission that he had failed to reflect the popular support of the people he still commanded. But it was difficult to enliven the two bodies. The Egyptian people lacked conviction in them. He spoke to Boghdadi of administering a "shock" to the people,[19] a wake-up call to convince the Egyptians that a new revolution worth supporting was on the way. His analysis of the situation was sound, but the administering of the needed shock was beyond him.

To spur the people to participate in the government, Nasser imprisoned hundreds of members of the bourgeoisie. But that move didn't work. The Egyptian people remained indifferent, more interested in improving their economic conditions. The majority of them were with him and could have provided a counterweight to the army, but the army was organized and the people were not. To make the people's support into a source of power meant that he had to organize them. He needed organizations able enough to gather them into solid entities. He needed an effective way to speak in their name. To appeal to the people, in 1964 he introduced the National Charter and also a new constitution. This too didn't work. In fact, the only developments of interest to the people were rumors about more Muslim Brotherhood conspiracies to kill him (this was a nonstop activity, and the Brotherhood's Secret Apparatus had actually sentenced him to death), and reports that he had suffered a number of heart attacks. Even turning the economy in a distinctly socialist direction, though it generated much interest by the people, stopped short of affording him a civilian socialist base.

The National Charter called for universal health care, the provision of housing to the poor, the building of vocational schools, providing all of Egypt with clean drinking water, widening the Suez Canal to handle larger tankers, and, as much as possible, keeping a check on the civil service to stop it from inflating and becoming an even larger burden on the state. He went further and began developing an extensive program of family planning despite expected opposition from Al Azhar. Women's rights, expanded in the past, got more of his attention, and for all practical purposes women became equal to men. Clearly he was a man who understood the needs of Egypt and was looking for ways to address them. But the fact that he had not completely given up on his Arab position became clear when he decided to continue to use the Arab Republic as a name for Egypt. To implement these ambitious reforms Nasser needed time. He was elected to another six-year term in early 1965. Of course he was the only candidate for the position; the old ruling pashas were forbidden by law from running for office, and his comrades had been reduced to mere followers.

There was a clarity in the way Nasser faced some domestic problems which was absent from the two other issues which dogged him throughout his political career, the Arab-Israeli problem and his relationship with the Islamic movement. In fact, his real attitude toward these two questions during this period remains somewhat of a mystery to this day. The evidence that he wanted a peaceful solution to the Arab-Israeli problem is considerable: there were no border incidents, he refused to back raids against Israel, and for a while he stopped making fiery anti-Israeli speeches. Even if he had doubts about provoking Israel in the past, they became more apparent during the early 1960s. The accusation that he used the presence of UNEF to justify total inactivity against Israel, hurled against him by other Arabs, was not untrue. Moreover, his use of the Kennedy years to turn his attention to domestic issues encouraged him to continue with most of those reforms. Nasser believed that Hammarskjöld and Kennedy would not allow Israel to take advantage of his inclinations to initiate a massive reform program in Egypt and to devote himself to internal problems.

The complexity of this internal reform pales in comparison with the tangled relationship he had with the Muslim Brotherhood and other Islamic organizations. In this, too, the dichotomy between his personal and political behaviors was considerable. He was an observing Muslim, and following the tenets of his religion came naturally to him. But his opposition to political Islam was rock solid, and from that he never deviated, nor did he consider compromise. He believed that you could not run a moderate state on the basis of the Koran.[20] The relative moderation with which his regime treated political enemies never included its treatment of the members of the Muslim Brotherhood. When it came to political Islam, something in him went into high gear and his inherent inclination toward nonviolence was set aside. As far back as 1957, a small incident involving the Muslim Brotherhood members of a work gang in one of his prisons became a major incident when he ordered the security people to respond with force. The police killed twenty-one prisoners,[21] and Nasser never expressed regret over the handling of the incident.

This was as shocking as the treatment of the Brotherhood's

chief ideologue, Sayyed Qutub. Qutub was imprisoned several times, but that didn't stop him. During one of his prison stays, he wrote the definitive book about the aims of the Islamic movement and its attitude toward Nasser and his secular government. Called *Signs Along the Way,* the book accused Nasser of taking the country into another *Jahiliya,* meaning ignorance, and what the Arabs and Muslims called the pre-Islamic movement. The book was a best-seller and was reprinted five times. Although living in the shadow of death, Qutub did not mince his words. To him Nasser was the representative of a new age of ignorance. The book came out at a time when Nasser was trying to reorganize the government and introduce socialist schemes modeled after the Soviet Union. Unable to silence Qutub even in prison, Nasser imprisoned him again in 1965, then linked him to a Saudi-sponsored conspiracy in 1966, rearrested him, sentenced him to death, and executed him. In turn, the Brotherhood passed a death sentence against Nasser.

Why he behaved in a divided way toward both the Arab-Israeli conflict and political Islam can only be explained in terms of the power politics of the Middle East, but that still falls short of explaining the depth of personal feeling he had toward both. According to Mohamed Heikal, Tahseen Beshir, and Nasser's daughter Huda, Nasser was convinced that peace with Israel was impossible. Both Heikal and Beshir (who were in positions to know) state that this feeling was always with him. Huda Abdel Nasser supports this contention.[22] His detractors think that the contacts of his representatives with the Israelis during 1954–55 were nothing but a charade. In reality, the contacts were genuine; although he went back and forth from hawk to dove a number of times, it was Israeli intransigence that eventually drove him to think peace with Israel was impossible. He spoke of Israel being an expansionist country that viewed the Arabs with disdain. His resentment of Israel's attitude would also cover his other indirect contacts with Israel. Even his supposed conversion by UN secretary-general Dag Hammarskjöld and his acceptance of the principle of a negotiated peace amount to no more than another futile exercise. But why did he do it? Why did he pretend that he was seeking a political solution to the problem? Examining the history of the period produces no acceptable answers. Nothing depended on his appearing as if he were making peace with Israel. On the contrary, in terms of the Arab street, he would have been better off not undertaking the contacts with Sharett's government and appearing to agree with Hammarskjöld. Whatever his real thinking was, his negotiations with the Sharett government were a major policy setback; he didn't get the peace he wanted, and he endangered his standing with his constituency.

The situation with the Muslim Brotherhood was equally twisted. The Brotherhood's checkered past and its politics do not recommend it, and there is little doubt that it had cooperated with outsiders, both Arab and Western governments, to assassinate him, overthrow him, or both. But the bloodthirstiness that marked his reactions to anything the Brethren did puts him on a par with the likes of Saddam Hussein. And his handling of peace moves with Israel was equally flawed. There were periods in the late 1950s when he could have tried to reach a genuine accommodation with Israel. Again, his advocacy, in this case his attempts to martial the energy of the people to establish a semidemocratic system, could have provided him with a solid base in Egypt that would have given him a vehicle for trying. He could have sold the idea of peace with Israel to the Egyptian people. He did not. Nor did he show any desire to convert the Muslim Brotherhood to his way of thinking. He stood firmly behind a policy equating the Muslim Brotherhood with violence, and his own reaction to that, his official policy, was violent. Even the early trials of members of the Brotherhood, the ones that took place before they tried to kill him in Alexandria and an untold number of other assassination attempts, were a sham, a farce that harmed the regime without eliminating the danger of the Brotherhood.

If the mercurial handling of the issues of reforms within Egypt, Arab unity, opposition to Western and Communist interference in the Middle East, and energizing the Arabs and bringing them into the twentieth century were marked by lack of planning, then the handling of the Israeli problem and the Islamic threat had no cohesion whatsoever. The commitment to face Israel militarily, in which he believed, fell victim to his "special" relationship with Amer. For years Amer's was the only voice he listened to. The required regimentation of the people, the potential of which always fascinated him, never happened. The Egyptian people were hard to regiment, and he never pursued any idea long enough for it to take root. And in the case of the Muslim political movements, his adoption of oppression without a sound policy to counter the Islamic threat backfired. Not only did he fail to eliminate the Islamic threat, the Muslim Brotherhood gained support throughout the country. His oppression of Islamic groups became no more than a personal campaign similar to what bedevils the behavior of most criminal dictators. He too failed to understand the limits of oppression, how once begun it is difficult to stop or contain, and in relying on it he tarnished his own record and achievements. By 1965, the Brotherhood was stronger than ever before, strong enough to try to mount another attempt to overthrow his regime in a complex but feasible plot.[23]

And what was it that justified his significant efforts to settle the Arab-Israeli problem despite a belief that peace with Israel was not possible? In a typical example of Arab doublethink he did both: he tried to reach a peace agreement while not thinking he could achieve one. The division in his thinking included fear of Islamic political movements that could oppose peace with Israel, in particular the Muslim Brotherhood.

His only competitor for the honor of wanting to settle the Palestinian problem peacefully was probably Israeli prime minister Moshe Sharett. My exclusion of Sadat and Begin, the two men who signed the Camp David peace agreement, as peacemakers takes this into consideration. Unlike Nasser and Sharett, neither Sadat nor Begin, who both won the Nobel Peace Prize, was a man of peace. They were the products of world politics, and their efforts were due more to circumstances than to a belief in peace. Moreover, their efforts were not groundbreaking. Nasser had received the Israeli dove Nahum Goldman years before. His friendship with Hammarskjöld couldn't have been as good as it was unless the austere Swede was convinced of Nasser's peaceful intentions.

The anti-Israeli atmosphere of the Nasser years was very strong in the 1950s and 1960s, much stronger than in the late 1970s, when Sadat was president. In addition, there is little doubt that the abortive Nasser-Sharett initiative made Sadat's and Begin's agreement possible. Records of some of the discussions between Nasser and Hammarskjöld exist, but they have not been opened for inspection. Sadat had them classified because he thought going public with them would diminish the perception of his achievement. Begin's attitude was similar. The overall Israeli attitude called for classifying the documents because their release would enhance Nasser's reputation and undermine their justifications for their bloody raids and perhaps for starting the 1967 War.

While the Suez Crisis and the 1967 War steal the limelight in terms of both newspaper headlines and direct impact on the Middle East and the rest of the world, it is the middle years of Nasser's career which tell us more about him as a person and as a political leader. In the case of the Suez Crisis, the event itself and the emergence of a global consciousness were the heroes of the drama, and in a way this was repeated in the 1967 War. But the less dramatic middle years, 1957–66, were the period when Nasser's behavior was the determining factor in what was swirling around him. Although he could have done whatever he wanted because he was so popular, he wanted to reflect the will of the people. On the other hand, Sadat and Begin expressed a feeling which was already there. Accepting this makes it possible to see the differences between them. Nasser was a more genuine believer in democracy.

It was the early 1960s that exposed Nasser and that now allow us to judge him. It was a period when outside powers were not manipulating the region and when his personal behavior determined what was happening. The first question which comes to mind concerns the cost to Egypt of the ceaseless state of combat against all the forces which opposed the country and its leader. Perhaps more appropriately, one should speak of the forces which he opposed. Taking into consideration the enormity of the powers that were pitted against him, the news of his deteriorating health, which he tried to keep secret, comes as no surprise. He could have resisted the temptation to confront his opponents, or settled some of the problems facing him through compromise. His refusal to do either suggests that he enjoyed confrontational politics, despite his claims to the contrary. The effects on his health of the constant state of war which seemed to surround him become understandable. Beginning with the dissolution of the UAR, Nasser lived on painkillers. His diabetic condition led to other health problems and high blood pressure, of which even his family was not aware.[24]

Surely he could have avoided certain activities. He could have refrained from shipping arms to Congolese rebels, limited his involvement in the Yemen, stopped interfering in the internal politics of Syria and Iraq, ordered his followers in Jordan to reach an accommodation with King Hussein, reduced his backing for the Arab press in Lebanon and other places, tried to settle some issues with the Islamists, toned down his anti-Israeli rhetoric, lessened or disguised his antipathy toward President Johnson, limited his hounding of the local Communists. He could have rewarded competence instead of relying on personal friendships. He could have given more attention to his personal health and reconciled his declared ambitions with his reduced secret ones. None of these steps was acceptable to him, and his only reason for rejecting them was his boundless enchantment with promoting what people wanted—the very same thing which led him to conclude that Arab unity was no more than an unattainable dream, what produced his deserved lack of faith in the Arab people. Only the man who was responsible for all these things could decide whether they were achievable or not.

However, all these problems together amounted to less than Nasser's failures within Egypt itself. The major failure was his inability and his lack of desire to make peace with the Brotherhood and the Communists. He refused to consider some sort of a truce with them but failed to crush them. The failures in his other ventures were made intolerable because of his failure to develop a working political system which eased the economic and, in later days, political pressure on the Egyptian people. Improving the lot of the average Egyptian would have given him a safe base of operations. But making sense out of Egypt proved elusive. Not even knowing about Amer's corruption, he couldn't conceivably be in a position to take the corrective steps needed. Not only was he unable to develop an effective internal political system, he didn't even know the people who could have helped him implement one. He lived and died a man apart, out of the mainstream of Egyptian life, a stranger whose heart was in the right place but whose policies were too weak to cope with the problems he faced.

To be understood, the period following the Mosul Rebellion and Syria's reclaiming its independence has to be judged by what Nasser was trying to do in Egypt. It was within Egypt that he tried developing a system of government in a country he knew well. Egypt was home territory, unlike Syria and the Yemen, and the mistakes of Nasser could be judged in an absolute sense. Not only that, but his handling of Egypt and the degrees of success and failure affected Nasser's regional and international policies and standing. Conditions within Egypt reflected themselves in everything he did. It was the need for American wheat which colored his relations with President Johnson, almost as much as his need for financing the Aswan High Dam determined his eventual amity with the USSR. Additionally, he was always hampered by what

Egypt could afford, and Egypt itself was governed by his ability to finance a regional policy. Thus the country's poverty placed limits on what he could do.

The shock of Syrian secession had immediate effects on Egypt. According to Abdel Latif Boghdadi, Nasser's reaction to Syria's departure included an attempt to reorganize the army. His previous attempts to distance himself from the army and leave it to Amer were replaced by a desire to improve "the management of the army."[25] For the first time he began referring to Amer's shortcomings and inability to run the army. Boghdadi records that Nasser considered several alternatives, including replacing Amer with Kamal Eddine Hussein, one of the original Free Officers. It was an indication of how much the loss of Syria produced a loss of direction, and a loss grave enough to convince Boghdadi to resign. Clearly, Boghdadi did not think that Nasser was capable of solving the problems facing him. Boghdadi was one of the few who knew how unwell Nasser was and how his mental state affected his diabetes until he practically lived on painkillers.[26]

This is when the idea of "a new revolution" was adopted by Nasser. This idea made him revert to his old ways and he pretended to consult with his old comrades. Boghdadi, Hammroush, and others were struck by Nasser's acceptance, for the first time, of the idea of oppression as a legitimate instrument of governance. Furthermore, his new revolution was thoroughly socialist; his old friends considered it an attempt to reclaim his popularity by adopting socialist methods. "The people opposed to the revolution will be subjected to violence," he was supposed to have told Boghdadi. The people he had in mind existed both outside and within Egypt. Outsiders included on and off enemies like Kings Saud and Hussein. In Egypt, the attack on the centers of reaction included the old landowning class and new people who had acquired their positions through nepotism and the loopholes in what had been implemented since 1952. This new attitude led to the rearrest of some people who had been imprisoned and freed, and of others who had been overlooked during earlier "cleansing" campaigns. Official steps—the adoption of a new constitution, formation of a new cabinet, introduction of arbitrary arrests, creation of a new revolutionary council, introduction of a legislative committee, organization of local legislative assemblies in all villages and cities, and seeming reversion to group rule—were introduced. But none of them worked. The idea of a new revolution never assumed the importance or urgency it deserved. However, this attempt to reorganize the state did expose the existence of a power struggle between Nasser and Amer. The incompetent Amer had gathered enough power in his hands to oppose all measures which limited his extensive authority, exercised through the committees in all walks of life which he had collected. Even Nasser's assumption of the position of commander in chief of the armed forces was a strictly decorative measure, and Amer continued to run the army unencumbered. He threatened to resign a number of times, most notably about reorganizing the army in September 1962, and this was enough of a threat to deter Nasser from implementing his plans. This confirmed the existence of "two states," the one led by Nasser and the shadowy one headed by Amer. The division between them was so great that Amer could continue to place officers loyal to him in key positions. Nasser's main response—dismissing about twenty Amer loyalists and placing many others in new positions—added to the weakness and unpreparedness of the army. Until then the army had suffered from Amer's general incompetence and military inexperience; after that it fell victim to constant subordination of fitness for command to favoritism.

Alone because his old comrades viewed his problems with Amer as a family feud and expected the two to kiss and make up, in 1963 Nasser resorted to proposing the creation of a presidential council as the supreme executive of the state. When Amer opposed the move, Nasser began implementing it in steps. With the Yemen War still in progress, the Egyptian state supporting the ineffective and manifestly backward revolutionary regime in that country was split down the middle. To Boghdadi and others, Nasser had only himself to blame, and the discovery that his own telephones were tapped by the pro-Amer security apparatus did nothing to allay their fears.[27] To them the tapping of Nasser's telephone lines meant that Amer considered himself secure enough to challenge Nasser. In fact, in addition to expecting that the Nasser-Amer split would be healed, they were afraid to get involved in the highly personal struggle for power on Nasser's side because they didn't think he would win. There is little doubt that this division in Egypt's leadership affected the performance of the Egyptian army in the Yemen, the overall competence of the officer class, and Nasser's ability to introduce his new revolution. Soon, fear of Amer's power began to consume most of Nasser's time; he started many protective moves, including attaching Zakkaria Mohieddine as chief of intelligence to his office. To most members of the old Free Officers, it was too late for Nasser to assume the role of a reformer because it was his 1953 original appointment of Amer which had undermined the new state and what it stood for.

The one thing in Nasser's life that never caused him trouble was still his home life. By the 1960s his daughters were in their early teens and the boys were nearing that landmark. The records of the Madrassa al-Kumieh (the National School) clearly describe them as model students. They were treated as equals by their fellow students. Unlike the sons and daughters of his cabinet members, Nasser's children had no bodyguards. Ever the loving father, Nasser, though he told Heikal that people like himself don't live long, concealed his illness from his children, even continuing to play football with them.[28] Their first inkling of any health problems he had didn't come until September 1969, when he suffered a massive heart attack and was forced to rest at home for two weeks. When not playing with them during his afternoon break, he still continued to read, mostly in English. Today, although proud of his legacy, his children still cannot reconcile his simple ways with the glory seeking usually associated with men of his position and standing.

Nasser's risk taking in his confrontations with both the West and the USSR contradicted the picture of the devoted family man who kept his family out of the limelight. His personal magnetism and crowd appeal allowed him to bridge the natural contradictions between the private and public man. His natural leadership of Egypt and the Arab world, the extensions of the public man, never reflected itself in his achievements. Nor did his "cleanliness" inspire the rest of the region, or even the other Egypt under Amer's control. To Nasser, the 1952 revolution was a social rather than a military movement. He so believed this that his private thoughts on battling Israel appear to have depended on a desire to raise the standard of scientific knowledge among his people, the kind of thing neither Amer nor Arafat understood. But he never went public with such thoughts. Like many another leader, he dealt with what appealed to crowds. In his case, even the discovery that the Arab people were unreliable and utterly incapable of helping him achieve his aims didn't interfere with his desire to do things aimed at keeping and claiming their loyalty.

Though still maintaining a state of war with Israel, he did have a long period of peace, 1956–67. But the most popular Arab leader since Mohamed and Saladin failed to create a structure which gave his ideas content. His reform programs never got anywhere. Attaining military parity with Israel proved impossible. Involvement in the affairs of other Arab states did nothing but drain the budget of Egypt. The Islamists, both parties and those Arab leaders who thought Islam came ahead of Arab nationalism, were gaining ground against him. His feud with Amer was ruinous, and it was of his own making. His initial rejection of police-state methods eventually gave way to an adoption of similar measures. He failed to impose his interpretation of his relations with the United States and the USSR on both sides. Bereft of helpful friends, he listened to his own voices, the inner urges which governed his behavior. His aloneness left him out of touch and dented his inherent pragmatism. His self-education took him so far and no further. He lacked a global view of power politics, and though he read widely, his mind was not the disciplined mind of an educated man. The need to inject ideology into Arab nationalism came too late, after his exclusively personal approach proved unequal to the problems facing him. Unable to manipulate Arab leaders, he borrowed ideas from Tito and Hammarskjöld. He was the most popular failure in history. He destroyed the dreams of the Arab nation and the people who made him. All this happened before the 1967 War, one of the most humiliating defeats in Arab history.

# 9

# The Politics of Decline

The Six-Day War, as the Israelis call it, is the war the Arabs would rather forget. The *naxa,* setback, was so unexpected in its totality, stunning in its proportion, and soul-destroying in its impact that it will be remembered as the greatest defeat of the Arabs in the twentieth century. The Arabs are still undergoing a slow process of political, psychological, and socio-logical recovery. It is easy to trace all that afflicts the Arab world today to the defeat which the 1967 War produced. To the Arabs it was and is more than what the First World War, the only comparable event in European terms, meant to France, Britain, and Germany.

Even comparison to the "lost generation" of post–World War I Europe is apt. The Arab generation which was lost as a result of the 1967 War didn't die in the trenches or rebelling against an already disintegrating Ottoman Empire, or even while trying to reverse the Anglo-French Sykes-Picot Agreement, which divided the Arab world into countries that had to depend on the support of the colonial powers to exist. They became a lost generation because they lost their honor and because they were as much to blame as their leaders and the governments the leaders ran. The setback was enormous and all-inclusive.

Unlike the 1948 Arab-Israeli war, the 1967 naxa cannot be attributed to the corruption consuming the Arab world and the traitorous behavior of some Arab leaders. It was the Arab people and the most popular Arab leader in at least five hundred years, Nasser, who lost the 1967 War. In fact, because there was enough information available to Arab governments and the PLO which should have told them that they were not ready to do battle with Israel, it resembled an act of mass suicide. In Egypt, despite assurances by Amer that the Egyptian army was ready to confront Israel, Nasser thought otherwise and believed that his army would not be ready for a new war until 1970.[1] Among other considerations, Egypt was short of pilots.[2] As such, though unable to predict its enormity, most Arab leaders knew what the outcome would be. Yet, the 1967 War was unavoidable. It was a defeat foretold.

If a whole people, or the governments that represent a whole people, could go to war expecting defeat at the hands of a merciless enemy, then the mass suicide of a religious cult, in this case a cultural entity, is an accurate way of describing what happened. In 1967, the Arabs, belatedly acting as one just before Israel attacked them, sanctioned the idea of cultural suicide. The Arabs of today, of the twenty-first century, are living in the shadow of that event, just as individuals live in the shadow of the suicide of family members. They are tainted and haunted by it, unable to reverse, justify, or even accept it. Any comparison to how other wars affected a whole culture falls short of explaining the impact of the 1967 War on the Arabs. Were it subject to mathematical analysis, a generous multiple has to accompany any such comparison. For the Arabs, nothing has been the same since. In all likelihood, nothing will ever be the same.

I am aware that I am starting with the colossal consequences of the event before telling what actually happened. But explaining the 1967 War demands that. Compared to its consequences, what happened in the field of battle pales and becomes a nonevent. The collective suicide Egypt, Jordan, Syria, and the PLO committed with the rest of the Arabs behind them becomes a simple transitory act of stupidity—an act of stupidity that Nasser understood more than other Arab leader because he was the *primus inter pares,* the chief of chiefs, of the Arabs. King Hussein and the army officers who ran Syria held on to their reduced positions, and Arafat's comparative position was actually enhanced, but Nasser never recovered from the defeat. After 1967 his celebrated and undisputed leadership of the Arabs receded almost imperceptibly until it became nothing more than a memory. Nobody spoke of the dignity and pride of the Arabs after the 1967 setback. Nobody does now.

Why and how this came about is a source of pain to every Arab. To repeat, it was the Arab people and their demands and pressures on their leaders that made the war and consequent Arab defeat inevitable. No other conclusion is possible. Judging the results of the 1948 and Suez wars was easy for the Arab people: the first defeat was blamed on their feuding leaders, and the second, Nasser justifiably turned into a victory. As a people, the Arabs felt that they were not involved in the outcome of either, though the price of the 1948 War was the loss of most of Palestine. In fact, in 1967 the Arab people were anxious for war, and the Israelis, always ready to start one and comfortable in the knowledge that the United States supported them and that they would win, gave them one. The Israelis have always used the shouts and noise generated by the Arab street to justify their actions, to appear as if they were threatened and fighting for their very existence.

It was a series of small incidents which escalated in 1967 that made the naxa inevitable. As such it is impossible to give a date for when things spun out of control. The deterioration began when a number of CIA operatives in Yemen, working under the cover of being economic-aid personnel, were attacked by local partisans of Nasser. Both the CIA and the U.S. government were enraged. The Johnson administration (unlike that of Kennedy) was under the influence of a group of committed Zionists, Arthur Goldberg and Walter and Eugene Rostow among others. This group believed that Nasser was out to control the Middle East and felt that American interests in the Arab world were threatened. Johnson believed that the USSR was behind Nasser's Yemen adventure and that it was part of a Soviet strategy to achieve regional hegemony over the Arab world. When Congress decided to punish Nasser and voted to suspend the shipments of wheat to Egypt in 1965, the issue was joined. Nasser's fiery retort did not help the situation. Choking with anger, he resorted to an old Arab saying and declared, "If they don't like our behavior then they can go drink the sea."[3] The "drink the sea" Arab phrase meant "go and get lost," and it inflamed his followers' anti-American passions throughout the Arab world. The Yemen attack on the agents, spontaneous as it was, did reflect the feeling of the Arab nationalists. After years of playing an intermediary role in the Yemeni civil war, the United States had changed course and joined the UK in supplying anti-Nasser royalists with arms, enough to tip the balance against the Egyptian forces supporting the republican side. The link between Nasser and America became more fragile, and Lyndon Johnson, already opposed to Nasser, became more committed to cutting the Egyptian leader to size.

In March 1967 the tension between Israel and Syria, which had gone on for years, grew worse over grazing rights in the no-man's-land separating the two countries. The Syrians claimed that the demilitarized land was theirs, that demilitarizing it did not alter its ownership. The expansionist Israelis viewed the land as a strategic area too near the source of the Jordan River to be overlooked, and they were determined to deny the Syrian claim. Ambush followed ambush, on the Arab side mostly by the Syrians but with occasional participation by the Palestinians; the Israelis, claiming the right of hot pursuit, chased the guerrillas into Syria, with both ground troops and their air force. Neither side would give in, and the world helplessly watched the slide toward war. The UN did nothing, the U.S. government supported the Israelis, and Nasser was alone in trying to control the Syrians without appearing to be an appeaser of Israel. To control the Syrians he went as far as stating that he would not be provoked into war before he was ready.[4] On the other hand, the Arab people expected him to aid militarily the Syrians and the PLO. The escalation reached the danger point in 1965, but for two years, he did nothing.

But early in 1967 Soviet premier Aleksey Kosygin sent Nasser a warning through Sadat, who was visiting Moscow, that Israel was about to carry out a large-scale attack on Syria. Other Soviet warnings followed over a period of several months. What convinced the USSR of this has never been established beyond doubt, although everybody accepts it as an intelligence failure. Whether Israel or the United States was behind misleading the Soviets and intentionally dragging Nasser into the fray is also unknown, though most writers, notably Anthony Nutting,[5] believe Israel was the culprit. However, given the bad relations between Nasser and President Johnson of the United States and Johnson's decision to oppose Nasser in the Arab world, U.S. involvement in this critical piece of disinformation, or provocation, should not be ruled out. Belatedly, in April 1967, King Hussein claimed knowledge of what was happening and warned Nasser against being dragged into war.[6]

King Hussein's awareness that things were slipping out of hand came too late. Besides, he himself was a member of the de facto anti-Nasser coalition that was pushing Nasser into a corner. Hussein's propaganda machine was run by CIA agent John Fistere and the distinctly anti-Nasser Wasfi Tel; a trusted adviser of Hussein's who later became prime minister and who never lost a chance of accusing Nasser of cowardice. The Saudis weren't far behind, and in their case it was money that spoke loudly. Operating under the supervision of Kamal Adham, Saudi intelligence followed the Jordanians by repeating the paper-tiger accusation, that Nasser was hiding behind UNEF, the UN force stationed between Egypt and Israel since the Suez War. The Saudis too took their instructions from the CIA, in this case from James Critchfield, the CIA's regional director. For a different reason, even Syria and the PLO accused Nasser of being an escapist, especially after the April 1967 aerial battle in which the Israelis downed six Syrian planes in a matter of minutes. Intense and sophisticated, the combined taunts of the two countries threatened Nasser's standing with the Arab people. Despite having given up on the Arab people as the constituency that would help him achieve Arab unity, Nasser continued to respond to the street and behaved as if he could not live without the people's support. In the middle of the crisis with Israel he wrote Lyndon Johnson telling him, "I obey the summons of the people."

On May 16, 1967, convinced that Israel was determined to attack Syria, Nasser asked UN Secretary-General U Thant to withdraw UNEF. There was no question that Nasser had the right to do that. UNEF was deployed on the Egyptian side of the border only, and its presence there required Egyptian approval. On May 18 U Thant announced that all UN forces stationed in Egypt would be pulled out. He did very little to persuade the Egyptian leader to withdraw his request, and he didn't even call for a meeting of the General Assembly, which everybody, including the Israelis, expected him to do.[7] In fact, Israel believed that Nasser wanted a way out of the developing confrontation, a new UN resolution that would provide him with a face-saving way of allowing the UN forces to stay.[8] Moreover, there is disagreement as to whether the Nasser request included the UNEF units at Sharm al-Sheikh, the gateway to the Gulf of Aqaba and the Israeli port of Elat. While the request itself is rather vague on this point, most historians and Egyptians who were in a position to know believe that Nasser did not want to reoccupy Sharm al-Sheikh and that his request was limited to the UN forces separating Egypt and Israel. Nasser had no plans to reoccupy Sharm al-Sheikh because he did not intend to close the Gulf of Aqaba to Israeli shipping, to impose a blockade. International law on blockading countries is clear—it is an act of war.[9] It was Secretary-General U Thant who adopted the all-or-nothing policy. U Thant refused to contemplate a partial withdrawal. Had he kept the UN forces at Sharm al-Sheikh he would have denied the Israelis the legal right to retaliate. There is no evidence whatsoever that U Thant tried to restrain the Israelis.

Because they had not counted on reoccupying Sharm al-Sheikh, and in a sign which betrays reluctance on Nasser's side, the Egyptian forces which moved into the town took three days to do it.[10] Acting with unusual consistency, Nasser had assured the United States and the USSR that he would not commence hostilities. He still thought the chance of war was remote because the United States and the United Nations would not let it happen. Even Yitzhak Rabin, then chief of staff of the Israeli Defense Force, and with a reputation as a hawk, admitted later that "Nasser did want not war."[11] However, the reoccupation of Sharm al-Sheikh by the Egyptians and the closure order which followed and denied passage to Israeli shipping made war likely. Thus caught in a trap not of his own making, Nasser stopped being cautious. After the blockade he gave a speech to the National Assembly on May 29, in which he stated that "the issue was not UNEF or closing the Strait of Tiran; the issue is the rights of the Palestinian people."[12] Five days before, Nasser had made practically the same speech at an air force base in Sinai. Obviously he had decided that war was inevitable. The Nasser who emerged from this transformation was a throwback to another Nasser, a pre-Hammarskjöld, young Nasser whose main concern was to endear himself to the average Arab by reflecting his opinion. He sounded like a local politician seeking popularity.

But all of Nasser's crowd-pleasing moves and speeches aside, it was U Thant who failed to rise to the occasion. The UN had been effective as a buffer between Egypt and Israel, but for a long time the secretary-general made no effort to meet Nasser, and by the time he got to Cairo it was already too late.[13] The decision to withdraw from Sharm al-Sheikh was the only one he had taken speedily, and he made it without consulting Nasser or the major powers. His lack of will and absence of foresight were so apparent to everybody that UN Security Council members Canada and Brazil felt compelled to ask him to get involved. Meanwhile, even after Nasser had assured the United States that Egypt would not fire the first shot, President Johnson still held a lengthy meeting with Israeli diplomat Abba Eban on May 23. Eban told Johnson what everybody knew, that the Israelis considered the closure of the Strait of Tiran an act of war to which they had to respond. In other words, Israel would attack Egypt.[14]

Amazingly, Amer read the situation correctly, anticipated an Israeli attack, and advocated a first strike.[15] And Amer was not alone in advocating a preemptive policy. Among others, onetime Syrian prime minister Amin al-Hafez was a first-strike advocate. But Nasser held the line for a long time and went as far as rejecting raids against Israel organized by Egypt and Syria. The Syrians never forgave him for this—from then on he was a tainted man. Nasser did, however, order the Egyptian army into the Sinai Peninsula, while making it clear that it would be deployed defensively. Nasser acted on two pieces of advice, one from the U.S. administration that Israel would not attack[16] and another from the Soviet Union warning him against starting hostilities. However, Shams Badran, the incompetent Egyptian minister of defense and Amer partisan, was in Moscow just before the outbreak of hostilities and told Nasser that the USSR was solidly behind him. Whether Badran's statement was an outright lie—and his career was full of them—or based on a misunderstanding of what the leaders of the USSR told him remains unknown to this day. Anyway, it was irrelevant. The evidence available suggests there were several changes in Soviet policy during the crisis period, and it is possible that the USSR was inclined to back Nasser, then changed its mind. After the war the USSR claimed that no such assurance had been given to Badran. Meanwhile, the Syrians and the PLO, happy with the drift toward war, increased their activity and continued to provide Israel with the justification it needed. On this subject the Israeli writer Moshe Shemesh makes an unqualified statement: "The PLO contributed toward the war."[17] But it was U Thant who was blamed most, and he will probably go down in history as the least competent secretary-general the United Nations ever had.

Every other development pointed toward war. On June 2, 1967, Moshe Dayan, a hawk who advocated attacking Egypt as a way of undermining Nasser, joined the Israeli cabinet as minister of defense, along with Menachem Begin, who became minister of state. Their appointments were a blow to the dovish Prime Minister Levi Eshkol. In fact, Eshkol, reluctant to start a war, was threatened with a coup by some Israeli generals who considered Nasser a long-term threat to their country.[18] But the biggest sign that war was imminent was the arrival in Cairo of King Hussein of Jordan on May 30. Having contributed to the crisis by criticizing Nasser's acceptance of UNEF, he now feared being toppled by his pro-Nasser people unless he joined the Egyptian-Syrian military alliance which had been in existence since 1966. Hussein acted after Israel openly warned him to stay out of the fray. To Hussein, and indeed to others, the signs that Israel intended to start a war were unmistakable. Still, how he and Nasser expected to integrate their armies and effectively coordinate their activities in such a short time was indeed a mystery. Meanwhile, the CIA, still angry over the attack on its offices in Yemen, got Johnson to approve its cooperation with Israel and told the Israelis to strike first. CIA director Richard Helms assured the president that Israel would prevail. Meanwhile, and against all evidence to the contrary, Nasser still believed war was avoidable and dispatched messages reflecting his belief to Johnson and French president Charles de Gaulle. He also accepted an American invitation for Zakkaria Mohieddine, the onetime prime minister and one of his most trusted aides, to visit Washington.

In view of what followed, Nasser's position at the outbreak of the war merits repeating in depth. In 1964, the Muslim Brotherhood issued a fatwa against Arab nationalism that condoned the idea of assassinating him. A year later it almost succeeded. And at the outbreak of the 1967 War Egypt was still recovering from the most serious attempt by the Muslim Brotherhood to overthrow the Nasser government.[19] There were numerous attempts, according to Heikal at least fourteen, including an ambitious one to blow up the Alexandria–Cairo train carrying Nasser. At one point during its campaign the Brotherhood did manage to blow up sixteen bridges.[20] The Brotherhood went further and recruited members of Nasser's Special Forces. Saudi Arabia acted as financial backer, and the Saudi government and the CIA were cosponsors of the Brotherhood and other Islamists. Amazingly, the Islamic groups were so lacking in ideological belief and determined to remove Nasser that on occasion they even cooperated with the local Communist Party. Saudi Arabia managed to smuggle light arms through the Sudan to the Brotherhood's Special Apparatus. The U.S.-Islamist alliance created an odd situation which was to repeat itself in later U.S. dealings with Saddam Hussein of Iraq and Muammar Qaddafi of Libya. Then as now the Americans were acting against Arab leaders who exploited popular Islam against the political Islam backed by the House of Saud, the CIA, and the State Department. Nasser had become aware of the eventual dangers of political Islam as a young man, when he got to know the Islamists when he was looking for a political direction. His animus against them was so strong that he executed their chief ideologue, Sayyed Qutub, in 1966 with little justification. But even with Qutub's books and other writings available to everybody and advocating an unmistakably anti-American Islam, the Americans saw Nasser as more immediately dangerous to their Middle East position and so backed the Islamists against him. There was a great deal to prompt the United States to refrain from supporting and helping the Muslim Brotherhood, including the terrorism of the Special Apparatus, but its preoccupation with Nasser stood in the way. The same shortsightedness led the Americans to support Osama bin Laden years later.

Simultaneously, Egypt was facing a financial crisis. The Egyptian treasury was so empty that Nasser couldn't afford a war of even a few days. When Nasser told the United States that he would not start a war, the economic problems of Egypt, which were known to America, suggested that he was telling the truth, and President Johnson had every reason to believe him. In addition, Nasser refused to accept Amer's first-strike option because of their different appraisals of the readiness of the Egyptian army. Nasser thought the army was in no position to undertake a preemptive strike. He knew that the air force lacked pilots and the army reserve lacked training, and he doubted the competence of the army officers, Amer's handpicked cronies. He had also not accepted at face value the information he had received from Shams Badran on the position of the USSR in case of an outbreak of hostilities. Later it became known that no promise of assistance had been made. Furthermore, the Arab armies that came under the newly created United Arab Command—Egypt, Syria, and Jordan—had no time to coordinate their plans. Essentially the joint command was no more than a last-minute attempt to form a defensive force; nothing in its makeup suggested it had any plans to attack Israel. And most of Nasser's Special Forces were in faraway Yemen.

Finally, Nasser was in bad health. He had suffered a massive heart attack in 1966, was racked by diabetes, and had to drag his right leg when he walked. According to his bureau chief, Abdel Magid Farid, he was living on painkillers. There had been several occasions when his poor health made him consider resigning. He spoke to Heikal about his physical inability to carry the burdens of office and told his confidant that "people who live like me don't live long." But once again, his illness, though he could no longer disguise it completely, was something his family knew little about.[21]

Nasser's change of position from doing everything to avoid war to giving speeches in which he stated that war was unavoidable was a remarkable yet typical change of direction. With everything going against him, he reverted to the Nasser of old, set aside his lack of belief in the Arab masses, and time and again wrote President Johnson about obeying the "voice of the masses." Psychologically he became totally Arab, a believer in his own words regardless of their unreality. For someone whose faith in the masses had suffered an irreversible setback and who no longer believed in the people, it must have been a painful hankering for something he once believed in, perhaps an attempt to prove himself wrong in his original condemnation of his only source of support. But he knew that he was not ready to do battle with Israel, and the loyalty of the Arab masses, despite the psychological lift it gave him, made no difference in his ability to wage war. What mattered above all else, what had a direct effect on the outcome of the battle, was his disastrous reliance on Amer. The support he consistently gave his closest friend after Amer demonstrated lack of ability and military competence condemns him.

Nasser's chief Arab enemy, Saudi Arabia, watched developments from a distance, but showed no inclination to participate in a war or help the Arab cause, certainly not while Nasser still led Araby. Despite the outbreak of pro-Nasser, anti-American riots in Dhahran and other Saudi cities, the Islamist King Faisal had Nasser where he wanted him. The United States, the leading intermediary in avoiding war in the past, behaved differently now than it had under Eisenhower and Kennedy. Johnson did send the unimpressive Robert Anderson to Cairo to try to settle the crisis in U.S.-Egyptian relations, but it was too late, and the CIA's James Jesus Angleton was already orchestrating the Israeli military plans with Tel Aviv. *The New York Times* of June 5, 1967, came out in favor of the Nasser allegations, accusing the American government of providing the

Israelis with satellite pictures showing the disposition of the Egyptian air force. Years later, in 1980, CIA officer Wilbur Eveland, a committed member of the anti-Nasser camp within the agency, confirmed the allegation. "The United States connived in 1967,"[22] wrote Eveland in a book the agency tried to suppress.

The combination of Arab disunity and undivided American support couldn't have been better for the Israelis. In the words of Nasser biographer Anthony Nutting, "If they [the Israelis] could have planned every Arab movement, they could not have organized things better."[23] But even after the U.S. government warned King Hussein against getting involved and advised him to try to save his regime, Nasser still suffered from the same old division regarding America and thought there was a way of avoiding war. Yet at the same time Nasser, behaving as if he had a foot in every camp, set aside all he had learned from past experience and everything he believed in and listened to the voice of the masses. His *Voice of the Arabs* led the way; like him, it was responding to the calls of the Arab people for vengeance. Except for the noticeable absence of Iraq, a country that had an impressive army, not much was expected from the others. As usual, the Arabs came out ahead in the war of words. Radio Cairo and its many branches knew how to address the Arabs, how to appeal to them. A state of near hysteria prevailed throughout the Arab world, and to the average Arab what was on the way was an Arab-Israeli war that would avenge all wars.

Why the signs that Israel was preparing to attack were dismissed cannot be explained except by Nasser's belief in the "world opinion" that had saved him in 1956. Among the many indications he should not have ignored was the May 9 Knesset decision to grant the government the right to go to war. The Israeli army was concentrating along the Syrian border and didn't try to conceal it. Both Prime Minister Levi Eshkol and Chief of Staff Yitzhak Rabin had issued clear threats of retaliation against Syria. The USSR, concerned but refusing to afford Nasser the support he needed, transmitted several secret messages to Nasser that Israel was determined to start hostilities. Former British minister Anthony Nutting told him that an Israeli attack was imminent. Nasser himself believed that the closure of the Gulf of Aqaba would lead to war. He even told his colleagues that the United States was colluding with Israel to overthrow him. Yet, he still refused to accept that Israel would attack him, at least not by itself. The belief in world opinion aside, there is only one other explanation that makes sense. He still acted to please the people, and despite Mosul and the loss of faith in them it produced, he still wanted to be the people's champion. When the chips were down he was one of them. It was an emotional response, perhaps a psychological one that he couldn't control. Very much like Willy Loman in *Death of a Salesman,* Nasser failed to get what he knew wasn't worth having. There are pictures of him waiting to deliver one of his fiery speeches which show that he was an unwell man. He brooded and looked tired, almost spent, while waiting for his turn to speak. He definitely looked like a man suffering considerable pain. But all that disappeared the moment he was in front of a crowd; whatever energy he had within him surfaced. He went through a metamorphosis in a matter of minutes.

On June 5, 1967, Israel struck at 7:30 in the morning. It was the time of duty shifts, and the attack was timed to produce confusion and take advantage of the sun, which was against the Egyptians. In the words of Israeli politician Shimon Peres, "It took 80 minutes to execute a plan which had been in the making for ten years."[24] Out of 419 Egyptian planes, 304 were destroyed in the first two hours, most while on the ground. Amer and General Mohamed Sidki, the commander of the United Arab Command (Egypt, Syria, and Jordan), were on a plane on their way to the front when the Israeli attack took place. For all practical purposes the war was over by the time they returned to Cairo (the immediate confusion forced them to circle Cairo several times looking for an airfield to land). Nor had the Egyptian preparations included a substitute command structure. During the initial, most destructive phase of the onslaught, the Egyptian army was leaderless. There were Egyptian claims that most of the air force had escaped the blitz and others that accused the U.S. Air Force of fighting alongside the Israelis, but neither was true. In fact, the Israelis used most of their aircraft in the effort, leaving only twelve planes behind to protect Israel proper against a possible Egyptian response. Not a single Egyptian plane reached Israel. For the first two days the Iraqis managed to penetrate the Israeli defense net, but their numbers were small and the Israelis eventually shot them down.

The Israelis followed their victory in the air by another on the ground. Israeli armor cut through Egyptian lines along the whole border. By the evening of June 5 they had occupied the strategic town of Al Arish. Three days later the Israelis reached Al Qantarah

East, well into Sinai, and the Egyptian garrison at Sharm al-Sheikh faced the possibility of being cut off. According to Sadat this finally made Nasser aware of the gravity of the situation. The Supreme Executive Committee set up by Nasser to oversee the conduct of the war met time and again without producing anything to reverse the tide of defeat. Most of its members—old comrades from the RCC—attributed the rout of the army to the Nasser-Amer conflict, and in particular to Amer's lack of leadership qualities, corruption, and overall incompetence. In the two days following the Israeli attack Amer insisted that the army would stop the Israelis and force them back. When this didn't happen, it was Amer who thought of attributing the collapse of the Egyptian armed forces to American participation on the side of Israel. At first Nasser refused to accept this, but later he adopted it and spoke of it publicly. Yet, he still didn't remove Amer or assume command himself.

The simple Egyptian soldiers fought bravely here and there, but they lacked leadership in a situation which cried for it. The Mitla Passes in Sinai were a natural line of defense and the Egyptians could have made a stand there, but there was no plan to do it. Most of their officers ran back to Cairo and left their troops behind. Tens of thousands of Egyptian soldiers were stranded in Sinai. Many of them were without shoes, and the hot sand blistered their feet. The Israelis showed no mercy, gave the Egyptians no humanitarian assistance in accordance with international law, and many Egyptian soldiers died of thirst and sunstroke. It took Israel six days to finish the job and occupy all of Sinai, Gaza, and the West Bank. When the guns fell silent after the June 10 ceasefire Israel had occupied Gaza, Sinai, and the West Bank, and later, on June 12, Israel followed these conquests with a successful attack on the Syrian Golan Heights. The campaign to occupy the Golan Heights was a difficult one; nature provided the Syrians with natural protection—the Golan Heights' rush from sea level to the sky and gave the Syrians an exceptional advantage. But the Israelis prevailed, on occasion in hand-to-hand fighting. Here too, despite the courage of the Syrian soldier, most of Syria's elite units were back in Damascus trying to decide whom to support as the country's strongman: Defense Minister Hafiz al-Assad, who eventually prevailed, or Salah Jedid, who lost out and spent twenty-five years in prison.

For nearly four days the military defeat and its extent were unknown to most Arab people, including the Egyptians, who continued to believe the fabrications of *Voice of the Arabs,* which always purported to speak for all Arabs, and thought victory was on the way. Of course, the rest of the Arab news organizations followed Cairo's lead and proclaimed an Arab victory. In some places, including Jidda in Saudi Arabia and on a smaller scale in Cairo, there were victory celebrations. But the euphoria was short-lived, and soon the devastating reality began to dawn on the Arab people. Their armies were defeated—the Egyptian army had collapsed within hours of the Israeli attack. Even the Jordanian army, British trained and better led, didn't put up a credible fight. Arab history was rewritten in a matter of days, if not hours. The Arabs looked as if they had been attending a funeral. The usual din in the souks disappeared. Men cried openly, pregnant women aborted, and some people committed suicide. The defiant *Voice of the Arabs* had so little to say that all the Arabs turned to Israeli radio to hear the truth. In the middle of it all, Amer continued to generate a barrage of nonsense aimed at convincing Nasser that the army would fight and eventually hold the line. But even Abdel Latif Boghdadi, one of the leaders of the 1952 coup, found himself listening to Radio Israel to get the true picture. On June 8, Nasser appeared on television to tell the Arab people the truth and explain the causes of defeat. After reviewing the speech written by Heikal a few hours before going on the air, he amended it in a serious way. He insisted on adding words accepting all responsibility for the outcome of the war. Looking tired and almost lifeless, he announced that he was resigning in favor of Zakkaria Mohieddine, amazingly without telling the heir apparent, and that he was ceding all power to Mohieddine immediately. Feeling that his name had been used and abused, Mohieddine, an able administrator and a gentleman, resigned his position as minister of interior in protest and rarely saw Nasser again.

During the battle, more accurately the Israeli walkover, Nasser told Mohamed Heikal that he intended to resign. In a gesture of a nobility which never left him and which contrasted with the reality which followed his withdrawal of his resignation and assumption of greater dictatorial powers, he not only blamed himself for the disastrous results of the war, he adamantly refused to mention how Syria, the PLO, Jordan, and Saudi Arabia had goaded him into a war he did not want and for which he was not prepared. After he heard of Israel's dawn attack and personally watched Israeli aircraft roam the skies of Cairo unopposed, he rushed to army headquarters to inquire about the overall military situation. When Amer treated him with disdain in the presence others, what had been a secret conflict between them burst into the open. The two men conducted a nonstop, embarrassing shouting match. Nasser still hoped that his army would put up a fight, but he got unsatisfactory answers to all the questions he asked Amer. The inept field marshal, as unqualified a military commander as had ever led an army, continued in his self-delusion, or lied unashamedly. As with his reaction to the tripartite invasion of Suez in 1956, he suffered what amounted to a nervous breakdown. Even with defeat staring him in the eye Amer kept doctoring the reports from Sinai and asking Nasser for more time to redress the balance. He had lost track of where most army units were; and his communications with Jordan had broken down because they had adopted a new communications code which both sides could not use. His military coordination with Syria, despite a military alliance which had been in place for nearly two years, never worked. Not only was there no coordination, but the Syrians never forgave Amer for contributing to the breakup of the UAR, and they too were puzzled by Nasser's reliance on him. But more tellingly, even with Israel administering one of the greatest defeats of Arab history, Amer instinctively tried to keep Nasser in the dark by giving him false and vague answers. It was in the middle of the battle that the two former friends became enemies. The bitterness of their public exchanges amazed the people who heard them, and it became obvious that they had ceased to be friends well before the 1967 War brought the animosity to the surface. A few hours after the Israeli attack, the stage was set for each of them to saddle the other with responsibility for what followed. The one thing all the people who were there remember is Nasser's eventual on-the-spot assumption of command and his utterly brilliant instructions to the Egyptian army regarding their withdrawal from Sinai. The only sensible decision was made by Nasser against Amer's advice. Of course, none of the officers appointed by Amer to high command posts showed any stomach for combat. Most of the officers who fled from Sinai and left their troops behind to fend for themselves were Amer's "boys." Indeed, there is ample reason to state that the Egyptian army divided between those who performed with distinction and honor and those who didn't fight at all. And when the enormity of the defeat dawned on Nasser, he couldn't think of any excuse for the situation except to embellish his protégé

Amer's big lie and falsely accuse the United States of direct military collusion with Israel.

A new version of the 1967 War events just surfaced in August 2001. According to this record of what happened, the USSR's position on providing Egypt with direct military assistance changed from day to day.[25] The biggest indication of this took place on June 10 after Egypt's defeat became total and the Israelis turned their attention to Syria. The USSR reacted when the Israelis destroyed Syrian armor and poised to strike at or occupy Damascus. Fearing that a total collapse of the Arab armies might backfire and reduce their influence in the Middle East, the USSR's leadership issued an ultimatum to the Israelis, through a message transmitted to the U.S. government, to stop their advance. The Russians demanded an immediate cessation of the Israeli attack on Syria and stated that they would feel obliged to help their Syrian clients. The Americans took the warning seriously and feared the Israelis would continue and provoke an East-West confrontation. The situation was saved by Israel's agreement to stop fighting after occupying the Golan Heights and achieving all they had wanted. People close to Nasser at the time, including confidant Mohamed Heikal and Abdel Magid Farid, support this story. They claim the position of the USSR regarding the Egyptian front was not as solid as its support for Syria. They assert the Communists changed several times and that at one point an offer to provide Nasser with air cover was made, but it was withdrawn forty-eight hours later.[26]

On June 12, two days after both sides accepted a UN call for a cease-fire, one of the strangest episodes in the war took place. The attack on the U.S. warship *Liberty* occurred hours after the Israelis had decided to spare Syria an even more humiliating defeat. The Israelis attacked the *Liberty*, killed over thirty American sailors, and nearly sank the intelligence-gathering ship.[27] The United States accepted the Israeli version of events and tried to hush up the whole episode. But little doubt exists that it was a deliberate attack. Most available data suggest that the Israelis were disturbed by the *Liberty*'s ability to track, through the use of elaborate electronic gear, what was happening to the Egyptian soldiers in Sinai. They didn't want the world to know that they were refusing to give whatever was left of the Egyptian army food and water. The hawkish Israeli government feared a backlash in the United States and Europe against their inhumane behavior, which ran against the Geneva and other conventions. (Nutting claims that this period of just five days saw the death of twenty thousand Egyptians.) Years after, when Saddam was still a friend of America, Iraqi aircraft attacked an American warship in the Persian Gulf, and this incident too was not adequately reported. Saddam was "a friend" who was waging war against America's enemy Khomeini. When it came to the Middle East, America has had one policy for friends, Israel and later Iraq, and another policy it used to oppose foes, or friends who became enemies.

During the 1967 War, Nasser, the incurable believer in American goodwill, publicly spoke of the Americans "not leaving us alone," something he had confided to Heikal and Farid months before. Later he explained how he was going to behave toward the Soviet Union by using the Arab maxim "The enemy of my enemy is my friend." His final alienation from America made him go as far as expressing willingness to reach "a secret or open treaty" with the USSR.[28] The Soviets never acted on the offer because they suffered from ambivalence about how far they should go in embracing the defeated Arabs. The pro-Soviet leaders of the Arab world, the Algerians and Iraqis in particular, were offended by the policy of their Communist ally. They expected the Soviets to match the total support Israel received from the Johnson administration. Conversely, one reason behind the Soviets' reluctance to act was the Egyptian inability to master the weapons the USSR had given to Nasser. Nasser's new, openly anti-American posture goes a long way toward explaining his exceptionally harsh rhetoric. He meant what he said. He could not, would not, accept Johnson's policies. To Nasser, it was Lyndon Johnson who had made war inevitable. According to Anthony Nutting, because of his hate for Johnson, Nasser had "declared war on America in 1966." What he said after 1967 was a typical Arab response, answering through suicidal histrionic threats. Above all his reaction was a response to the successful American support for the enemies of his Arab nationalism, Faisal of Saudi Arabia and Hussein of Jordan, the two men who cooperated with and contributed more toward the growth of Islamic fundamentalism than any other leaders in modern Arab history.

What emerges from interviewing Egyptians, Nasser's old associates, and even his enemies, is a Samson-like figure willing to bring the house down on himself and everyone else. Never mind his loss of belief in the Arab masses and Arab unity, they still represented his fallback positions on all fronts, and his words moved the people. The Muslim Brotherhood challenge on street level, sponsored as it was by America's Arab allies, would have defeated a lesser man. U.S. opposition, finally in the open, would have made other Arab leaders rethink or remold their position. The success of Faisal's efforts to forge an Islamic front was a major defeat, but it failed to make Nasser change his mind about political Islam. Developing a domestic policy that would inspire the people and make them want to participate in the running of their country eluded him. His domestic policies never amounted to more than wishful thinking. The alliance with the USSR, always based on mutuality of interest, failed to provide him with critical support in 1967. His old comrades in arms were corrupted by power. His closest associate turned against him and undermined his efforts in all fields. Turning the Egyptian army into a fighting force never got anywhere. Outside of a model family life, the only thing which was his and which never slipped out of control was his remarkable ability to command the loyalty of the Arab masses. Examined thus, his reversion to the young Nasser, his recommitment to the people even when they proved unworthy, is not surprising. As usual his adoption (in this case readoption) of a cause was total. Knowing the Arab masses couldn't save him didn't stop him from relying on them. His followers could make trouble for America, shake the thrones of Jordan and Saudi Arabia whenever he ordered them to do it, and take over the streets of Baghdad at will. He was still the leader of the Arabs. If unifying them was not possible, then leading them gave him stature.

Yet, all these things together affected the course of events in the Arab world less than did Nasser's disastrous reliance on Amer. The fun-loving field marshal, a lightweight by any yardstick, was a major factor in destroying Nasser and what he represented. Even the Yemen disaster, something Nasser could and should have avoided, produced less damage than Amer. Indeed, there was no excusing his sentimental attachment to a most undeserving man. The Israeli politician and political writer Jon Kimche described Nasser's hold on the Arabs as a second Arab awakening, and distinguished him from other Arab leaders by stating that he was the only Arab of modern times to run Egypt and lead the Arabs. But the West, America in particular, had decided to get rid of him, both in the late 1950s and during the Johnson years. With the CIA in the lead, America's experts on the Arab world concluded that a military defeat in 1967 would be the end of him. Certainly Lyndon

Johnson expected him to fall. He was humbled by the defeat; but he was not overthrown. He proved irreplaceable because the people were behind him. At long last they did give him a victory.

With the Arabs stunned and licking their wounds, what followed in Egypt came close to being a civil war. The Amer challenge was infinitely more serious than any Nasser had faced before. Alone except for his popular standing, he faced a new Amer who was determined to clear his name and that of the army. To Amer, Nasser was behind what had happened in Syria, Yemen, and the 1967 defeat. The army stood with Amer, not only the officer class, but the simple soldiers, who became convinced that Amer's call for a first strike had made sense and would have saved them from what followed. Nasser himself wanted to avoid a confrontation, and he was willing to forgive Amer, Chief of Security Salah Nasr, and Minister of Defense Shams Badran, the unholy trio who ran a government within a government in Egypt without his knowledge and approval. He made no public accusations against them and did not arrest or remove any of them. In fact, he devoted himself to preparing for an Arab summit conference in neutral Sudan. He was not the dashing figure of old, the man who towered above all his contemporaries, the leader who aroused Arab hopes in a way never seen or heard before; he went to Khartoum on August 28 as a defeated leader, to explain the dismal performance of his army to the rest of the Arab leaders. And indeed his old enemies thought that they had nothing to fear anymore.

Despite Nasser's continuing popularity, the 1967 War confirmed Egypt's decline and the emergence of the oil states as the arbiters of Arab affairs. Not even Nasser advocated the use of the oil weapon, and the Khartoum heads-of-state conference adopted a unanimous stand against using it against the major powers. There was a selective embargo against some European countries such as Holland and Germany, but it lasted only a month, continuing it was opposed by a Faisal favorite, Saudi Arabian oil minister Ahmad Zakki Yamani, and it had no effect whatsoever. For decades the target of the Arab nationalists, who thought oil belonged to all the Arabs and considered it a major threat to use against the West, the control of oil was ceded back to its rightful but somewhat backward owners without a fight. Everybody, America above all, thought that Saudi Arabia would use its new primary position and oil wealth to replace Nasser, assume regional leadership, and put an end to the anti-West feelings of the average Arab. But though Saudi Arabia's foreign policy did depend on money from oil, what the Western promoters of Saudi leadership of the Arab world forgot were the long-term consequences of its Islamic policies. Political Islam, what the Saudis espoused, represented more long-term dangers from within than did the followers of Nasser. Saudi-backed Islamic fundamentalism began replacing Nasser's secularism. The United States in particular celebrated Nasser's humiliation, and talk of a Muslim confederation attached to America became more frequent.[29] What America pretends nowadays, that it was unaware of the inherent danger of the growing Islamic movements, is patently untrue. Among others, Professor Zein Zein of the American University of Beirut warned vehemently against it.

All this despite Nasser's dramatic resignation on television on June 10, when the handsome but tired-looking Egyptian lacked the zest that was his trademark. But amazingly, he turned his apology to the Arab people into a masterful speech. Thousands of Arabs cried in open sympathy with his position, which was also theirs, and he managed to recapture the Arab people through his humility and by speaking to them as his equals. Immediately after the speech was over thousands upon thousands of Arabs throughout the Middle East and North Africa demonstrated in his support. They adopted the slogan that was used by the Cairo crowds; "We are your soldiers, Gamal." The people's response to the speech exceeded his most optimistic expectations, and he followed that response with an incredible piece of theater, written, directed, and produced by him. He was a superior showman, and any suspicion that his past performances were the work of Heikal and Minister of Information Abdel Khader Hattem disappeared. Even his nomination of Zakkaria Mohieddine to succeed him was a piece of theater.

A highly respected former prime minister and minister of the interior, the no-nonsense Mohieddine was known for his superior sense of organization. To many outsiders Zakkaria Mohieddine was totally pro-American. It is intriguing to speculate as to what might have happened had he replaced Nasser. As it were, he heard about Nasser's offer to make him president of Egypt on radio. For the Egyptians and the rest of the Arabs, accepting

Nasser's resignation was the equivalent of accepting Israeli demands. Even had he coveted the position, Mohieddine could not ignore the huge spontaneous demonstrations that broke out throughout Egypt and the rest of the Arab world. Not only is there no evidence that these demonstrations were sponsored by the government, most observers believed that the Egyptian government's inefficiency precluded its organizing the huge demonstrations, which grew by the hour. All foreign journalists stationed in Cairo at the time, and even the diplomats of unfriendly countries, accepted the genuineness of the demonstrations. Moreover, there was no way to ignore the size of them or the demands made by the demonstrators. They wanted Nasser to continue to lead them. Seizing the moment, Nasser retracted his resignation after a mere twenty-four hours.

The show of force by the people, and his retraction of his resignation, his response to the call of the souk and street, gave Nasser enough space to arrest a good number of army officers. But he committed a major blunder; Amer, Badran, and Nasr remained free. The chief culprit, Amer, not only remained free, he behaved as if nothing had happened to justify Nasser's acceptance of the people's demands. And he was free enough to return to his native village of Istal to relax. Given a hero's reception by the natives of Istal, the man behind the major Arab setbacks in Syria and Yemen and against Israel had reason enough to feel safe. Nasser's refusal to arrest him was tantamount to declaring him innocent.

The August Khartoum summit took place while the people of Egypt and the Arab world wondered about the outcome of the now known internal struggle inside Egypt. Syria, as perverse as ever, boycotted the meeting. But there is little doubt that it was Faisal's finest hour. Everybody expected him to lead. With Nasser disqualified by defeat, it was natural to expect backward but wealthy Saudi Arabia to assume the leadership of the Arabs. The triumph of Saudi Arabia was a victory for those who believed in Faisal's Islamist policy. They too were elevated by Nasser's humiliation. Unsurprisingly, outside interference was a major factor in the continuing problem of Yemen, and Saudi Arabia and Egypt easily signed an agreement of mutual withdrawal. The USSR, contrary to American expectations, did not try to continue the civil war or to control the Arabian peninsula. The CIA's claim that Egypt was no more than a front for Communist penetration of the

Arabian Peninsula proved to be naive.[30] Neither Nasser nor Faisal, the real combatants, had an interest in perpetuating the conflict.

In fact, Khartoum marked the death of Arab nationalism and secularism and the emergence of Islam as the paramount regional ideology of the Arab world. The demise of Arab nationalism was to be expected because the Arabs are apt to follow individual leaders rather than ideology, and though most Arabs manifested an attachment to the movement's ideals, Nasser's reduction in status left them with no leader worthy of their affection. Moreover, there were no institutions to adhere to as a substitute. Islam, however, was part of their everyday life and, like other religions, provided the disaffected with a refuge. Khartoum also produced a common Arab policy against Israel: no peace, no negotiations, and no recognition of the state of Israel. In the absence of a concrete anti-Israeli policy accepted by "united" Arab countries, what Israel feared most, the "three nos," as they became known, played right into Israel's hands. Tel Aviv hurriedly declared its willingness to negotiate a peace agreement and blamed Arab intransigence for the continuing stalemate. The Israelis called for negotiations with individual Arab countries instead of with all of them together, and it was against this Israeli demand that the three nos were aimed.

How the 1967 defeat had changed the whole political picture and regional balance of power did not escape Nasser. While paying lip service to the three nos and aware that negotiations by individual countries weakened the Arab position, he still advised King Hussein to try to negotiate with Israel through America. Nasser wanted Hussein to try to recover as much of his lost land as possible. Rightly, he expected the Israelis to try to colonize the West Bank and small parts of the Gaza Strip. Whatever knowledge he had of Hussein's direct but secret contacts with Israel was set aside. Grateful to Hussein for his support and his participation in the fighting, Nasser overlooked Hussein's perfidy. This resembled his position vis-à-vis Amer—he placed personal relations ahead of all else.

To most Arabs even the three nos meant little; what mattered to them was the supposed amity that marked the proceedings, the fact that Faisal and Nasser kissed and made up. They celebrated the willingness of Saudi Arabia, Kuwait, and Libya to offer Egypt, Syria, and Jordan financial subsidies to the tune of $200 million a year. Nasser's financial dependence on the rich Arab countries was so great that it was unavoidable that they would use it to keep him in line. To exaggerate the fabricated Faisal-Nasser amity at the end of the conference, the two heads of state roamed Khartoum in an open-top car while clasping hands and raising them to the cheering crowds. Compared to the realities on the ground, these were empty, audience-pleasing gestures. But gone forever was Nasser's ability to use the hopes and fears of the Arabs and meld them into an Arab nationalism which hooked into the racial, linguistic, and cultural identity of the Arab nation. The negative aspect of the three nos exposed the Arabs' inability to develop new plans to continue the confrontation with Israel. Instead of taking steps to truly represent the Arab side, the Arab leaders gave the masses empty gestures. Many had grown accustomed to the pro-West leaders resorting to this kind of tactic, but this time it was their popular hero who was succumbing. Except for the vague "by all means," not a word was said about how the Arabs intended to recoup what they had lost. The quests for reclaiming Palestinian rights and Arab sovereignty died at Khartoum.

But even after the phony results of Khartoum became obvious, there was no way out of the developing confrontation between Nasser and his onetime close associate. Amer had set his heart on confronting Nasser, and the Egyptian army was a reliable source of support for the field marshal. By the time Nasser returned to Cairo from Khartoum in early September, Amer had convinced himself that Nasser was removable and that he was ready to take his place. His clique was psychologically ready for moving against Nasser, but characteristically, there was no planning. Instead of reporting to army headquarters or taking charge of army units willing to back a coup against Nasser, Amer and his friends and generals continued to meet at his home, which had been turned into a fort protected by units of the special forces.

There was one significant regional development: the Arab countries that met in Khartoum deputized Algerian president Huari Boumeddien and Iraqi president Abdel Salam Aref to visit Moscow to clarify the position of the USSR. The mission produced nothing to alter Arab-Soviet relations. Brezhnev, Kosygin, and the rest of the USSR's leadership refused to give the Arabs the open commitment of support they needed. Communist leaders, military and civilian, visited Egypt, but not a single one of them deviated from the official policy, the determination to stop the Arabs from dragging them into a war with Israel that could expand and create a superpower confrontation. The most the USSR provided was an air bridge to resupply the Egyptian army with military hardware in great quantities, about half of what the Egyptians had lost during the fighting. They even stopped short of supplying Nasser with the most sophisticated weapons in their arsenal. The USSR and its Communist cohorts did break diplomatic relations with Israel, but they refrained from following Nasser and breaking relations with America. The hybrid policies followed by Nasser since 1952, playing the superpowers against each other, came to an end after the 1967 War.

But Nasser's natural inclinations not to punish Amer and his corrupt clique ran into strong and spontaneous opposition from the Egyptian people. It was a bizarre situation where the people actually knew more about and were more condemning of Amer and his group's misdeeds than was the president of the country. A mere month after they pressured Nasser into withdrawing his resignation in a show of support the likes of which the Arab world had never known, the Egyptian people were clamoring for punishing the guilty. For someone who had always been hampered by the people's apathy toward institutions which would represent them, it was a very dangerous sign. The average Egyptian was beginning to demand participation in the running of the country, albeit for negative reasons. And once again Nasser accepted the demands of the people. Moreover, as usually happens in stressful situations and in the absence of belief in governments' programs, Nasser feared the developing tilt toward religion. The officers' club Nasser ran, the Free Officers, whose recognized leader he became in 1954 and which ran the country unopposed, was being held accountable. Yet, it still took Nasser some time to act. Unlike in the past, what the people wanted was directed against his government, above all against his closest colleague. To Nasser the number one enemy was colonialism in its varied forms, followed by Israel, and then the Muslim Brotherhood. Suddenly—and the extent of what the war produced was unexpected and included retarding the relatively successful industrialization plans he had set in motion—the war exposed the built-in weaknesses of Nasser's regime, the way September 11, 2001, exposed the divisions within countries like Saudi Arabia.

The divisions separating the Arab leaders from their people widened. For example, even with Nasser agreeing to play second fiddle to Faisal, the shock of what happened in 1967 left many Saudis unhappy with their government's policies. Serious riots broke out in several Saudi cities, and they were followed by what many consider the most organized plot ever to remove the House of Saud. In September 1967 several air force units identified by the CIA as operating under the command of pro-Nasser officers rose in open rebellion. Forty air force officers were executed, hundreds were cashiered, and the Saudi government adopted a policy which made officership in the air force the exclusive domain of members of the royal family and their relations. In Jordan rumors that King Hussein had secretly collaborated with the Israelis widened the divide between the government and the people. Hussein sent the army into the streets in a show of force, and Amman looked like an army camp. Syria grew more neurotic and ungovernable. Iraq split down the middle between militant Ba'athists and Nasser supporters. The Islamists aside, the only known Arab group to benefit from the debacle was the PLO. People were so desperate that they began championing the organization which promised most and did least. Its role in starting the war unknown, the PLO became a magnet for the disaffected.

Meanwhile, whether, as Nasser and his supporters alleged, there was a real Amer-led conspiracy to unseat him a mere month and a half after the war, cannot be verified or denied. But there is little doubt that Amer was putting up a fight, perhaps for the first time in his life. He was adamant in his refusal to accept blame for the shortcomings of the army. Supporters of the theory that a coup against Nasser was in the making at the end of August 1967 believe that the Amer camp was planning a coup which surpassed in its chances of success all the anti-Nasser efforts of the Islamists over two decades. Amer, Chief of National Security Salah Nasr, and Minister of Defense Shams Badran were the chief culprits. Except for Amer they had no street following, and even his was thin. But they knew that the street was turning against Nasser, and there was no doubting the decline in his popularity. Amer's strength among the officers of the armed forces was augmented by his control of many nonmilitary institutions such as the Higher Censorship Bureau, the office in charge of relations with the Sufis, and even the soccer union. The spontaneous reaction to Nasser's resignation was instinctive and reflected popular nonacceptance of the defeat. This, however, evaporated in a short time.

There was also the possibility that the anti-Nasser camp was in touch with or considered cooperating with America. The accomplished British diplomat and Arabist Sir Anthony Pearson always insisted that since 1965 U.S. policy had called for getting rid of

Nasser.[31] The confession by Defense Minister Badran during his trial spoke of Amer's loyalists wanting to contact the United States. Even Anwar Sadat's memoirs, arrogantly short on praise for any person beyond Sadat himself, spoke of U.S.-Amer contacts.[32] However, if that was indeed the case, then the contacts between the two sides were very preliminary, and in all likelihood they took place after the Egyptian defeat rather than before it. Certainly the two sides never had an action plan. The personal behavior of Amer is much more revealing than all of the accusations and counteraccusations. His refusal to accept the blame was totally in character—he had done the same during the Suez War and when he governed Syria and during the Yemen War. The only surprise was his defiant posture.

The way Amer turned his house into a fort is hardly an indication of his having had a plan to seize power. Indeed, even in this case his lack of organization was obvious. There were hundreds of officers who offered him support, but they milled around his house aimlessly. According to Sadat, Amer had the loyalty of six hundred officers and two generals. They were all cashiered later, but Amer, Commander of the Air Force Sidky Mahmoud, and nine other generals, including the commanders of the three branches of the armed forces, were eventually arrested and tried at different times. Had there been a conspiracy there would have been a response to Nasser's crackdown against the "conspirators." Instead, the whole thing looked like a minor case of disobedience by a petulant group. In fact, all of Amer's postwar moves betrayed total confusion on his part, and none of his supporters was capable of pushing him into action or acting by themselves. Even his visit to Nasser's home after the latter invited him to a meeting, and his subsequent arrest when he tried to leave, looked like the work of an amateur. Measured by any yardstick, Amer's attempt to confront Nasser and perhaps replace him was the brainchild of a shallow, inexperienced man rather than a conspirator. And although it represented the most serious challenge to Nasser since his 1954 confrontation with Naguib, when it became obvious that Amer had to go, Nasser moved decisively against his old friend and showed no concern regarding assuming greater dictatorial powers and no inclination to stop the slide into darkness.

Nasser took his time—three months—before arresting Amer and the senior members of his entourage. But later, when the courts gave Commander of the Air Force Sidky Mahmoud and fellow officers light sentences, Nasser personally ordered retrials and instructed the courts to give them heavier prison sentences. Among the justifications he used for this arbitrary behavior was the claim, in all likelihood apocryphal, that Sidki Mahmoud didn't even know that the war had broken out for several days. True, the decision to retry the officers and give them heavier sentences resulted from pressure on Nasser in the form of violent demonstrations by the labor unions in Helwan and the students of Cairo and Alexandria Universities; but he showed no hesitation in behaving dictatorially. The protestors didn't understand the long-term implications of what Al Rayyes did to human rights and individual freedoms. The man who was dismissive of the courts and ordered them to behave differently was a new Nasser who followed when he should have led. It was a Nasser who was assuming more and more dictatorial powers and who had given up his commitment to political reform. The adoption of dictatorial powers occurred at a time when Egypt was desperately in need of a new political direction, when the death of Arab nationalism gave him an opportunity to replace it with something satisfactory to his people.

There is more than one answer to the riddle of Nasser's weakness in dealing with Amer and his clique despite the field marshal's obvious faults, which included corruption and stupid behavior. Huda Abdel Nasser, now in charge of the Center for the Study of the 1952 Revolution, refuses to accept the word "weakness," which I used to describe her father's behavior toward Amer. To her, Amer was very much "part of the system, one of the original Free Officers" and a close friend of her father's. Without actually using the word, she thought that her father was a loyal person. *Cairo Times* editor Hisham Kassem attributes Nasser's toleration of Amer's behavior to his being "completely out of touch." Chief of Security Salah Nasr, a close friend of Amer's and also someone whom Nasser liked and trusted, was supposed to have "kept Nasser indoors, without a link to the people." While the accusation that Nasser was out of touch can be argued, in essence it is true. While Nasser felt untainted enough by the behavior of this group to put them on public trial without hesitation, the overall result of excusing Amer's behavior for so long was a negative one for which he personally was responsible. His destruction of the judicial system was but one response to the near collapse of his authority in the face of the unhappiness of the Egyptian people. But other moves toward creating a dictatorship followed, including making himself prime minister and commander in chief of the armed forces. With that disappeared the last chance to create a semblance of democracy, and now there was little talk of democratic reform. What had been a de facto dictatorship with benevolent inclinations became an ordinary Middle Eastern dictatorship with an inherent bent toward arbitrariness. After that Nasser stopped dreaming.

Continuing to blame outsiders for his total defeat meant pointing the finger at an American betrayal, an idea he borrowed from Amer. The unambiguous accusation led to the first break in Egyptian diplomatic relations with the United States. To the USSR, the break between Nasser and America represented an opportunity not to be missed. Along with Israel, the Islamic movements, and the PLO, the Communist bloc was a winner of the 1967 War. Anti-Western feelings among the Arabs were genuine and ran deep. The arrival of Russian arms immediately after the cease-fire by boat and aircraft to replace what had been lost to the Israelis was an act of friendship which the Communists publicized.

For the first time, Nasser's tilt toward the Communist bloc became the cornerstone of his foreign policy. The Arab street accepted the arms shipments and the Communist bloc's severance of diplomatic relations with Israel as friendly acts. The Nasser balancing act between the West and the Communist world became a thing of the past. American envoys trekked to Cairo to contain the drift toward the USSR. Some of them knew the Arab world well and realized the long-term implications of the strained relations between Nasser and America. But the opinions of Assistant Secretary of State William Rountree, Ambassador Charles Yost, and Policy Planning Council member and occasional special envoy to the Middle East William R. Polk—all accomplished diplomats for whom Nasser had a great deal of respect—did not determine the direction of America's policy. Their warnings against the dangers inherent in supporting Islamic movements went unheeded, though Polk's reflected a lifetime of dealing with the Arabs. America had no intention of changing its foreign policy. Johnson had nothing to offer Nasser and was more inclined to listen to his pro-Israeli advisers and special envoy Robert Anderson (amazingly, used by Eisenhower, Kennedy, and Johnson as an emissary despite an obvious lack of understanding of the problems of the Arab world). So even without believing in Israeli-U.S. collusion, there was very little to expect from the United States, certainly nothing from President Lyndon Baines Johnson.

On September 14, 1967, Abdel Hakim Amer committed suicide while in detention. That he was *allowed* to do it is undoubtedly true, but little hard evidence exists as to how it was organized.[33] Boghdadi's diaries are open in accepting the accusation of the Amer family that "they" (the government) killed him. The only suicide over an issue of honor to take place in any of the Arab armies for years, it was a way out of the Nasser-Amer crisis for everyone. After Amer's suicide, Nasser was left with the mediocrities of the original RCC. The thinkers (Khalid Mohieddine, Zakkaria Mohieddine, Boghdadi, and Ali Sabri) had either become estranged from him or accepted his assumption of dictatorial powers as inevitable. Later Zakkaria Mohieddine and Sabri had short stints as prime minister, though Mohieddine seldom met his leader alone and was treated as an outsider by Nasser. Boghdadi, the most independent-thinking officer among the heavyweights, had parted with Nasser in 1962 to protest the latter's friendship with the USSR. Denied the support of the talented members of the RCC, Nasser decided on two weaklings to serve as vice presidents, the colorless Hussein Shafi and the one everybody, including the Israelis, never took seriously and whose appointment was an afterthought, Anwar Sadat.[34] Before this unexpected elevation, Sadat had been a minor member of the RCC and on occasion had occupied ceremonial posts.

Despite the reasons behind it and the obvious involvement of the government in arranging it, the suicide of Amer was something Nasser felt deeply. He spoke of losing "the person closest to me."[35] Indeed, it was a psychological blow from which he never completely recovered. Not for the first time, his were the deeds of a divided person, as always someone whose dictatorial behavior was in direct conflict with his very genuine commitment to the honor and dignity of the common man. Of course, the Amer suicide was used by his Arab opponents as an example of his inherent perfidy. The expression most used to describe his handling of this sordid affair is an old Arab one, "*Be uktel al wahid we be ymshi fi janazto,*" "You kill the man and walk in his funeral." The Saudis in particular went as far as authoring phony memoirs which they attributed to Amer and which blamed Nasser for the state of unreadiness of the Egyptian army and the strategy that produced the naxa.

The phony Amer memoirs were the invention of Saudi intelligence, in all likelihood with CIA help. They were given to my *Time* magazine correspondent father by Prince Nawaf bin Abdel Aziz, then an aide to his brother King Faisal, who pretended he was favoring an old journalist friend. My father and the readers he hired to examine the document decided it was genuine. *Life* magazine ran three excerpts from it before discovering that it was a work of fiction, to my father's and *Life*'s editors' surprise. The head of Jordanian intelligence, General Radi Abdallah, told them that he had helped prepare it. This, along with other activities such as continuing to provide financial support for the Brotherhood, must have convinced the Egyptian leader that, Khartoum aside, the Saudis were determined to remove him, or at least reduce him. Khartoum had been no more than a ploy aimed at appeasing the Arab people.

The determination of the other anti-Nasser Arabs to continue undermining Nasser showed in increased Jordanian support for the Muslim Brotherhood and a more open Saudi attempt to assume regional leadership. This despite Nasser's open appreciation of King Hussein's role during the war and his decision to withdraw from Yemen ahead of the date agreed upon with Faisal. Of course, the militants, such as the Syrians, the Algerians, occasionally the Iraqis, and the PLO, had another anti-Nasser ax to grind. They continued to blame Nasser for accepting defeat and refusing to continue the war with Israel. They wanted him to go from full military confrontation and traditional warfare to guerrilla action. This was the reason behind Syria's boycott of Khartoum. Beyond helping the Saudis and Jordanians, the latter through offering financial support for the Muslim Brotherhood–Jordan alliance, the CIA was still looking for a Muslim Billy Graham in Egypt itself. (One inevitably wonders whether this was behind their backing of Islamic movements and Osama bin Laden years later.) Meanwhile, on November 27 the United Nations finally acted, and it did so through the efforts of the seasoned British diplomat Lord Carradon and with little help from Secretary-General U Thant. It adopted Resolution 242 and appointed the Swedish diplomat Gunnar Jarring to mediate a final solution between the Arabs and Israel.

From the very beginning, the resolution suffered from ambiguity. In English it called for Israel to withdraw from "territories" acquired by force by Israel. But both the French and Spanish versions of the same resolution used "the territories." The difference between the two had and has huge implications. Naturally, the

Israelis accept the English-language version and believe it allows them to retain some of the land they conquered in 1967 under the concept of "belligerents' rights." How much and what they want to retain of the West Bank and what justification they use for Gaza differ from one year to another and certainly from one politician to another. Meanwhile, the Arabs insist on an interpretation based on the French and Spanish versions and demand the return of all land (the territories) occupied as a result of the 1967 War. The argument remains unresolved. Years later, even the author of Resolution 242, Lord Carradon (Hugh Foot), the British diplomat who sponsored it, was unclear as to what he had in mind, whether he meant "the land" or "land." Support for the Arab position on Resolution 242 comes from another part of the very same resolution, the part which unequivocally rejects the acquisition of land through conquest. Indeed, international law not only rejects the acquisition of land by force, it is also very clear about how people in occupied territories should be treated. The Israelis—and they have defied more UN resolutions than any country in the world—pay little attention to this.

Nasser accepted UN Resolution 242 in November 1967. To his loyalists, this was no more than a ploy to gain time and prepare for the inevitable future confrontation with Israel. To his detractors his acceptance of 242 was yet another sign that he wanted a negotiated solution of the Palestinian problem, which was no longer at the top of his agenda. The anti-Nasser militants refused to accept the notion that he was trying to gain time. There is ample evidence to support the points of view of both his supporters and his detractors—once again, there was a divided Nasser approach to a problem. Reequipping and retraining the army took priority over other requirements, and he personally took control of this. Nasser also worked very hard to establish an eastern front, to have Syria, Iraq, and Jordan operate under a unified command capable of threatening Israel from the east.[36] It was not an original idea—others had seen its merits and potential and had unsuccessfully tried to implement it. Furthermore, in a reversal of policy, he also began advocating using oil as a strategic weapon against the West.

What the six months following the 1967 War produced was not the old Nasser who acted and forced the rest of the Arab leaders to follow him, but a new Nasser who consulted with them and tried to reinvigorate the policy of common Arab aims. He even admitted that he needed more money from Saudi Arabia and Kuwait, though both of them turned down his request. He maintained good relations with both in spite of their refusal to provide him with more financial help. In fact 1968–69 was a period when he did have good relations with the pro-West Arabs. It was his traditional backers, Algeria, Syria, Iraq, and the PLO, who opposed his obvious acceptance of something considerably less than a military solution and formed a "rejection front."

In many ways the Nasser of this period presents a clearer image than the Nasser of old. Internally he was following a more doctrinaire socialist line. His direct personal control of the army was tantamount to accepting the inevitability of another war with Israel. For the first time he allowed the presence in Egypt of a huge military mission from the USSR. Regionally his abandonment of the dream of uniting the Arabs became obvious, and eventually his former Arab enemies believed him. This was especially true of King Hussein, toward whom Nasser showed sudden, genuine warmth. Internationally, to the surprise of Washington above all, he unexpectedly stuck to his newly acquired anti-American policy. The one-way love affair had truly come to an end. Cooperation with the USSR was the order of the day, but his true personal feelings on the subject remained unknown. He chain-smoked, and visited Tito more often than ever before. He was still the loving husband and father who spent a great deal of time with his family. Outwardly, he was still an overwhelming personality, a man who bore the qualities of leadership easily. But he was alone and unwell, and now the effects of both showed when he was not in the public eye. He stooped, and his hair was graying fast, and it wasn't the old gray temples which had made him look mature and handsome—at forty-nine, it was the gray of old age.

The one problem which still haunted Nasser was that of Palestine, and he felt guilty because of his role in it. Then in March 1968, less than a year after the 1967 War, two months after he ordered his forces to begin harassing the Israelis on the eastern side of the blocked Suez Canal, Nasser's world spun out of control and changed beyond recognition. The PLO and Arafat had moved to Jordan, where they stationed themselves along the river and began infiltrating Israel and unbalancing the Jewish state despite huge sacrifices. Nine out of every ten Palestinians who managed to cross the Jordan and attack the Israelis never came back. But this didn't stop them. After several unsuccessful attempts to knock out the Palestinian encampments through the use of heavy artillery in February 1968, the Israelis decided to strike across the river.

On the night of March 21 they attacked the Palestinians in force. They used paratroops, tanks, armored personnel carriers, helicopter gunships, jet fighters, and bombers. General Moshe Dayan, Israel's defense minister, predicted an easy victory in a number of hours. But the ill-trained Palestinians held their ground tenaciously. For a few hours they fought alone, manifesting remarkable courage. But later, when the pressure on the Palestinians intensified, they were joined by the Jordanian army acting on the orders of the local commander, who couldn't reach King Hussein. Facing unexpected resistance, the Israelis withdrew, but not before suffering heavy losses: twenty-eight dead and seventy wounded. True, the Palestinians suffered over a hundred dead, but the Battle of Karamah was an Arab-Palestinian victory. Suddenly the Arabs had new heroes, the Fatah organization and a relatively unknown man by the name of Yasser Arafat.

Nasser watched from afar and obviously not without pain the emergence of his replacement. Volunteers from all over the world flocked to join Fatah, including hundreds of Egyptians. This was Nasser's chance to cede the leadership of the Arabs without being accused of abandoning the Palestinians and their cause. Moreover, the Palestinians themselves, since the days of the mufti and his Arab Higher Committee, had insisted on being independent and insisted that they be allowed to speak for themselves. The argument as to whether the problem of Palestine was a Palestinian-Israeli one or an Arab-Israeli one was never settled to their satisfaction. After all, it was because Nasser limited their freedom of action when they were in Gaza that Arafat and his original Fatah group had moved to Kuwait. A week or so after the Battle of Karamah, Nasser dispatched his trusted friend Mohamed Heikal to Jordan to invite Yasser Arafat to Cairo. He had decided to cede the leadership of the conflict with Israel to the Palestinian resistance. Because the confrontation with Israel had been what united the Arabs for fifty years, he was giving up Arab leadership. Perhaps Anwar Sadat's assessment of his predecessor was close to the truth. Summarizing the results of the 1967 War, Sadat wrote, "He [Nasser] didn't die in September 1970, he died on 5 June 1967, exactly one hour after the war broke out."[37]

# 10

# We Are Defeated

In accepting defeat in the three dramatic words that will inevitably repeat themselves in this chapter, Nasser once again set a new standard of behavior for Arab leaders and foretold the emergence of his replacement. The Battle of Karamah catapulted Arafat and his Fatah group into the limelight and provided Nasser with a more acceptable way out than trying to have the Arab leaders share the weight of responsibility for the Palestinian problem with him, or his earlier selection of Zakkaria Mohieddine as his heir. Fatah's rise was a godsend, an almost perfect solution to what was uppermost on his mind, and he quickly invited Arafat to Cairo to be crowned the new guardian of the Palestinians.

Ostensibly Nasser was making the ultimate sacrifice. Having succeeded in turning his mea culpa speech into victory there was no immediate pressure on him to do more. But after talking to trusted advisers for a number of years, he finally made up his mind without deferring to any of them. Because of that, his resignation after the defeat, the climax of his leadership, was remarkable in its simplicity. However, it represented another defiance, indeed another major violation, of Arab tradition, certainly a redefinition of it. Once again, he felt entitled to proffer a redefinition, and once again it was a masterstroke.

Amer's suicide, whatever the exact circumstances, was not Nasser's personal decision. As such the attempts by conservative pro-West Arab leaders, and many in the American government, to link the suicide to Nasser's ceding of leadership, to bundle them as one package which the naxa had made inevitable, was an illogical interpretation of the Egyptian leader's judgment. Like many times before, none of Nasser's Arab contemporaries understood what he had in mind. Certainly none of them would have acted similarly; in their case, losing a war would have prompted the people to make them pay for their failure. Of course, Nasser's opponents saw something sinister in his decision, but then they always did. They had not expected him to survive the 1967 debacle and were amazed when he did. Now he was exceeding himself and confusing them. No Arab leader in the twentieth century had ever questioned his own paramountcy. The House of Saud in Saudi Arabia, the Hashemites (King Hussein's family), and others took their antiquated legacies for granted. Even had it occurred to them to purify themselves through sacrifice, they would not have done it so openly. Nasser was as different from them in defeat as he was in his confrontational prime, when a simple word from him challenged them and shook their governments to the roots. Now he was forcing them to examine their own positions, because they had never accepted their own feebleness, incompetence, and lack of solid policies popular with their people as major contributors to his success. They opposed his policies without understanding what he represented and how he intended to implement these policies. As such they simply were holding the line against any threat to their status.

Although Nasser had not created the opportunity, the timing was perfect, and he knew it. If most Arab leaders saw his earlier success with the Arab people as something alien, this was even stranger. By promoting Arafat and asking the PLO to assume a position of leadership in the Arab confrontation with Israel, he was absolving himself of future blame for the shortcomings of the Arabs' efforts against Israel. The other Palestinian groups which operated under the PLO's umbrella, the ANM included, were compromised. Most of them were leftists who had supported Nasser and resented Fatah's policies of compromise. Their disdain for and mistrust of the little man Nasser chose to lead them, Arafat, was legendary. There was cynicism in Nasser's decision, but he did admire Arafat's pragmatism. He saw the Fatah leader as less likely to cause him trouble than the Palestinian ideologues of the Palestine Liberation Front and the Popular Front for the Liberation of Palestine.

All the Arab leaders had gone out of their way to celebrate Fatah's Karamah victory, and, thirsty for the smallest triumph, their propaganda departments exaggerated the battle's results and meaning. Rightly, Nasser assessed the situation in terms of their inability to oppose him, to accuse him of being a Pilate for acting in a manner similar to theirs. Yet, the difference between him and the rest of the Arab leaders was obvious. His support for Arafat was of greater significance. Arafat could do without the backing of the others, but not without Nasser's endorsement. Nasser's decision changed the nature of the Arab-Israeli conflict. It reduced the Arab conflict with Israel to a Palestinian-Israeli one. The subsidiary positions of the other Arab leaders didn't endow them with such power. Consequently, what they did was tantamount to supporting Nasser's "abdication." It merits repeating that the other Arab leaders responded to their Western sponsors and creators of their dynastic positions rather than to their people and Arab concerns. Their support for Fatah was a popular move which neither infringed nor disturbed their relationship with the West.

If Nasser's original rise to Arab leadership represented a menacing stance which they did not understand, then his decision to accord Arafat and the PLO new status was no less challenging. On the surface, his new move was easy to understand, and Nasser and his Arab detractors appeared to be doing the same thing, for they too wanted to transfer whatever subsidiary responsibility they had toward the Palestinians to Fatah and Arafat. This is why they showered the new PLO with considerable sums of money. In reality, their accepting Arafat was insignificant. Unlike Nasser's, their decisions made no difference. Their financial gifts aside, the political support that followed was an act of mimicry.

In the middle 1950s power had changed Nasser. His emergence as the leader of the Arabs erased the brooding look he wore as a young man, gave him the broad, attractive smile which he wore when he spoke to Arab audiences, and added to the natural sparkle in his eyes. The rise to power and the change in his persona were behind the remarkable development of his unique speech-making style, his incredible ability to sense the wishes of, and thereby manipulate, his audiences. His imperceptible reliance on a middle Arabic which transcended local dialects and made all the Arabs understand what he was saying was a major element in his assumption of Arab leadership. After 1967 signaled the end of his pan-Arabism and his reduction to the man behind the naxa, he changed for the second time. It was a forced and unattractive change which took place under duress. The political fallout of the 1967 War was followed by a worsening of his ailments, black diabetes, diabetic neuritis, and arteriosclerosis. The stress of the battles to survive and maintain honor he was waging on the domestic, regional, and international fronts showed. His limbs were affected and he began dragging his right leg, and there were boils all over his back. Rest could have helped him, but resting was alien to his nature.

But even when suffering the consequences of involuntary change, he was lucky in knowing himself enough to assess his reduced position and to accept it and incorporate what was left of him into a new position. He was no longer the "loud, strident, and romantic"[1] figure of old; he knew he couldn't be. Stooped, graying speedily, visibly preoccupied, and extremely lonely, he still enjoyed taking risks. Once again he turned the haunting and painful remnants of defeat into an asset. His gift of relating to all Egyptians and Arabs orally (and he preferred the spoken word to the written one) remained superior in defeat to what other Arab leaders could offer in moments of glory. He stayed ahead of them. The knowledge that he was no longer young, constant stress, his various illnesses, and working over fourteen hours a day were taking their toll. He became prone to repeating the refrain "People like me do not live long." Even after he won in Egypt and relegated the Amer challenge to the dustbin of history, his sense of his new position was correct. For a change, it was the insoluble problems of Egypt which preoccupied him. With Amer gone, and the success of the new chief of staff, General Mahmoud Fawzi, in arresting four hundred officers loyal to the incompetent field marshal, Nasser no longer needed to create a working internal governmental system as a counterweight to the army. Nevertheless, Amer's disappearance did nothing to lessen his belief that the naxa had awakened the Egyptians from a long slumber, and he wanted to respond to this by addressing Egypt's economic and social problems. It was the people of Egypt, mostly its young students, who had forced him to face up to Amer and his collection of charlatans, and the very same group who had given him a victory against Amer were making demands on him. The internal problems did not lessen the demands on him from the Arabs and the West. His elevation of Arafat fell short of the latter's assuming responsibility for the strategic questions of the Arab-Israeli conflict, and of course there was the issue of the control of oil and the consequent Western fear that Nasser would help Russia threaten the oil fields. Palestine continued to top the list, and Nasser sought to deal with it first. Palestine had made and destroyed many an Arab leader before him, but the risk taker in Nasser dictated his course of action. As always, he got his inspiration from the people, who still deferred to him and not to Arafat. He still led.

Because defeat accelerated the growth of pan-Islamism, in this case a return to religion in the wake of secularism's defeat, it took Nasser a while to articulate his new, endangered position. But, despite Islamic rumblings amounting to blaming secularism for the defeat, and just like when he assumed *all* responsibility for the naxa, Nasser faced the Palestine problem head-on. Though he was somewhat discredited, abandoning Palestine would have meant surrender to the more vocal than ever Islamists. Once again he had it right. He was a young Lear confronting dizzying adversity. "I have no personal dreams," he told *New York Times* columnist Cyrus Sulzberger early in 1968. He didn't mean that he'd never had dreams, but that he had given up his ambitions. Only a few years before, he'd had one of the biggest dreams of them all, arguably one the likes of which the world had not seen for centuries. Now he was abandoning the revolutionary dream and taking refuge in behaving like a statesman. He moved into the breach he created, assumed responsibility for the aftermath of the naxa. Karamah aside, Arafat was not the stuff of heroes, and Nasser knew that he had to "make him." And contrary to the interpretations of his Arab opponents and the Johnson administration, the reasons behind his words and deeds were crystal clear and had no conspiratorial aspect. He wanted Arafat to assume the day-to-day problems of Palestine. He wanted out. Only fifty years old, he was tired and broken. In a most un-Arab way he wanted to spend more time with Tahiya and his children, who by now had become aware of how ill he was.

His desire to lighten his work schedule was temporarily helped by transferring some parts of the problem of Palestine onto the PLO and Arafat. But that wasn't enough. Despite following this desire with open eyes, he remained an incurable workaholic, and he had a yen to lead. His disdain for the Arab people didn't stop him from considering them "his army." He couldn't help himself. He needed them. The strategic decision to use the PLO was made without hesitation, but not without psychological pain. What he feared most was being sidelined and eventually sliding into nothingness. It was another manifestation of his divided self. The other Nasser who still wanted to occupy center stage resented what the defeated Nasser was doing. Arafat was elevated openly by a defeated Nasser, but the second Nasser, the egoist, found Arafat unworthy and was pained by the latter's dishonesty and amateurishness.

The Arafat who came to Cairo to see Nasser was not yet the chairman of Fatah, he was a member of a committee of eight which ran it. But he was the head of the military wing of Fatah and the movement's innovator, and even before Karamah he was the movement's de facto leader. He arrived to see Nasser with two other comrades of the Fatah central committee, Abu Iyyad and Farouk Qaddoumi. But both he and Nasser knew the meeting was about Arafat and Fatah's place in the struggle against Israel. It was the flamboyant five-foot-four Arafat who had led the Palestinians at Karamah and made the most of the Palestinians' victory. He was the only one among Fatah's leaders contacted by Heikal. To see Nasser, he wore his customary military fatigues, and his kaffiyeh was painstakingly shaped to resemble a map of Palestine. The world would eventually grow accustomed to this look, but then most of the time he wore a cap and American-style large sunglasses, and for more drama he carried a stick. Hidden from people but always around his neck was a sura from the Koran. He was without what later became another trademark, his stubble.

Nasser was in his customary business suit. Despite later Arafat claims to the contrary, the two had never met, and for Nasser the new hero of the Palestinians and Arabs was just another name. He did not remember that he had imprisoned Arafat in 1954 over Arafat's Muslim Brotherhood connections and his unauthorized raids into Israel from Gaza, which had forced Arafat to move to Kuwait. The difference in looks and style between the two men was accentuated by differences in behavior. Somewhat rigid, Arafat offered a military salute. Nasser smiled and offered him his hand. Nasser called Arafat by his first name, while Arafat addressed Nasser as "Your Excellency." The other two PLO officers were equally deferential but contributed little. It was a Nasser-Arafat meeting.

Not a single Arab leader, regardless of political color, had missed the chance to celebrate Karamah and send a congratulatory message of "brotherly" support to Fatah. But because Nasser was the one Arab leader in a position to make or break Fatah, Arafat had prepared an open plea for support and an end to the squabbles that had separated them. He had no inkling of what was on Nasser's mind. Also, unlike other Palestinian groups, among them the ANM and the Syrian-backed Palestine Liberation Front, Fatah was a nationalist movement without an ideology. Practical in their approach, Fatah's leaders did not distinguish between pro-West and anti-West regimes. Arafat thought Fatah's acceptance of help from all Arab governments regardless of their political color would be held against him by Nasser. After all, the original Fatah members had been driven into exile by Nasser. They had started in Kuwait, hardly the right base for revolutionary movements, which showed in Kuwait's refusal allow the ANM to operate on its soil. In fact, the Fatah policy of noninterference in Arab affairs and befriending all Arab governments was a deliberate one which was adopted after months of debate.

Unlike other Palestinian movements, Fatah had no Nasser followers or partisans among its leaders. The differences between them before the 1967 War were deep enough for Fatah to defy Nasser and provoke Israel. Nasser knew that ceding power to Fatah, instead of to the ANM or other believers in his Arab nationalism, would stop accusations of ideological favoritism. The kings, presidents, sheikhs, and emirs preferred Fatah to the radicals. Nasser realized this and tried to please them. Saudi Arabia had supported Arafat and his group before Nasser did by imposing a 7 percent tax on the income of the Palestinians working there and remitting the proceeds to Fatah. The other Gulf states had followed Saudi Arabia. Nasser's acceptance of the heroes of Karamah completed the picture.

During their meeting Nasser asked Arafat whether he thought he could win a war against Israel. Arafat said yes. Nasser then asked him what he needed to achieve his aim. Arafat asked for arms and financial support. When Nasser promised to provide both, Arafat's bulging eyes almost popped out. Then, not without a touch of irony, the Egyptian leader stared at Arafat and asked, "How many years do you need to destroy Israel and set up your state?"[2] When the Palestinian leader stuttered and stammered without producing a coherent reply, Nasser smiled and told him to think about peace.[3] He advised Arafat to consider a Palestinian state comprising the West Bank and Gaza. Then came another piece of advice. Nasser asked Arafat to maintain the independence of Fatah and to stay out of Arab entanglements. This was what Fatah had always advocated; Arafat accepted it on the spot.

To reward Arafat and confirm what all this meant, Nasser then ordered that the name of Voice of Palestine radio, which he sponsored, be changed. Both agreed to call it Sawt al-Assifa (Voice of the Storm, the name used by Fatah's military organization in its bulletins). Nasser asked Arafat and his colleagues to take immediate control of Sawt al-Assifa and suggested that it be run by Palestinians. Nasser also told Arafat that he would push Fatah onto the international stage, and invited the Palestinian leader to join him on a planned visit to Moscow. Arafat and his colleagues had come to Cairo to demand less.

Arafat never answered Nasser on the ideas of making peace and limiting Fatah's ambitions to the West Bank and Gaza. But he accepted the invitation to accompany Nasser to Moscow as a member of the official Egyptian delegation. He was issued a passport in the name of Muhsin Amin. By all accounts, Arafat appreciated Nasser's generosity, liked him as a person, and—most unusually for him—trusted Nasser. In Moscow in July 1968, Nasser went out of his way to see that Arafat was accorded special treatment.[4] He took the Palestinian with him to all the high-level meetings he held with the Soviet leaders. The two men's need for each other transcended the differences in their thinking. They formed a strategic alliance. In February 1969, the interregnum leader of the Nasser-sponsored Palestinian movement, another handpicked Nasser nonentity by the name of Yahya Hammoudeh, who had replaced the bombastic Ahmad Shukeiri immediately after the 1967 War, resigned his post. With Nasser's blessings Fatah joined the PLO, and Arafat became chairman of both.

Among the Palestinians Arafat was addressed as "the leader," on occasion as "the old man," and more often by his nom de guerre, Abu Ammar. Soon he became visible and identifiable worldwide, particularly after he appeared on the cover of *Time* magazine. But Arafat never commanded the pan-Arab loyalty that belonged to the irreplaceable Nasser.[5] "I am only a soldier," he told the three correspondents who interviewed him for the *Time* cover story. The double-talk went deeper than that. He continued to refuse to clarify his position on war and peace, believed Western backing for Israel would eventually give way to realism and greater deference to the Arabs, and insisted on creating a false identity for himself which included being born in Jerusalem as a member of the mufti's renowned Husseini family. Much more tellingly, he referred to all Arab leaders as "brothers." Arafat's embrace of the conflicting strains among the Arabs was explained by him thus: "We have the same aim, the liberation of Palestine."[6] Nasser frowned on Arafat's double-talk, and knew that the emergence of Fatah would help the Arab establishment to reassert its claim to leadership of the Arab world. He was right; but when it came to running the day-to-day affairs of the Palestinians he never wavered, tried to reclaim his old position, or challenged Arafat.

Like all Egyptian leaders to this day, Nasser found it easier to meddle in Arab affairs than to solve Egypt's problems. Saddling Arafat with much of the Palestinian problem provided him with a breather. Tilting markedly toward the USSR ended his playing the superpowers against each other. Combined, the two moves allowed him to concentrate on planning the war of attrition (about which more later) and to spend more time with his family. He even took the first three-week vacation in his life, though it was no more than a visit to Moscow for medical treatment. Nasser stopped trying to impose himself on the Arab world. To his discomfort, many believers in his pan-Arabism viewed his "retreat" on Palestine as temporary. They used his name to follow policies he had discarded. There is no evidence to link him with the efforts of Jordanian army officers to topple King Hussein or with Yusuf Tawil's serious plot to overthrow the Saudi regime late in 1967. In fact, both King Hussein of Jordan and King Faisal of Saudi Arabia believed the promises of noninterference Nasser gave them in Khartoum. They accepted his old maxim "I can't control the people who follow me."[7] Unlike Washington, they never accused him of backing the conspirators.

The hiatus of inter-Arab peace and some rest restored some of Nasser's vigor, but overall, his health continued to decline. The reduced workload was still too much for even a healthy man. In fact, he shouldn't have been working. He tired easily, and this made him irritable. Physical pain made his scimitarlike nose more prominent. Mohamed Heikal, Abdel Magid Farid, Tahseen Beshir, and a few other people openly and frequently asked him to take it easy, but he didn't. Instead, he started rechanneling his energy into preparing the war of attrition, the harassing of the Israeli army along the Suez frontier. When the same loyalist group suggested building him a rest and recreation villa in Beni Mur, he flatly turned them down and continued to live in the Manshiet al-Bakr house he had owned since he was an army colonel.[8] The Israelis, confused by his decision to support Arafat as a partial replacement for himself, dismissed intelligence reports of his new plans to confront them. Briefly, they thought he was a spent force. Essentially they never understood their enemy. Israel's legendary minister of defense, Moshe Dayan, summed up Israel's view in one simple sentence: "We don't know what Nasser's price is."[9] The naxa exposed a part of Nasser which changed his place in history. Even after ceding the day-to-day demands of the Palestinian problem and having given up the confrontations with the traditional Arab regimes, he still cast a larger-than-life shadow across the whole Middle East.

Even immediately after the 1967 War other Arab leaders continued to believe in Nasser's primary regional position. Abdel Salam Aref of Iraq and Huari Boumeddien of Algeria proudly deputized for him in the wake of the naxa. Disappointed with the USSR's behavior during the 1967 War, they journeyed secretly to Moscow to clarify Arab relations with the Soviets. But they were no replacement for Nasser or match for the USSR's leaders, and their mission was a disaster. Not only did the Soviet leadership, Premier Kosygin in particular, send them back emptyhanded, but the Russian premier turned the tables on them and demanded to know if the Arabs were willing to end the state of war with Israel.[10] The enormous benefits to the USSR as a result of the war had not materialized yet. But soon after, in January 1968, Nasser gave the USSR something it had wanted for years; naval facilities in Port Said, Alexandria, and Marsa Matruh. This preceded Karamah and his calculated "abdication." Only he could have opened the door for the USSR thus. It confirmed his deep disaffection with the United States and his loathing for Johnson. In another sign that he still led the way, the anti-West Arab leaders of Iraq, Algeria, and Syria followed their idol's new line. The Soviet navy was offered facilities in Oran and Algiers in Algeria, Latakia in Syria, and Basra in Iraq.

He was still the pioneer and pacesetter. In Khartoum Nasser had told King Hussein of Jordan to use his friendship with America to try to reclaim as much of the territory he lost in 1967 as possible. Fearing that Hussein would view this as an ephemeral thought, Nasser reconfirmed this upon his return to Cairo. Hussein adopted the offer and promised to apprise him of all developments. Shortly thereafter, Hussein told Nasser that the United States was pressuring him to sign a separate peace treaty with Israel. Nasser advised him to turn them down. Grateful to Hussein for his role during the 1967 War and for cooperating with him, Nasser even overlooked Hussein's secret negotiations with the Israelis.[11] As with Amer, Nasser placed his new personal friendship with Hussein ahead of higher Arab considerations. Later the political analyst in him bundled all the pieces of his new policy toward Israel and reduced them to one sentence, which he forced on all the Arabs: "Without a peace treaty Israel hasn't won the war."[12] Arab leaders accepted this as their standard. He followed this with another simple declaration which underscored the feelings of most Arabs toward Al Quds, "the Holy," as the Arabs call Jerusalem. "Al Quds cannot be relinquished," Nasser declared. Indirectly, he supported King Faisal's declared wish to pray in a Muslim Jerusalem. The Saudi king was pleased.

In fact, despite his open acceptance of UN Resolution 242 and the consequent emergence of the steadfast front of Arab states (Syria, Iraq, Algeria, and the Sudan) which rejected it, and his later loss of the valuable support of the Palestinian-led Arab Nationalist Movement, Nasser had set the parameters for the post-naxa Arab position with exceptional clarity well before his meeting with Arafat. Abdel Magid Farid records, with a hint of dismay, that Nasser had decided, "The people are not up to the task of war."[13] This casts doubt on the reasons behind his elevation of Arafat and Fatah and creates the suspicion that his concession to Arafat was nothing but an act of convenience. If it wasn't deliberate cynicism, then it was the usual situation of Nasser planning to do something, then instinctively behaving in character and doing something else. Coupled with his unceasing forays to play guide to the Arabs regarding Palestine, Nasser's behavior amounted to a virtual retraction of his earlier decision. But Nasser still supported Arafat's day-to-day management of Palestinian affairs because he wanted to be relieved of them. It is quite possible that his behavior resulted from the United States' and the other Arab countries' habitual deference to him and his implied nonacceptance of Arafat. Of course, there was also the discovery that the Palestinian leader was a back-alley politician and not up to the task Nasser had given him.

Even his uncharacteristic, somewhat bitter statement to King Hussein, "We don't go to war for the sake of war,"[14] found its place in determining Arab recognition of the new reality. Judged together, Nasser's statements amounted to writing a constitution for Arafat. And there was no other way for the Palestinian but to accept the Nasser-authored constitution. Arafat was the new king, but Nasser made sure that it was a constitutional monarchy which followed the legacy of the old king, himself. Even Nasser's big diplomatic adventure, his unambiguous acceptance of UN Resolution 242, the call for return of Arab land occupied in 1967 in return for a comprehensive peace agreement, was aimed at creating parameters for Arafat. Accepting UN Resolution 242 included accepting the mission of Gunnar Jarring, the UN-appointed Swedish diplomat entrusted with bringing the Arab-Israeli conflict to an end. The Jarring mission was unambiguous. Nasser had opted for peace.

If, as some observers insist, it is never difficult to divide the Arabs against themselves, then the Nasser who emerged from the ashes of the 1967 War, the self-appointed unifier who persuaded and pressured, was as rare as the young Nasser who condemned, confronted, and came close to destroying the Arab establishment and the traditional systems of government. Sami Sharaf, for a number of years Nasser's closest aide but a member of Amer's circle, sees the post-1967 period as Nasser's golden age. "Ever since then, God has been testing us [the Arabs], so we might learn his [Nasser's] value."[15] Mohamed Heikal, the unwavering supporter turned protector of Nasser's populist legacy, agrees, but for different, more intellectual reasons. Heikal believes Nasser "won all the battles he fought after 1967." Nasser's daughter Huda is another supporter of the golden age theory. "There were no secrets in what my father did; what he did in public and what he did privately were one and the same." It is clear that, along with many others, she believes that defeat turned her father into a statesman of exceptional stature.

Attractive as all of the justifications for this theory are—and Heikal's admirable loyalty, mixed as it is with selective memory, has done much to create an angelic legend—the explanations do not fully answer why political Islam emerged as the replacement for the man who tried to destroy it. Nor do the apologists and their justifications, even when we attribute extraordinary powers to Nasser's seriously flawed successor, Anwar Sadat, explain the ease with which this happened. Sadat—corrupt, pretentious, and judged by his colleagues and the obvious exaggerations in his memoirs an outright liar—was preoccupied with erasing the Nasser image and destroying his myth. To do that Sadat switched sides. Lacking a constituency of his own, he chose to rely on the Islamic movements (his first act was to release thousands of Islamists from prison), leaned toward the West, and tried to undo Egypt's Arab identity in favor of an exclusively Egyptian one.

It is only through examining what Sadat did and what Hosni Mubarak tries to do nowadays that the significance of Nasser as an Egyptian and Arab leader is clarified. Neither Nasser nor Sadat created institutions for us to judge. It is unlikely that Mubarak will. A comparative analysis based on their achievements and failures becomes the best method of judging all three of them and sheds light on Nasser's final years. In fact, whatever their achievements, it is still too early to accord them a place in history or to consider them transitory. Other biographers of Nasser, especially the non-Arab ones, ignore one of his great achievements. What allowed Nasser to play unifier was there from the beginning. He had never wanted full and complete union among the Arab states. As detailed before, the union with Syria was forced on him, and its results reinforced his instincts against total mergers. Essentially he was more interested in confronting the West through controlling the Arabs' foreign policy.

In 1980, Abu Dhabi Television, government owned and run, aired a commemorative program on the tenth anniversary of Nasser's death. The small, wealthy sheikhdom has no particular political ax to grind. Its ruler, Sheikh Zayyid, is populist and traditional, remarkable for never losing touch with his people, and his realm is small enough for him to follow the Arab traditions of mourning the dead and celebrating the living. He seldom misses a wedding or a funeral, and often dances at the first and weeps at the second. What was aired on his television reflects Sheikh Zayyid's attractive persona. It is safe to accept the Abu Dhabi Television appreciation of Nasser as an Arab judgment of an Arab leader. In revealing Nasser's Egyptian and Arab roles, the documentary automatically contained a comparison with Sadat. Selective Western judgment of Nasser, the assessment accepted by the world because of Western dominance in formulating world opinion, is inherently biased. When it comes to the Arab world, the Western media have consistently been most unenterprising. The Western press has never stopped being anti-Nasser, and it spoiled Sadat and elevated him to statesman status. Nothing was ever reported about Sadat's alcoholism and hashish smoking, his corruption and unattractive subservience. Unlike Nasser, Sadat was the master of banality, very often talking to journalists about their salaries. Western journalists ignored all this.

Because the Palestine problem and controlling the flow and price of oil were behind Nasser's anti-West regional dominance, Abu Dhabi Television judged him by an exclusively Arab yardstick. It showed the faces of people listening to him give a speech—women, girls, old and young men, looking as if they were seeing something messianic. The narrator didn't mince his words: Nasser was described as the most popular Arab leader of the twentieth century and the conscience of the Arab world. Conversely, Nasser's Arabness has never been understood by the West. So, with the benefit of hindsight, the question of what Nasser represented is reduced to an argument between his Western detractors and his Arab supporters. Were the final years his finest? What happened after Nasser wrote the constitution on future Arab relations with Israel? How real and significant was the assumption of Arafat of Palestinian leadership? These questions were not answered by the Abu Dhabi Television program, but the spacious question of what he represented was. "He comes to mind whenever Arab interests are threatened," said the narrator of the program. Then, in a voice thick with emotion, he concluded, "Eternity is yours, Nasser." It was a tribute the West should study.

Despite the massive difference in their personalities and policies, and the after-the-fact enmity which Sadat created in an attempt to elevate himself to being Nasser's equal, it is beneficial to examine Sadat's record of Nasser's final years as presented in his memoirs, *The Search for Dignity.* Sadat vividly underscores the damaging effects of the Amer-Nasser conflict as a major contributor to the defeat of Egypt and the Arabs in 1967. Sadat minimizes Arab considerations because he himself was never popular with the Arabs.

But he details the violent anti-Nasser student demonstrations of February 1968, which protested against the light sentences given to the negligent air force officers and members of Amer's inner circle. Sadat's presentation of how Nasser bowed to the students and the street, in fact how Nasser used them to assume wider dictatorial powers, is most revealing. In responding to the internal unrest, Nasser issued what became known as the March 30 Statement. In this declaration Nasser tried to "bribe" the Egyptian people by promising them a semidemocratic constitution. The promise was no more than a diversion.

The Arab dimension of Nasser's leadership is reduced by Sadat, but he puts it in context. It was the internal problems which erupted in Egypt as a result of the 1967 War which determined Nasser's decision to promote Arafat and adopt a new Arab policy. However, it still was a personal decision. A lesser man would have avoided making it. What it represented was a serious suppression of ego by a leader who belonged to a race of believers in individual genius. At long last, Nasser devoted himself to Egypt and put its problems ahead of other issues. His use of Arafat and King Hussein, and his hasty departure from Yemen to please King Faisal of Saudi Arabia, were natural results of his new inward look. The one problem he couldn't cede to others was the Israeli occupation of Sinai and its control of the eastern bank of the Suez Canal. Without any effort by the United States (and he never stopped believing that America held all the cards),[16] he hurried and started the war of attrition, the fighting along the canal from fixed positions, in September 1968. In need of arms and ammunition that he couldn't obtain from other sources, his dependence on the USSR increased.

The Israeli response resembled what we have witnessed during the past two years between Arafat and Sharon. Instead of caving in, the Israelis resorted to massive retaliation. Egyptian shelling produced an Israeli air force response which included attacks on Egyptian power stations deep inside Egypt, at Naji Hammadi. The vital Qena Bridge was also attacked. The fierce Israeli attacks on Egyptian cities on the western bank of the Suez Canal, especially Port Taufiq, which was practically razed, and Ismailia, and the departure to safety of most of their populations, created a huge refugee problem. In fact, Israel's disproportionate response produced immediate results. Nasser ordered a cessation in all military activity, but he had not given up the idea. He ordered the building of a network of internal defenses at breakneck speed, and the war of attrition was resumed in March 1969. In the background, Arafat continued his pinprick efforts to infiltrate and disrupt the Israelis, and King Hussein pursued a diplomatic course to get back the West Bank. The rest of the Arabs provided "the fighting Arabs" with financial support while avoiding direct military involvement. Military clashes have a natural tendency to escalate, and the war of attrition was no exception. Although the Israelis had the upper hand, and Israeli raids on the Nile Delta produced hundreds of Egyptian casualties, Nasser wouldn't stop. He was convinced that the Israelis couldn't afford the losses he was inflicting on them. When he eventually deployed SAM missiles against the Israeli air force, the war of attrition was relabeled the missile crisis.

The Abu Dhabi Television documentary dealt with what Sadat tried to minimize, the Arab dimension of Nasser. The program was a celebration of Nasser's Arabness and his leadership of the Arabs. To Abu Dhabi Television it was the thrust of his personality that dazzled the Arabs and the rest of the world. It was an effusive Arab celebration of *Time* magazine correspondent James A. Bell's statement about Nasser having whatever it takes to be a leader, "The man had it, and in droves."[17] Dismissive of Nasser's failure to create institutions or a political organization, the documentary inevitably judged him by his own words. Like the Saudi taxi driver mentioned in the introduction to this book, Abu Dhabi Television accepted the importance of his "search for dignity," which Sadat shamelessly used as the title of his book. The strength of the television program was in comparing like with like. It didn't say that the Arabs would have been better off under him; it reached its conclusion from the opposite direction. Among other things it stated that the only way to judge Nasser as an Arab is to consider the decline of the Arab position vis-à-vis Israel since his death. The implications were even larger. That it was aired by a small pro-West country like Abu Dhabi demonstrated the inherent Arab double-think and suggested that the Arab position toward the West was better with him at the helm. Implicitly it said that Faisal, Sadat, Hussein, and the rest simply didn't measure up.

---

In 1969 three events forced the rest of the world to react to another Middle East slide toward disaster. The first was the USSR's agreement to provide Nasser with SAM3 missiles against the deep incursions of the Israeli air force shortly before he restarted the attrition war. More important was Russia's eventual dispatch of pilots to protect Egypt's skies, and they did down a number of Israeli planes. Combined with the finishing of the last stage of the Aswan High Dam, these moves gained the Russians some popularity among the Egyptians, but not enough to bridge the Egyptians' inherent antipathy toward the austere Communists. Nasser's attempts to endear the Russians to the Egyptian people never worked. The fun-loving Egyptians had little in common with the dour Russians. Nasser himself was never enamored of them on a personal basis.

Then, in July 1969, came the burning of Islam's third holiest shrine, the Mosque of Omar in Jerusalem, by Christian fundamentalist Denis Michael Rohan. Soon after, in early September, Colonel Muammar Qaddafi, a Nasser worshiper, assumed power in Libya. According to Hakim Abdel Nasser, the emergence of Qaddafi made his father visibly happy; it gave him a victory without offending the other Arabs.[18] The Russian decision to supply him with modern weapons strengthened his resolve. The burning of the Mosque of Omar prompted him, however momentarily, to want to reassume his old position and issue a call to arms by all Arabs. Unintentionally, it was King Faisal of Saudi Arabia who now saved Nasser from himself. Faisal's adoption of the issue of Jerusalem was a tactical setback for Nasser, but it also absolved him of a major responsibility.

Using the opening provided by the crazed Australian Rohan, Faisal called for a conference of Muslim heads of state in Rabat, Morocco. The uncharacteristic speed with which Faisal moved (the Saudis are known for their slow reactions) was an attempt to wrest the responsibility for Jerusalem from Nasser and end the primacy of Arab nationalism once and for all. Faisal succeeded. The issue of Jerusalem became an Islamic instead of an Arab one. Western-sponsored Islamic fundamentalism was on the march. Despite Faisal's obvious purpose, Nasser attended the Rabat conference. According to Sadat, he was worried that the conference might take decisions which diminished his position further.[19] It was then, in December 1969, that he appointed Sadat and Shafi vice presidents.

None of the other living comrades of the original RCC wanted to work with him anymore. Occasionally old friendships, even with Boghdadi, turned into enmities. Having become an absolute dictator, Nasser was suddenly afflicted by what accompanies dictatorship, pettiness and disregard for the law. Unexpectedly he started using his old comrades' known trespasses against them. At one point, angry with Ali Sabri over the latter's outspokenness, he ordered that his baggage be searched when the latter returned to Egypt from a holiday in Europe. The expected followed, and Sabri was charged with trying to smuggle goods into Egypt. Eventually the whole thing was dropped, but not before Sabri's reputation was destroyed. Except for Amer, Nasser never tried to eliminate his old comrades the way most Arab dictators do, but he got into the habit of humiliating them.

Rabat was Faisal's Muslim show. But inevitably there was much that was exclusively Arab. Admitting in a speech that the Arabs were not capable of military action against Israel,[20] Nasser confronted the rejectionists of UN Resolution 242 and the Jarring peace mission and demanded that they reveal their plans to defeat Israel. When, like Arafat before them, they had no answer, he pressed the attack vigorously. He insisted that they tell him whether they were willing to fight a long war and asked each of them specific military questions regarding their armed forces. For example, he wanted to know if Algeria was willing to commit all of its air force against Israel.

But once again his open policy was accompanied by a secret one. His aides spread the word that his acceptance of 242 and Jarring was no more than a ploy to gain time.[21] In fact, Tahseen Beshir recalled Nasser telling him that there was no way out of the conflict with Israel except through war.[22] Huda Abdel Nasser supports this recollection fully, as does Mohamed Heikal. To make his public position palatable to both the anti-242 governments and the Arab people, Nasser's Rabat speech focused on the escalating war of attrition. He told them that he was in the middle of a bloody war. And his attempt to please went further when he placed the recovery of the West Bank and the Arab part of Jerusalem ahead of the return of Sinai. Despite this, his new approach didn't work, mostly because the rest of the Arabs remained skeptical about his motives for accepting 242. However, their rejection of his public policy gave him the freedom to act without deferring to them.

Yet Nasser never used the freedom he gained through his firm stand against the rejectionists. He never retreated from his Arab position and assumed an Egyptian stance. Strangely, this period reveals some hitherto hidden elements of his character. For example, shortly after the Ba'ath returned to power in Iraq in July 1968 under the leadership of Ahmad Hassan al-Bakr, Saddam, and their group, the Iraqis announced the discovery of a spy ring and executed eight people, six of whom were Jews. When the Ba'athists made a show of leaving the bodies of the executed hanging in Baghdad's main square and called on Iraqis to view what happened to traitors, Nasser's anger surfaced. With nothing to gain, he publicly condemned the gruesome show and the people behind it.[23] Simultaneously, Nasser intervened in the budding conflict between the PLO and the Lebanese over the Palestinians' use of Lebanese territory to raid Israel and the massive Israeli retaliations. Early in 1969 he chaired a meeting which produced an agreement between the Lebanese and the PLO, what became known as the Cairo Agreement. The agreement allowed the PLO to use Lebanese soil to attack Israel without infringing on the sovereignty of Lebanon. While the agreement essentially self-destructed, obviously Nasser thought of himself as the arbiter of Arab disputes and, in the case of the Iraqis, Arab behavior.

In the background the United States and the USSR were preoccupied with arresting the escalation of fighting along the Suez Canal. For both, the disagreement in Arab ranks represented an opportunity to entice Nasser into unequivocal support for moves toward peace. The Russians, as always, feared the war of attrition might eventually lead to a confrontation with the United States. But they had no intention of abandoning Nasser. The United States, by 1970 under the internationalist Richard Nixon, was concerned by the same prospect, and determined to reassert an acceptable American presence and contain the Communists. Unlike the United States, the USSR did not depend on treaties for whatever relationships it had with the Arabs. Also, the Soviets had no free press to criticize the policies they were pursuing. Convinced that they had finally gained a foothold in the Arab world, the Russians didn't want to provoke the Americans. Although America's eventual reemergence on the Middle Eastern scene pleased him,

Nasser was very sensitive to the endless taunts of the American press.[24]

In fact, America's interest in controlling the Nasser drift toward Russia began when the USSR was given the port facilities, followed by the dispatch of 1,500 military advisers to Egypt. But the initial reaction to these events, under Lyndon Johnson, was, to say the least, unimaginative. The American president sent fellow Texan Robert Anderson on another diplomatic tour of the Middle East. As usual, Anderson failed. Why Anderson was used by Eisenhower, Kennedy, and Johnson as a special envoy to the Middle East is baffling. Having personally known Anderson, I can testify that the folksy Texan's knowledge of the Middle East bordered on the nonexistent. Nor was he an accomplished diplomat or an imposing person. Yet, at the time, America was rich with knowledgeable diplomats in the area. In fact, the U.S. ambassador to Egypt, John Badeau, was a very talented and able man. But for a long time his government did not authorize him to reestablish a sensible dialogue with Nasser.

It finally fell to William R. Polk, academic and sometime member of the State Department's Policy Planning Council, an accomplished Arabist and a gentleman admired by Nasser and other Arab leaders, to break the deadlock. In Jerusalem to attend a conference at the Hebrew University, Polk was approached by an aide to Israeli prime minister Golda Meir, Mordecai Gazit, and asked to arrange a cease-fire with the Egyptians. Polk knew the Middle East well enough to want to verify the authenticity of the request. Satisfied that it had Meir's support, he was surprised by the Israeli request not to share his knowledge with National Security Adviser Henry Kissinger. Operating behind people's back was hardly the style of the seasoned diplomat, but what was at stake was considerable enough for him to do it. Polk's first move was to arrange a meeting with Nasser's national security adviser, Hassan Sabri al-Kholi, in Beirut. The Egyptian thought it was a serious enough development to dispatch a special messenger to Moscow, where Nasser was visiting. When Nasser returned to Cairo he made a speech which contained a signal of acceptance to the Israelis. He also sent Polk a message thanking him for his efforts. The cease-fire came into effect soon after.[25] Capitalizing on the hiatus created by Polk's successful efforts, Secretary of State William Rogers embellished UN Resolution 242 and presented it to both sides in what became known as the Rogers Plan.[26]

---

The internal situation in Egypt, though it occupied most of Nasser's time, still took a backseat to his efforts in the larger Arab arena. Inside Egypt, the Muslim Brotherhood, with Saudi and Western financial aid, became a greater threat than ever before. U.S. financial help to the Brotherhood reached unprecedented levels, with tens of millions of dollars transferred into the Swiss bank account of Said Ramadan, the Brotherhood's supreme guide.[27] Saudi Arabia joined the United States in this policy despite improving relations with Nasser, and King Hussein succumbed to American pressure and provided the leadership of the Muslim Brotherhood with logistical support, which included giving them diplomatic passports.[28] Even after Nasser imprisoned over thirty thousand Brethren without legal justification, their numbers as well as their ability to infiltrate the army and the police continued to expand.

Nasser's second internal problem was his failure to entice his people to participate in the business of governance. "The people believe I can do it all alone," Nasser told Abdel Magid Farid.[29] Despite many signs showing popular dissatisfaction with the harsh economic conditions, and popular anger over the failure to recover Sinai, he still thought he personally was above parties and organizations. This encouraged him to continue his efforts through changing the nature of his appeals. "We must wipe out corruption," he stated on radio in 1969. But when there was no popular response to this either, he again turned to the war of attrition. But even this failed to capture the people's imagination. Refusing to be discouraged, he attacked the United States, accusing it of planning to create both a regional and a purely Egyptian U.S.-Islamic alliance. Again there was no response.

It was a dialogue of the deaf. After Amer, Nasser's personalization of power was so complete that it precluded all else. Before 1967, in Egypt, his strength of personality and character and the mediocrity of most of his comrades had helped him tower above others. Even his changes of prime ministers, deliberately neglected by this book because they were irrelevant, were ornamental in nature. After 1967, his almost total control of the state was expanded through the use of dictatorial methods. One could say this was the point when he created the police state. The natural lethargy of the Egyptian people, which showed in their lack of interest in his semidemocratic schemes in earlier years, turned into an implicit belief that no serious reform could take place with him at the helm. If the reasons for their lack of interest had changed, the result—his inability to create institutions—remained the same. What did change was the expansion of police statism and the adoption of the tyrannical methods of Arab dictatorships. He was still popular, but not nearly as popular as before, and he was more popular with Arabs than with the Egyptians. The latter suffered from his oppressive methods. For them, rhetoric and promises no longer worked. His instincts as to what mattered to his people had failed him.

With Israel no longer carrying out deep-penetration air raids into Egypt, and the deployment of sophisticated SAM defense systems and the use of Soviet pilots in operational missions at a standstill, Secretary of State William Rogers, an able diplomat and underrated secretary of state, realized the timeliness of what William Polk had initiated. Early in 1970 he started promoting his plan with vigor. Outwardly the plan was a revival of UN Resolution 242, but now it was more detailed, was explicit in its adoption of the land-for-peace principle, and had the weight of the United States government behind it. This meant that Israel could no longer depend on the United States to support its expansionist policies.

Israel's opposition to the Rogers Plan was open and immediate.[30] So was the rejection of the plan by the Arabs who had opposed 242: the PLO, Syria, Iraq, Algeria, the Sudan, and Libya. Nasser tarried, made sure that King Hussein was with him and that Saudi Arabia would not oppose him, and then in June 1970 dropped his bombshell. He accepted the Rogers Plan without the ifs and buts that traditionally accompanied his major diplomatic moves. Undoubtedly, it was the most critical point of departure ever from traditional Arab policies and the resolutions of the Khartoum conference. But Nasser once again demonstrated a hard-to-judge ambiguity. Heikal, Farid, Bashir, Hammroush, and Huda Abdel Nasser insist that this major step was no more than a tactical move aimed at exposing Israeli intransigence, that Nasser expected the Rogers Plan to fail. Surprisingly, Nasser's various biographers have consistently accepted this version of events. Among the evidence used to support this was Sadat's vocal refusal of the Rogers Plan and his retreat to his home village in protest against his boss's position.[31] Nowadays, everybody agrees that yes-man Sadat would never have taken such a stand unless he believed that Nasser was inclined to reject the plan or, at most, give it ephemeral support.

But here again, Nasser the divided leader didn't leave us with a clear picture. His support for the plan was strong enough to prompt him to crack down on PLO activity in his country, and he shut down the Cairo-based Radio Sawt al-Assifa when Arafat foolishly used it to criticize him. Even the ANM came out solidly against Nasser in what looked like a final breach.[32] As pointed out by the believers in the tactical-acceptance theory, he also used the lull in the fighting along the Suez Canal to move the SAM batteries forward.[33] The believers in Nasser's acceptance of the Rogers Plan as no more than a tactical move have nothing to say about the Soviets' critical position regarding the American initiative. In fact, their wish to avoid a confrontation with America came into play, and the Soviets, without openly accepting Rogers and forcing Nasser's hand "pushed him into accepting Rogers."[34] Considering Egypt's near total dependency on the USSR, this is a plausible explanation for his actions. Both Farid and Heikal were aware of the Soviet position and readily accepted it.

Furthermore, we now have another explanation for Sadat's behavior. Nasser was openly planning to remove Sadat as his vice president because he considered him a poseur who on many occasions had received bribes from the Saudis. His original selection reflected Nasser's need for someone safe, but Sadat had become a liability.[35] According to Nasser's close associates during this period, Nasser had already sounded out Boghdadi about rejoining the government and becoming his second in command in mid-1970, a short time before the Rogers initiative. Because Boghdadi's 1962 resignation was a protest against Nasser's closeness to Russia, Boghdadi asked to determine at first hand the nature of the new Egyptian-Soviet informal alliance. He and Nasser agreed that he should visit the Soviet Union alone in an attempt to make sure that there were no differences in perception of what the new relationship between the two countries meant. Boghdadi feared the existence of a secret alliance. It is likely that Sadat had heard about this, and aware of Boghdadi's unfriendly position toward the USSR, used Nasser's acceptance of the Rogers Plan to endear himself to the Soviets by rejecting the American proposal.

Important as the reaction toward the Rogers Plan was in Egypt, and the American-financed Muslim Brotherhood was among its harshest critics, Nasser's acceptance of it had a greater impact on the Arab world and internationally. Because it was unexpected, the Rogers Plan had not been prepared for by Nasser. Overnight, the Rogers Plan became the main target of the PLO. Arafat and all the Palestinian groups lost sight of the simple fact that Golda Meir, Eshkol's uncompromising replacement as Israeli prime minister, had turned down the Rogers Plan. It wasn't the first time the attitudes of the PLO and Israel coincided, but the PLO rejection did provide Meir with a way out. Furthermore, the PLO was reacting to more than Rogers; Arafat was very concerned about the new Nasser-Hussein alliance which had emerged out of Khartoum. But Arafat took little notice of the behavior of his rabble. As always Arafat manifested an inability and a lack of will to curb his followers. In July 1970, King Hussein had made Nasser aware of the PLO's unacceptable behavior in detail. The Palestinian guerrillas drove cars without license plates, vandalized stores, levied taxes, and insulted members of Hussein's army and security forces. Some of them attempted to assassinate Hussein, while others made alliances with officers of the Jordanian army who were willing to overthrow the king. After Arafat went as far as convening the Palestine National Council in Amman and asking its members to debate the replacement of Hussein within earshot of the royal palace, Nasser needed no convincing. He supported Hussein and condemned the Palestinians.

In Lebanon a different but equally revealing situation was unfolding. Continued infiltration from Lebanese soil was producing massive Israeli retaliation which threatened the structure of the country. The Christians considered the Palestinians an alien force and wanted them controlled and removed. The Muslims saw in them allies against Christian dominance. Arafat refused to control his forces. As with Jordan, the responsibility for controlling the behavior of the Palestinians was Arafat's but mending the situations developing between the PLO and other governments fell to Nasser, the creator of the PLO, architect of the Cairo Agreement, and new arbiter of inter-Arab conflicts. What the Palestinians were doing in undermining Jordan and Lebanon was the most serious challenge to Nasser by Arafat. He was destabilizing Jordan and Lebanon to serve notice that the PLO was capable of acting without Nasser. It was his way of undermining the Rogers Plan.

Syria was another problem for Nasser and Rogers. Strategically it was needed to make the plan work. In addition, it was the home of many Palestinian groups, and it openly encouraged them to redouble their activities against Israel. The other Arab states opposed to Rogers—Iraq, Algeria, and Yemen—had less of an impact on what was happening because of their remoteness. But they supported the PLO's hard line, increased their financial aid to Arafat, and expanded their training facilities for the Palestinians. The rest of the Arab countries, especially the oil producers, were looking for a way out of the developing confrontation between the Palestinians on one side and King Hussein and the Lebanese on the other. In reality the confrontation was between Nasser and the Palestinians. To him, the adopted child had become an embarrassing relation. On the other hand, Arafat considered Nasser's acceptance of the Rogers Plan as nothing less than a betrayal. While Nasser's position within Egypt remained relatively secure, his Arab position was under attack by the PLO. In fact, Washington was beginning to doubt his ability to deliver peace. To the Israelis, Arafat was a godsend.

If Arafat's personal behavior was unacceptable, then the behavior of the leftist Palestinian groups belonging to the PLO was abominable, and they accused Arab leaders of treason. Of course, Arafat did nothing to curb them. Senior Fatah leaders repeatedly warned Arafat against going too far, but he wouldn't listen. At one point King Hussein called his bluff and asked him to form a government in Jordan, but that was beyond Arafat's capacity. After that, Hussein's several concessions to avoid a civil war fell on deaf ears. Even his dismissal of his minister of the interior, Mohamed Rasul al-Keilani, and of his own uncle and cousin, both generals in the Jordanian army who opposed making any concessions to the PLO, failed to impress Arafat. The PLO leader was doing little against Israel, but he was destroying the foundations of the Jordanian and Lebanese states and plunging the Middle East into chaos. Nasser was in pain. His various messages to Arafat to cease and desist went unanswered.[36] The behavior of most of his troops was akin to the behavior of a rabble out of the film *The Wild Bunch*. Another leader would have been ashamed of the behavior of his fighters, in fact mostly habitués of Beirut bars and extortionists, but Arafat was always callous and lacking in gentlemanly behavior. He was born and raised in Cairo, and he was no more than a street Cairene.

On September 6, 1970, the Popular Front for the Liberation of Palestine (PFLP), acting on instructions of "the Master," Dr. Wadi Haddad, carried out one of the most memorable hijackings in history. They began with the simultaneous diversion to Jordan of a Swissair DC-8 and a TWA Boeing 707, and these were followed six days later by the hijacking of a BOAC VC-10. The aircraft were forced to land at Dawson Field, thirty miles from Amman, which was renamed Revolutionary Airport. Meanwhile another PFLP hijack team which had failed to hijack an El Al plane managed to hijack a Pan American 747 to Cairo and, in direct defiance of Nasser, blow it up while the media recorded the incident for a gasping world audience.

The PLFP put on a circus with planes replacing animals. There was no intention of harming the passengers; it was a clear attempt to dramatize the plight of the Palestinians and undermine those who pretended to speak in their name (i.e., Nasser). The PFLP people on the ground issued statement after statement condemning everything, including the Rogers Plan. Of course, there were more immediate demands, including the freeing from European prisons of hijackers who had failed during previous attempts. It is true that there was no irrefutable evidence to connect Arafat with the events, but what was happening supported his narrow thinking. But the association of Arafat to the hijackings became clear when he and Haddad declared Dawson Field a liberated area. This suggested that Arafat intended to liberate the rest of Jordan. But if that was so, then—as usual with him—he had no plan for the liberation.

Nasser fumed and issued condemnations of the hijackers, but Jordan had a more immediate problem: what to do about them. There were many politicians in Jordan who had supported the PLO, former premiers Abdel Munim Rifai and Bahjat Talhouni among them, and who still wanted a negotiated settlement with Arafat. On the other hand, Hussein; his brother, Crown Prince Hassan; and the Bedouin elements of his army favored a crackdown. The Palestinian leader, as he had many times in the past, misread the reaction his actions would produce. Even the destruction of the planes on the ground on September 15 did not move him to act against the hijackers. Instead, in another slight to Nasser, he had a few days before rushed to Baghdad to seek the support of the Iraqi government against Hussein. But though he had read several manifestos which called for Hussein's removal on the improvised radio of the PLO, in reality Arafat had no specific plan in mind. When it looked as if Hussein was tilting toward using force to discipline the Palestinians, Arafat started attributing the crisis instigated by the hijackings to "outside influences" and pointed the finger at the CIA. At this point, Hussein, possibly with Nasser's approval, put his own plan into action. The Jordanian army's attack against the Palestinians began on September 16.

The savagery of combat between the Jordanians and Palestinians resembled what had happened during the Mosul Rebellion. Neither side took prisoners; individual scores were settled, and the Jordanian army shelled several Palestinian refugee camps totally occupied by civilians. Five thousand Jordanian troops defected to the Palestinian side, but luckily for King Hussein, the defections were individual—no whole units defected. The fighting began with an attack by the Jordanians on the Palestinian stronghold of Zarga and spread throughout Jordan in hours. The Palestinians acquitted themselves well. Arafat stormed around Amman encouraging his troops, but by the third day the Palestinians' lack of coordination and organization was giving the well-trained Jordanians the edge. With victory slipping away, Arafat began making accusations of "genocide." Units of the Iraqi army stationed in Jordan didn't come to his help as he had expected. On September 19, units of the Palestine Liberation Army stationed in Syria and supported by Syrian armor crossed into Jordan and made a dash toward Amman. Arafat the ever changing propagandist now declared the areas they occupied "liberated areas."

Suddenly Pakistani aircraft sent to prop up Hussein's shaky position, undoubtedly with American prompting, went into action against the invading force. The Israelis mobilized, and the American Sixth Fleet positioned itself between Cyprus and Syria. The Middle East was in flames. In the midst of the fighting, on September 22, an Arab League delegation nominated by Nasser managed to get to Amman and establish contact with Arafat. It was made up of Sudan's President Ja'afar Numeiri, the Tunisian prime minister, the Kuwaiti minister of defense, and the Egyptian chief of staff. Nasser's instructions to them were "not to return to Cairo without getting the two sides to agree to a cease-fire."[37] The Arab delegation was successful. But no sooner had the delegates returned to Cairo, and a mere one day after he agreed to the cease-fire, than Arafat renounced the agreement and renewed his call for the overthrow of the Jordanian monarchy.[38]

It was vintage Arafat. Given the retreat of his forces against the disciplined Jordanians, it was an act of daring. When, on Nasser's prompting, the Arab League delegates returned to Amman, they had to resort to signals and secret messages because Arafat was in hiding. Eventually they appealed to King Hussein for help locating his enemy. When they reached Arafat they finally prevailed on him to go to Cairo with them. His version of what happened renders him heroic, but in fact King Hussein looked the other way and allowed him to leave. Interestingly, the Egyptian president didn't receive Arafat. Instead, Nasser concentrated on getting King Hussein to Cairo for a meeting of Arab heads of state. It took an emotional personal plea by Nasser for Hussein to join the meeting in Cairo on September 27. To Nasser's utter dismay, Arafat and Hussein attended the Arab meeting with their side arms.

As expected, the meeting was lacking in decorum. Hussein accused Arafat of trying to overthrow him, and Arafat went into histrionics and table pounding. Nasser pleaded with both men "to stop it," and when they didn't he suggested they call a psychiatrist. Saudi King Faisal retorted by accepting the facetious suggestion provided he, Faisal, was the first to be examined. Qaddafi of Libya joined the fray by telling Hussein that he was mentally just like his father. (Hussein's father, King Tallal, had been forced to abdicate because of mental illness). But when it came to invective, Arafat had the upper hand. His was a virtuoso performance that day, dredging up every vulgarity he had learned on the streets of Cairo.

It was left to the ailing, tired Nasser, who had suffered several heart attacks since 1967 and had been ordered by his doctors not to work, to hammer out an agreement between Arafat and Hussein. Several hours later, after saying good-bye to the emir of Kuwait, the last Arab leader to leave, Nasser suffered a massive heart attack, was taken home, and died a short while later. Tahiya was with him, along with Heikal and Sadat. Sadat opened his hands and read a sura from the Koran. Tahiya looked at the people gathered around her husband's bed and appealed to them to refrain from allowing the media and the new government to focus on her. "He was the only thing I ever wanted and now he is gone; my only wish is to be buried at his side,"[39] she told them. Then she knelt beside the bed, held his hand, and kissed it. An hour later, the Arab world came to a standstill. Most Arabs were in a state of shock. In faraway California, I heard the news while driving a rented car. Momentarily I lost control of it. After I finally managed to stop it, I put my head in my hands and sobbed uncontrollably. A state trooper stopped to ask the reason I had parked the car so awkwardly, but after he had a look at me, he asked, "What seems to be the matter, sir?"

"Officer, there has been a death in my family. I've just heard it on the radio."

# EPILOGUE

## "You Live, Abu-Khalid, You Live"

Hakim Abdel Nasser: *"The Aswan High Dam is my father's greatest achievement. Without it we would have had floods and years of drought."*

Dr. Huda Abdel Nasser: *"My father set the standard for future Arab leaders."*

Diplomat Tahseen Beshir: *"When it comes to cleanliness, we are not likely to see his like again."*

Journalist and writer Mohamed Heikal: *"Overall, there hasn't been anyone like him, nor are we likely to see anybody like him."*

French premier Guy Mollet: *"Nasser is a Hitler."*

Wilton Wynn, Nasser's first biographer: *"For me there were two Nassers and one of them was a tyrant."*

*The Times* of London, September 30, 1970, obituary: *"Whatever the ultimate verdict of history, he will be remembered as one of the outstanding rulers of Egypt."*

Nuri Said, prime minister of Iraq, speaking to British prime minister Anthony Eden in 1956: *"Hit him, hit him now, and hit him hard."*

Israeli author Eliezer Be'eri: *"Among the outstanding leaders."*

BBC World Radio (talking about Nasser): *"There are a lot of Hitler jokes."*

BBC correspondent Douglas Stewart: *"Haji, haji, haji baba."*

Israeli prime minister David Ben-Gurion: *"I have a great respect for Nasser."*

French writer André Malraux: *"He will enter history as representative of Egypt, the same as Napoleon of France."*

Egyptian political activist Sherrif Hatatta: *"Nasser's greatest achievement was his funeral. The world will never again see five million people crying together."*

Robert Gibbons of Robert Gibbons Associates, onetime Nasser public relations representative: *"He was an extremely charming man."*

American diplomat William R. Polk: *"He was the John Kennedy of the Arab World."*

Saïd Aburish, on the BBC World Television program *Hard Talk*: *"My generation was orphaned when Nasser died."*

*Al Ahram* newspaper: *"He is dead and the whole world is weeping."*

Nasser was not one person. As attested to by the above statements, he was different things to different people. Hundreds of equally poignant summations describing the life and death of Gamal Abdel Nasser came to my attention during three years of researching and writing his biography. Accepting the multiplicity of Nasser's persona allows me to turn the basic question of his place in history on its head. Were the many Nassers he embodied the creations of a cynical politician who responded to whatever confronted him selectively and derived boyish satisfaction out of being unpredictable, or were these divisions within him beyond his control? His achievements and failures do not provide us with an answer. The one Nasser who is always present regardless of whatever persona he adopted to cope with a particular situation was the dreamer. As a boy, an army officer, a leader of Egypt, and then the most popular Arab leader in centuries, Nasser never stopped being a dreamer. But he failed to achieve any of his ambitions because all of them were beyond his reach.

There is an enormous difference between his dreams and his ambitions. Having dreams is a psychological condition. Being ambitious can be judged in the realistic terms of success and failure. Nasser reached the conclusion that his ambitions were unattainable well before his followers did. He realized that he could not unite the Arabs because the Arab masses he so loved lacked the necessary social cohesion that could produce such a result. The Arabs failed him. But he never stopped dreaming. It is this, the abandoning of ambition without stopping to dream, which distinguishes him from the run-of-the-mill Arab dictators. It was Saddam Hussein's inability to make this critical distinction which produced his ruin. And the separateness of dream from the realities of ambition is why Arab nationalism has ceased to exist as a realistic political ideology and now is no more than an intellectual exercise.

If people remember where they were when Kennedy was shot, then Sherrif Hatatta's statement that Nasser's funeral was his greatest achievement holds true, as does the subsidiary fact that the world is unlikely to see anything like it again. In the Arab world people remember it. Five million mourners followed his cortege, and, like participants in an Irish wake, they told his life story in improvised, memorable chants. Even when we ignore the tens of millions of Arabs who were there in spirit, the ones who wept in coffeehouses, at home, alone, in groups, silently, loudly, through prayer, in cars in faraway California, or who suffered the pain of his death in frozen numbness, Hatatta still has it right. Hatatta, imprisoned by Nasser the tyrannical dictator for four years, obeys the sense of history the funeral contained.

Covering the story for CBS from Cairo, the greatest American broadcaster of the time, Walter Cronkite, was infected by the sense of occasion, and for a moment he faltered. King Hussein of

Jordan sobbed like a baby. Muammar Qaddafi of Libya fainted twice. Arafat shed silent tears while his trembling lips prayed. Sadat, Sabri, the Mohieddine cousins, Heikal, and other Nasser comrades were there. But there were no major Western dignitaries. Premier Aleksey Kosygin represented the USSR. In essence it was an Egyptian-Arab funeral even in its unruliness, as when the crowd almost hijacked the coffin. The only exception to the thick sense of grief enveloping Cairo, the entire Arab world, and even some Muslim countries came from the Muslim Brotherhood. Sheikh Omar counseled his followers, "Do not pray for the faithless Nasser."

The dirges, the absence of Western dignitaries, and the callousness of Sheikh Omar sum up Nasser's life. The broadcasts of his funeral told the same story; the Arab tribe had lost its head. The Palestinian poet Fadwa Toukan eulogized him for a whole generation. "The wind told us he would come," she wrote. Samih al-Kassem's poem was more explicit; he asked the Arabs to weep. Even years after, in 1975, the Lebanese writer Nejla Abu Izzidine pointed out that Nasser died on the same date as the prophet Mohamed and issued an Arab challenge to all of Nasser's detractors: "He was no accident." To this day, the statement of the Saudi taxi driver who placed Nasser ahead of all other Arab leaders before and after him is echoed by Iraqi farmers, Syrian shop owners, Jordanian waiters, Moroccan tourist guides, Palestinian refugees, Lebanese housewives, Tunisian students, and Arabs everywhere. According to Dr. Zakki Badawi, the head of the Muslim College in London, "The Muslim Brotherhood, the very same organization which tried to assassinate him so many times, has finally, three or four years ago, issued a directive advising its followers to refrain from criticising Nasser."

Nasser has endured even without leaving us with a recognizable inheritance except for the Aswan High Dam, or solid institutions with which to judge him. Nasser, multifaceted as he was, lives up to the statement of Abu Dhabi Television and "comes to mind whenever the Arabs face a problem." What I selected from thousands of available assessments, what members of his family, his old comrades, his implacable Islamic enemies, Arab leaders, poets and writers, and Western statesmen comparing him to Hitler, what all of them said was true. *The Times*'s obituary spoke of his place in history after saying that it was too early to judge him. The contradictions contained in my list of statements are true today, even after September 11, 2001, and the consequent realization that the Middle East is a bigger mess than we had thought.

The five million mourners were hardly satisfied with Hussein's obvious grief and Arafat's customary cynical performance. Their universal dirge was "You live, Abu-Khalid, you live." Some said it in anger, women shrieked it, boys and girls echoed it, and older men, as if infected by it, joined in. It was a defiant statement which combined mourning with promise. Then, echoing a mourner who responded to the presence of Hussein and Arafat by saying they were behind the meeting which exhausted their leader to death, the millions of marchers began demanding, "What have you done to him, what have you done to him?" The women of Cairo adopted this question readily and shook their fists. From there the millions bidding him good-bye reverted to praise and keening: *"Ya Gamal ya nour el ain sayyeb al Arab o rayyeh fein"* ("Gamal, light of our eyes, you're leaving the Arabs and going where"). Judged by Western standards this was histrionics, but the Arabs are people who express themselves emotionally. To them shows of grief are a form of reverence. But perhaps it was Chou En-lai, the Chinese premier who met Nasser at Bandung and recognized the power within him, the man who helped him with the arms deal with the Czechs, who delivered the ultimate judgment: "He died of sorrow, he died of a broken heart."

However impressive the funeral and overwhelming the emotions of the people who mourned Nasser in person or from afar, analyzing his legacy, entering into his various personae, requires a writer to go through a process of elimination of possibilities until they are reduced to the manageable. His passions, loves, hates, compromises, intemperance, and statesmanlike behavior and even his ultimate discarding of the noble attributes of the young believer in democracy and becoming a dictator reflect the three major faces he presented to the world. There was the face of Nasser, the quintessential Arab; there was another one which he used in dealing with the West; and there was a third, which he used to deal with the East. Unbelievably, his policies toward Israel originated from rather than formed and determined his three faces.

In the relatively short period of sixteen years, Nasser faced the Arab establishment and came close to defeating it. Would the House of Saud have continued its antiquated ways if Nasser had lived on? I think not. I think that his mere existence would have acted as a check on their unacceptable political and personal ways. Nor was his advocacy of mild socialism and justice for the common man confined to words. Perhaps his hopes in this area were part of his dream. But the dream has not been forgotten by the Saudi taxi driver. The dream lives, and it waits for the race of individual genius to produce another person to embody it. Without a leader, Arab dreams become frustrations.

The reason for confronting the West was a simple one which resulted from his opposition to colonialism, direct as in the case of Britain and France, indirect as in the case of the oil companies determining America's Middle East policy, or by proxy as in Israel playing the role of a Western implant deserving the affection of all who dredge up ancient and recent history in an effort to demonize the Arabs and Muslims. We are back to Western support for Judaic Israel and the control of the oil by its users rather than producers as key factors in Nasser's face toward the West.

The on and off quarrel with the East was a natural result of Nasser's intrinsic Arabness. Believers in individual genius do not make good Communists or socialists. Nasser's opposition to Communism was no different from that of the average Arab. In 1958, Britain was right and America was wrong. There was no Communist threat to the Arab world from the local Communist Parties, not even in Iraq. It was Nasser who threatened the oil concessions and the traditional regimes of deputy sheriffs. In a way, it was the British who defeated him by making a stand in Iraq, even when this policy required supporting the mentally unbalanced Abdel Karim Kassem. Historically, losing the Suez campaign was just that, losing a campaign, but defeating Nasser in Iraq was winning a war. Britain won the war. Nasser knew it.

But in accepting that there are no self-perpetuating institutions in the Arab world the West reaches the wrong conclusions. To Britain and France, from after the end of the First World War to the late 1950s, the absence of institutions meant that whatever was represented by any Arab leader disappeared with his death. So to them, the dreams of Arab unity which followed the Arab rebellion against Turkey during the First World War disappeared with the death of Sherrif Hussein, the man who allied himself with Britain and inspired it. America followed this flawed maxim when it replaced Britain and France as the leading power in the Middle East in the late 1950s. In making the same mistake, America too thought that whatever Nasser represented died with him.

The West saw no link between the Arab rebellion of 1914 and Nasser. This is a grievous error, made even worse by America's lack of understanding of Islam and the dangers of politicizing it. This is why America's understanding of September 11, 2001, is a superficial one that concentrates on who did it and ignores the reasons for it. The former *Times* of London Middle East correspondent James Morris (before he changed persona and became Jan) summed it all up in the 1950s by proclaiming that Islam was inflamed. Gamal Abdel Nasser personalized the blazing fire of Islam like no other person since Saladin. He failed. He failed in Egypt. He failed in the Arab world. He failed in his confrontation with Israel. He failed in building institutions that would outlast him. Eventually he became a petty dictator, the one thing he feared most when he was young. It wasn't a case of power corrupting; it was the direct result of failure.

But his dreams live. His dreams have been hijacked by the Islamic movements the West created to defeat him. Although dreams are not a replacement for ambitions, we still owe his dreams a great deal. But for them, we would have had many vile September 11s. Abu Dhabi Television was right in thinking of him in terms of the state of the Arabs today, be it the elevation of a Tikriti thug to Arab leadership in Iraq or the absence of control over a wanton murderer. Nasser told Arafat to think of peace in 1968. In 1969 he lashed out at the Iraqi leadership for making a show out of brutality; then, after making his speech, he went home to play soccer with his young children. In his case, the eventual dictator was a victim of the people who failed him, the Arabs.

# NOTES

## Introduction: The Painful Truth

1. Tewfic Farah, editor, *Pan-Arabism and Arab Nationalism: The Continuing Debate* (Boulder, Colo., 1987), p. 42.
2. Interviews with Egyptian activists Dr. Sherrif Hatatta and Mohamed Sayyed Ahmed, Cairo, November 2001.

## 1. The Dreamer from Nowhere

1. Jean Lacouture, *Nasser* (London, 1973), p. 20.
2. Joachim Joesten, *Nasser: The Rise to Power* (London, 1960), p. 19.
3. Butheina Abdel Rahman Tikriti, *Gamal Abdel Nasser: Beginning and Evolution of Nasserite Thought* (in Arabic) (Beirut, 2000).
4. Desmond Stewart, *The Middle East: Temple of Janus* (London, 1971), p. 328.
5. Stewart, p. 328.
6. Robert Stephens, *Nasser* (London, 1971), p. 32.
7. Lacouture, p. 42.
8. Stephens, p. 22; Huda Abdel Nasser, interview, Cairo, November 2001.
9. Lacouture, pp. 30, 32, 43, 46, 47, 48, 49, 368.
10. Joesten, p. 62.

11. Joesten, p. 19.
12. Eliezer Be'eri, *Army Officers in Arab Politics and Society* (London, 1970), p. 77; Peter Mansfield, *Nasser* (London, 1969), p. 21.
13. Robert St. John, *The Boss* (New York, 1960), p. 33.
14. Anouar Abdel Malik, *Egypt's Military Society* (Arabic) (Cairo, 1982), p. 206.
15. Lacouture, p. 39.
16. Lacouture, p. 43.
17. Anwar Sadat, *In Search of Identity* (London, 1978), pp. 98–105.
18. Anwar Sadat, *Revolt on the Nile* (London, 1957), p. 15.
19. Khalid Mohieddine and Mahmoud Hammroush, original Free Officers members, interviews, Cairo, November 2001.
20. Stephens, p. 48.
21. Stephens, p. 54.
22. Woodward, p. 17.
23. Lacouture, p. 48.
24. Mansfield, p. 56.
25. Khalid Mohieddine, interview, Cairo, November 2001.
26. P. J. Vatikiotis, *Nasser and His Generation* (London, 1978), pp. 36–37.
27. Lacouture, p. 49.
28. Tikriti, p. 18.
29. Sadat, *Revolt on the Nile*, p. 64.
30. Salah Nasr, *History of the 23 July Revolution* (Arabic) (Cairo, p. 65 1986); The late Kheiry Hammad, official spokesman for King Abdullah in 1947, reporter's notebook, conversation.
31. Stephens, p. 74.
32. Stephens, p. 75.
33. Mohamed Heikal, *Secret Channels* (London, 1994), p. 75.
34. Lacouture, p. 61.
35. Hammroush, pp. 12–13.
36. Larry Collins and Dominique Lapierre, *O Jerusalem* (New York, 1972), p. 535.
37. Abdel Latif Boghdadi, *Diaries*, 1977, p. 28.
38. Avi Schlaim of St. Anthony's College, Oxford, wrote a whole book on this subject, *Collusion Across the Jordan* (Oxford, 1982).
39. Lacouture, p. 66.
40. Stewart, p. 36.
41. *Al Hayat* (London), September 30, 1992.
42. Vatikiotis, p. 105.
43. Miles Copeland, a former CIA operative involved in the Syrian and

the later Egyptian coups, reporter's notebook, conversation in the late 1970s.

44. Joesten, p. 82; Richard P. Mitchell, *The Society of the Muslim Brotherhood* (Oxford, 1982), p. 100.
45. Anwar Sadat, *Revolt on the Nile*, p. 80.
46. Hammroush, pp. 14–17.
47. Boghdadi, pp. 60–90.
48. Stewart, p. 339.
49. Mohamed Heikal, interview, Cairo, November 2001.

## 2. The Encounter with Power

1. Abdel Latif Boghdadi, *Diaries* (in Arabic) (Cairo, 1982), p. 40.
2. Anthony Nutting, *Nasser* (London, 1972), p. 20.
3. Nutting, p. 30.
4. Paul Parker, former U.S. Treasury representative, reporter's notebook conversations, London, 1984–85.
5. Karem Thabet, *The End of the Monarchy in Egypt* (in Arabic) (Cairo, 1968), p. 431.
6. Abdallah Imam, *The Muslim Brotherhood* (in Arabic) (Cairo, 1986), p. 7.
7. Derek Hopwood, *Egyptian Politics and Society* (London, 1991), pp. 23–24. The author attributes this to Anwar Sadat.
8. Khalid Mohieddine, interview, Cairo, October 2001.
9. Anwar Sadat, *In Search of Identity* (London, 1978), p. 103.
10. Sadat, *In Search of Identity*, p. 101.
11. Nasser, *The Philosophy of the Revolution*, pp. 12–14 (booklet produced by many people and the pages differ from one edition to another); Salah Nasr, *The Revolution of 23 July* (in Arabic) (Cairo, 1980), p. 84; Sadat, *Revolt on the Nile* (London, 1958), p. 112.
12. Boghdadi, p. 41.
13. Robert St. John, *The Boss* (New York, 1960), p. 33; Peter Mansfield, *Nasser* (London, 1968), pp. 38–42.
14. Boghdadi, pp. 45–52.
15. P. J. Vatikiotis, *The History of Modern Egypt* (London, 1991), pp. 378–379.
16. Khalid Mohieddine, interview, Cairo, October 2001; Boghdadi, pp. 46–52.
17. Khalid Mohieddine interview.
18. Nutting, p. 38.
19. Mansfield, pp. 46–48.

20. Butheina Abdel Rahman Tikriti, *The Growth and Evolution of Nasserite Thought* (in Arabic) (Beirut, 2000), pp. 156–158.
21. Khalid Mohieddine and Mahmoud Hammroush interviews, Cairo, October 2001. Mohamed Labib is supposed to have told the Muslim Brotherhood, and Hammroush himself told the Communists.
22. William Lakeland, correspondence, April–June 2001.
23. Eliezer Be'eri, *The Arab Armies in Politics and Society* (London, 1970), p. 89.
24. Salah Nasr, *The 23 July Coup* (in Arabic) (Cairo, 1986), p. 107.
25. Sadat, *Revolt on the Nile,* p. 28.
26. Jean Lacouture, *Nasser* (London, 1973) p. 97.
27. Imam, p. 33.
28. Nutting, p. 38.
29. Hammroush interview.
30. Mansfield, p. 53.
31. Mohieddine interview.
32. Stephens, p. 107; Nutting, p. 41.
33. Dr. Rashidd al-Barawy, *The Military Coup in Egypt* (London, 1952), p. 31.
34. Miles Copeland, reporter's notebook conversations, 1977–79.
35. Tikriti, p. 159.
36. Vatikiotis, p. 108.
37. Mohamed Heikal, interview, November 2001.
38. Nutting, pp. 42–43.
39. Mohamed Heikal, *For Egypt Not for Abdel Nasser* (Beirut, 1988), p. 74.
40. Imam, p. 47; Zakki Baddawi, interview, London, August 2000.
41. Nutting, p. 54.
42. Mourad M. Wahba, *The Role of the State in the Egyptian Economy* (Ithaca, N.Y., 1994), p. 49.
43. Geneive Abdo, *There Is No God but God* (Oxford, 2000), p. 49.
44. Sadat, *Revolt on the Nile,* p. 19.
45. Boghdadi, p. 70.
46. Kennett Love *Suez—The Twice-Fought War* (London, 1969), p. 48.
47. Love, p. 13.
48. Hammroush, *The Story of the 23 July Revolution,* (Arabic) (Cairo, 1977), p. 16
49. Imam, p. 68; Mitchell, p. 28.
50. Joachem Hippler and Andre Lueg, *The Next Threat* (London, 1997), p. 67.
51. Mohamed Fayyeq, interview, October 2001.
52. Nasr, p. 107.
53. Hammroush, p. 101.

54. Hammroush, pp. 18–20.
55. Avi Schlaim, correspondence, April 2001. Schlaim is an authority on the subject, the author of *The Iron Wall.*
56. Boghdadi, p. 110.
57. Boghdadi, pp. 156–57.
58. Be'eri, p. 116.
59. Khalid Mohieddine, interview, October 2001, Cairo.
60. Hisham Kassem, *Cairo Gazette* editor, interview, Cairo, October 2001.
61. Imam, p. 74.
62. Imam, pp. 74–77.
63. Anouar Abdel Malik *Egypt's Military Society* (London, 1968), pp. 119–35.
64. Abu Saïd Aburish, *Time* magazine correspondent, interview, Seattle, April 1999. Aburish reported this at the time.
65. Tahseen Beshir interview; Mohamed Heikal interview.
66. Boghdadi, p. 64.

### 3. The Road to Suez

1. Khalid Mohieddine, interview, Cairo, October 2001
2. Dr. Huda Abdel Nasser, interview, Cairo, November 2001.
3. Hakim Abdel Nasser, interview, Cairo, October 2001.
4. Miles Copeland, CIA agent, reporter's notebook conversations, 1981–82; Khalid Mohieddine, former RCC member, and Mahmoud Hammroush confirm this.
5. Stewart Stevens, *The Spymasters of Israel* (London, 1981), p. 61.
6. Ian Black and Benny Morris, *Israel's Secret Wars: A History of Israel's Intelligence Service* (London, 1991), p. 117.
7. Correspondence with Mr. Bar-On, who supplied the writer with a copy of his lecture to the Bruno Kreisky Institute in Vienna, October 1999. Avi Shlaim, *The Iron Wall: Israel and the Arab World* (London, 2000), p. 53.
8. Shlaim, p. 78.
9. Black and Morris, pp. 113–14.
10. Dan Raviv and Yossi Melman, *Every Spy a Prince* (New York, 1990), p. 56.
11. General Abdel Fatah Riyadh, former security officer under Nasser, interview, Cairo, October 2001.
12. General Abdel Fatah Riyadh and Colonel Salah Dessouki, interviews, Cairo, October–November 2001.

13. Shlaim, p. 51.
14. Riyadh interview.
15. Kennett Love, *Suez—The Twice-Fought War* (London, 1969) p. 80.
16. Riyadh interview; Salah Dessouki interview.
17. Anwar Abdel Malek, *Egypt's Military Society* (London, 1968), p. 182.
18. Malek, pp. 102–3.
19. Miles Copeland, conversations, 1970s and 1980s.
20. Rashid al-Barawy, *The Military Coup in Egypt* (London, 1952), p. 209.
21. Jon Kimche, *The Second Arab Awakening* (London, 1970), p. 102.
22. Dr. Huda Abdel Nasser, interview.
23. Sherrif Hatatta and Salah Dessouki, interviews, Cairo, October–November 2001.
24. Jean Lacouture, *Nasser* (London, 1973), p. 161.
25. Sherrif Hatatta; interview, Cairo, November. 2001.
26. James A. Bell, conversations, 1970s and 1980s.
27. Najla Abu Izzidine, *Nasser of the Arabs* (Beirut, 1980); p. 201.
28. Copeland, reporter's notebook conversations.
29. Khalid Mohieddine, Mahmoud Hammroush, and Mohamed Heikal, interviews, Cairo, October–November 2001.
30. Mohieddine interview.
31. Geoffrey Aronson, *From Sideshow to Center Stage: U.S. Policy Toward Egypt, 1946–1956* (New York, 1986), p. 200.

## 4. Give Them Dignity

1. Dr. Zakki Badawi, interview, London, June 2001.
2. Fawaz A. Gerges, *Arab Politics, Islam, and the Clash of Cultures* (Cambridge, 1998), p. 40.
3. Miles Copeland, CIA agent, conversations, London, 1970s and 1980s.
4. Hakim Abdel Nasser, interview, Cairo, October 2001.
5. P. J. Vatikiotis, *Nasser and His Generation* (Cairo, 1978), p. 250.
6. Nasseddine Nashasshibi (former editor of Cairo's *Akhbar*), "Memoirs," *Sharq Al Awsat* newspaper, August, 24–September 15, 2001.
7. Mohamed Heikal, interview, November 2001. Heikal recalled that he mentioned this in his *Cairo Documents* (New York, 1973), p. 94.
8. Heikal, p. 76.
9. Aburish, *A Brutal Friendship*, pp. 259–61.
10. Miles Copeland, CIA agent, conversations, London, 1970s and 1980s.
11. Stephen Dorril, *M16: Fifty Years of Special Operations* (London, 2000), p. 612.

12. Jordanian Interior Minister Radi Abdallah, conversations, 1960s and 1970s.
13. Dorrit, p. 612.
14. Jean Lacouture, *Nasser* (London, 1973), p. 140.
15. Kennett Love, *Suez—The Twice-Fought War* (London, 1969), p. 123.
16. Moshe Shemesh, *The Palestinian Entity, 1959–1974: Arab Politics and the PLO* (London, 1988), p. 3.
17. Love, p. 141.
18. Geoffrey Aronson, *From Sideshow to Center Stage: U.S. Policy Toward Egypt, 1946–1956* (Boulder, Colo., 1986), p. 188.
19. Love, p. 3.
20. Salah Dessouki, Nasser security aide, interview, Cairo, October 2001.
21. Abu Saïd Aburish, *Time* magazine correspondent, interview. The author's father remembers asking the Egyptian ambassador to Lebanon what the new policy meant only to be told he had not been briefed on the subject.
22. Anthony Nutting, *Nasser* (London, 1972), p. 126.
23. Love, p. 305.
24. Aronson, p. 256.
25. Anthony Gorst and Lewis Johnman, *The Suez Crisis* (London, 1997), pp. 50–51; a reproduction of PROFO 371/118862, C. A. E. Shuckburough to H.M. Representatives, MAY, 28, 1956.
26. Aronson, p. 227.
27. Aronson, p. 228.
28. Mohamed Heikal, interview, Cairo, November 2001.
29. Abdel Latif Boghdadi, *Memoirs* (Arabic) (Cairo, 1982), p. 321.
30. Lacouture, p. 166.
31. Boghdadi, p. 321.
32. Boghdadi, p. 321.
33. Love, p. 340.
34. Hugh Thomas, *The Suez Affair* (London, 1966), p. 38.
35. Charles D. Cremeans, *The Arabs and the World: Nasser's Arab Nationalist Policy* (New York, 1963), p. 156.
36. Thomas, p. 67.
37. Nejla Abu Izzedine *Nasser of the Arabs* (Beirut, 1975), p. 166.
38. Dorril, p. 210.
39. Thomas, p. 47.
40. Thomas, p. 181.
41. Thomas, pp. 34–35.
42. Nutting, p. 47.

43. Salah Dessouki, interview, November 2001.
44. May Oueidah, "An Examination of Some Structural Elements in the Speeches of President Nasser," unpublished thesis for a master's degree at the American University of Beirut, 1981, p. 26.
45. Derek Hopwood, *Egypt, Politics, and Society, 1945–1990* (London, 1993), p. 51.
46. Dorril, p. 627.
47. Thomas, p. 70.
48. Boghdadi, p. 328.
49. Boghdadi, p. 328; Thomas, p. 68; Robert Stephens, *Nasser* (London, 1992), p. 208.
50. Thomas, p. 78.
51. Nutting, p. 158.
52. Nutting, p. 171.
53. Thomas, p. 13.
54. Thomas, p. 90.
55. Love, p. 433.
56. Love, p. 433.
57. John Mecklin, *Time* magazine correspondent and witness to the incident, conversation, reporter's notebook.
58. Stephens, p. 231.
59. Boghdadi, pp. 344–45.
60. Boghdadi, p. 354.

## 5. The Dark at the End of the Tunnel

1. Mufti, reporter's notebook interview, Beirut, 1960.
2. Kennett Love, *Suez—The Twice-Fought War* (London, 1969), p. 8, attributes it to Tom Little, head of Reuters in Cairo, p. 15.
3. Abdel Latif Boghdadi, *Diaries* (Cairo, 1982), p. 191.
4. Keith Whitlock, *Nasser's New Egypt* (New York, 1996), p. 282.
5. Mahmoud Hammroush, interview, Cairo, October 2001.
6. Rashid Khalidy, *The Palestinian Identity: The Construction of Modern National Consciousness* (New York, 1997), p. 183.
7. Geoffrey Aronson Boulder, *From Sideshow to Center Stage: U.S. Policy Toward Egypt, 1945–56* (Colo., 1985), p. 245.
8. Andrew Tulley, *Inside the CIA* (London, 1986), p. 108.
9. Roger Owen, *State, Power and Politics in the Middle East* (London, 1988), p. 95.
10. Saïd K. Aburish, *The Rise, Corruption, and Coming Fall of the House of Saud* (London, 1997), p. 50.

11. Robert Stephens, *Nasser* (London, 1971), p. 257.
12. Mohamed Heikal, interview, Cairo, October 2001.
13. Wilbur Eveland, *Ropes of Sand* (New York, 1982), p. 177.
14. Private source.
15. Mohamed Heikal, *For Egypt, Not for Abdel Nasser* (Beirut, 1988), p. 15.
16. James Critchfield, interview, Washington, D.C., 1996.
17. Mohamed Heikal, interview, Cairo, November 2001.
18. Stephen Dorril, *The Silan Conspiracy* (London, 1993), p. 87.
19. Mohamed Heikal, *For Egypt, Not for Abdel Nasser*, p. 15.
20. Saïd K. Aburish, *A Brutal Friendship: The West and the Arab Elite* (London, 1997), p. 130.
21. Dilip Hiro, *Inside the Middle East* (London, 1987), p. 320.
22. Hanna Batatu, *The Old Social Classes and the Revolutionary Movements of Iraq* (Princeton, N.J., 1978), p. 862.
23. Hammroush interview.
24. Mohamed Sayyed Ahmed, interview, Cairo, November 2001.
25. Boghdadi, p. 279.
26. Hammroush interview.
27. Mohamed Heikal, interview, Cairo, November 2001.
28. Charles Issawi, *Egypt in Revolution: An Economic Analysis* (Oxford, 1963), p. 47.
29. Issawi, p. 197.
30. William L. Cleveland, *A History of the Modern Middle East* (Boulder, Colo., 1994), p. 323.
31. Gilles Kepel, *Muslim Extremism in Egypt* (*The Prophet and the Pharaoh*) (Berkeley, Calif., 1985), pp. 37–42.
32. Daniel Pipes, *The Long Shadow* (New York, 1985), p. 125.
33. Love, p. 647.
34. Dr. Zakki Badawi, interview, London, June 2000.
35. Eveland, p. 250.
36. Jean Lacouture, *Nasser* (London, 1973), p. 182.
37. Robert Lacey, *The Kingdom* (London, 1981), p. 312.
38. David Holden and Richard Johns, *The House of Saud* (London, 1982), p. 188.
39. Eveland, p. 244.
40. Dr. Huda Abdel Nasser, interview, Cairo, October 2001.
41. Andrew Cockburn and Leslie Cockburn, *Secret Liaison* (London, 1992), p. 237.
42. Batatu, p. 795.
43. Boghdadi, p. 35.
44. Boghdadi, p. 35.

45. Boghdadi, p. 35.
46. Anthony Nutting, *Nasser* (London, 1972), p. 219.

## 6. And I Shall Divide Your Araby into Two

1. Anthony Nutting, *Nasser* (London, 1972), pp. 223–230.
2. Nutting, pp. 213–232.
3. Abu Saïd Aburish, the author's father and a *Time* magazine correspondent then, verified this with a Syrian cabinet member.
4. Abdel Latif Boghdadi, *Diaries* (Cairo, 1982), p. 51.
5. Wilbur Eveland, *Ropes of Sand* (New York, 1980), pp. 139–140.
6. Miles Copeland, *The Game Player* (London, 1989), p. 215.
7. Eveland, p. 273.
8. Saïd K. Aburish, *The St. George Hotel Bar* (London, 1987), pp. 54–56.
9. Eveland, p. 263.
10. The mufti, off-the-record interview, reporter's notebook, Beirut, 1960.
11. Abdel Magid Farid, executive director of Nasser's office, interview, London, June 2000.
12. Boghdadi, p. 53.
13. Robert Stephens, *Nasser* (London, 1982), p. 289.
14. John Chancellor, who eventually broke the story, told it off the record to Canadian newsman Donal Gordon and the author sometime around July 21, 1958.
15. The late Wasfi Tel, then a Jordanian attaché in Iran but later prime minister of Jordan, told the author of this. He had bought the intercept from an Iranian intelligence officer in Beirut in 1959, and it was verified.
16. Boghdadi, p. 55.
17. May Oueidah, telephone interview, December 2000.
18. Richard Parker, former American diplomat and Arabist, correspondence, July 17, 2001.
19. Boghdadi, pp. 60–65.
20. Saïd K. Aburish, *Saddam Hussein: The Politics of Revenge* (London, 2000), pp. 42–43.
21. Ismael Aref, *The Revolution of 14 July and Establishment of the Iraqi Republic* (Arabic) (London, 2000), p. 284.
22. Boghdadi, p. 82.
23. Boghdadi, p. 83.
24. The author was at the Syrian-Iraqi border town of Kamishly when many of the pro-Shawaf injured were brought into Syria.
25. William McHale, conversation, reporter's notebook, April 1958.

26. Boghdadi, p. 83.
27. Aref, p. 284.
28. James Critchfield, interview, Washington, D.C., 1997.
29. The mufti, reporter's notebook, interview, December 1958.
30. Attributed to Saddam by his half-brother Barazam, conversation with the author, Baghdad, 1982.

## 7. Search for an Honorable Exit

1. Mohamed Heikel, interview, Cairo, October 2001.
2. Tahseen Beshir, interview, Cairo, October 2001.
3. Dr. Huda Abdel Nasser and Hakim Abdel Nasser, interviews, October–November 2001.
4. Professor Avi Shlaim (St. Anthony's College, Oxford), interview by correspondence, May 2000.
5. Charles D. Cremeans, *The Arabs and the World: Nasser's Arab Nationalist Policy* (New York, 1963), p. 63.
6. P. J. Vatikiotis, *Nasser and His Generation* (London, 1978), p. 159.
7. Miles Copeland, CIA agent, conversations, 1970s and 1980s.
8. Mohamed Heikel, interview, Cairo, October 2001.
9. Mohamed Heikel, *Nasser—The Cairo Documents* (New York, 1973), p. 140.
10. Mohamed Heikel, interview, Cairo, October 2001; Vatikiotis, p. 304.
11. Anovar Abdel Malek, *Egypt's Military Society* (London, 1968), p. 359.
12. John Waterbury, *The Egypt of Nasser and Sadat* (Princeton, N.J., 1983); p. 302.
13. James Critchfield, interview, Washington, D.C., 1998.
14. Dana Adams Schmidt, *Yemen: The Unknown War* (London, 1968), p. 257.
15. Richard Beeston, *The Daily Telegraph*, July 8, 1963.
16. Mohamed Heikel, interview, Cairo, November 2001.
17. Mohamed Heikel, interview, Cairo, November 2001.

## 8. Leader of the Arabs

1. Moshe Shemesh, *The Palestinian Entity, 1959–1974: Arab Politics and the PLO* (London, 1988), p. 3.
2. Saïd K. Aburish, *Arafat: From Defender to Dictator* (London, 1998), p. 57.
3. Aburish, *Arafat*, p. 43.
4. Yezid Sayigh, *Armed Struggle and the Search for State* (London, 1999), p. 108.

5. Private sources who spoke on a not-for-attribution basis.
6. Mohamed Heikal, *Nasser—The Cairo Documents* (Beirut, 1972), pp. 187–188.
7. Heikal, Ibid. The whole book is on this subject.
8. Professor Avi Shlaim, an authority on the subject, verified this in correspondence with the author.
9. Sayigh, p. 155.
10. Wilbur Eveland, *Ropes of Sand* (New York, 1980), pp. 244–245; conversation with the author, London, 1982.
11. James Critchfield, regional CIA director, interviews, Washington, D.C. June–July 1994.
12. Joachem Joesten, *Nasser: The Rise to Power* (London, 1960), p. 221.
13. Saïd K. Aburish, *A Brutal Friendship: The West and the Arab Elite* (London, 1997), pp. 61–63.
14. Malik Mufti, *Sovereign Creations* (Ithaca, N.Y. 1996), p. 156.
15. Mohamed Heikal, interview, Cairo, November 2001.
16. Abba Eban, *Personal Witness* (London, 1993), p. 253.
17. Mohamed Sayyed Ahmed, interview, Cairo, November 2001.
18. Heikal, *Nasser—The Cairo Documents*, pp. 204–205.
19. Abdel Latif Boghdadi, *Diaries* (Cairo, 1982), pp. 120–140.
20. Jean Lacouture, *Nasser* (London, 1973), p. 128.
21. Gilles Kepel, *Muslim Extremism in Egypt* (Berkeley, Calif., 1985), p. 28.
22. Interviews, Cairo, October–November 2001.
23. Mahmoud Hammroush, interview, Cairo, October 2001.
24. Abdel Magid Farid, executive head of presidential office, interview, London, August 2000.
25. Boghdadi, p. 142.
26. Abdel Magid Farid, interview, London, July 2001.
27. Boghdadi, Ibid., pp. 120–140.
28. Hakim Abdel Nasser, interview, Cairo, October, 2001.

## 9. The Politics of Decline

1. Mahmoud Hammroush, interview, Cairo, October 2001; Ian Black and Benny Morris, *Israel's Secret Wars* (London, 1991), p. 211, state that Israeli military intelligence, Aman, also felt Nasser would not be ready for a military confrontation until 1970.
2. Abdel Magid Farid, *Nasser, The Final Years* (Reading, U.K., 1994), p. 12.
3. Dr. Butheina Abdel Rahman Tikriti, *Gamal Abdel Nasser: Beginning and Evolution of Nasserite Thought* (Beirut, 2000), p. 268.

4. Farid, p. 16.
5. Nutting, *Nasser* (London, 1972), p. 397.
6. Nutting, p. 106.
7. Martin Gilbert, *Israel: A History* (London, 1998), p. 367.
8. Gilbert, p. 390.
9. Derek Hopwood, *Egypt: Politics and Society*, 3rd ed. (London, 1991), p. 73; Nutting, p. 402.
10. Nutting, p. 400.
11. Tikriti, p. 290.
12. Walter Laqueur and Jerry Rubin, eds., *The Israeli-Arab Reader* (London, 1991), p. 159.
13. Jean Lacouture, *Nasser* (London, 1973), p. 304; Tikriti, p. 143.
14. Abba Ebban, *Personal Witness: Israel Through My Eyes* (London, 1993), p. 369.
15. Peter Woodward, *Nasser* (Profiles in Power series) (London, 1992), p. 106.
16. Nutting, p. 406.
17. Moshe Shemesh, *The Palestinian Entity, 1959–1974: Arab Politics and the PLO* (London, 1982), p. 55.
18. Nutting, p. 406.
19. Abdallah Abdel Imam, *Abdel Nasser and the Muslim Brotherhood* (Arabic) (Cairo, 1986), pp. 100–110.
20. Imam, p. 126.
21. Lacouture, p. 148.
22. Wilbur Eveland, *Ropes of Sand* (New York, 1980), p. 323.
23. Nutting, p. 426.
24. Mahmoud Hammroush, *The Autumn of Gamal Abdel Nasser: The Story of the 23 July Revolution* (Arabic) (Beirut, 1977), p. 107.
25. *The Guardian*, August 18, 2001, article by Isabela Ginor reporting from Jerusalem.
26. Mohamed Heikal and Abdel Magid Farid, interviews, Cairo and London, 2001.
27. Andrew and Leslie Cockburn, *Dangerous Liaison: The Inside Story of the U.S.-Israeli Covert Relationship* (New York, 1991), p. 146.
28. Abdel Magid Farid, interview, London, 1999.
29. David Holden and Richard Johns, *The House of Saud* (London, 1981), p. 192.
30. Stephen Dorril, *MI6: Fifty Years of Special Operations* (London, 2000), p. 681, cites James Critchfield as claiming, "The Soviets are waging war [in Yemen]."

31. Hammroush, p. 107.
32. Anwar Sadat, *In Search of Identity* (London, 1978), p. 175.
33. Nutting, p. 429; Woodward, *Nasser*, p. 114.
34. Eliezer Be'eri, *Army Officers in Arab Politics and Society* (New York, 1970), p. 120.
35. Be'eri, p. 127.
36. Tikriti, p. 328.
37. Sadat, p. 179.

## 10. We Are Defeated

1. Faud Ajami, *The Dream Palace of the Arabs* (New York, 1998), p. 246.
2. Hassan Khalid Hussein, *Abu Iyyad: Unknown Pages from His Life* (Arabic) (Beirut, 1977), p. 154.
3. Jean Lacouture, *Nasser* (London, 1973), p. 323.
4. Abdel Magid Farid, former aide to Nasser, interview, London, July 1997.
5. John Bulloch, *The Making of a War: The Middle East from 1967 to 1973* (London, 1974), p. 165.
6. Abu Saïd Aburish, the writer's father, was one of Arafat's interviewers and made available his and his colleagues' notes to the author.
7. Mohamed Heikal, interview, Cairo, October 2001.
8. Tahseen Beshir, Mohamed Heikal, and Hakim Abdel Nasser, interviews, October–November 2001.
9. Abdel Magid Farid, *Nasser, The Final Years*, (Reading, U.K., 1994), p. 114.
10. Farid, p. 31.
11. Private Jordanian intelligence source.
12. Mahmoud Hammroush and Mohamed Heikal, interviews, October–November 2001; Farid, p. 121.
13. Farid, p. 57.
14. Tahseen Bashir and Mohamed Heikal, interviews, Cairo, November 2001.
15. Sami Sharaf, former aide to Nasser, telephone interview, Cairo, October 2001.
16. Anwar Sadat, *In Search of Identity* (London, 1978), p. 198.
17. James A. Bell, conversation with the author, New York, 1969.
18. Hakim Abdel Nasser, interview, Cairo, October 2001.
19. Sadat, p. 190.
20. Farid, p. 63.
21. Farid, p. 48.

22. Tahseen Beshir, interviews, Cairo, October–November 2001.
23. Nutting, *Nasser* (London, 1972), p. 287.
24. Robert D. Murphy, *Diplomat Among Warriors* (Garden City, N.Y., 1964), p. 506.
25. William R. Polk, interview, Vence, France, October 2002.
26. William R. Polk, interviews, Vence, France, August–October 2002.
27. Georges Corm, *Abdel Nasser and the Muslim Brotherhood* (London, 1986), p. 109.
28. General Radi Abdallah, King Hussein's chief of intelligence and minister of interior, conversations in the 1960s and 1970s.
29. Farid, p. 129.
30. Abba Eban, *Personal Witness: Israel Through My Eyes* (London, 1993), p. 428.
31. Moshe Shemesh, *The Palestinian Entity, 1959–1974: Arab Politics and the PLO* (London, 1988), p. 100.
32. Harold M. Cubert, *The PFLP's Changing Role in the Middle East* (London, 1997), p. 42.
33. Farid, pp. 183, 199.
34. Bulloch, p. 173.
35. Mohamed Heikal, Mahmoud Hammroush, Kahlid Mohieddine, interviews, Cairo, October–November 2001; Abdel Magid Farid, interview, London, July 1998.
36. Private source within Arafat's entourage.
37. Mohamed Heikal, interview, Cairo, October 2001.
38. Saïd K. Aburish, *Arafat: From Defender to Dictator* (London, 1998), p. 112.
39. Lacouture, p. 347.

# INTERVIEWS

Abdallah, General Radi, reporter's notebook, Beirut, 1959–1960.
Abdel Nasser, Hakim, Cairo, October 2001.
Abdel Nasser, Dr. Huda, Cairo, October–November 2001
Abu Saïd, Aburish, Seattle, April 2000.
Ahmed, Mohamed Sayyed, Cairo, November 2001.
Badawi, Dr. Zakki, London, June 2001.
Bahieddine, Ziad Ahmad, Cairo, October 2001.
Bar-On, Dr. Mordechai, correspondence, June–September 2001.
Bell, James A., talks, New York, 1972–1980.
Beshir, Tahseen, Cairo, October–November 2001.
Copeland, Miles, reporter's notebook, London 1972–78.
Critchfield, James, Washington, D.C., June–July 1994.
Daoud, Dia Eddine, Cairo, October 2001.
Dassouki, Salah, Cairo, October 2001.
Eveland, Wilbur Crane, London, 1982.
Farid, Abdel Magid, London, July 1998 and July 2001.
Fayyeq, Mohamed, Cairo, October 2001.
Firzli, Suleiman, London, June 2001.
Hammad, Kheiry, reporter's notebook, Beirut, 1960.
Hammroush, Mahmoud, Cairo, October 2001.
Hatatta, Dr. Sherrif, Cairo, November 2001.

Heikal, Mohamed, Cairo, November 2001
Kassem, Hisham, Cairo, October–November 2001.
Lakeland, William, correspondence, June 2001.
Mohieddine, Khalid, Cairo, October 2001.
Parker, Paul, reporter's notebook, London, 1992–93.
Polk, William R., Vence, France, 2002.
Riyadh, General Abdel Fatah, Cairo, October–November 2001.
Sharaf, Sami, telephone interview, Cairo, October 2001.
Shlaim, Avi, correspondence, April–July 2001.
Tel, Wasfi, reporter's notebook, Beirut, 1959.

# SELECT BIBLIOGRAPHY


Abdel Malek, Anouar. *Egypt's Military Society*. London, 1968.

Abdo, Geneive, *No God but God: Egypt and the Triumph of Islam*. Oxford, 2000.

Abu Izzeddine, Nejla M. *Nasser of the Arabs*. Beirut, 1975.

Aburish, Saïd K. *A Brutal Friendship: The West and the Arab Elite*. London, 1997.

Ajami, Fouad. *The Arab Predicament: Arab Political Thought and Practice Since 1967*. Updated ed. Cambridge, 1992.

Aronson, Geoffrey. *From Sideshow to Center Stage: U.S. Policy Toward Egypt, 1946–1956*. Boulder, Colo., 1986.

Awadah, Mohamed, *Farouk: Beginning and End* (Arabic). Cairo, 1992.

el-Barawy, Dr. Rashed. *The Military Coup in Egypt: An Analytical Study*. Cairo, 1952.

Be'eri, Eliezer. *Army Officers in Arab Politics and Society*. New York, 1970.

Bishri, Tarek. *Democracy and the Revolution of 23 July* (Arabic). Cairo, 1991.

Black, Ian, and Benny Morris. *Israel's Secret Wars. The Untold History of Israeli Intelligence*. London, 1991.

Boghdadi, Abdel Latif. *Diaries* (Arabic). Cairo, 1982.

Bulloch, John. *Final Conflict: The War in Lebanon*. London, 1983.

Copeland, Miles. *The Game of Nations*. London, 1969.

———. *The Game Player: The Confessions of the CIA's Original Political Operative*. London, 1989.
———. *The Real Spy World*. New York, 1972.
Cremeans, Charles D. *The Arabs and the World: Nasser's Arab Nationalist Policy*. New York, 1963.
Daoud, Dia Eddine. *Years with Abdel Nasser* (Arabic). Cairo, 1980.
Dawisha, Karen. *Soviet Foreign Policy Towards Egypt*. London, 1979.
Dorril, Stephen. *M16: Fifty Years of Special Operations*. London, 2000.
Eden, Sir Anthony. *Full Circle*. London, 1960.
Farah, Tawfic E., editor, *Pan-Arabism and Arab Nationalism: The Continuing Debate*. Boulder, Colo., 1987.
Farid, Abdel Magid. *Nasser: The Final Years*. Reading, U.K., 1994.
Finer, S. E. *The Man on Horseback: The Role of the Military in Politics*. London, 1962.
Gerges, Fawaz A. *The Superpowers and the Middle East: Regional and International Politics, 1955–1967*. Boulder, Colo., 1994.
Gilbert, Martin. *Israel: A History*. London, 1998.
Glubb, Sir John Bagot. *A Soldier with the Arabs*. London, 1957.
———. *Britain and the Arabs*. London, 1982.
Gorst, Anthony, and Lewis Johnman. *The Suez Crisis*. London, 1997.
Hammroush, Mahmoud. *The Autumn of Abdel Nasser* (Arabic). Beirut, 1978.
Heikal, Mohamed. *Autumn of Fury: The Assassination of Sadat*. London, 1983.
———. *Cutting the Lion's Tale: Suez Through Egyptian Eyes*. London, 1986.
———. *Secret Channels: The Inside Story of Arab-Israeli Peace Negotiations*. London, 1996.
———. *Nasser—The Cairo Documents*. London, 1972.
Herzog, Chaim. *Living History: A Memoir*. London, 1997.
Hopwood, Derek. *Egypt: Politics and Society, 1945–1990*. 3rd ed. London, 1991.
Hourani, Albert. *A History of the Arab Peoples*. London, 1991.
Imam, Abdallah Abdel. *Nasser and the Muslim Brotherhood* (Arabic). Cairo, 1986.
Issa, Salah. *Learned and Soldiers* (Arabic). Cairo, 1986.
Issawi, Charles. *Egypt in Revolution: An Economic Analysis*. London, 1963.
Joesten, Joachim. *Nasser: The Rise to Power*. London 1960.
Kamle, Rashad. *The Life of Abdel Hakim Amer* (Arabic). Cairo, 2001.
Kerr, Malcolm H. *The Arab Cold War: Gamal 'Abd al-Nasir and His Rivals, 1958–1970*. 3rd ed. London, 1971.

Kimche, Jon. *The Second Arab Awakening*. London, 1970.

Lacouture, Jean. *Nasser*. London, 1973.

Laqueur, Walter. *The Struggle for the Middle East: The Soviet Union and the Middle East, 1958–68*. London, 1969.

Love, Kennett. *Suez—The Twice-Fought War: A History*. London, 1969.

Lunt, James. *Hussein of Jordan: A Political Biography*. London, 1989.

Marlowe, John. *Arab Nationalism and British Imperialism: A Study in Power Politics*. London, 1961.

Mohieddine, Khalid. *Now I Speak* (Arabic). Cairo, 2001.

Nasr, Salah. *The Revolution of 23rd July: Between Destiny and Forward Movement* (Arabic). Cairo, 1980.

Nasser, Gamal Abdel. *The Speeches of President Gamal Abdel Nasser*. Cairo, 2001.

Neff, Donald. *Fallen Pillars: U.S. Policy Towards Palestine and Israel Since 1945*. Washington, D.C., 1995.

Nutting, Anthony. *Nasser*. London, 1972.

———. *No End of a Lesson*. London, 1967.

Quandt, William B., editor. *The Middle East: Ten Years After Camp David*. Washington, D.C., 1988.

Raviv, Dan, and Yossi Melman. *Every Spy a Prince: The Complete History of Israel's Intelligence Community*. Boston, 1990.

Rabinovich, Itamar. *The Road Not Taken: Early Arab-Israeli Negotiations*. New York, 1991.

Raghib, Dr. Nabil. *An Israeli Testimony* (Arabic). Cairo, 1996.

Rubin, Barry M. *The Arab States and the Palestinian Conflict*. Syracuse, N.Y., 1981.

el-Sadat, Anwar. *In Search of Identity: An Autobiography*. London 1978.

———. *Revolt on the Nile*. London, 1957.

Said, Edward W. *Culture and Imperialism*. London, 1993.

Sayigh, Yezid. *Armed Struggle and the Search for State: The Palestinian National Movement, 1949–1993*. Oxford, 1997.

Searight, Sarah. *The British in the Middle East*. Rev. ed. London, 1979.

Shemesh, Moshe. *The Palestinian Entity, 1959–1974: Arab Politics and the PLO*. London, 1988.

Shlaim, Avi. *The Iron Wall: Israel and the Arab World*. New York, 2000.

Steven, Stewart. *The Spymasters of Israel*. London, 1981.

Thomas, Hugh. *The Suez Affair*. London, 1967.

Tikriti, Butheina Abdel Rahman, *Gamal Abdel Nasser: Beginning and Evolution of Nasserite Thought* (Arabic). Beirut, 2000.

Vatikiotis, P. J. *The History of Modern Egypt*. London, 1991.

Wahba, Mourad Magdi. *The Role of the State in the Egyptian Economy, 1945–1981*. Reading, U.K., 1994.

Wilson, Keith M., editor. *Imperialism and Nationalism in the Middle East: The Anglo-Egyptian Experience, 1882–1982*. London, 1983.

Woodward, Peter. *Nasser* (Profiles in Power series). London, 1992.

Yapp, M. E. *The Near East Since the First World War*. London, 1991.

# INDEX